JESUS

MIRIAM'S CHILD, SOPHIA'S PROPHET

ELISABETH SCHÜSSLER FIORENZA

JESUS

MIRIAM'S CHILD, SOPHIA'S PROPHET

CRITICAL ISSUES IN FEMINIST CHRISTOLOGY

CONTINUUM • NEW YORK

1999

The Continuum Publishing Company
370 Lexington Avenue, New York, NY 10017

Printed in the United States of America

Library of Congress Cataloging-in-Publication Data

Schüssler Fiorenza, Elisabeth, 1938–
    Jesus : Miriam's child, Sophia's prophet : critical issues in
feminist Christology / Elisabeth Schüssler Fiorenza.
        p.   cm.
    Includes bibliographical references.
    ISBN 0-8264-0671-8 (hbd.)
    ISBN 0-8264-0858-3 (pbk.)
    1. Jesus Christ—Person and offices.   2. Wisdom (Biblical
personification)   3. Feminist theology.   4. Bible.   N.T.—Criticism,
interpretation, etc.   5. Women in Christianity—History—Early
church, ca. 30–600.   I. Title.
BT205.S324   1994
232'.082—dc20
                                                            94-35571
                                                                CIP

To Chris
on her twenty-first birthday

Bless you, my sister
Bless you on your way...
So go gently, my sister
Let courage be your song.
You have words to say,
In your own way
And stars to light your night
   And if you ever grow weary
   And your heart's song has no refrain
   Just remember we'll be waiting
   To raise you up again
And we'll bless you our sister....

From *Blessing Song*
by Marsie Silvestro

Contents

Acknowledgments

When I was putting the last touches on this manuscript, Francis placed on my desk an article from *Time* magazine that starts with the rhetorical question: "What is feminism and is it likely to ruin your daughter's life?" My answer to the latter question is, obviously, that I do not think so. Yet it costs much psychological and spiritual energy to write a feminist theological book at a time when the backlash against feminists is in full swing. Hence, I am especially grateful to all who have steadfastly supported me in this endeavor.

Over the past five years I have worked on and off on *Jesus: Miriam's Child and Sophia's Prophet*. The idea for a book grew out of the interest in the chapter on the Jesus movement in *In Memory of Her*. It has been nourished through lectures and panel discussions in the United States, Switzerland, Germany, England, Israel, and Hong Kong. Specifically I want to express my thanks to the Faculty of Theology of the University of Nottingham for inviting me to give the Firth Lectures in the Fall of 1992. Since the charter of the Firth Lectures stipulates the lecturer should explore "the relation of some aspect of Christian faith to contemporary problems," I chose as a theme for this lecture series: "Re-Visioning Christ: Feminist Explorations of Biblical Christology." I am also greatly indebted to Professor Martin Stöhr and Vikarin Gabriele Zander for inviting me to give a seminar on feminist christology in the Studienjahr in Israel Programm.

In the Spring of 1992 I taught a seminar on "New Testament" theology, which attracted students from a variety of academic backgrounds and social locations. I am very grateful to all seminar participants — Peta Ruth Blake, Karen Fraioli, Melanie Graffam-Minkus, Clare Hickmann, Jane Iwamura, Melanie Johnson De Baufre, Cathy Kelsey, David Kyuman Kim, Heather Kirk, Shelly Matthews, Lynn Miller, Ralph Moore, Laura S. Nasrallah, Solveig Nielsen-Goodin, Peter Paik, Yon Pak, and Fairbairn Powers — for their probing questions and challenging insights. Their critical feedback was invaluable.

Werner Mark Linz of Continuum Publishing Company offered not only encouragement but also added "Jesus" and "critical" to the title, while my editor, Frank Oveis, shepherded the manuscript through its various stages of production. I am grateful to both for their lively interest in and steadfast support of my work over the years. Thanks are also due to Stephan Killen for the jacket design.

The willingness of Cheryl Froderman and Margaret Studier to use an unfamiliar word processing program has greatly benefited the final form of this text. I am thankful for their careful attention to the minutiae of style and form as well as their expert labor. In addition, I am greatly indebted to three other people who have patiently read and corrected drafts of individual chapters: Cathy Kelsey, who volunteered to read two crucial chapters, my assistant Julie Miller, who corrected several drafts of all chapters, and Chris Schüssler Fiorenza, who helped at a point when I was desperately struggling to meet the deadline. To all three my heartfelt thanks!

Last but not least, I want to thank the community of Notre Dame de Sion in Ain Karim, and especially Sister Donna Purdy, for their gracious and enriching hospitality. As always, I am in great debt to Francis Schüssler Fiorenza for making it all become possible.

On the feast day of Mary of Magdala,
July 22, 1994

Part I

The Invitation of Wisdom

Chapter 1

THE ORATORY OF EUPHEMIA AND THE EKKLĒSIA OF WO/MEN[1]

In those days Mary set out and went with haste to a Judean town in the hill country, where she entered the house of Zechariah and greeted Elizabeth. (Luke 1:39–40)

Wisdom has built her house, she has set up her seven pillars. She has slaughtered her animals, she has mixed her wine, she has also set her table. She has sent out her women servants, she calls from the highest places in the town, "You that are simple minded, turn in here!" To those without sense she says, "Come, eat of my bread and drink of the wine I have mixed. Lay aside immaturity, and live, and walk in the way of Wisdom." (Prov. 9:1–6)

The two epigraphs introducing this chapter mark the imaginative and theoretical space in which the christological reflections of this book move. By naming Jesus as the child of Miriam and the prophet of Divine Sophia, I seek to create a "women"-defined feminist theoretical space that makes it possible to dislodge christological discourses from their malestream frame of reference. The hermeneutical-rhetorical creation of such a space intends to decenter hegemonic malestream christological discourses and to reframe them in terms of a critical feminist theology of liberation. The investigations of this book seek to uncover the hidden frames of meaning that determine malestream as well as feminist christological discourses. What Edward Said has affirmed about the task of the intellectual with respect to human rights discourses equally applies to feminist christological investigations:

> For the intellectual to be "for human rights" means, in effect, to be willing to venture interpretation of those rights in the same place and with the same language employed by the dominant power, to dispute its hierarchy and methods, to elucidate what it has hidden, to pronounce what it has silenced or rendered unpronounceable.[2]

3

The "hidden" frame of meaning that generally governs malestream as well as apologetic feminist christological discourses is that of the modern kyriarchal sex/gender system (see p. 14 below for a definition of "kyriarchy.") This theoretical and theological frame of meaning understands Jesus primarily as the Divine Son whom G*d,[3] the Father, sent to redeem us from our sins. By evoking the images of Divine Wisdom's table and Mary's "visitation" of Elizabeth as metaphorical boundary markers for determining feminist christological understandings, I attempt metaphorically to reconfigure hegemonic malestream discourse about Jesus the Christ.[4]

In the past couple of years a host of books about Jesus has appeared,[5] ranging from the very scholarly to the very popular.[6] The Newest Quest for the Jesus of history seems to be bearing a variety of fruits. Less numerous but still very significant are the books on feminist christology that gather new and very diverse theological voices around the table of Divine Wisdom.[7] Hence, one would be justified in asking why anyone would want to write another book on Jesus the Christ. Do we not already have enough accounts about Jesus of Nazareth that seem to mirror the image and likeness of their authors more than that of Jesus the Galilean?

It is important, therefore, to state from the outset that this book is not and does not pretend to be another Christian Testament[8] study about Jesus. Neither have I set out to compose a "revolutionary biography" of Jesus,[9] nor do I want to write a "postpatriarchal christology."[10] Instead, I seek to employ a critical feminist hermeneutics in order to explore the theoretical frameworks of various discourses about Jesus the Christ, and I do so from the social location of a biblical scholar who works from within the critical interpretive discourses of a critical feminist theology of liberation.

I am writing these christological analyses in Ain Karim,[11] a former Arab village near Jerusalem, where rich Palestinians used to have their summer homes. Today, tourist guides to Jerusalem recommend the town as a Jewish artists' colony known for its ceramics and visual arts as well as its contributions to the performing arts.[12] Ain Karim, meaning "spring of the vineyard," is said to be the birthplace of John the Baptist. Here, according to legend, his parents had their summer home, and the pregnant Miriam of Nazareth is believed to have visited Elisheva, the mother of John. Commemorating this visitation there is a drinking fountain called "Mary's Well" or "Spring of the Virgin" near the church. A sign in Hebrew and English warns the visitor: "Do not drink! Water may be contaminated."

This warning has become a metaphoric imperative for the conceptualization of this work. I attempt not only to explore whether a feminist articulation of christology is possible but also to investigate whether and how feminist christological discourses may be "contaminated" by their social location in academy and church. I am concerned here with the "politics" of christological discourses, to invoke a much used but little understood phrase.[13] A politics of discourse seeks to investigate the links between feminist christological articulations and those theoretical, historical, cultural, and political conceptual frameworks that shape biblical as well as feminist christological discourses. Bible, history, and theology are important not only for religious communities. Rather, as "master narratives" of Western cultures, they are always implicated in and collude with the production and maintenance of systems of knowledge that either foster exploitation and oppression or contribute to a praxis and vision of liberation. As critical interpretive practices, feminist theology and biblical interpretation must assess the implications of their own impregnation by hegemonic knowledges and discursive frameworks that make "sense" of the world and produce what counts as "reality" or "common sense."

In short, in this chapter I seek to make visible the contesting interests and theoretical frameworks that determine the christological articulations of feminist studies. In order to do so I need first to locate such feminist christological discourses in their sociopolitical rhetorical contexts. Second, I will sketch my own feminist method of systemic analysis of domination and, third illustrate the kyriarchal embeddedness of christological discourse. Finally, I will elaborate the notion of ekklēsia of wo/men as the hermeneutical center of feminist christologies.

The Sociopolitical Context of Christological Discourses

Hegemonic christological discourses are Western articulations that claim universal significance. They shape the self-identity and religious horizons not only of Christians but also of Western culture. Since education and religion are the primary institutions by which subjects are fashioned, feminist theologies must critically investigate how biblical studies and Christian theologies collaborate in producing subjects malleable and usable in the growing service economy and consumer culture of the late twentieth century.

Such a global identity formation is accomplished by an explosion of international communication possibilities and ideology techniques. Global media discourses have fostered the development of a multinational economy[14] that has engendered corporate internationalism, with its service industry in the West and the displacement of industrial production to the so-called two-thirds world. These economic developments go hand in hand with an "informatics of domination,"[15] which seeks to discipline the explosion of communication technologies through the control of information.

Every time we turn on our TV sets we meet our neighbors in the "global village." National and international "town" meetings discuss issues of the day. "Revival" meetings, a typical American phenomenon, reach an international audience. The telecommunications explosion,[16] rapid transit, and mass tourism have made us business partners in the global village. The broadcast of national and international ecological disasters, the threat of nuclear accidents and biological-chemical warfare, the displacement of whole populations because of war, hunger, occupation, and political or religious persecutions should have increased our awareness of global interdependence and our resolve to find ways to improve the conditions for our "neighbors" in the global village.

However, this is often not the case. Rather, the explosion of information has engendered tendencies to political protectionism and nationalist isolationism instead of a spirit of responsible global citizenship. These effects are the results of the control of the "News," not by overt censure but by the saturation, proliferation, and regionalization of information. The news media claim simply to report the "facts," not to shape them. Hence they do not enable readers or viewers to observe critically how they construct these "facts."[17] Generally, they also do not make systemic global connections between the discrete items they have selected for the "News." One day we hear about earthquakes in the Philippines, civil war in Bosnia, military dictatorship in Haiti, and starvation in Somalia. The next day these are forgotten as if wiped from the face of the globe. The "News" has moved the center of attention to the problem of "illegitimate" children, teenage welfare mothers, economic difficulties in Russia, street crime in Chicago, problems in Castro's Cuba, the visit of the German chancellor to Washington, or the antics of Arafat jeopardizing the Israeli-Palestinian peace agreement. Every day the news media overwhelm us with reports about new disasters happening around the world. They saturate the public with broadcasts of endless talks by political pundits and intellectual experts skilled in mystifying rather than clarifying the political interconnectedness of our lives.

Hence the effects of the "News" are not an increase in global awareness, international literacy, human solidarity, or an active contribution to the solving of such problems. Rather, media discourses generate great anxiety and the sense of absolute powerlessness in the face of such complex problems. They foster a quiet resignation and create political paralysis that concerns itself with little beyond individual survival. The media achieve this conservative political effect by news proliferation that regionalizes human suffering. They seldom provide critical systemic analyses that would make the connections between our own lives and those of peoples thousands of miles away — or even of those living in our own neighborhood. The explosion of popular books on Jesus as well as on women's spirituality and the feminine are part and parcel of a politics of meaning that operates by proliferating and simultaneously compartmentalizing knowledge and information.

Feminist and liberationist movements and theologies seek to intervene in this struggle over the control and commodification of knowledge and information. They aim to keep the knowledge of liberation and the vision of radical equality alive before the eyes of the disenfranchised and disempowered whose radical democratic dreams have been subverted.[18] In the past, radical democratic movements around the globe have fought for this dream of freedom and the empowerment of the people. Today, many of these movements are being wrecked because of ruthless economic exploitation and nationalist strife.

Economists point out that only the highly skilled upper 15–20 percent of the world population benefit from the global economy, whereas two-thirds are increasingly relegated to the status of the working poor, the unemployed, and welfare recipients.[19] This economic and educational erosion of the so-called middle classes creates a geopolitical situation in which the dividing line is no longer drawn between the so-called first and third worlds but rather runs across the world, dividing the have and have-nots living in the same city, county, or country. In other words, my neighbor who works for an international computer firm has more in common with her counterparts in Europe, Latin America, or Japan than with the woman on welfare who lives three blocks away. Accordingly, at this moment we are confronted by this alternative: either the emerging global village will be fashioned into a radical democratic confederation that is governed by interests in favor of the economic well-being and political rights of all its citizens without exception, or this global situation will become subject to a tightly controlled, "soft-gloved" dictatorship that concentrates all economic and cultural resources in the hands of a few and relegates the majority to a permanent impoverished and dehumanized underclass.[20]

This context of global struggle compels feminist studies and liberation theologies to reassert the need for a global systemic analysis not only of culture but also of religion.[21] In the face of postmodern "ludic" (i.e., playfully relativistic proliferation) and often nihilistic theories, feminist

theologies and religious studies must rearticulate their critical liberationist visions in such a way that they contribute to the fashioning of
subjects dedicated to a radically democratic praxis. They must confront
these issues and assess whether christological discourses make possible
a critical mode of thought, radical democratic politics, and committed
solidarity in the struggles for economic justice and global well-being.

Otherwise, religion in general and christology in particular will remain a dangerous weapon in the hands of the powerful who use it to
conservative, oppressive ends. In the United States, religion, for instance,
is used to encourage a nationalist "bunker mentality" and for scapegoating the disadvantaged "underclasses" or single "welfare mothers"
with "illegitimate" children.[22] Around the globe conservative political
forces continue to claim religion as a cover for the interests of those who
are economically better off, those whose anxieties have increased because their economic and educational potential has been steadily eroded
during the 1980s.

Fundamentalist right-wing movements around the world — whether
the electronic churches of the United States, Islamic fundamentalist
groups,[23] Jewish ultraright movements,[24] biblicist and revivalist movements in Latin America, or emergent religious movements of Hindu
nationalism[25] — all exhibit common traits: They employ modern media
technologies in very sophisticated ways and generally advocate nationalist or religious exclusivism. While they embrace modern technological
science as well as modern industrialism and nationalism, they reject
many of the political and ethical values espoused by modern democracy:
basic individual rights, pluralism, freedom of speech, the right to hous-
ing, health care, and work, equal compensation for equal work, social
market measures, a democratic ethos, the sharing of power and political
responsibility, and especially equal rights for women.

These fundamentalist movements are a political-religious response to
the struggle of democratic movements around the globe. The political-
religious right claims the power to name and to define the true nature of
biblical religions against liberation theologies of all colors and geograph-
ical locations. Its well-financed think tanks are supported by reactionary
political and financial institutions that seek to defend kyriarchal capitalism. The interconnection between religious antidemocratic arguments
and the debate concerning women's place and role is not accidental nor
of only theological significance.[26]

In the past decade or so right-wing fundamentalist movements
around the globe have insisted on portraying emancipated women as sig-
nifiers of Western decadence or of modern atheist secularism, but they
have presented masculine power as the expression of divine power.[27]

Whether it is possible to transform androcentric exclusivist forms of religion[28] and whether religion will contribute to the global struggles for a more democratic world order will depend for the most part on whether it will engage feminist and liberationist theologies for articulating a different spiritual vision in this situation of globalization. Struggles for radical democracy and for women's religious-theological authority are intrinsically intertwined. The power of the gospel for salvation and well-being in a global context, I argue, depends on the Christian articulation of a liberating critical vision as well as a theological commitment to liberation.

In this context of struggle, the "postmodern" proliferation and production of Jesus-books for popular consumption by malestream biblical and theological studies seems to function as the reverse side of the fundamentalist literalist coin. In a literalist dogmatic reading, fundamentalist christologies seek to "fix" the pluriform expressions of Christian Scriptures and traditions, particularly the ambiguous metaphors and variegated texts dealing with Jesus Christ. They attempt then to consolidate them into a single, definite, one-to-one masculine discourse of meaning. In response to such literalist readings "liberal" theological scholars seem to relativize their own Jesus research in such a way that it becomes simply one more privatized religious expression. Ironically, their publishers often employ marketing techniques that assert historical positivism to shore up the scholarly authority and universal truth of Jesus research.

For instance, *Jesus: A Revolutionary Biography* — John Dominic Crossan's popularized version of his scholarly *The Historical Jesus: The Life of a Mediterranean Jewish Peasant* — is advertised as a "revolutionary biography by the world's leading expert on the life of Jesus."[29] The publisher assures readers that this book is the work of a world-renowned scholar who gives a comprehensive account "of what we can know about the life of Jesus."[30] Consequently, the proliferation of "new" Jesus books does not undermine and undo the literalist masculinist desire of christological fundamentalism for an "accurate" and reliable christology. Rather, it tends to reinscribe such a christology in terms of historical positivism.

Feminist literary analyses of the Gospels or histories of Jesus that espouse the positivist strategies of biblical scholarship[31] do not interrupt but play into the hands of such authoritarian fundamentalism. Those discourses that advocate christological "regionalism" in turn tend to serve the interests of liberal pluralism. Studies written from a professedly "ethnic" local point of view — like "white" European, Australian, American, African American, Asian, African, or Latin American articulations of feminist christology — are also in danger of postmodern co-optation.[32] They turn into the "reverse" of malestream readings and become "regionalized" whenever they grow into exclusive articulations that belong only to a discrete ethnic group.[33] Such discourses are in danger of reinforcing the oppressive divisions of class, race, gender, religion, nation, and age that have been articulated by Western colonialist powers.

If feminist theologies relinquish the claim that their critiques and insights have universal validity, they are in danger of feeding into postcolonial attempts of crisis management that operate through the particularization, fragmentation, and regionalization of the disenfranchised and oppressed. Feminist christological articulations that do not argue for their theoretical significance[34] but rather relinquish claims that their insights are valid for everyone unwittingly foster such a regionalization and privatization of emancipatory political struggles. As a result, it becomes important to disentangle such feminist christologies and their validity claims from the colonialist racist frameworks that they seek to reverse but continue to inhabit. It is, therefore, mandatory to reflect critically on feminist methods of analysis and on theories of interpretation that provide the discursive frame of feminist christological (re)constructions.

In such a context of political-ideological struggle over the "power of naming," religious renewal movements and feminist theologies must not concede the power of naming to reactionary forces by respecting conservative claims to ownership of biblical religions. Hedwig Meyer-Wilmes has proposed that the boundaries between academy and church are the best site for a Christian feminist theology of liberation to engage in a political struggle over the power of religious "naming."[35] She suggests that feminist scholars in religion distinguish three discrete discourses in which we participate, namely, theology, feminism, and science. She goes on to argue that we must locate our critical christological practices on the boundaries between these three discourses, constantly moving between them. She is right, in my opinion, to maintain that as feminist theologians we should not have to choose between academic scholarship and the women's movement, between theory and practice.

While I agree with her politics of discourse, I would like to place a different metaphor at the center of attention. The image I want to suggest is that of the feminist theologian as troublemaker, as a resident alien, who constantly seeks to destabilize the centers, both the value-free, ostensibly neutral research ethos of the academy and the dogmatic authoritarian stance of patriarchal religion. Feminists can do so, I suggest, by rewriting and refashioning academic and ecclesial discourses from a critical feminist perspective of liberation. Feminist theologians should not situate their theological work on the boundaries and in the margins but should move it into the center of academy and religion.[36] Women, who for so long have been excluded from the production of scientific and theological knowledge, must claim the center of theory and theology in order to transform it.[37] We must do so in order to undermine the tendencies of androcentric world views and theological languages that have relegated us to the margins, the periphery, and the boundaries for much too long.

In order to intervene effectively in malestream theoretical and theological practices, feminist discourses must become bilingual, speaking the languages of our intellectual-theological "fathers" as well as the dialects of our feminist "sisters." Hence feminist theologians must remain firmly rooted in diverse women's movements for change. We can speak as insiders-outsiders, as resident aliens of church and academy, only if we continue to be challenged and nurtured by the women's liberation movements in society and religion. These movements cannot relinquish the modern emancipatory claim to be recognized as subjects and agents in church and academy, in society and university. While it is true that feminist scholars in religion participate in four quite different discourses, those of the university, organized religion, feminist theory, and the feminist movement, I do believe that we have to privilege feminist movements for change in order to integrate all of them — and many more — into our life and work. We are not able to speak as feminist theologians if we have not integrated these discourses with each other and thereby changed them, their boundaries, and their centers.

Feminist scholars in religion must be careful not to reinscribe among ourselves the old divisions between church and academy, between theory and practice, that the malestream ruling center of academy and church has enacted and still seeks to reinforce today either by silencing or by co-opting our feminist work. It may sound somewhat quaint but in my opinion we are able to bring about change only if our work remains a part of a movement of solidarity and struggle. Commitment to the vision of a different church and world must remain the hallmark of a Christian feminist theology.

I do not want to be misunderstood: I do not argue that like battered women, feminists must remain in situations that are oppressive and abusive of our human rights and dignity. Rather, those of us who have experienced and are committed to the liberating power of traditional Christian vision must claim and exercise our own spiritual-theological authority and power of naming for the sake of life in the global village. In short, critical feminist christological discourses of liberation must remain rooted in the diverse radical democratic feminist struggles as the political-religious site from which we speak.

A Critical Systemic Analysis of Domination

In my own work I have sought to develop a critical systemic analysis that can lift into consciousness the realization that multiplicative structures of oppressions determine wo/men's lives.[38] Such a systemic analysis is essential to a critical feminist theology of liberation committed to transformation. Its articulation must be critical rather than apologetic and start with a hermeneutics of suspicion rather than with a hermeneutics of undiscriminating acceptance of Scripture and tradition. It begins with women's experience but insists that this experience must be systemically reflected upon if it is to become the starting point for critical feminist reflection.

Such a critical theology of liberation has an explicitly feminist commitment in that it announces its political goals rather than claims to be simply a descriptive academic study of women or an unbiased cultural analysis of symbolic gender constructions. Although a feminist liberation theory is able to engage the incipient feminism of women's and gender studies in religion, it does not share their academic posture of detached objectivity. Its own explicit self-understanding is not simply theoretical. Rather it understands itself as a political practice not only for personal transformation but also for structural change. Since wo/men are not merely innocent victims but also collaborators in perpetrating prejudiced mind-sets and exploitative social structures, a feminist politics must first of all change the internalized self-hate of women and cultural disrespect for wo/men.

In consequence, a critical feminist theology of liberation does not simply seek to analyze and explain the socioreligious structures of domination that marginalize and exploit women and other nonpersons, to use an expression of Gustavo Gutiérrez.[39] Instead, it aims to change entirely structures of alienation, exploitation, and exclusion. Its goal is to transform theoretical and theological-religious knowledges and sociopolitical systems of domination and subordination. Such a feminist theology understands itself as a critical theology of liberation because its critical systemic analyses and its intellectual practices for the production of religious knowledge seek to support struggles for wo/men's liberation around the world. Hence, its articulations are diverse and often in tension and conflict with each other.

In contrast to malestream liberation theologies, a feminist liberation theology does not privilege a Marxist class analysis but seeks to comprehend the multiplicative structures of women's oppression — racism, class exploitation, heterosexism, and colonialism — that determine and diminish all of our lives. Unlike some other forms of white European and North American academic women's or gender studies in religion, its analysis does not rely on a theoretical framework of symbolic gender dualism. As its basic analytic categories it does not simply employ androcentrism and patriarchy, which are generally understood in dualistic terms as the oppression of all women by all men. Rather, a critical feminist analysis radically shifts its focus from gender analysis to a complex systemic analysis of the multiplicative structures of oppression.

Such a liberationist theological analysis is best developed in dialogue with materialist, postmodern-resistance feminist theories that articulate a "social analytic," meaning a theoretical accounting of how the social order is conceptualized.[40] In contrast to the postmodern rejection of all so-called master narratives, like patriarchy or capitalism, a social analytic insists that feminism cannot relinquish its systemic critique of totalities. In the face of increasing global violence against women[41] as well as the growing neocapitalist exploitation of the so-called two-thirds world and the explosion of an "informatics of domination," feminist theory cannot stop with the postmodern "subject-in-language" and its permanent destabilization, global dispersal, and atomizing regionalization.[42] Instead it must develop a theoretical discourse and analytic framework that can account for the interaction between cultural-religious, economic, and political spheres of production.

For that reason, a global social analytic does not shrink from conceptualizing the social order in terms of a global system of exploitation in order to counter the logic of regionalization.[43] It does not understand power simply as diffused networks[44] of forces but rather articulates power as energy that can be used for liberation or exploitation. Such an articulation "allows us to consider how power operates hierarchically and systemically," as well as "how patriarchal and racist oppressions are deeply involved in the unequal control and distribution of social assets." Such a theoretical framework further allows us to understand the subject as "multiply and contradictorily positioned." Every "individual" subject is positioned across "multiple social coordinates of race, class, gender, sexuality, and ethnicity among others."[45]

Challenged by women of the so-called two-thirds world and utilizing the insights of biblical scholarship, I began in the late 1970s to articulate such a "social analytic" in historical-political terms. Since then I have argued for a redefinition of the concept of patriarchy to mean not simply the rule of men over women but rather a complex social pyramid of graduated dominations and subordinations.[46] Because feminist discourses continue to use the term "patriarchy" in the sense of gender dualism, I introduced in *But She Said* the neologism "kyriarchy," meaning the rule of the emperor/master/lord/father/husband over his subordinates. With this term I mean to indicate that not all men dominate and exploit all women without difference and that elite Western educated propertied Euro-American men have articulated and benefited from women's and other "nonpersons'" exploitation.[47] As a consequence, the hermeneutical center of a critical feminist theology of liberation cannot simply be women. Rather, it must be constituted and determined by the interests of women who live at the bottom of the kyriarchal pyramid and who struggle against multiplicative forms of oppression. The term "kyriocentric," in turn, refers to ideological articulations that validate and are sustained by kyriarchal relations of domination. Since kyriocentrism replaces the category of androcentrism, it is best understood as an intellectual framework and cultural ideology that legitimates and is legitimated by kyriarchal social structures and systems of domination.

Since my own work has focused on biblical studies, I have sought to develop such a theory of kyriarchy and kyriocentrism primarily in historical terms. In Christian Scriptures we find a series of texts that advocate the subordination of freeborn women and wives, slave women and men, young people, and the whole Christian community as such to the master/lord/father/emperor. Although such a "patriarchal politics of submission" is inscribed in Christian Scriptures and mediated by them, biblical scholarship on the so-called household code texts has shown that this politics of submission did not originate with them.[48] It was not invented by Christian theology but rather was first articulated in the context of the Greek city-state and mediated by Greco-Roman philosophy.[49]

In ancient Greece the notion of democracy was not constructed in abstract, universal terms but rather was rooted in a concrete sociopolitical situation. According to the theoretical vision — but not the historical realization — of democracy, all those living in the polis should be equal citizens, able to participate in government. In theory, all citizens of the polis are equal in rights, speech, and power. As the assembly of free citizens, the ekklēsia should come together to deliberate and decide the best course of action for achieving its own well-being and the welfare of the polis. Democratic political practice was not to be disengaged and detached. On the contrary, by engaging in the rhetorical deliberation of the ekklēsia, i.e., the democratic voting assembly, citizens were to promote the well-being of all.

However, the socioeconomic realities in the Greek city-state were such that only a very few freeborn, propertied, educated Greek male heads of households actually exercised democratic government. Greek kyriarchal democracy constituted itself by excluding the "others" who did not have wealth or a share in the land but whose labor sustained society. Freedom and citizenship were measured against slavery and also restricted in terms of gender. Active participation in government was conditional not only upon citizenship but also upon the combined privilege of property, education, and freeborn male family status. As Page duBois has succinctly pointed out: "The ancient democracy must be mapped as an absence. We have only aristocratic, hostile representations of it.... The dēmos, the people themselves, have no voice in history; they exist only as figured by others."[50]

The philosophies of Plato and Aristotle, who actually were critical of Athenian democracy, have been articulated to exclude certain groups of people, such as freeborn women or slave women and men, as not capable of participating in democratic government.[51] These groups, such a philosophical legitimization maintained, were not fit to rule or to govern because their natural powers of reasoning were deficient. In short:

> To secure order, Plato and Aristotle turned away from the politics of democracy. The alienation, conflict and narrow self-concern charted by Thucydides and confronted by Democritus prompted Plato to bind the pursuit of the good to the existence of a stable, unified, hierarchical society, the earthly embodiment of a cosmic order. In restructuring society, so as to provide a firm foundation for order, Plato and Aristotle abandoned the aims of democratic politics and democratic thinkers.[52]

It was this conflict between the politics of democracy and the societal order, the contradiction and tension between the logic of the democratic ideal and actual sociopolitical kyriarchal structures that produced the kyriocentric (master-centered) ideology of "natural" or "God-given differences." Such "natural" or "divinely ordained" differences are supposed to exist between elite men and women, between freeborn and slaves, between property owners and farmers or artisans, between Athenian-born citizens and other residents, between Greeks and barbarians — both women and men — and, last but not least, between the civilized and the uncivilized world. Such an explicit ideological justification of kyriarchy on "natural" or "God-given" grounds always appears to be necessary at points in history when radical democratic notions are introduced and put into practice in kyriarchal societies.

The early Christian injunctions to kyriarchal submission, which seek

to adapt the egalitarian and therefore subversive Christian movement to
Greco-Roman patri-kyriarchal society and culture, are best understood
as a part of this ancient cultural rhetoric.[53] These injunctions would
not have been necessary if from its very inception Christian community and self-understanding had existed solely as a kyriarchal formation.
The Hellenistic paradigm of kyriarchal submission encoded in Christian
Scriptures — together with the Roman imperial paradigm — developed
into the hierarchical cultic structures of the Roman church in the second
and third centuries. This conjunction of ancient kyriarchal structures determined the self-understanding of the post-Constantinian "orthodox"
church.

Although the Greek aristocratic/oligarchic and the Roman imperial/
colonialist forms of kyriarchy were modified under changing socioeconomic and political conditions, they seem to have been the two
prevailing forms of kyriarchy in the history of Western Christianity.
The hierarchical institutions of Roman Catholicism tend to resemble the imperial kyriarchal pyramid of Rome.[54] For instance, like the
Roman emperor, the pope is called *pater patrum* and believed to represent G*d on earth.[55] In contrast, some churches of the Reformation
conform more to the classical Greek form of kyriarchy insofar as
they adopted institutional structures resembling those inscribed in the
Pastoral Epistles.

Since modern capitalist democracy was modeled upon ancient Greco-
Roman philosophical notions of democracy, it has inherited this contradiction between actual sociopolitical structures of domination and ideal
democratic self-understandings.[56] At first modern American democracy
excluded all women and men who were slaves, immigrants, or poor
from full democratic participation. Property and elite male status by
birth and education, not simply biological sex, entitled men to participate in the government of the few over the many. At the same time
the modern form of democracy based civil rights on the belief that all
people are created equal and hence entitled to the pursuit of freedom
and well-being.[57]

This contradiction between radical democratic ideals and their kyriarchal actualization has engendered emancipatory movements seeking
full citizenship. In the last two centuries the struggles over "equal
rights" have gained political and civil rights for all adult citizens. However, these movements for political and civil rights have not been able
to radically change kyriarchal economic exploitation or sociopolitical
stratifications along lines of race, gender, class, immigrant status, and
heterosexual orientation. Liberal theories of formal "equal rights" thus
prove to be kyriarchal discourses in disguise. By using the language

of democracy but actually reinforcing the structures of kyriarchy, they make the democratic liberal circle appear to be coextensive with the kyriarchal pyramid of oppression rather than to be in tension and contradiction with it.

The feminist philosopher Joan Cocks has pointed out that modern political thought elaborates two aspects of masculine power: one, based in the family, seeks to secure control of species reproduction; the other, based in ideology, desires sexual gratification.[58] In the first place, patriarchal right, or father-right, operates on the side of the kyriarchal order, wielding control over wives, children, wealth, institutions of knowledge, and social-cultural-religious institutions by exercising public political rule and deploying the force of law. In the second place, masculine power has articulated itself as the phallic right over the objects of its desire. It is based on male physics, on a particular type of body, and on the penis representing masculine power.[59]

This distinction between the two aspects of the kyriarchal regime is important, but in my opinion it must be understood differently. Rather than positioning the kyriarchal logic of father-right in the family, I would suggest that patriarchal power as kyriarchal power operates on an institutional-political structural level, while phallic power as kyriocentrism functions on a linguistic-ideological systemic level. These two levels are not separate but interact with each other in perpetrating wo/men's oppression.

White European and American elite males have produced the kyriocentric politics that not only has defined elite white women as the "other," but also subordinated classes, races, and peoples as the "others" in order to colonize and exploit them under the guise of modern kyriarchal democracy and civilization.[60] In short, knowledge as the way we make sense out of the world is not simply gendered but also racialized, class-dominated, colonialized, and Eurocentric. The African American cultural critic bell hooks has likened this "politics of domination" to a building, where the interlocking systems of oppression share the ideological ground "which is a belief in domination and a belief in notions of superior and inferior. . . . For me it is like a house; they share the foundation but the foundation is the ideological beliefs around which notions of domination are constructed."[61]

Just as in antiquity so also in modernity philosophies of "natural differences" are ideological justifications of dominance that seek to exclude from full citizenship certain people who are considered inferior. They are created by the contradiction between the ideal of democratic self-definition and its actual kyriarchal socioeconomic practices of domination. Modern democracy perpetrates many of the ideological practices

first articulated in classical philosophy and theology. Insofar as it claims
that its citizens are "created equal" and are entitled to "the pursuit
of liberty and well-being" but at the same time justifies "natural" social stratifications and economic inequalities, its philosophical, political,
and religious rhetoric of "equality" for a few "eminent and great men"
serves to exclude all the "others" from full democratic participation.

The Sociopolitical Location of Christological Doctrine

Christological doctrines were shaped at a moment when those segments
of the ancient church that became hegemonic "orthodox" Christianity
pivoted into a place of prominence in the Constantinian imperial Roman
Church. Moreover, in modern times they have been mediated through
liberal theological discourses that were created by the modern form
of kyriarchy articulated in the sex/gender system. Classic christological
dogma expresses the imperial desire for the unification and control of a
church created by the diverse understandings of Jesus developed in the
beginnings of Christianity.[62] Keeping in mind that such a historical context of powerful interests is inscribed in christological discourses helps
to explain why feminist interpretations that address the kyriarchal imperial expressions of Jesus' divinity or the centrality of the atonement in
the understanding of Jesus' death often provoke intellectual protest and
emotional resistance.

Liberal Enlightenment christologies of Jesus, the greatest man who
ever lived, the exceptional individual hero, or the true religious genius to
be imitated in turn have resurrected the "divine man" of ancient Greece
who is always male, autonomous, and defiant, and stands above and
beyond all human limitations.[63] They have backed

> the unchallenged rise to political power of a genius, supported by the
> ideological agreement of a large part of the population.... The Christian
> tradition and the interpretation of its heritage today is full of the belief
> in the divine man, from the understanding of its heroes, such as Jesus
> and Luther, to the suggestion that true piety will also carry the reward of
> human greatness and extraordinary accomplishments for ourselves, both
> as individuals and as a nation. That we are under the spell of this idea
> also implies the pervasiveness of male and white imagery — and nothing
> is lost if we add a few female and black heroes to this gallery of religious
> geniuses.[64]

The following experience can illustrate how deeply ingrained are notions of Christian dogmatic superiority and orthodox belief in Jesus'

singular greatness. This summer I came to Jerusalem for a workshop on feminist christology with German students, mostly Lutheran, who were studying for a year in Israel. To my great surprise, the most heated discussions came in reaction to my mentioning Jacob Neusner's insistence that Judaism, Christianity, and Islam are three distinct religions.[65] Consequently, he argues, we need to avoid the expression "Judeo-Christian tradition" because it construes the relation of Judaism and Christianity as a single religious tradition. This concept manifests Christian supersessionism and bespeaks the Christian "will to power."

Since this workshop on "feminist christology" was held toward the end of their study year in Israel, I had expected that the students had recognized by then that the very common Christian insistence on a single continuous Judeo-Christian tradition was not acceptable to many Jews because its will to power funds Christian notions of superiority vis-à-vis Judaism. Despite their liberal pro-Jewish intentions, however, some of the students did not want to relinquish the expression "Judeo-Christian," probably because the notion of Christian superiority is undergirded by classical christological dogma and Enlightenment notions of Jesus as singular religious genius.[66]

It was not surprising that communication completely broke down when we began to discuss an article by the Swiss theologian Regula Strobel outlining feminist critical discussions of the "maleness of Jesus" and of the theology of the cross.[67] Rather than attempt to address these feminist debates critically and to explore the roots of their discontent, some students unilaterally declared them "heretical." Since the same students opposed Strobel's feminist critical insights by resorting to "confessions of faith," it proved impossible for other students to enter into critical reflection and dialogue on the issues. An exploratory discussion of feminist concerns about the religious misuse of cultural gender stereotypes and the theology of the cross — often used for compelling women to accept suffering, male family authority, and violence — turned out to be impossible.

Withdrawing to an "orthodox" position without being able to articulate it coherently, some students simply refused to deal with theological-historical arguments — and not simply feminist ones — arguments that maintain that classical christologies are rooted in an imperial kyriarchal theology. They were able to authorize their refusal with appeals to orthodoxy because "classical" christologies not only are interrupted by modern liberal christological discourses but often are also continued in them. Insofar as contemporary liberal christologies share in the kyriocentric pathology of modernity, they — like classical theology —

reinscribe the various discourses of kyriarchy against or in line with modern interests of power.[68]

That classical christological doctrines were shaped by imperial interests is generally recognized. The Roman emperor Constantine, whose military victories had recently reunited the empire, summoned the first Christian council at Nicea on May 20, 325 C.E. In his opening speech he stated that he considered the "disunion in the Church an evil more terrible and more grievous than any kind of war" and went on to exhort the assembly of bishops to "banish all causes of dissension" and to "solve controversial difficulties according to the law of peace." This imperial "law of peace" did not value or tolerate difference, disagreement, or diversity but imposed rules and standards of uniformity that could be enforced by the state.[69] Similarly, the decision-making process of the Council of Ephesus (431), which Leo of Rome called the "Robber Synod," was totally under imperial control.[70]

The Chalcedonian promulgation of the doctrine of Incarnation is a good example of how kyriocentrism and kyriarchy feed on and reinforce each other. This doctrine was formulated by the Ecumenical Council of Chalcedon (451) and proclaimed in the name of the Council Fathers and the Roman emperors Marcian and Valentinian. The Latin word *incarnatio* meaning to "enflesh" (*in* + *caro* [flesh]) translates two separate Greek words in the text of the council: *enanthropēsin* and *oikonomia*. *Enanthropēsin* is used only once in the text as meaning to live among (*en*) or to have the appearance of a human being (*anthrōpos*).

The other Greek expression, *oikonomia,* translated into Latin as *incarnatio* is a compound form of *oikos* (house/household) and *nomos* (law/order/management). Its original meaning is household management/order/administration. The modern word "economy" is derived from it. *Oikonomia* is used three times in the council document of Chalcedon: "some dare to corrupt the mystery of the Lord's incarnation for us"; "those who attempt to corrupt the mystery of the incarnation" and "those who presume to rend the mystery of incarnation." What is translated as the "mystery of the incarnation" would better be rendered as the "mystery of the Lord's (household) management/order/law/ economy."[71] Such a translation would demystify the Latin derivation and disclose that the mystery of "incarnation" is that of kyriarchy, since in antiquity the kyriarchal order of the house was the paradigm of the order of the state and the whole universe. Kyriarchal rule accordingly is the method of the Lord's government and dispensation.

How then does the council decree articulate this new world order and Christian dispensation?[72] This section abounds in exclusive terminology. A whole range of condemnations of various christological formulations, which according to the Council Fathers must be rejected, introduces the promulgation of the "mystery of incarnation." The Synod Fathers "oppose, expel, withstand, drive away, anathematize and reject, exclude and damn to hell" those who hold different positions. The orthodox politics of meaning decrees, bans, and legalizes. Its rhetoric discloses that it is a product of struggle over words and conceptualizations. Its language reveals that the council exercises its authority here by means of imperial kyriarchal power that excludes and vilifies its opponents.

While bitter struggles over meaning are inscribed in the writings of the Christian Testament, these writings bespeak internecine "sectarian" struggles more than they assert ruling power. The christological dogmas of the fourth and fifth centuries, to the contrary, are generally recognized as articulated under Roman imperial pressures. They exercise normalizing functions by which the increasingly imperialized church establishes its rule, sanctions its violence, and sacralizes its power. This shift in theological process and politics of meaning is clearly inscribed in the Chalcedonian council document. It can be traced in its introduction and is expressed in the statement of purpose articulated in the second paragraph of the doctrinal definition:

> The Holy, Great and Ecumenical Synod, by the grace of God and the command [better, divine decree] of our most orthodox and Christ-loving Emperors, *Marcian* and *Valentinian* Augusti [emphasis mine],... had decreed as follows....[73]

The same conjunction between emperor and G*d/Christ can be seen in the council's definition:

> Our Lord and Savior Jesus Christ, confirming the knowledge of the faith to his disciples, said, "my peace I leave with you, my peace I give to you," to the end that no one should differ from his neighbor in the doctrines of orthodoxy, but that the proclamation of the truth should be shown forth equally by all.[74]

This text is noteworthy not only because it employs the imperial titles "Our Lord and Savior" but also because it cuts short the quotation of John's Gospel, which it uses to establish its "common-sense" scriptural authority. By replacing the following Johannine Gospel statement, "not as the world gives, do I give to you," with a statement of purpose, "to the end that no one should differ from his neighbor in the doctrines of orthodoxy," the synod's promulgation exchanges the peace of Christ with the peace of the emperor, the Pax Romana.

The "mysterious *oikonomia*," that is, the household/world order/ management, is here identified as the true "nature" of the Lord Jesus Christ. It asserts the "common-sense" givenness of the imperial order

as Christian "reality" by substituting for the "grace of God" and the
"peace of Christ" the "divine decree" of the emperors, which the Synod
Fathers promulgated at the instigation of the imperial administration.[75]
The articulation of the "mysterious economy" is, however, not a submerged memory and trace of valued differences, as Odell-Scott argues.
Although he suggests that "the doctrine of the mysterious economy of
God and world in Christ has parallels in and is mirrored by the mysterious union of God and the Emperors in the theo-political configuration
of the time,"[76] he nevertheless argues that the doctrine

> is subversive of the powers that be, both the political powers-that-be
> (the Emperor and the Imperial Church) and the onto-theo-logical powers-
> that-be. It is a subversion which "accommodates," "conceals," "hides,"
> "shelters," and "gathers" differences in violation of law and order and in
> defiance of reason and reality.[77]

In my reading, such an argument mistakes the formulation of dualistic difference for a multiplicity of differences (plural).[78] The long
list of Chalcedon's condemnations clearly indicates that the "mysterious
oikonomia" does not tolerate differences. Rather its doctrinal formulation enshrines the dualism of human and divine difference in the identity
construction of Jesus Christ as the union of opposites and requires
acceptance without question and deviation. Commanded here is not *theologia*, i.e., reflection and exploration of the human-divine relationship,
but rather mystified *oikonomia*, i.e., kyriarchal ruling and ordering of
the expressions of faith. Moreover, although the confessional formula of
Chalcedon clearly expresses such kyriarchal gender dualism, it is often
overlooked[79] that the imperial ordering is starkly gendered:

> Begotten of the Father eternally as to Divinity,
> Born of the Virgin, Theotokos, temporally as to Humanity.[80]

The Chalcedonian doctrine of christology is not "unnatural." It is
political. It shaped and was shaped by the imperial politics of meaning
that legitimated kyriarchal domination and exploitation. Its kyriocentric formulation of the dual nature of Christ attributes his divinity to
the "eternal begetting of the Father" and his humanity to the temporal birth by the Virgin Mother of G*d (*Theotokos*). This christological
doctrine thereby inscribes into Christian orthodox self-understanding
and identity the "mysterious economy" of kyriarchal relations and imperial domination. By associating fatherhood/masculinity with divinity
and eternity and by firmly placing motherhood/femininity in the temporal realm of humanity, it introduces not only gender dualism but also
the dualism between church and world, religion and nature, heaven and
earth.

At the behest of the imperial court, the Council Fathers not only inscribe these dualisms doctrinally as oppositions but also forbid anyone to say or think otherwise under threat of expulsion and damnation. The promulgation invokes the "grace of God" and the "peace of Christ" in order to secure the political unity and religious power of the empire. As doctrinal discourse the kyriarchal politics of the Chalcedonian promulgation continues to shape Christian "orthodox" identity as kyriarchal. Such kyriocentric identity has become "common" sense in orthodox Christian communities and provides the "preconstructed,"[81] unreflective frame of reference for biblical as well as feminist christological articulations today. This frame of reference is determined not only by imperial relations of domination but also by the kyriocentric sex/gender system of Western culture.

Imperial christological discourses do not undermine the kyriarchal sex/gender system. Rather, for their operation they need the ideological construct of the *feminine* as well as the active collaboration of women. The "Oratory of Euphemia" in the title of this chapter provides a potent metaphor for characterizing such an enabling cultural-religious feminine space, which is essential to the operation of the Western kyriarchal politics of meaning. It refers to an oratory named after a woman saint. There the final form of the Chalcedonian christological doctrine was brokered. As Grillmeier explains:

> It was only under constant pressure from the Emperor Marcian that the Fathers of Chalcedon agreed to draw up a new formula of belief. Even at the fourth session of the Council, on 17 October 451, the delegates of the emperor heard the synod once again endorse its purpose to create no new formula over and above the creeds of Nicea and Constantinople.... But the imperial commissioners — together with the Roman delegates — brought about the turning point.... The bishops gave way and expressed themselves agreeable that a committee, to be formed at the Emperor's pleasure, should work a new formula.... Thereupon twenty-three bishops assembled with the imperial commissioners, in the oratory of St. Euphemia. When they returned to the full assembly, they were able to put before the synod a long declaration of faith.[82]

This reference to St. Euphemia's Oratory may be historically insignificant. It characterizes the space of Chalcedon as marked by the name of a woman saint whose memory might or might not have had any influence upon the actual deliberations of the Council Fathers. Nevertheless, a feminist reading can utilize this information as a symbolic expression for signifying and disclosing that kyriarchal discourses need to construct the ideological space of the cultural-religious "feminine" as the enabling ground of their articulation. Hence, feminist critical practices of interpretation must not only pay attention to the "maleness" of cultural-religious discourses but also reflect on their "feminine" frameworks. Feminist theologies will be able to change "stable" Christian kyriarchal identity formations, I argue, only if they destabilize such kyriocentric forms of christology, both by dislodging them from their embeddedness in kyriarchal relations and by critically examining the cultural-religious space of "the feminine" in which such kyriarchal discourses operate. Whether feminist theological discourses will change Christian belief systems and practices depends to a large extent on whether feminist scholars are able to develop a theory of a feminist subject and replace the kyriarchal space of the feminine with a political counterhegemonic space where critical practices for change can become operative.

The Ekklēsia of Wo/men as the Hermeneutical Center of a Feminist Critical Practice of Transformation

In my own work I have attempted to delineate such a space that is counterhegemonic to kyriarchy by developing the notion of the ekklēsia of wo/men as a critical practice and vision of radical democracy in society and religion. The title of this chapter juxtaposes the expressions "Oratory of Euphemia" and "Ekklēsia of Wo/men" to tease the reader's imagination. This conjunction of the construct ekklēsia of wo/men with the place where the christological doctrine of Chalcedon was brokered is intended to function as a metaphor for feminist struggles to reconfigure societal and religious kyriarchal discourses. Critical postmodern feminist studies have explored the function of the signifier "woman/feminine." Critical cultural and liberationist studies in turn have challenged feminist theoretical gender analyses not to abstract from their sociopolitical function and so reinscribe the cultural ideal of the "Lady."[83]

This critique of the basic categories of feminist analysis has introduced a crisis into feminist self-understanding and the practices of the feminist subject. In order to mark this crisis in my writing I introduce here a particular spelling of "wo/men" that seeks to indicate that women are not a unitary social group but rather are fragmented and fractured by structures of race, class, religion, heterosexuality, colonialism, age, and health. Nonetheless, I do not think that feminists can relinquish the analytic category "women" entirely and replace it with the analytic category "gender" if we do not want to marginalize or erase the presence of women in our own feminist discourses.[84]

Among the various feminist theories, I have found Rosemary Hennessy's work most helpful for critically reflecting on this categorical crisis in feminist discourse. Hennessy has developed a theory of feminist critical practice for bringing about change in the lives of women by elaborating on Louis Althusser's notion of ideology and Antonio Gramsci's concept of hegemony. She begins by positioning her own materialist feminist theory between two feminist discourses in the West and asks how French feminist theory and North American standpoint theory construct the fundamental feminist category "woman." Whereas French postmodern feminism focuses on the "priority of systems of significa- tion, takes the unconscious as a privileged area of exploration, and in some versions, contends that women have no position in the symbolic order from where to speak," North American feminism "treats women as a 'self'" and language as a "transparent communication." North American standpoint theory "anchors critical undertakings in experience and posits feminism primarily as a prescription for action." Hennessy critically evaluates both feminist discourses as unsatisfactory if feminism is understood both as a political movement and as a theory that can "make sense" out of the world of oppression.

By reading French feminist and American standpoint theories criti- cally against each other, Hennessy seeks to develop an "analytic" that extends postmodern and feminist critiques of the centered subject with- out giving up a commitment to the possibility of transformative social change.[85] To that end she critically evaluates Althusser's notion of ide- ology as overly functionalist and his concept of interpellation as too subversive of agency. Nevertheless, she finds his theory of language help- ful because it understands language as "social action" and as the means through which subjects are fashioned. Ideology produces discourses that can be seen, heard, spoken, proclaimed, printed, believed, and valued, in other words, all that counts as socially determined reality.

> To say that ideology is a material force in that it (re)produces what counts
> as reality suggests that other material forces, both economic and political,
> are not merely reflected in ideology but that they too are at least in part
> shaped by ideology.[86]

Such a conception of ideology also seeks to correct empiricist- positivist understandings of "reality" as outside of discourse. It does so "by including the discursive within the materiality out of which the social is produced." Hence, we must distinguish between the "raw material," the real object (i.e., the actual world), on the one hand

and the discursively elaborated real as the object of knowledge on the other. The clear implication for feminist christological discourse consists in the insight that "reality," whether that of the historical Jesus or that of women's experience, is always an ideological-rhetorical construct shaped by the cultural languages and theoretical framework of particular historical moments.

Hennessy goes on to elaborate this notion of ideology in terms of the concept of hegemony that Gramsci developed. In Gramsci's theory hegemony is understood as a process whereby a ruling group comes to dominate by establishing the cultural "common sense." Cultural power is not simply exercised from the top down, but rather is negotiated and contested in a process of discursive articulation.[87] By combining the insights of both Marxist theorists and confronting them with feminist theories, Hennessy seeks to develop a theoretical framework that can offer a fruitful way out of the crisis introduced by the postmodern notion of "the subject-as-constructed-in language."

If what becomes cultural or religious "common sense" is engendered[88] by a process through which those in power establish and maintain their rule, then christological dogmas must be understood as the result of a political process through which the imperial church, under the pressures of the political interests of the Roman emperors, came to dominate. Christological discourses must be investigated to determine how much they continue this kyriarchal process and how much they interrupt it. Hence feminist theology that engages in ideology critique as a social practice does not simply reject the entire ideological formation of christology but engages in theoretical struggles in order to reconfigure it. Feminist theology is able to do so, I suggest, only if it no longer conceptualizes christology as a monolithic totality but rather understands it as an aggregate of contesting, rival, often contradictory discourses that produce what comes to count "as the way it is."

The theoretical work of Hennessy sheds light on my own attempts to address the dualistic either/or alternative — *either* identify with patriarchal institutions (such as biblical religions) *or* leave them — which is inscribed in feminist discourses in religion. It also is helpful for "reconfiguring" feminist christological discourses in such a way that they can disrupt the kyriarchal socioreligious practices that are discursively constructed. In *But She Said* I attempted to develop a feminist theory of a critical interpretation for liberation so that it might work with the postmodern insight that the category "woman" is discursively constructed and at the same time articulate women's historical agency for change.

I did so, however, not primarily in terms of abstract philosophy but in terms of the historical-theological interaction between the practices of kyriarchy and democracy in antiquity. I thereby sought to intervene in the preconstructed notion of "how things were" and attempted to disrupt the "common-sense" assumption of biblical and theological scholarship that uncritically holds that kyriarchal relations were all-encompassing as well as the "culturally given" common-sense fact in antiquity.

The notion of the "ekklēsia of wo/men," that is, the full democratic assembly of wo/men, attempts to conceptualize a feminist space and discourse, counterhegemonic to that of imperial or democratic kyriarchy in antiquity and modernity. This paradoxical expression seeks to articulate a critical democratic space from which feminists can speak in order to change hegemonic "common-sense" theological discourses. The notion of the ekklēsia of wo/men constitutes the enabling ground for feminist discourses to articulate christological images for change. Such a discursively constructed and historically specific articulation, I have argued, is able to disarticulate and replace the religious constructions of the cultural sex-gender system.

When I speak of the ekklēsia of wo/men as the hermeneutical center of feminist biblical interpretation and christological construction, I do not speak of a women's church that excludes men. Nor do I speak of one group of women as a unitary entity or mean to argue for women's integration into the kyriarchal institutions of the church. Nor do I want to restrict the notion of the ekklēsia of wo/men to the interpretive theological community that articulates christological discourse. Rather, the "reality" and vision of the ekklēsia of wo/men is a hermeneutical, discursively constructed articulation that seeks to make conscious that cultural "common-sense" patriarchal religion and malestream democracy have been exclusive of women, be they human or divine.

Theologically, the expression "ekklēsia of wo/men" asserts that "salvation" is not possible outside the world or without the world. G*d's vision of a renewed creation entails not only a "new" heaven but also a "renewed," qualitatively different earth freed from kyriarchal exploitation and dehumanization. To articulate ekklēsia, i.e., the assembly of full citizens, means to name an alternative reality of justice and well-being for all, without exception.

In contrast to fundamentalist or liberal modern theologies, feminist liberation theologies of all colors do not see the threat of secularization as the greatest problem for faith today. Rather the greatest problem consists in the fact that life on earth is jeopardized by the multiform practices of dehumanization, violence, exploitation, and extinction. Like other liberation theologies, feminist liberation theologies shift their focus from the modern question, How can we believe in G*d? to the questions, What kind of G*d do Christians proclaim? and Do religious faith and community make a difference in the struggle for the well-being of all in the global village? Are the Bible and christology used to sustain hegemonic kyriarchal discourses or are they deployed to reconfigure them so that they support wo/men's struggles for liberation and transformation? Which christological articulations legitimate the status quo and which promote G*d's intention for the welfare of every wo/man?

Through feminist political-religious struggles for liberation the ekklēsia of wo/men seeks to mediate divine "revelation"; it makes experientially available the "reality" of the life-giving power of G*d in the midst of the death-dealing power of kyriarchal oppression and dehumanization. G*d's power for salvation must "reveal" itself as active in the struggles for survival and well-being of women living at the bottom of the kyriarchal pyramid of oppression. Feminist christological discourses therefore have to pay special attention to those theological articulations of the ekklēsia of wo/men that explore situations of multiplicative oppressions. They may, however, not construct these articulations as regionalized, isolated struggles but rather take the measure for all feminist christological construction from them.

In short, I argue that within the logic and rhetoric of radical democracy we can conceptualize the ekklēsia of wo/men as the metaphoric space[89] that can sustain critical practices of struggle for transforming societal and religious kyriarchal institutional discourses. Such a theoretical space and frame of meaning seeks to displace the feminist anthropological construct "woman" or the "feminine" to replace it with a political construct that is at once a historical and an imagined political religious reality, already partially realized but still to be struggled for. Historically and politically the metaphor of the ekklēsia of wo/men is an oxymoron, a combination of contradictory terms for the purpose of articulating a feminist political site from which to speak.

As the intersection of multiple public feminist discourses and the site of "ideological" contradictions, feminist alternatives, and as yet unrealized feminist possibilities, the ekklēsia of wo/men requires a rhetorical articulation of theological interpretation in general and of christology in particular. Taking the ekklēsia of wo/men as their discursive frame of reference, feminist christological articulations can move back and forth between different rhetorical strategies and historical contexts. They do not need to construct christological discourses as fixed positions that exclude each other. In such a way critical feminist theological practices can make available polyglot discourses through which individual wo/men can shape their own narratives of interpretation in conversation and debate with other christologies and discourses of liberation.

The following two examples seek to show how critical feminist readings and christological discussions function when positioned not within kyriarchal discursive frameworks but within the space and horizon of the ekklēsia of wo/men.

First, in my book *In Memory of Her* I argued that feminist historical reconstruction must begin with the assumption of women's presence and agency rather than with the preconstructed kyriarchal discourse of women's marginality and victimization.[90] Such an argument seeks to shift "the burden of proof" to kyriocentric hegemonic biblical scholarship that contends that women were not active and present in the development of early Christian life and theology. Only the presumption of women's historical and theological agency, I contended, will allow us to read the slippage, ambiguities, gaps, and silences of androcentric, i.e., grammatically masculine, texts not simply as properties of language and text but as the inscribed symptoms of historical struggles. Hence I insisted that feminist inquiry change its methodological focus from the "study of women as objects and of what men have said about women (gender constructs)" to a feminist systemic analysis of oppression and struggle for change.

Such a change of theoretical frameworks or hermeneutical "binoculars" makes it possible to understand early Christian beginnings as shaped by the agency and leadership of Jewish, Greco-Roman, Asian, African, free and enslaved, rich and poor, elite and marginal men and wo/men. Those who hold the opposite view that, for instance, slave wo/men were not active shapers of early Christian life would have to argue their point. Shifting from a kyriarchal preconstructed frame of reference to that of the ekklēsia of wo/men we can no longer argue that, for instance, women might or might not have been members of the communities that produced the hypothetical Sayings Source Q.[91] If one cannot show definitely that women were *not* members of this group, one needs to give the benefit of the doubt to the textual traces that suggest that they were. Rather than taking the grammatically androcentric text at face value, one must unravel its politics of meaning.

The objection that this is a circular argument is valid, but it applies to all hermeneutical practices. For instance, social scientific studies that presuppose the preconstructed dualistic opposition of "honor and shame" as given "facts" of Mediterranean cultures will read early Christian texts "about women" within this theoretically "constructed" kyriocentric frame of reference.[92] Their narratives, however, appear to be more "realistic" and "objective" than feminist ones only because kyriocentric discourses function as ideologies, that is, they mystify the "constructedness" of their account of reality.[93] Therefore hegemonic narratives of "how the world of early Christianity really was" are easily accepted by readers as "common-sense," "objective," "scientific," historical accounts, although they are as much a "construction" as feminist accounts are — if not more so.

For my second example I want to return to my short analysis of the politics of discourse that shaped the doctrinal articulation of the Council of Chalcedon and the interpretations of Chalcedon by Odell-Scott and Studer.[94] My argument refers to the same text as theirs but reads it quite differently. Since both acknowledge the political interventions and pressures of the imperial administration, this difference does not consist in our political readings. Rather it is rooted in the different frames of interpretation with which we approach the text.

Odell-Scott's text is positioned within a postmodern Heideggerian theoretical discourse and moved by Protestant interests. Within a Roman Catholic hermeneutics Studer in turn argues that the christological doctrine is in line with Christian Testament texts. He seeks to give a positive interpretation of the council text, arguing that it expresses Jesus' solidarity with G*d and with humanity.[95] As elaborated, my own text is positioned within the hermeneutical space of the ekklēsia of wo/men and moved by the interests of feminist liberation theologies. Whereas a "scientific" positivist framework and method argue for the "objectivity" and thereby superiority of a single interpretation — usually one's own — a liberal pluralist frame of reference tends to proliferate examples of different readings. It refuses to adjudicate between them and instead calls for a ludic (playful) intellectual engagement with them.

Christological discourses that position themselves within the hermeneutical space of the ekklēsia of wo/men, I argue, can adopt neither a positivist nor a postmodern "ludic" politics of discourse. Rather they must adopt a hermeneutics of suspicion as a method of investigation in order to lay open the kyriocentric strategies of texts and discourses. Such a hermeneutics of suspicion seeks to assess critically the kyriarchal effects of christological articulations on the lives of wo/men in the global village. My own text has underscored not only the imperial context that shaped the doctrinal pronouncement of Chalcedon but also the "politics of meaning" inscribed in the intellectual conundrum of the "mysterious *oikonomia*" of Jesus Christ. As doctrinal formulation it reinscribes again and again the dualistic kyriarchal order/law into Christian self-understanding as "common-sense" and as "revealed," "given" truth of "how the world is."

For such a critical assessment of the "politics of meaning" inscribed in christological discourse a critical feminist theology of liberation derives its criteria of evaluation neither from appeals to the universal

divine feminine and woman's nature nor from assertions of essential femaleness and salvific sisterhood. Rather, positioned in the horizon and
space of the ekklēsia of wo/men, it undertakes a critical systemic analysis of kyriarchal oppression for such a critical dialogue. To that end it
positions itself explicitly within wo/men's particular historical-religious
struggles against the systems of oppression operating on the axes of
class, race, gender, ethnicity, religion, and sexual preference, among
others. Historical political-religious struggles to change the exploitative structures of kyriarchy — and not sexual difference — constitute
the "qualitative threshold" of feminist christological articulations in the
ekklēsia of wo/men.

The chapters of this book seek to engage various christological discourses in order to intervene in their politics of meaning. I particularly
wish to link the struggles over christology articulated in biblical studies
and feminist theologies. My reflection focuses on the construct or image
of Jesus the Lord and Savior to investigate how the "reality" articulated by this signifier has become "common sense" and remains deeply
embedded in contemporary religious and political processes of domination. In short, I seek to lay open for critical reflection how much the
interpretive frames of even feminist theologies remain implicated in this
kyriarchal process.

By placing feminist and biblical christological discourses alongside
each other as well as by reading them in dialogue and conflict with each
other I do not seek to defend my own reading as the only "correct"
or possible reading. Neither do I want to relativize my interpretation in
such a way that it loses its power of argument. Rather, my critical discourses seek to stage a critical conversation and public debate among
those gathered around the christological table set by Divine Wisdom.
In this way I hope to contribute to the refiguration and rearticula-
tion of both feminist and hegemonic christological discourses within the
social-political contexts of struggle in the global village under the radical
democratic horizon of the ekklēsia of wo/men.

Chapter 2

AND MARY WENT
INTO THE HILL COUNTRY
Issues in Feminist Christology

In those days Mary set out and went with haste to a Judean town in
the hill country, where she entered the house of Zechariah and greeted
Elizabeth. (Luke 1:39–40)

Introducing the concept of gender into feminist thought was an important
political move. It meant that we did not have to argue our way at every
step out of the biological connection implicit in the concept of sex. But
the already givenness of "gender" and "difference" creates problems for
sociology. . . . Difference is already there. The seams, cracks, varieties and
contradictions in the multiple sites and modes of being a woman or being
a man are reduced and homogenized.[1]

The Lukan statement "and Mary went into the hill country," which introduces this chapter, does not function as a historical reference so much
as a hermeneutical metaphor and interpretive key for a critical feminist
theology. Thereby I seek to position feminist christological discourses
neither in the "wilderness"[2] nor in a deadly "minefield"[3] — two metaphors used for characterizing the situation of feminist literary criticism.
Rather I want metaphorically to figure feminist christological discourses
as wandering in the "hills," the "ups and downs" of feminist struggles
for liberation.

Thus, in this chapter I seek to explore the hardships and difficulties
of a feminist journey into the intellectual territory and "hill country"
of hegemonic christology. I will particularly focus on those malestream
theological "roadblocks" that the cultural and religious constructs of
maleness/masculinity and femaleness/femininity place in the way of a
feminist meeting. Only after such an arduous intellectual journey, guided

33

by a critical hermeneutics of suspicion, I submit, are wo/men able to meet on their own terms and in their own space. For the scriptural metaphor of this chapter's title not only evokes an arduous journey but also the joyous embrace of two women pregnant with the possibilities of new life. Hence, I have chosen the woodcut *Heimsuchung* (Visitation) by the German socialist artist Käthe Kollwitz for the cover of this book to visually announce the protective strength and communicative power of women talking to and blessing each other. The Shekinah, G*d's Presence, will grant such meetings of minds and hearts where two or three are gathered in her name.[4] Instead of "listening in" on the historical conversation of biblical women by imaginatively reconstructing it, I will attempt to enter into contemporary feminist christological debates in order to assess their power for change.

European and American feminist theologians have raised the problem of Jesus' "maleness" as one of the most central issues in christology.[5] In the present chapter I will explore feminist christological proposals and argue that even feminist discussions are constructed on and remain positioned within the terrain of the preconstructed cultural-religious sex/gender frame of meaning often taken for granted as "commonplace." As I outlined in the first chapter, the notion of a "preconstructed" frame of meaning is methodologically helpful for exploring the conditions of this christological terrain. Hence I will first sketch the cultural-religious sex/gender system as the prevalent frame of meaning affecting both malestream and feminist critical discourses. In a second and third step I will critically discuss feminist theological proposals for addressing the problem of Jesus' maleness in order to argue for a paradigm shift in feminist christological discourses.[6] In a concluding section I single out a famous and much-quoted speech of the black abolitionist Sojourner Truth as a hermeneutical guide for such a paradigm shift. Since this speech was written down by a white suffragist, it represents a common womanist/feminist christological tradition that could provide a different hermeneutical frame of reference.[7]

The Sex/Gender System[8]
as Discursive Frame of Meaning

Christological discourses are best understood as social rhetorical practices that produce and reconstruct religious-theological identity in an ongoing intertextual and intercultural process. Christological gender constructions thus are a distinctive effect of a complex of social relations specifically defining femininity [and masculinity] and organizing, in and across actual local sites of people's lives, the homogeny of gender difference.[9]

The following experience might illustrate what is meant by this abstract sociological language. When Chris was four years old she came home from kindergarten crying and very upset. After much prodding she related that she had been in an argument with other children at school about the newborn baby whose birthday we celebrate on Christmas. Her playmates claimed that Jesus was a boy while Chris insisted that the Christ-child was a girl. When the teacher intervened and confirmed that Jesus was a boy, Chris was devastated. Since we had always stressed how happy and fortunate we were that she was born a girl and had given her the name Christina, she simply had taken it for granted that all the fuss about the newborn babe was due to its being a girl. Her tears and rage testified to the invisible scars left on women by the often subconscious realization that boys, not girls, sons, not daughters, are the center of our cultural and religious heritage and celebrations.

The assumption of "natural" sex/gender differences informs such everyday experience and turns it into "common-sense" knowledge that makes gender difference appear to be "commonplace" and "G*d-given." It serves as a preconstructed frame of meaning for feminist biblical and theological readings. It understands the modern sex/gender system of masculine and feminine difference in positivistic terms either as a natural-historical fact or as a metaphysical essence that is revealed rather than socially constructed. By presenting the sex/gender system of male/female or masculine/feminine as universal and "common-sense," this preconstructed frame of meaning obscures and mystifies the reality that the very notion of two sexes is a sociocultural construct for maintaining kyriarchal domination rather than a biological "given" or innate essence. This preconstructed framework makes us forget that not so long ago racial and national differences were considered to be natural biological facts or to be ordained by G*d — as they still are considered by some today.

Feminist theory has explicated that the Western sex/gender system operates simultaneously on four discursive levels: first, on the social-political level; second, on the ethical-symbolic level; third, on the biological-natural level; and finally, on the linguistic-grammatical level. These levels are interactive and mutually reinforce each other. Different feminist approaches enter their critical analysis at different nodal points of these interlocking discursive levels and hence emphasize different aspects of the sex/gender system. They generally distinguish the terms "male"/"female," which mean to classify human beings on the basis of anatomical differences; "man"/"woman," which are understood as based on social relations; and "masculine"/"feminine," which are seen as the cultural-religious ideals, norms, values, and standards appropriate to one's gender position.

As I maintained in the first chapter, feminist theologies must adopt a social analytic that can break through the sex/gender system's totalizing and mystifying dualistic frame of reference. An analytic of kyriarchy rather than simply an analytic of gender, I argued, provides a more adequate conceptual tool of analysis. Such an analytic enables us to interpret christological androcentric texts and kyriocentric traditions as socioreligious constructions rather than as revealed "givens" and also to see how gender, race, class, and colonialist structures are multiplicative and interdependent. In order to distinguish such a feminist liberationist analytic from the prevalent dualistic feminist understanding of patriarchy as domination of men over women, in *But She Said* I coined the word "kyriarchy" in analogy to the German term *Herrschaft*. This neologism, I submit, is historically more adequate and theologically more appropriate than "hierarchy," which is commonly used in English to designate a pyramidal system of power relations. Whereas much of feminist thought still locates the root of misogyny and patriarchal oppression in gender dualism, I have consistently argued to the contrary that *kyriocentric* symbolic gender constructions shape and legitimate the sociopolitical system of kyriarchal oppression that in turn produces such ideological constructions. This can be shown with respect to all four levels of the sex/gender system.

 First Level: A critical feminist theology of liberation begins its analytic work with the *sociopolitical* level of the sex/gender system. If we conceptualize reality not in terms of gender dualism, but rather as a socially constructed web of interactive structures, we are better able to understand dichotomies such as world-church, human-divine, profane-sacred, politics-religion, orthodox-heretic, earth-heaven, male-female. We are able to recognize that our cultural-religious position and intellectual perspective are determined by our social location if we understand oppression not in terms of dualistic opposites but as diverse social, interactive, and multiplicative structures of power. Hence, the categories "male"/"female," "masculine"/"feminine," or "man"/ "woman" do not signify dualistic opposites or fixed gender slots but socio-political-religious discursive practices that are defined not only by anatomical sex, but also by features of race, class, and culture. The social relations that give rise to gender differences are socioculturally constructed as relations of domination and are not simply biological givens. In other words, the world is determined by relations of domination. Sex/gender is a part of such relations of ruling, which also ground other divisions such as class or race.

Although maleness and femaleness are supposedly natural-biological "givens," they are in fact cultural norms that are backed by social sanctions. Since sex/gender differences are grounded in kyriarchal arrangements, they are articulated differently in different historical periods and cultures but nonetheless are taken to be "commonplace," universal, natural "facts," or ordained by God. Whereas in antiquity, for instance, menial service was seen as appropriate to the nature of slaves and serfs, in modernity it is construed as a "feminine" ideal appropriate to the nature of women. Public political service in turn is conceptualized as "masculine," appropriate to the nature of men. This kyriarchal separation between the public male sphere and the private female domain has generated a separate system of economics for women[10] that has resulted in the increasing feminization of poverty and the destitution of female-headed households[11] — a development with devastating effects especially on women of the so-called two-thirds world and their children.

The modern sex/gender system must be scrutinized not only for its heterosexist economic-cultural biases but also for its classist, racist, and colonialist underpinnings. Aristotle argued that the freeborn, propertied, educated Greek man was the highest of moral beings and that all other members of the human race were defined by their functions in his service.[12] Modern political philosophy continues to assume that propertied, educated elite Western man is defined by reason, self-determination, and full citizenship, whereas women and other subordinated peoples are characterized by emotion, service, and dependence.[13] They are seen not as rational and responsible adult subjects but as emotional, helpless, and childlike. In short, in order to function kyriarchal societies and cultures need a "servant class," a "servant race," or a "servant people," be they slaves, serfs, house servants, kulis, or mammies. The existence of such a "servant class" is maintained through law, education, socialization, and brute violence. It is sustained by the belief that members of a "servant class" of people are by nature or by divine decree inferior to those whom they are destined to serve.[14]

Second Level: As the first chapter elaborated, such kyriarchal relations of domination and subordination were explicitly articulated in Western political philosophy in the context of Greek patriarchal democracy. They have been mediated by Christian scriptural-theological traditions and have decisively determined modern kyriarchal forms and ideologies of democracy. Among other feminist political philosophers Genevieve Lloyd has documented that modern (and postmodern) understandings of rationality and of the world have been articulated by white European-American elite educated men.[15] These men have defined not only white women as "others," but also all "other" nonpersons who lack human, i.e., masculine qualities. The definition of other races and peoples as "feminine Other" has enabled colonial Western powers to exploit and utilize religion in the colonial capitalist quest for identity and property.

The modern bourgeois ethos of "femininity" prescribes that "good" wo/men perform unpaid services in and outside the family with selfless love, nurturing care, and patient loving-kindness. The ethos of "true womanhood," romantic love, and domesticity defines wo/men's nature as "being for others" in actual or spiritual motherhood. Whereas men are measured by the masculine standards of self-assertion, independence, power, and control, wo/men are called to fulfill their true nature and destiny through self-sacrificing service and loving self-effacement. The cultural socialization of wo/men to selfless femininity and altruistic behavior is reinforced and perpetuated by the Christian preaching of self-sacrificing love and humble service.

Since the industrial revolution in Europe and America church and religion have been pushed out of the public realm and relegated to the private sphere of individualistic piety, charitable work, and the cultivation of home and family. Nevertheless, both religion and women also have been crucial in maintaining public interest in the antithetical "other" and in shaping American self-identity.[16] Like the "white lady," Christianity as a "missionary religion" had the function of "civilizing" the savages, who were understood as "untamed nature." The Western discourses on femininity and female nature have here their sociopolitical and religious contexts in the colonial exercise of power.[17]

In the process of religious privatization and cultural "feminization," the clergy lost their privileged status and came to be treated like "women" in polite society. This feminization of religion has emphasized the service role of the church. It has led both to the emasculation of the clergy in society[18] and to the reassertion of their masculine roles in theology, church, and home. The debates on women's ordination and the profession of the "maleness" of Jesus have here their "setting in life."[19] Women's recent access to professional ministry and theology is resisted by male clerics because the ministry is culturally typed as "feminine." Hence, male clergy fear that the church will be totally feminized and become a "women's church" if women join the ranks of male clergy.

Third Level: Although "maleness" and "femaleness," as well as "man" and "woman," are figurative categories and symbolic constructs of the cultural sex/gender system, they *appear to be "natural"* or *"factual" sex differences* in commonplace discourse and everyday under-standing. The oppression of women is not achieved by force but through individual socialization and public discourses. Like education, religion has a major role in the discursive construction and symbolic legitimiza-tion of such sex/gender relations as heterosexuality. For instance, biblical religion has applied the metaphor of patriarchal marriage relationships to the relation between G*d and the individual soul as well as between Christ and the community. Early Christian theology continued prophetic discourses that understood God as the groom/husband of his bride/wife Israel. In Western mysticism and piety, men, like women, have taken up the "feminine" position of receptivity and surrender with respect to G*d, conforming to a masculine G*d's desire for the feminine while at the same time sustaining masculine practices of control and superiority with respect to the world.

This analogy between G*d-Christ-husband-male on the one hand and soul-bride-female on the other has become "naturalized" and biologized in modern theological discourse.[20] Although Christians did not continue the practice of male circumcision as the core symbol of corporeal elec-tion, the Christian churches excluded women from ordination until very recently — and my own church still does so today on grounds of ana-tomical sex. It is female sex that disqualifies a person from representing Christ. Whereas traditional theology had rationalized the exclusion of women on Aristotelian and scriptural grounds of subordination, mod-ern theology argues that women cannot physically resemble Christ, the bridegroom of the church.

In order to undo such modern "naturalizing" sex/gender tenden-cies feminist theologians have insisted that christological discourses must distinguish between biological sex and kyriarchal symbolic gender constructions. For instance, Elizabeth Johnson asserts:

> Let me be very clear about what is at issue here. The fact that Jesus of Nazareth was a man is not in question. His maleness is constitutive for his personal identity, part of the perfection and limitation of his historical reality, and as such it is to be respected. His sex is as intrinsic to his his-torical person as is his race, class, ethnic heritage.... The difficulty arises, rather from the way this one particularity of sex...is interpreted in sex-ist theology and practice. Consciously or unconsciously, Jesus' maleness is lifted up and made essential for his christic function and identity, thus blocking women precisely because of their female sex from participating in the fullness of their Christian identity as images of Christ.[21]

Although such an attempt to separate biological sex from gender is common in feminist theological discourse, it is nevertheless problematic since it does not sufficiently reflect that the cultural sex/gender system "naturalizes" the category of "sex" as biologically given rather than as discursively constructed. It does not take into account that primary and secondary physical sex differences are not "biological facts" but are also discursively constructed. For instance, common sense has it that facial hair is a male physical secondary sex characteristic. This commonplace assumption conceals, however, that it is discursively constructed. In order to uphold this ostensibly male sex standard, a multibillion dollar cosmetic industry strives to eradicate all facial hair in women. Anatomical physical differences are as discursively constructed and socially maintained as are cultural sex differences. Moreover, different cultures construct the meaning of anatomical differences differently. For instance, it might be argued that boy and girl children are physically more alike than girls and nursing mothers. In addition, biological differences receive different significance if they are discursively constructed on a continuum rather than in terms of dualistic oppositional taxonomy.[22]

As long as this cultural and theological sex/gender politics of meaning remains operative in feminist christological reflection, it will continue to provide a sociopolitical "modern" frame of reference in which the masculine sex/gender of Jesus as well as that of grammatically "generic" language remains a central problem and obstacle for feminist christological reflection. This theological naturalization of gender and its reduction to anatomical sex conceals its social location in a modern biosocial science of human variation. According to nineteenth-century scientists:

> lower races represented the "female" type of the human species, and females the "lower race" of gender. . . . By analogy with the so-called lower races, women, the sexually deviate, the criminal, the urban poor, and the insane were in one way or another constructed as biological "races apart" whose differences from the white male, and likeness to each other, "explained" their different and lower position in the social hierarchy.[23]

Fourth Level: A theology that asserts biological sex/gender differences as natural and God-given can do so because its readings of Scripture and tradition engages in a linguistic-symbolic process of "naturalizing" grammatical gender. Not only religious language but also androcentric language in general repeatedly reinscribes the cultural-religious prejudices and social-kyriarchal relations that in turn undergird its disciplinary practices. The term "grammatical gender" derives from Latin *genus,* which means "class, kind, or category." The grammatical noun classification system of masculine/feminine is said to have been introduced by the fifth-century B.C.E. Sophist Protagoras. If Protagoras had used a different classification system such as, for instance, long/short, the devastating conflation of grammatical gender with biological sex in Western symbolic universes might have been avoided.

According to the grammarian Dennis Baron, association of grammatical gender with human generation was developed by medieval grammarians into Latin species, an association that later grammarians imposed on Old English by arguing for it in cultural-religious terms.[24] For instance, in his *Theory of Language* published in 1788 James Beattie argued on theological grounds for the distinction of biological sex as the primary basis for noun classification:

> Beings superior to man, although we conceive them to be of no sex, are spoken of as masculine in most of the modern tongues of Europe, on account of their dignity; the male being according to our ideas, the nobler sex. But idolatrous nations acknowledge both male and female deities; and some of them have even given to the Supreme Being a name of the feminine gender.[25]

A few years later the very influential grammarian Lindley Murray also argued on cultural grounds for such a sex-based classification:

> Figuratively, in the English tongue, we commonly give the masculine gender to nouns which are conspicuous for the attributes of imparting or communicating and which are by nature strong and efficacious. Those again are made feminine which are conspicuous for the attributes of containing or bringing forth, or which are particularly beautiful or amiable. Upon these principles the sun is always masculine, and the moon, because the receptacle of the sun's light, is feminine. The earth is generally feminine. A ship, a country, a city...are likewise made feminine, being receivers or containers.[26]

In 1850 the British Parliament passed an act declaring that henceforth the pronoun "he" would be used as including reference to women as well as to men, thereby replacing the use of "they" as generic with the pseudogeneric "he."[27] The Western linguistic sex/gender system that uses gender classifications as rooted in biological sex cannot but reify and naturalize sociopolitical gender constructs. In such a linguistic system, masculine terms function as "generic" language in which "man"/"male"/"masculine"/"he" stands for human *and* male whereas "woman"/"female"/"feminine"/"she" denotes femaleness. Grammatically androcentric "generic" Western languages that are based on the classical grammatical systems of Greek and Latin explicitly mention women only as the exception to the rule, as problematic, or specifically as particular individuals. In all other cases one has to adjudicate in light of contextual linguistic markers whether women are meant or not.

Western androcentric languages and discourses do not simply marginalize women or eliminate them from the historical cultural-religious record. As kyriocentric languages they also construct the meaning of being "women" or being "men" differently. What it means to be female/

woman/feminine does not depend on one's sex so much as on one's location in the social-symbolic system of multiform kyriarchal oppressions.
The meaning of "women" is unstable and ever shifting,[28] depending
not so much on its sex/gender relation but on its sociosystemic contextualization.[29] The category "woman" today is used interchangeably
with "female"/"feminine" and thus has become a "naturalized" generic
sex-based term, although until very recently it was utilized as an appellation for lower-class females only. A statement such as "slaves were not
women" offends "common-sense" understandings, whereas a statement
such as "slaves were not ladies" makes perfect sense. We can perceive
the slippages, cultural constructedness, and historical ambiguity of the
meaning of "woman" much more easily in the term "lady," because this
discursive appellation readily "reveals" its race, class, and colonial bias.
"Lady" has been restricted to women of higher status or educational re-
finement until very recently. It also has functioned to symbolize "true
womanhood" and femininity.

In Western kyriocentric language systems the lady/mistress/mother is
"the other" of the lord/master/father whereas all other women who are
marked as "inferior" by race, class, religion, or culture are the "others
of the other."[30] Hence they are not mentioned in historical kyriocentric
records at all. Read in a kyriocentric way, for instance, the famous text
of Galatians 3:28, which states that in Christ there are "neither Jews
nor Greeks, slaves nor free, male and female," is usually interpreted as
referring to three different groups: Jew and Greek as religious ethnic
characterizations, slave and free as sociopolitical determinations, and
male and female as anthropological sex/gender definitions. However,
such a reading does not take into account the obfuscating strategies of
kyriocentric language when it tacitly infers on the one hand that "Jews,"
"Greeks," "slave," and "free" are terms pertaining solely to men and on
the other that only the third pair, "male and female," refers to women.

Such a cursory discussion of the Western sex/gender system explains
why proposing to address the "maleness" of Jesus from a feminist perspective usually raises great, albeit repressed, anxieties among men and
women. Since religious men are culturally stereotyped as "feminine,"
they need to establish their cultural-religious self-identity by profess-
ing and upholding masculine standards. Women in turn uphold the
ideal of femininity, which in modernity was formulated, for instance, by
Rousseau, who argued that men are to be educated to be "their own
man," whereas women are to be educated to be "women for men."[31]
Accordingly, women fear a loss of their cultural-religious feminine self-
identity and prestige if they no longer can model their relations to men
on the paradigm of their relation with Jesus, the perfect man for whom

they live.[32] A recent poll has shown that almost 70 percent of U.S. women consider "feminist" to be a negative label evoking the image of bra-burning "crazies." Although many of the women interviewed actually subscribe to many goals of the feminist movement and have benefited from its socioeconomic achievements, they still feel compelled to distance themselves from feminism as much as possible. This cultural compulsion affects *all* women and not merely middle-class white women. Indeed the media often charge that feminism is "racist" or "colonialist" in order to compel women of the so-called two-thirds world to distance themselves from feminism as a political movement for change.

In short, the form and shape of feminist christological inquiry has been conditioned not only by its biblical-dogmatic location but also by its rhetorical-theological location within the preconstructed modern frame of the sex/gender system. It is apparent that feminist theological explorations of Jesus' masculinity are positioned in the collusion between the kyriarchal doctrinal discourses of the ancient church and the modern sex/gender discourses of Western culture. Because it is generally believed that christology is at the heart of Christian identity, biblical and theological scholarship today is compelled to articulate christological discourses in response to the rationalist and positivist challenges of modernity articulated by the "Man of Reason." Liberal theological reflections and feminist discourses on Jesus have here their "setting in life."

If we consider this rhetorical location of christological discourse in general, it is not surprising that feminist christological explorations are caught up in the same dynamics of the sex/gender system. They center on the maleness of the historical Jesus and its significance for Christian identity, since the masculinity of Jesus has been underscored in modernity in order to secure the masculine identity of male clerics and to legitimate their authority claims. In line with this, Rosemary Radford Ruether has concisely summed up the central problem of feminist christological discourses in the rhetorical question: "Can a male savior redeem and save women?" Feminist theologians have responded to this question in two distinct ways: they have either emphasized the humanity of Jesus or stressed relationality and connectedness as feminist frames of meaning.

"Full Humanity" as Interpretive Framework

Rhetorically situating the masculinity of Jesus as the central feminist christological problem is not new or the result of the second wave of feminism. Mary Daly pointed to the historical roots of this question in the nineteenth century by introducing her christological reflections in *Beyond God the Father* with a quote from Elizabeth Cady Stanton:

> Take the snake, the fruit tree and the woman from the tableau, and we have no fall, no frowning Judge, no Inferno, no everlasting punishment — hence no need of a Savior. Thus the bottom falls out of the whole Christian theology. Here is the reason why in all the biblical researches and higher criticisms, the scholars never touch the position of women.[33]

In the last century suffragists asserted that Christendom would tumble like a house of cards if the misogynist doctrinal trump card of female sinfulness and male salvific efficacy were pulled out; in this century, however, the theological import of Jesus' male gender is at the heart of feminist christological debates. This shift in emphasis points to a shift in the theological-political contextualization of the feminist christological controversy.

The misogynist theology of woman's sinfulness, cunning, and weakness no longer takes center stage today because it has lost its persuasive power in a sociopolitical context in which women's equal rights and dignity are accepted, in theory if not always in practice. Hence, patriarchal articulation of christology and its religio-political contextualization has shifted its emphasis to the sociocultural discourse on natural gender difference. Since hegemonic patriarchal gender discourses assume essential gender difference as a "common-sense" biological given, patriarchal theology can persuasively advance the maleness of Jesus as divinely revealed and historically given. The ecclesiastical arguments against women's access to all levels of church leadership through ordination have endowed the biological sex of the historical Jesus with theological significance.

Malestream theology insists that the Bible proclaims G*d as male and reveals his incarnation in the man Jesus of Nazareth and that such an assertion does not deny women's dignity and invaluable contributions to church and society. Rather, it simply upholds the particularity of G*d's historical revelation in Jesus Christ. To be a Christian requires one to believe that masculine G*d-language and the historical maleness of Jesus constitute ultimate revelation. Such a politics of essential revealed gender difference is not only advocated by the Vatican today but also found in some feminist discourses. It argues that women and men are of equal worth or even that women represent human qualities and relations more fully. Women and men are essentially different by nature or by the divine order of creation. Apologetic Christian feminist attempts to prove that Jesus was a feminist or to ascribe to him androgynous status and to claim that he was the perfect man who integrated his masculinity and femininity remain caught up in the androcentric-patriarchal framework of Western culture. The question "Can a Male Savior Save Women?" makes sense only when contextualized in a frame of reference that assumes that femininity and masculinity are ontologically predetermined natural or revealed differences.

Post-Christian feminist scholars in religion rightly have objected to such a Christian feminist apologetics, but they often presuppose the same theoretical framework of gender essentialism and historical positivism. Like Cady Stanton they assume, without critically questioning their own presuppositions, that at the heart of the christological system is an intrinsic connection between original sin and female gender as well as between redemption and male gender; therefore they cannot but reject Christian faith as intrinsically misogynist. A feminist Christian response in turn is justified in pointing out that such a post-Christian reading resorts to fundamentalist literalism when it insists on the biological-cultural maleness of the historical Jesus. By rejecting christological doctrine without questioning its theological-cultural framework, post-Christian theological discourses are in danger of reproducing and reinscribing rather than destabilizing the patriarchal politics of christology that they oppose.

This christological debate between Christian and post-Christian feminist theology has been paradigmatically staged in a dialogue between the American feminist theologian Rosemary Radford Ruether and the British feminist theologian Daphne Hampson, which took place in 1986 in Westminster Abbey. Hampson contended that a feminist can be religious but not a Christian because Christian religion is intrinsically sexist; it cannot allow for the equality of women because it is bound up with a particular historical person Jesus Christ, who was male. Because Christianity sees certain historical events as revelation, it cannot be freed from its sexist historical context:

> If one was to remove the history of Israel, the history concerning Jesus, the resurrection in some form, the early church, and the Bible as a particular literature, the foundation of Christianity would be lost. . . . The religion cannot be freed of this historical context. The sexism of that context is always going to be present together with the religion.[34]

In her book *Theology and Feminism* Hampson clarifies that the problem "is not that Jesus was a man, but that this man has been considered unique, symbolic of God, God Himself."[35] Hampson therefore repeatedly insists on the historical *fact* of the maleness of Jesus and points to the masculinity of Christian G*d-language as essential to Christianity. It becomes the criterion for assessing whether a feminist theological proposal is Christian or not.

In her response Radford Ruether objects to such a positivist notion
of Christianity "as enclosed in a past revelation." She points to the
conservative theological underpinnings of such an argument.

> The chief defect of your argument seems to me to be your definition
> of Christianity as a historical religion. I am sure that this is the way
> conservatives use the idea of Christianity as a historical religion to resist
> change. But in fact, such an idea is thoroughly ahistorical. It is ahistorical
> because being historical means first of all being a living community of
> people.... Secondly the search for absolutes in past historical experience
> is ahistorical, since history is ever partial, relative and limited.[36]

In confronting the dogmatic assertion of the masculinity of Jesus Christ
within a discourse framework of gender, Radford Ruether argues that
an unmediated feminist recourse to Scripture or to the historical Jesus is
in danger of solidifying Christian identity as male identity in historically
and theologically positivist terms.

Radford Ruether's own wide-ranging and multifaceted work has decisively shaped feminist christological discussion.[37] Her by now almost
classic articulation of the central problem facing a feminist christology — "Can a Male Savior Save Women?"[38] — is repeated in the chapter
on christology of her book *Sexism and God-Talk*. This formulation reveals its sociohistorical location within the nineteenth-century feminist
christological discourse rearticulated by Mary Daly as a challenge to
Christian theology. Radford Ruether approaches the question by tracing the historical roots of christology in the Ancient Near East, Judaism,
and the ministry of Jesus. In a second step she discusses the patriarchalization of christology in the first five centuries of the church; this
is followed by a review of alternative christological articulations such as
androgynous and Spirit christologies. She concludes this chapter with
her own constructive answer, which relies heavily on an understanding of the historical Jesus as a prophet, liberator, and representative of
liberated humanity:

> In this sense Jesus as the Christ, the representative of liberated human-
> ity and the liberating Word of God, manifests the *kenosis of patriarchy,*
> the announcement of the new humanity through a lifestyle that discards
> hierarchical caste privilege and speaks on behalf of the lowly.[39]

Radford Ruether is careful not to limit the "new humanity" to the
historical Jesus when she asserts "redemptive humanity goes ahead of
us, calling us to yet uncompleted dimensions of human liberation."[40]
Nevertheless, her heavy reliance on the historical Jesus together with her
use of the concept of "humanity" — which manifests the "kenosis" but
not the abolition of patriarchal power and still conceptualizes Jesus in

masculine terms — are troublesome. They also indicate that her christological argument remains caught up in that feminist politics of meaning
whose frame of reference is determined by the preconstructed sex/gender
system.

As other feminist theologians have frequently pointed out, Radford
Ruether's concept of "new humanity" does not challenge the Western
cultural sex/gender system and its androcentric language, according to
which the male Man is the paradigm of being human whereas woman is
either his inferior or complementary "other."[41] Humanity and maleness
have been synonymous not only in Western cultures. Radford Ruether's
argument reveals that she still codes Jesus' humanness in culturally masculine terms when she claims that his lifestyle discards hierarchical caste
privilege. One can discard only what one has! It seems not an accidental
slip that she does not add here "male" because such a qualifier would
show that she reads the figure of Jesus as male.

Any feminist use of the concept "humanity" that does not radically
displace the Western kyriarchal frame of reference, which understands
gender as a biological given and masculinity as the paradigm for being
human, is bound to reinscribe the sex/gender system in feminist terms.
Most importantly, it neglects to address the issue that Christian women
read the Gospels as stories about Jesus, the great hero and exceptional
man, to whom they can relate in culturally feminine terms with love
and sacrificial service. In other words, stories about Jesus the liberator continue to function for religiously inculcating feminine romance
attitudes and to legitimate kyriarchal relations of dominance and submission. Most importantly, such a Christian feminist interpretation of
Jesus as the paradigmatic human being and liberator of women univer-
salizes him in such a way that his Jewish particularity becomes irrelevant
once again.

The African American theologian Jacquelyn Grant rightly has critiqued the dualistic sex/gender framework of "white" European and
European-American feminist christological discourses as an approach
tainted by racism. She distinguishes between three types of feminists:
biblical or evangelical feminists, feminist liberation theologians, and rejectionist feminists, who repudiate biblical tradition and faith. Grant
argues that all three directions in feminist theology have unintentionally
promoted a white supremacist frame of reference, insofar as they universalize the experience of European-American women and do not take the
experience of women of color or poor women into account. Although
liberation theologians such as Letty Russell, Carter Heyward, and Rosemary Radford Ruether analyze racism and classism, in Grant's judgment
they nevertheless remain caught up in the dominant European-American

gender framework. She summarizes the position of Russell and Radford
Ruether as follows:

> The historical Jesus was a man, but men do not have a monopoly upon
> Christ, and Eve was a woman but women do not have a monopoly on
> sin. For "Christ is not necessarily male, nor is the redeemed community
> only women, but new humanity, female and male." The maleness of Jesus
> is superseded by the Christness of Jesus. Both Russell and Ruether argue
> that the redemptive work of Jesus moves us toward the new humanity
> which is in Jesus Christ. But whereas Russell still holds to the unique
> Lordship of Jesus, Ruether raises the possibility that this Christ can be
> conceived in nontraditional ways — as in sister.[42]

Far from being inclusive, she concludes, sisterhood is a construct that
remains within the dominant gender framework, which does not acknowledge the differences between women. Grant proposes, first, that
white feminist christologies must be scrutinized to determine whether
they employ a one-dimensional gender analysis or instead develop a
multisystemic analysis of sexism, racism, and class exploitation. Such
a criterion, I would add, must be applied to *all* christological constructions, not only to those of white feminist theologians.

Second, Grant argues that feminist christology must emerge from the
experience and situation of the least, because "Jesus located the Christ
with the outcast."[43] Therefore she insists that the experience of black
women as women of color must become the second norm by which
the limitations of feminist perspectives in theology and christology are
to be judged. Her second argument, however, raises two problems. On
the one hand it does not take seriously the differences of class, culture,
age, and religion that also exist — including those among black women
themselves and between black women and other women of color. On
the other hand it theologically legitimates this norm with reference to
the historical Jesus.

However, such a methodological move is more than problematic. I do
not think that we can derive the criterion and norm of a feminist Christian theology from the option of the historical Jesus for the poor and
outcast. Rather, we must ground feminist theology in wo/men's struggles for the transformation of kyriarchy. Although in these struggles
wo/men may experience moments of liberation, on the whole no woman
is free and liberated unless all women without exception are liberated
from kyriarchal oppression. Feminist movements and theologies must
seek to overcome the oppression of all persons exploited by kyriarchy,
women *and* men, but they nevertheless must focus their efforts especially
on the liberation of women who live on the bottom of the pyramid of
multiplicative oppressions.

Although I consider Grant's critique of white gender theology to be very important, I do believe that it is somewhat misplaced when it is directed toward Russell's and Ruether's christological work. Instead, I submit that Grant's own proposal is much closer to that of Radford Ruether than she is willing to recognize. Like Radford Ruether she advocates a complex theological analysis of patriarchy but does not sufficiently develop it theoretically. Although Russell's and Radford Ruether's proposals remain caught up in the anthropological sex/gender frame of reference, I am not so sure that Grant has transformed their analysis of oppression.

In contrast to post-Christian feminists and Christian gender feminists who assume an essential or natural gender difference between women and men, feminist liberation theologians in general have asserted that it is Jesus' historical practice and humanity that is theologically important, not his manhood. Jesus' practice as a Galilean prophet who sought to renew the Jewish hope for the reign of G*d, his solidarity with the poor and despised, his call into a discipleship of voluntary service, his execution, death, and resurrection, in short, Jesus' liberating practice and not his maleness is significant. Jesus' action become the symbol and model of the full but not yet realized way of being human. What matters is not Jesus' masculinity[44] but his option for the poor and his solidarity with those who are marginalized.[45] Consequently, Grant sounds very much like Radford Ruether when she asserts:

> I would argue, as suggested by both Lee and Sojourner, that the signifi-
> cance of Christ is not his maleness, but his humanity. The most significant
> events of Jesus Christ were the life and ministry, the crucifixion and the
> resurrection. The significance of these events, in one sense, is that in them
> the absolute becomes concrete. God becomes concrete not only in the
> man Jesus, for he was crucified, but in the lives of those who will ac-
> cept the challenges of the risen Savior, the Christ.... For me, it means
> today, this Christ, found in the experiences of Black women, is a Black
> woman.[46]

If Christian proclamation and theology are to become credible in feminist terms, I would argue with Grant, all theologies — and not only white feminist theology — must be challenged to develop effective and powerful critiques and visions in the struggle to transform patriarchal structures. Scripture, tradition, theology, and christology must therefore be critically analyzed and tested for their ideological-political functions in legitimating or subverting kyriarchal structures and mind-sets of domination. They must be judged on whether and how much they articulate Christian identity and faith in the service of kyriarchal oppression or in the service of emancipatory subversion and transformation.

Relationality as Interpretive Framework

Isabel Carter Heyward in the United States and Mary Grey in Europe, among others, have sought to create a paradigm shift in feminist christological discourse from a "heroic individualistic" or "heroic liberationist" christology to a christological construction that privileges right relation, connectedness, mutuality, and "at-one-ment." This feminist christological discourse uses key concepts such as redemptive connectedness, power-in-relation, dynamic mutuality, erotic creativity, the language of lovers, mutual interdependence, passionate creativity, inclusive wholeness, healing energy of existence, and the ontological priority of relationality. These terms and many more have become the coinage of the christological discourse of relationality. Although these concepts are "feminine"-typed, this approach does not consider them as part and parcel of the cultural sex/gender system.

In *Speaking of Christ: A Lesbian Feminist Voice,* Carter Heyward refers to "Christa," the name given to a statue of the female Jesus, arms outstretched as though crucified, sculpted by Edwina Sandys. She argues that the classical questions of christology — for example, Was Jesus divine? Was he human? and "the Jesus of history" vs. the "Christ of faith" debate — are dead. Instead "the christological task of Christian feminism is to move the foundations of christology from the ontology of dualistic opposition towards the ethics of justice-making."[47]

Such a reformulation of relational christology is conceptualized in existential terms. An existentialist goal is articulated in the following almost postmodern ludic statement: "To re-image Jesus is to claim the authority to play freely with both Scripture and subsequent tradition in order to comprehend our own existence."[48] In her more recent work Heyward critically challenges the dualistic conceptualization of christology either as "from below" or as "from above." She proposes to do christology *with Jesus* in order *to be in Christ.* It is Jesus with whom we stand in order to establish right relationships, whereas in community human beings create each other and give birth to the "body of Christ." "In our own Christian faith we know that in our shared commitment to human well-being, we are she: bearer and borne, mother and child. We are the Christa."[49]

If one seeks to integrate, as Heyward's later work attempts to do, an existentialist-relational christology with a liberationist-justice-oriented christology, one cannot simply combine them but must critically evaluate their contradictory tensions. If such a conceptualization is to lose its existentialist theoretical moorings, as I believe it must, it must be confronted with a systemic analysis of oppression. As far as I can see,

Heyward does not critically reflect upon the fact that such an existentialist framework stands in uneasy tension with a liberationist one. This is apparent in her definition of "relation":

> We come into this world connected, related, to one another — by blood and tissue, history, memory, culture, faith, joy, passion, violence, pain, and struggle.... To be related is essentially good, but not all relationships are good. There is right relation, that which in fact is true to itself — relation in which all parties are empowered to be more fully who they are as persons (or creatures) in relation. There is wrong relation, that which is literally perverse, "turned around" from its own possibility, distorted. In such a relation, all persons or participants are not empowered to be themselves.[50]

What does it mean for women to be "true to themselves?" Do women have to be true to their essential feminine nature or to "being woman" or to what? Without question we are all born into relationships and connections; these relations, however, are power structures that not only situate the self but also shape and define it. Since as a basic analytic category Heyward employs "relation," which is a "feminine"-typed category, but also codes it in moralistic terms of "good" and "wrong," her strong emphasis on justice cannot develop its transforming power.

Rita Nakashima Brock also utilizes Sandys's Christa figure to signify a relational christology. However, her central metaphor is not "right relation" but "broken-heartedness." Utilizing the work of the Swiss psychiatrist Alice Miller on the dysfunctional family, she argues that divine power should not be described in images of the patriarchal family, which fosters dependence, nor should it understand love as obedience to an outside authority and will. Particularly, atonement christologies are, in her view, problematic because they are based on some notion of original sin and haunted by the image of a father-god who in his latent, punitive aspects fosters dependence and advocates the divine abuse of the Son:

> Classical Trinitarian formulas reflect patriarchal family relationships between parent and child and husband and wife. In the patriarchal family all members are regarded as possessions and extensions of the reigning authority figure. The father and son become one person.[51]

Nakashima Brock criticizes the christology of Radford Ruether for its understanding of Jesus as a hero-savior figure who "defies established authority" by actualizing his father's will. According to her, Radford Ruether holds that Jesus' criticism of patriarchal relationships parallels that of feminist theology. Although Radford Ruether argues that the redeemer is one who is also redeemed, Nakashima Brock maintains that she gives no evidence as to how this was the case. Jesus, the messianic prophet, is the heroic individual and liberator who announces a new humanity and starts a new process.

In Nakashima Brock's view such an emphasis on Christ the liberator understands the oppressed as victims for whom Jesus speaks and acts. She concedes that anger at oppression is justified but argues that liberation is only one element in relationships. "The continual focus on political structures outside the self — on oppositional power — cuts off from important and potentially liberating insights through the self."[52] Instead she proposes that feminist christology should not be centered in Jesus, the heroic individual and liberator, but in Christa/Community as the "healing center of Christianity."

> Jesus participates centrally in this Christa/Community, but he neither brings erotic power into being nor controls it. He is brought into being through it and participates in the co-creation of it. Christa/Community is a lived reality expressed in relational images.... Hence what is truly christological, that is truly revealing of divine incarnation and salvific power in human life, must reside in connectedness and not in single individuals.[53]

The implications of such a paradigm shift to relational christology for feminist liberation theologies can be seen in how Nakashima Brock reworks my proposal of the ekklēsia of wo/men. In *In Memory of Her* I argued that Jesus can be known only in and through the witness of his disciples, women and men. Jesus and the Jesus movement are intertwined and cannot be separated. Nakashima Brock turns this epistemological/hermeneutical argument into the christological notion of Christa/Community, which she sees developed in the narrative of Mark's Gospel. Particularly, the stories of healing and exorcism, she argues, make present the Jesus of erotic power: "I find glimpses of this christology of erotic power in the Markan miracle stories, in exorcism and the healing of brokenheartedness — in the Christa/Community of erotic power."[54]

Hence, to my concept of the "ekklēsia of women," she prefers the expression "Christa/Community" to identify those empowered by the Spirit-Sophia of erotic power who live "by heart," because the church is only one manifestation of Christa/Community.[55] Such a shift seems to construe the notion of "ekklēsia" and "body of Christ" too narrowly in communal-anthropological terms. Thereby it is in danger of losing its political-global horizon. Nakashima Brock's alternative — either Christa/Community or ekklēsia of wo/men — thus seems to restate along similar lines the debate between Bultmann (existential/individual) and Käsemann (communicative/cosmological) on the notion of the "body of Christ."

Discussing relational christology in general and the work of Naka-shima Brock in particular, Susan Brooks Thistlethwaite has rightly pointed out that such a shift from sociopolitical to interpersonal in-terpretation emphasizes connectedness to the detriment of the struggle against sociopolitical structures of domination. Brooks Thistlethwaite no longer finds the existentialist concept of relationality appropriate for a feminist christological articulation of liberation since she believes "that there is both connection and destruction, creativity and evil at the heart of the cosmos."[56]

Aware of this critical assessment of the concept of relationality, the British scholar Mary Grey nevertheless continues to assert its usefulness. She recognizes that women have always been responsible for satisfying the relational needs of humanity, but she argues that the difference now is that it is "the passion for justice which empowers the relating and sees the hallowing of God, the God seeking justice for the oppressed, interconnected with the making of right relation."[57]

Like Nakashima Brock, Grey uses as her main metaphors per-sonal and structural "brokenness," "woundedness," "healing," "cre-ative love," and "wholeness." She asserts that the decisive quality of a christology of connectedness is the triumph of "being human-in rela-tion" over difference, otherness, and conflict. The essentially communal nature of healing and human wellness through the relational power of messianic Christian community, in all its cultural differences, makes clear that "connectedness" constitutes a deeper and after all more re-demptive reality than an ontology of struggle. "Compassion" — this stream of healing passion, which gives us all strength — moves people to act, because they are rooted in such a messianic community.[58]

Hence Grey's concept of "redemptive mutuality" does not challenge power relationships but reinscribes them. This comes to the fore in her discussion of the tension between mutuality and reciprocity, which, she says, "underlies this book":

> Mutuality considered as ethic of redemption is a far deeper concern than reciprocity. Relationships in the classroom are, unfortunately, far from egalitarian — teachers are paid, pupils generally do not want to be there — but by focusing on the value of mutuality, both teacher and pupil can participate in a profound creative enterprise.[59]

This statement indicates that redemptive mutuality does not require egalitarian relationships or even challenge hierarchical structures. With-out such systemic analysis and structural changes, however, "power-in-relation" is in danger of remaining another form of traditional feminine altruism, although it dresses up in terms of feminist liberation.

The German theologian Manuela Kalsky, who works in the Nether-lands, offers yet another version of a relational christology. She rightly argues that attention to the different contextualizations of particular christological articulations will enable feminists to make the historical experience of women central to their reflection. She suggests that the future of feminist christology lies in a "story" christology that elabo-rates the "messianic" stories of women, whether they are told in the Bible or in women centers, as a part of G*d's salvation history. Such women's stories are fragmentary, snapshot-like, and neither coherent nor consistent. Only the actual encounter with other women makes a mutual understanding possible. Relationality between individual women becomes here the catalyst for christological articulation.

Kalsky suggests that Nelle Morton's insight of "hearing each other into speech" provides a method for feminist christology that can respect differences and shape an ecumenical Christian identity that does not need to universalize its own particular notions of salvation. Dogmatic forms of christology are not the reference point of feminist christological concepts; rather the question of what salvation/liberation/redemption — i.e., in Christian theological terms, what Christ means in different contexts — is at the center.

In Kalsky's view feminist christologies cannot be developed in a sys-tematic way at a desk or in a study but emerge in the actual meeting of women and in their multidimensional, individual stories of oppres-sion. Not the search for a unified universal understanding of salvation but the communication of the actual desire for salvation would then be the goal of our common theological work.[60] Although Kalsky's sug-gestion of focusing on the messianic stories and experiences of women constitutes a significant advancement of the discussion, her conceptual and methodological framework is not positioned within the conscien-tizing praxis of liberation theology nor rooted in a systemic analysis of oppression. Rather it consists in the "sharing" of personal stories by feminist consciousness-raising groups, which often fail to progress to a systemic structural analysis.

In short, the approach of a relational christology has been widely ac-cepted and has almost become the "canonical" position among feminist theologians. While I agree with the shift from a "heroic" and "individ-ualistic" christology to a communal christological construction, I would insist, however, that such a reformulation must not be conceptualized in personalistic, individualistic terms as connectedness between individuals. Rather it must be articulated in sociopolitical categories.

Moreover, a relational christology seems to be determined and lim-ited by the same debilitating discursive framework that also has defined those "heroic" liberationist christologies that it seeks to replace. The same discursive structures of the sex/gender system inscribed in "heroic" christological discourses are also found in relational christology, except that they are now coded in "feminine" rather than masculine terms. What Cathie Kelsey has pointed out with respect to Nakashima Brock's work can also be applied to other feminist christologies of relationality:

> Brock's construction embraces many of the basic patriarchal gender constructions and calls them feminist. It is feminine to be concerned about relationality, so we have a feminist theology of relationship. It is common for women to be victims, so we have a feminist theology in which everyone is a victim. Women develop supportive groups among themselves, so we have a feminist theology in which the feminist community is the catalyst for healing. This construction intuitively feels "right" because it reappropriates patriarchal constructions of middle class Euro-American women's experience, but it only renames these constructions, it does not challenge their appropriateness.[61]

The cultural discourse of femininity inculcates "relationality" in two ways, either as romantic love or as women's personal responsibility for maintaining right relation. First, modern cultural discourses of femininity and masculinity ostensibly no longer construct sex/gender relationships as relations of domination and subordination but rather as erotic hegemonic heterosexual love relationships. Hence the fixation of feminist theology on the maleness of Jesus! Women who read the Jesus story or have a "personal" relationship to Christ take up the position that romance novels or films offer to women in relationship to men. As we have already seen, Rousseau insisted that men are to be educated for themselves whereas women are to be socialized for men. The tendency to conceptualize as intimate love relationship the relation between a believing woman and the exceptional man and singular hero, the beautiful Lord Jesus,[62] has a long theological tradition in the classical prophets, early Christian writings, and the spousal relationship of the mystics. Feminist research on romance literature and movies has elaborated the strategies of "feminine" internalization inculcated in such romance discourses.[63] No wonder that the figure of Jesus the Man takes center stage in feminist christological discourses. The "need" for a "personal relationship" with Christ that resists a politicization of feminist christology has here its deep cultural-religious roots.

Second, the cultural sex/gender system allocates responsibility particularly to middle-class women for cultivating and fostering personal relations. Middle-class "educated," "refined" women of all colors are encouraged to develop "power-in-relation" but not to claim their own power. Middle-class women are socialized for relational work (*Bezie-*

hungsarbeit): they are responsible for humanizing personal relationships in marriage, family, churches, and factories, and among relatives, business associates, and the wider community. They are responsible for preventing or managing any difficulties that have a negative impact on personal relations. Feminine relational work has a kyriarchal function insofar as it is supposed to create a "safe, peaceful world" and a protective community for those who belong.

Like the "Lady" in the Western sex/gender framework, so also religion and church have the function of cultivating and humanizing personal relations among people who belong to the same group so that the world of oppression in which they live becomes invisible or bearable. Whereas middle-class women are accountable for creating a haven for privatized relations and a safe space in a hostile world, multiply oppressed women must render such "relational work" in order to survive. Hence Jacquelyn Grant has rightly criticized a feminist relational christology of reconciliation as an instance of racist discursive practice.

In this light, women's identification with the "masculine" qualities and practices of Jesus — such as public preaching, power, authority, and divinity — can have positive functions in women's struggle against cultural gender-typing. The feminist critique of women's identification with Jesus the male overlooks that such an identification does not necessarily have to result in women's masculinization. It also can function in a "humanizing" way, enabling women to resist cultural-religious dictates that pressure them into accepting the ideals of middle-class white "femininity." On the other hand, to "feminize" Jesus by stressing his "feminine" rather than "masculine" qualities can have devastating effects on wo/men's self-identity. To my knowledge Julie Hopkins is the only feminist theologian who has pointed out this danger by investigating the "disastrous consequences" that the pietistic "feminization" of Jesus has had for women clergy, namely, "the pietistic Protestant stereotype of Jesus as servant and self-sacrificing child of God who proclaimed a personal conversion to a religion based on an ethic of care, love of God and emotional pietism."

> This has resulted in evangelical, pietistic, and Pentecostal Protestant circles in an idealization of the "feminine" and the so-called female virtues of charity, care, gentleness, patience, humility, self-negation and sacrificial love....Women ministers have inherited this double cultural stereotype. Through a complex process of socialization, projection, and internalization, they can feel called to embody the feminine virtues and the mission of the redemptive sacrifice of Jesus.[64]

This twofold demand of being a perfect woman and a perfect Christian, which especially women called to ministry have internalized,

Hopkins suggests, in the long run results in nervous breakdowns, illness, burn-out, or loss of faith. Women clergy, who follow this deep-seated drive to love, care for, and redeem everybody end up feeling like failures and frauds since they cannot fulfill either their own or their congregation's and fellow clergy's high expectations for perfect Christian (i.e., feminine) behavior.

As long as feminist christology uncritically reinscribes the preconstructed sex/gender frame of meaning, it will remain unable to take into account the experiences either of middle-class clergywomen or those of women who are poverty stricken or racially or ethnically discriminated against. Although the preconstructed discourse of cultural femininity is articulated with reference to elite white ladies, it is held up as an ideal for all women. An epistemology of relationality not only reinforces such feminine cultural ideals but also seems doomed either to see the "others" of the "white lady" as negative contrast or to uphold her as the romantic ideal to be imitated by all women.

Feminist christological discourse must abandon and replace with an epistemology of liberation both the christology of Jesus the great individual and its corrective conceptualization as "power-in-relation." Christology no longer has the need to determine identity in relation to "others" even if the "other" is Jesus Christ. Instead it must again and again critically evaluate religious identity in the process of the struggles for liberation. Identity, especially Christian identity, is always determined kyriarchally, and hence it must be repeatedly formulated anew in a permanent process of critical reflection and transformative solidarity.

Toward a Hermeneutical Paradigm Shift

Such a different theoretical frame of meaning undergirding christological reflection can be elaborated through a hermeneutical exploration of the extraordinary, often-quoted speech of Sojourner Truth. An African American woman and former slave who could not read or write, Sojourner Truth addressed a mostly European-American suffrage gathering in Akron, Ohio, in 1852:

> That man over there say
> a woman needs to be helped into carriages
> and lifted over ditches
> and to have the best places everywhere.
> Nobody ever helped me into carriages
> or over mud puddles
> or gives me best place....

And ain't I a woman?
Look at me!
Look at my arm!
I have plowed and planted
and gathered into barns
and no man could head me....
And ain't I a woman?
I could work as much
and eat as much as a man —
when I could get it —
and bear the lash as well,
and ain't I a woman?
I have borne 13 children
and seen most all sold into slavery
and when I cried out a mother's grief
none but Jesus heard me...
and ain't I a woman?
That little man in black there say
a woman can't have as much rights as a man
cause Christ wasn't a woman.
Where did your Christ come from?
From God and a woman!
Man had nothing to do with him!
If the first woman God ever made
was strong enough to turn the world
upside down, all alone
together women ought to be able to turn it
rightside up again.[65]

This address contains several insights to be critically elaborated in feminist theology and hermeneutics in general and feminist christology in particular. First, in distinction to the feminist critique of christology articulated, for example, by Elizabeth Cady Stanton and Mary Daly, Sojourner Truth does not apply her critical evaluation directly to the doctrinal christological system but to those who have articulated it. She points to the political interests of those who are the theoreticians of both the myth of "true womanhood" and also patriarchal christology and confronts them with her own concrete experience of slavery.[66]

Confronted with the experiences of a slave, the myth of the eternal feminine together with the cultural-religious sex-gender ideology turns out to enunciate the ideal of the "white lady" promulgated by white elite educated men. This myth of "true womanhood" serves not only sexist but also racist and classist interests. Such a racist and classist function of the construct of cultural-religious femininity cannot be fully recognized within the framework of gender theory but only within a complex theory of interlocking kyriarchal structures. The experience of the slave Sojourner Truth underscores that the theoretical construction of gender difference is not primarily anthropological but rather serves to maintain kyriarchal relations of domination. Thus Sojourner Truth inserts christology into the societal and ecclesial web of kyriarchal structures.

Second, Sojourner Truth's statement explicates the interconnection between the ideology of the "white lady" and kyriocentric christology by pointing out that elite clerical men ("that man over there say..."; "the little man in black there say...") continue to produce such a kyriarchal theology in order to maintain the status quo ("a woman can't have as much rights cause Christ wasn't a woman"). Against such a kyriarchal christology Sojourner Truth appeals to her own experience as a hardworking slave woman and mother whose children were sold into slavery. Her experience of exploitation and domination compels her to formulate two christological arguments with reference to the Bible, a book that she herself could not read because slaves were prohibited from learning to read and write. Both her criticism of the myth of femininity and her christological arguments are rooted in her own experience that Jesus alone heard her in the hour of her greatest exploitation and dehumanization when slavery robbed her of her children. This religious experience of liberation, which is unique and cannot be replicated, empowers her to articulate two counterarguments. These counterarguments anchor the articulation of christology in the revelatory struggle of women for survival and well-being.

Third, in her counterarguments Sojourner Truth points out, on the one hand, that the incarnation of Christ must be correctly understood as the collaboration of God and a woman. On the other hand she stresses that redemption from sinful structures can be experienced only when women come together and organize for turning the "world rightside up" again. She accepts the claim of patriarchal theology and traditional doctrine that woman caused original sin but draws a different conclusion from it. Precisely because a woman was implicated in the original fall, she insists, women must get together to right the perversion of the world since a woman was "strong enough to turn the world upside down."

Like Elizabeth Cady Stanton, Sojourner Truth understands incarnation and redemption as interconnected factors intrinsic to the patriarchal system of christology that perpetuates the marginality and oppression of women. However, she does not see this systemic interconnection of christology as intertwined with the cultural system of essential or natural gender difference. She understands women not as oppositional "others" who as innocent victims can disassociate themselves from the responsibility for kyriarchal relations of domination. Rather she sees women as deeply implicated in bringing about and sustaining the kyriarchal perversion of the world and of religion.

Sojourner Truth does not accept kyriarchal christology as normative for Christian experience and identity. Rather she unmasks such a christology as a rhetorical construction of male clerics. She does not, however, call for the development of a women's or a "feminist" christology in its place. Instead she insists that the best response to a kyriarchal christology is a praxis of liberation. Women must come together to "turn the world rightside up" again. The women's movement, she argues, can offset an oppressive kyriarchal christology by developing an emancipatory praxis.

A different christological rhetoric can emerge and develop its full power for change only as long as the discourses of the women's movement remain firmly rooted in an ethos of struggle for change. Whereas feminists who reject Christianity as totally patriarchal argue that christology engenders androcentric identity constructions and religiously deepens women's patriarchal self-alienation, Christian feminist theologies have sought to prove that this is not the case and to articulate a different christology within the traditional Christian theological frameworks. Sojourner Truth suggests a third alternative. She begins with her own experience of liberation from slavery and goes on to insist that women must come together to formulate a different christology for change, or, in her words, for turning the world rightside up again.

By invoking the christological experience of Sojourner Truth I do not want to subscribe to it uncritically nor suggest that feminists who call themselves Christians must express their liberation experience in similar terms. Instead, I want to propose that feminist christological reflection first must critically scrutinize its academic and doctrinal frames of reference to determine whether its own christological articulations break through the kyriarchal sex/gender system and hence inspire transformation and change rather than legitimate kyriarchal relations of domination.

The paradigm shift in theological discourse that Gustavo Gutiérrez, among others, has advocated must also be made in christology.[67] The reflections of liberation theology are no longer compelled by the modern question of whether G*d exists but rather are moved by the question of what *kind* of G*d Christians proclaim in a world of oppression.[68] In a similar way, feminist christological discourses should not spend their energy in explicating a systematic ontological account of christology proper but rather should test out the implications and elaborate the power of christological discourses either for legitimating or for changing kyriarchal relations of domination. Only a feminist christological approach concerned with justice and well-being for all can overcome the dualistic either-or alternative of feminist Christian or post-Christian theology. Only an approach that critically scrutinizes its own presuppositions, methods, interests, and social functions and their kyriarchal implications is able to lay open its own christological constructions for public discussion. Such a liberationist paradigm of interpretation challenges feminist christological discourses to perpetually inspect their own theoretical frameworks and methods to determine if they foster kyriocentric world constructions in language or legitimate kyriarchal relations of oppression. Such christological constructions should no longer, for instance, theologically reinscribe the maleness of Jesus, maintain the "femininity" of wo/men, or altogether skip over an analysis of the sex/gender system in favor of a universalization of "humanity" construed in elite male terms. Instead they must critically ask what kind of cultural-religious interests reify the "maleness" of Jesus or move feminist theologians to import "relational femininity" into christology. Accordingly, if we heed the challenge of Sojourner Truth, we cannot simply replace the dogmatic constructions of christology with a single normative christological reconstruction. Rather we must critically expose the rhetorical interests and theological implications that determine all Christian interpretations of Jesus the Christ.

A feminist christological hermeneutics oriented toward liberation praxis challenges biblical studies to assume responsibility for their methodological frameworks and the public functions of christological interpretations.[69] The alternative feminist approach implicitly advocated in Sojourner Truth's challenge requires the articulation and institutionalization of a rhetorical, praxis-oriented paradigm shift in biblical and christological studies. In consequence, a feminist liberationist exploration of Christian Scriptures does not begin its work with the biblical text but with a critical articulation and analysis of the experiences of wo/men. It does not restrict itself, however, to the experiences of a particular group of wo/men but proceeds from a broad range of experiences reflected upon in a systemic way. Such a critical biblical rhetoric of liberation seeks to articulate not only the ways in which women of different races, classes, and cultures endure oppression but also the ways in which they encounter liberation.

To that end a feminist liberation rhetoric has to adopt a systemic analytic that is adequate to critically explore the diverse "everyday" experiences of wo/men. Since wo/men's lives are not affected merely by gender oppression, the sex/gender framework of meaning is unsatisfactory for a christological analysis of Scripture. Nor does it suffice for a critical biblical interpretation simply to collect, analyze, and produce knowledge about Jesus or about his relationship to wo/men in Scripture or ancient history. Instead a critical feminist rhetorical approach to biblical interpretation adopts as its critical analytic frame of reference the struggles against kyriarchy, which it understands as the multiplicative interstructuring of systems of dehumanization in antiquity.

Since wo/men have experienced, marked, and named Christian Scriptures, traditions, and churches as oppressive, a feminist liberation hermeneutics first seeks to develop a critical analysis of biblical christological discourses. Yet such an analysis has positive ramifications for Christian self-understanding and theology, insofar as it deconstructs, in the interest of emancipatory praxis, kyriocentric texts and positivist christological readings of the Christian Testament that perpetuate a Christian kyriarchal identity formation. Thus the goal of a critical feminist liberation hermeneutics is not simply the collection and systematization of early Christian christological materials as "data" for systematic theological reflection in the interest of Christian identity formation. Rather it aims for a reconceptualization of christological biblical discourses and Christian identity constructions in the interest of emancipatory praxis. Such an interest in liberation and well-being, it maintains, must determine the theoretical framework of any biblical hermeneutics or Christian christology. Hence, its criteria of *validation* cannot be derived simply by observing the methodological procedures of biblical studies or by complying with the theological principles of dogmatics. Rather the theological criteria can be found in the embodied potential of texts and intellectual frameworks to engender processes of interpretation and praxis that can transform kyriocentric mind-sets and structures of domination. In short, such a theological interest in the liberation of all wo/men must determine all the intellectual frameworks of biblical studies in particular and of christological studies in general and not simply those of feminist studies.

Finally, a critical feminist reconstruction of early Christian christologies should not adopt doctrinal concepts as its organizing model if it wishes to avoid the "leveling in" effects of doctrinal interests in Christian identity formation. Instead, it must elaborate the multiplicity of christological images and arguments found in Christian Scriptures to make them available as theological resources for constructing feminist Christian identity formations in the struggle for liberation. Such identity constructions are not accomplished once and for all but are fragmentary, partial, and controversial. They must be reconstituted over and over again as emancipatory religious identity formations that are to be repeatedly negotiated, rearticulated, reshaped, and re-created in the diverse global struggles for liberation for all. In the following chapter I will critically investigate feminist biblical christological discourses and their implications for kyriarchal relations of domination in general and for the reproduction of Christian anti-Judaism in particular.

Part 2

The Children of Wisdom

Chapter 3

THE POWER OF NAMING
Jesus, Women, and Christian Anti-Judaism

"And truly, I say to you, wherever the gospel is preached in the whole world, what she has done will be told in memory of her." Then Judas Iscariot, who was one of the twelve, went to the chief priests in order to betray him to them. (Mark 14:9–10)

I find it especially disturbing, therefore, that the tendency to define Jesus as unique over and against Judaism remains even in feminists who do not make use of the Jesus-was-a-feminist argument, who are quite aware of Christian anti-Judaism, who are freely critical of Christian sources, who have gone very far in deconstructing Jesus' divinity.... It seems as if the feminist struggle with patriarchal christologies leads back into the trap of anti-Judaism. If Jesus is not the Messiah and the incarnate son of God on any traditional interpretation of these terms, then how does one articulate his uniqueness in a way that makes sense out of remaining a Christian.... Can Christians value Jesus if he was just a Jew who chose to emphasize certain ideas and values in the Jewish tradition but did not invent or have a monopoly on them?[1]

In this chapter I seek to respond to the query of Judith Plaskow and to investigate why "the feminist struggle with patriarchal christologies leads back into the trap of anti-Judaism." Such an investigation is important particularly because of the frightening increase of neo-Nazism, racism, and antiforeign sentiments in the United States and Europe. The worldwide increase of the practice of hate and the language of oppression[2] in the name of religion underscores the need for interreligious dialogues, especially dialogues between the so-called Abrahamic religions, Judaism, Islam, and Christianity.[3] Such interreligious dialogues are, however, of interest not only to religious people. Since religion often plays a divisive role in nationalistic and antidemocratic struggles, interreligious dialogue must fashion an ethos and ethics that can contribute to the solution of hostilities rather than continuing to fuel national and international conflicts.[4]

Christian-Jewish dialogue is advocated by liberal Jews and Christians but scorned by conservative Christians and Jews.[5] Although fundamentalist Christians usually have an immense interest in christological doctrines and in publicly confessing Jesus as Lord, they generally do not see the need for Jewish-Christian dialogue. Their understanding of Jesus Christ is shaped by the marriage of doctrinal and historical literalism insofar as they assume that biblical texts are directly revealed by G*d and that they exhibit the same christological understandings as later classic christological dogmas do. Hence, fundamentalist right-wing Christians have branded feminist theology as "secular humanism" because it challenges "revealed" kyriarchal relations of domination and subordination in family and church; they have also sought to convert Jews to "Jews for Jesus" in order to fulfill the Scriptures that expect the conversion of the Jewish people before the end of the world.[6]

Interreligious discourses encounter a different rhetorical problem in the general public. Religious discourses are frequently believed to be somewhat arcane and not of great significance to contemporary life. A feminist public in turn does not pay much attention to such discourses because it often considers religion and theology to be hopelessly oppressive and patriarchal. In short, the problem of how to articulate an emancipatory politics of religious meaning does not seem to be of much interest to either a pluralistic secularized public occupied with global economic decline and ecological disaster or to a secular feminist politics.

In such a situation, interreligious dialogues are challenged to articulate a public politics of meaning and to contest the ownership claims of right-wing religion in order to provide an alternative public spiritual vision of justice and well-being for everybody in the global village.[7] In their present form, however, such interreligious discourses are ill equipped to formulate such a liberating vision because they are still dominated by an educated male elite of priests, rabbis, ministers, and professors of religion. This situation continues despite the fact that in all religions feminist voices have been raised that challenge the collusion of religion in kyriarchal oppression. If religious traditions and visions are to advance toward a more just world and well-being for all, then religious communities and theologians have the formidable task of reconfiguring their self-identity and work.

If religious traditions and communities are to articulate a spiritual vision and theological knowledge that can help fashion a cosmopolitan ethos of justice and well-being, they cannot continue to relegate women to the margins of religious institutions and discourse. More-over, in order to contribute their own particular vision and specific ethos to such a spiritual project, religious communities must cease to define themselves against or in competition with each other. Today the one G*d of Jews, Christians, and Muslims calls women and men to engage their prophetic-messianic traditions of equity, freedom, dignity, love, and salvation in support of emancipatory struggles for a more just world.[8] Biblical religions are able to do so, however, only if they cease to suppress, exclude, and silence the voices of women.

In this chapter I will position feminist christological issues in the space of interreligious dialogues, particularly Jewish-Christian dialogues.[9] By placing the critical issues raised in the debates of Jewish and Chris-tian feminists within their wider malestream context,[10] I seek to avoid the impression that it is *solely or even primarily* feminist theology that engenders anti-Judaism. The claim of American Jewish feminists that Christian feminist theology has produced anti-Judaism has been used, particularly in Germany, by church and university men as an argument against feminist theology.[11] In the more openly liberal discourses of the American academy the complexity of the situation has prevented a co-optation of Jewish-feminist dialogues. More than ten years have passed since two Jewish feminists, Annette Daum and Deborah McCauley, critiqued not only feminist theology but also the institutionalized Jewish-Christian dialogue for its blatant androcentrism.[12] In the intervening years, Jewish-Christian discussions, however, have taken little account of the important contributions that feminist religious scholarship could bring to the agenda of malestream Jewish-Christian dialogues.[13]

For instance, in recent years the American Interfaith Institute has brought together scholars to debate "the tortured, yet intertwined his-tory of Jews and Christians"[14] and has published their conference papers. The second volume of conference papers is entitled *Jesus' Jew-ishness.* According to its editor, James Charlesworth, this volume brings together significant studies of the past two decades produced by "dis-tinguished scholars" employing the so-called disinterested method of historical inquiry. He stresses that these studies were gathered because they "are scientific and critical; they reflect the integrity of internation-ally renowned scholars."[15] Yet significantly, neither this volume nor the first contains a single contribution by a woman scholar, although in the first volume a male scholar had pointed to the importance of feminist discourse, especially Jewish feminist discourse, for the Jewish-Christian dialogue.[16] Nevertheless subsequent discussions have passed over his insight with silence.[17]

Exchanges between Jewish and Christian feminists on anti-Judaism have raised significant problems, which are important for Jewish-Christian dialogues in general. First of all, Jewish and Christian feminists insist that such dialogues must be based on substantive issues that the partners have in common rather than on attempts to reassert self-identity and engage in guilt-producing critiques of "the other." In the past two decades Christian, Jewish, postbiblical, and pagan feminists have worked together to articulate theoretical analyses and to form social movements for transforming patriarchal biblical religions. We have recognized that religious texts and traditions are formulated from the perspective of elite males and do not reflect the perspective and experience of women. Religious injunctions and projections as well as spiritual practices often have served to legitimate kyriarchal institutions that marginalize, silence, exclude, and exploit women. In the diverse struggles to claim our religious and intellectual "birthright" and to transform kyriarchal practices of the religious and academic communities to which we belong, we have learned from each other, supported each other, and criticized each other. Feminist Jewish-Christian dialogue partners argue that interreligious exchanges must take note of unequal power relations in the context of these common struggles.

The work of Jewish feminist theologian Judith Plaskow has pointed repeatedly to the long history of Christian domination and abuse. As early as 1978 Plaskow criticized women's biblical studies and feminist theology for asserting the liberation of women by Jesus and Christianity at the price of anti-Judaism.[18] Christian feminist theological discourses have engendered the antithesis: "Judaism equals sexism, while Christianity equals feminism."[19] Although Jewish feminists again and again have pointed out such anti-Jewish patterns,[20] scholarly as well as popular studies continue to stress the positive attitude of Jesus toward women and to draw "Jesus the feminist"[21] against the patriarchal background of Judaism, which generated the "depraved status" of Jewish women in the first century.

Although Jewish feminists have consistently pointed to anti-Jewish tendencies in discourses about Jesus, Christian feminist writings often unwittingly continue to reproduce them. Such anti-Jewish topics in feminist Christian writings include: Christian supersessionism, which claims the superiority of the "New" Testament over the "Old" Testament, the contrast between "law" and "gospel," and the contrast between the Hebrew tribal G*d of wrath and the Christian G*d of love. Postbiblical as well as Christian feminists often develop this contrast into the accusation that the tribal G*d of the Hebrews, the G*d of Jewish monotheism inherited by Christianity, was responsible for the death or suppression of G*ddess-religions.

If it is difficult for Christian feminists to perceive the power imbalance in Jewish-Christian relations and dialogues, then it is even more difficult for a general Christian public to do so. Anti-Judaism has become "commonplace" because Christians have held power over Jews through the centuries. My own experience confirms that such an imbalance is not easily acknowledged. Whenever I mention anti-Judaism in my lectures, someone in the audience is bound to point out that in the first century C.E. the situation was the other way around: Christians were the minority and Jews were the religious establishment at the time of Christian beginnings. It was Judaism, my interlocutors point out, that excluded and persecuted Christians, as the apostle Paul, who was himself a Jew, repeatedly states. Such an apologetic Christian defense, however, fails to consider that during the long Christian history of anti-Judaism, the power imbalance and violence between Jews and Christians has been quite different from that under Roman rule in the first century, which was the cultural-political seedbed of the religious competition and sectarian "family" strife between "Rebecca's children" — to use Alan Segal's expression.[22]

The fact of power imbalances, therefore, needs to be articulated as a central issue in any interreligious christological discourse. Christian feminists must acknowledge our collusion in Christian anti-Judaism and anti-Semitism. True, through the centuries Christian women were by law and custom excluded from public cultural and religious leadership in the churches and prevented from articulating theologies that produced Christian anti-Judaism and anti-Semitism. Nevertheless, women are implicated in Christianity's long prejudicial and death-dealing history of political violence and often continue to make theological superiority claims. Hence, Christian women must acknowledge our complicity in reproducing Christian anti-Judaism.

The obstinate persistence of veiled or explicit anti-Judaism in popular feminist arguments for the liberatory uniqueness of Jesus raises two sets of epistemological questions: the first is theological or ideological, the second historical. The first set explores what kind of theological interests compel Christian feminist reconstructions of the historical Jesus and his relationships to women. What is the meaning and function of the historical assertion that Jesus was a feminist or that he was shaped by his relation to women? How do such reconstructions function in Christian wo/men's struggles to transform patriarchal conditions today? Why is it necessary for Christians to define their religious identity against Judaism? The second set of questions asks not only *what* we can know historically about first-century Judaism and the relations between Jesus and women, but also *how* we know what we know, *who* has produced this knowledge, and to *what ends*. Why are Jewish feminist scholars compelled to hear any positive Christian feminist reconstruction of the Jesus movement in exclusivist and absolutist terms even when such a reconstruction seeks to underline in feminist terms the emancipatory elements of first-century Judaism?[23] Why is it that Christian feminists, despite their expressed intention to the contrary, end up reinscribing anti-Jewish arguments?

In the following, I seek to show that the answer to both sets of questions can be found if we pay special attention to the politics of meaning that determines the theoretical frames of feminist theological discourses and those of biblical scholarship. My contention is that the reproduction of the modern kyriarchal sex/gender system is the right hand and the reproduction of anti-Judaism the left hand of kyriocentric Christian theology. Hence I will look at the same historical-theological problems twice and with different lenses. My hope is that this way of proceeding will yield a bifocal exploration of the complex problem of anti-Judaism engendered by the Christian theological quest for the historical Jesus. If in the process of my discussion I disagree with some feminist proposals, such disagreements are never *personal* but always *methodological*. They are motivated by my concern for articulating a feminist theology and Christian identity that can contribute to interreligious discourses of liberation and a global politics of well-being for all.

To that end I will first attempt to locate the quest for "Jesus the feminist" and his relationship to women within the discourses of biblical scholarship. I will argue that discourses about "Jesus and women" operate within the preconstructed kyriarchal frame produced and sustained by the politics of meaning generated by the cultural-religious sex/gender system. In such a preconstructed frame of meaning even a text such as the anointing story, which gave my book *In Memory of Her* its name, can function to inculcate anti-Judaism while at the same time strengthening Christian women's male identification.[24] In a second step, I will place the Jewish feminist indictment of anti-Judaism in Christian feminist reflections on Jesus within the discursive space mapped by scientific research on the historical Jesus, which still is predominantly produced by male scholars. The historical "fact" of the maleness of Jesus produced by Christian biblical scholarship functions, I argue, to religiously inculcate cultural kyriocentrism and to legitimate kyriarchal structures of exclusion. In a third step I will approach the difficult problem of whether it is possible to articulate a model of historical reconstruction that does not continue to assert Jesus' superiority or uniqueness but also does not deny either his particularity nor our common — i.e., feminist — yet different Jewish and Christian struggles to transform kyriarchal relations of domination.

Biblical Christological Discourses:
Jesus and Women

Christian feminist concerns with Jesus and the proclamation of "Jesus the feminist" remain tinged with anti-Judaism, I suggest, because they have their roots in kyriarchal church practices and liberal theological apologetics. The liberal shift of christology from concern with the exceptional historical figure of Jesus, as Judith Plaskow has pointed out, as well as the preconstructed positivist frame of biblical inquiry continue to produce anti-Judaism in feminist Christian interpretation. Both modes of procedure, calling into question the maleness of Jesus as an "objective fact" of history and analyzing the ideological underpinnings of so-called value-neutral biblical scholarship, are necessary to combat anti-Jewish bias in feminist Christian interpretation.

Since the position of biblical studies as an *academic* "hard" (read masculine) science is precarious to say the least, biblical scholarship is compelled to demonstratively profess its high scientific, "stiff" standards and advocate an objectivist, value-detached mode of inquiry in order not to be relegated to the "soft" sciences. Accordingly, the ethos of positivist biblical scholarship does not allow critical reflection on its own ideological bias of anti-Judaism or antifeminism. Although biblical scholarship has officially established itself as an objective academic discipline against the doctrinal authority and hegemony of the church hierarchy, it nevertheless still employs a systematic theological frame of reference.[25] This frame of meaning defines the task of biblical scholarship as critically elaborating either the historical revelation of G*d in the person of Jesus Christ or the christologies of Christian Testament writers. Since the concepts and theoretical frameworks of the discipline called biblical "New Testament christology" are rooted in a doctrinal theological framework, the interests of this discipline conflict not only with the value-neutral ethos of biblical historical or literary scholarship but also with biblical scholarship's positivist claims to scientific methods of inquiry.

Aware of this problematic positioning of biblical studies, scholars have attempted in recent decades to find new methodological approaches and theoretical frameworks for articulating a theology or christology of the Christian Testament.[26] However, no new generally accepted method or theoretical framework that could integrate dogmatic-theological and scientific literary-historical methods has been articulated. Scholarly attempts to bring diverse and often contradictory Christian Testament materials about Jesus the Christ into a unified doctrinal or logical system have taken three methodological approaches — the doctrinal-historical, the literary-social, and the historical-apologetic approach.

Although these approaches are quite different from each other, they labor under the same presupposition. This assumption is apparent in the tacit aim of Christian Testament studies to articulate and refashion either modern Christian or Western cultural identity. Scholarly biblical discourses construct and propagate Christian and Western identity not only as a universally valid, masculine-determined, and canonical-theological or classic-cultural "given," but also as a preconstructed kyriarchal identity that has become both cultural and religious "common sense." Insofar as biblical scholars seek to construct christological discourses at all, they have as their goal to maintain Christian religious and Western cultural identity as preconstructed kyriarchal identity and to elaborate such identity formations in doctrinal-historical, spiritual-imaginative, literary-social, or historical-apologetic terms.

First, many of the studies on "Jesus and women" remain within the hermeneutical framework of the *doctrinal* paradigm of biblical interpretation, but now use scientific historical arguments for theological conclusions. In the struggle for Christian women's right to speak publicly or to be admitted to ordination, the opposing sides have resorted to the words and actions of the historical Jesus as "proofs" for their argument. For instance, as I am writing this, the pope has issued a statement in which he repeats that the Roman Church cannot ordain women because Jesus ordained only men. Such a declaration flies in the face of all serious biblical scholarship, which has shown that Jesus did not ordain anyone![27] Or, to give another example, the question of women and Jesus is usually discussed in terms of family status, since in antiquity like today the position of women in society and religion was defined largely by the patriarchal family. Although recent studies have shown that Jesus was critical of the patriarchal family and required his followers to sever their family ties, scholars nevertheless insist that Jesus did not intend to abolish patriarchal family structures but wished only to reform them.

Such an approach, which starts with church doctrinal teachings on, for example, incarnation or redemption, seeks to document that these doctrines were presaged in the Hebrew Bible and already elaborated in the Christian Testament. It then strives to order, systematize, and assess diverse early Christian texts in light of such dogmatic concepts. This approach argues, for instance, that Jesus was divine and that he could not have made a mistake. Since he did not choose women to be his apostles, he obviously did not intend for women to be successors of the apostles.

Such scholarly attempts to articulate a systematic biblical christology[28] not only are in conflict with the value-neutral ethos of the academy, but they also stand in tension with the aims of the historical, literary-critical, and sociological-critical methods of biblical studies that underscore the sociolinguistic particularity, historical-geographic limitation, and ideological-political contextualization of biblical texts and their worlds of meaning. If biblical christological reconstructions are presented as universally valid and as objective results of biblical scholarship, this tension between the dogmatic tendencies of systematizing universalization and the relativizing and particularizing tendencies of biblical-critical methods becomes obfuscated.

Hence the frequent recourse of systematic feminist theological discourses to Christian Scriptures is more than questionable because it uncritically imports the methodological tensions between biblical-historical and doctrinal-systematic christology.[29] For instance, Pamela Dickey Young insists with Schubert Ogden that the oldest or earliest layer of the christological tradition in the Christian Testament is the normative criterion by which the "Christianness" of feminist theology must be judged.[30] However, she overlooks that this earliest layer of the tradition is not a revealed "fact" but a historical expression and scientific construction. Without question, the central symbol of Christian faith is Jesus the Christ. However, what it means to say "Jesus Christ" is far from self-evident. Use of the Greek-based names "Jesus" and "Christ" in place of their Jewish equivalents "Jeshua" and "Messiah" already implies a certain interpretation, which then through usage becomes normative.[31] In addition, the "earliest" witness about "Jesus the Christ" is not a metaphysical "given" but a scientific-historical (re-)construction that tacitly presupposes certain theological assumptions and frameworks.

Feminist biblical christological discourses cannot but serve coercive, often anti-Jewish, interests if they hide their interpretive character and advance one possible historical-theological reading as the single *normative* criterion for being Christian. This attempt to secure Christian identity with the help of historical- or literary-critical christological readings of the Bible not only obscures that its hermeneutical strategy imports the presuppositions and ethos of positivist or scientistic interpretive frameworks into biblical-theological discourses. It also reproduces and reinscribes cultural masculine/feminine identity as Christian identity because it does not question the preconstructed sex/gender frame of meaning. For that reason, it stands in danger of ossifying Western kyriarchal identity constructions as Christian. By uncritically accepting cultural discourses of kyriarchal gender difference, christological discourse reinscribes the gender of Jesus as a static, universal "biological" and ontological "fact" rather than "revealing" it as a rhetorical-political construct.

The insistence that feminist christological discourses must be rooted in Christian Scriptures is encumbered by the same theoretical problems and methodological difficulties that have impeded the attempts of dominant biblical scholarship to reconstruct "New Testament" christology. It also burdens itself with the cultural-theological framework of essential or natural gender differences that often undergird biblical readings and reifies the masculinity of Jesus as a "given fact." Whereas biblical studies are rightly suspicious of doctrinal constraints in biblical scholarship that seek to reinscribe Christian identity and superiority claims, they have not been equally suspicious of the modern preconstructed frame of meaning sustained by the Western sex/gender system. Even feminist biblical studies often import this frame without critical reflection on it. Thus feminist christological discourse continues to remain imprisoned in the dominant essentialist discourse of gender difference.[32]

A second feminist approach to biblical christology operates within the constraints of the *liberal psychological-anthropological* paradigm in biblical studies that is likewise undergirded by the kyriarchal sex/gender system of modernity. This approach resorts to historical imagination and psychological elaboration for enriching Christian spirituality and identity.[33] Sermons and spiritual practices often rely on a psychologizing method that "fills in" and "fills out" with experiential colors the barren historical frame of our picture about Jesus for the sake of edification and motivation. From its inception feminist interpretation also has sought to actualize biblical stories in storytelling, poems, songs, role-playing, bibliodrama, and dance.[34] Such a hermeneutics of creative actualization has produced a host of imaginative stories about "Jesus and women" too numerous to mention here.[35] Two of the first such creative feminist accounts to appear were those of Rachel Conrad Wahlberg[36] and Elisabeth Moltmann-Wendel.[37]

Christian feminist theological interpretations also have sought to address the "datum" of Jesus' biological-historical maleness in different ways and with various methods. In line with Jungian psychology, such interpretations have argued, for instance, that the Jesus who preached love and compassion was the "feminine" and antipatriarchal man.[38] Such a feminist biblical apologetics is often permeated with anti-Jewish assumptions, since it construes Judaism in terms of patriarchal masculinity and Christianity in terms of feminine goodness and love. According to Christa Mulack Jesus is the "Anointed of Women" and has a very close relationship of love and caring with them. Through his education he was socialized into the honor code of maleness and the pride of Jewishness, but through his interaction with women he learned to correct his exclusive male (Jewish) behavior.[39] A similar feminist argument is made with reference to the Mediterranean notion of male honor: while Jesus' public ministry exhibited the "masculine" qualities of an honored Mediterranean male, his suffering and death displayed the "feminine" qualities of shame, passive suffering, and silent sacrifice.

Among others, Elisabeth Moltmann-Wendel has advanced the concept of "female/feminine" *relationality* as a key paradigm for a feminist biblical christology.[40] She argues that male self-understanding, which has shaped hegemonic christologies, stresses "person and work," whereas female self-understanding adds a third dimension, relationship. Hence, women have a special contribution to make to christology. When seen from the perspective of women, Jesus' story does not reveal the "man" but the "human" Jesus. Like Mulack, Moltmann-Wendel argues that Jesus learned from his close relationships with women and that women's serving, witnessing, and suffering shaped this relationship:

> We encounter a Jesus who had a direct closeness to women and the beginnings of a christology which is not yet influenced by claims of power-latent maleness.... Its content, which takes the women's experience as its example, is the illumination and healing of the cosmos through God who has entered into the creation.[41]

In her response to Moltmann-Wendel, Veronica Brady draws out the hermeneutical implications of this proposal for a relational feminist [feminine?] christology by quoting Hélène Cixous:

> If there is a "propriety of woman," it is paradoxically her capacity to depropriate unselfishly, body without end.... She doesn't bid it over her body or her desire.... Her libido is cosmic, just as her consciousness is world-wide.... She alone cries and wishes to know from within, where she, the outcast, has never ceased to hear the resonance of her fore-language. She lets the other language speak.[42]

Such an articulation of relational feminist christology reinscribes exegetically the "femininity" and "masculinity" of the cultural sex/gender system, which reproduces either a negative or a romantic understanding not only of women but also of Jews as "the others."

Deconstructive historical readings that reject christology as masculine ideology also reinscribe the Western kyriarchal sex/gender system when they revalorize rather than undermine the "feminine" pole of kyriocentric gender dualism. For instance, Gail Paterson Corrington examines female savior figures and the experience of salvation in the Jewish and Greco-Roman worlds of formative Christianity. She recognizes that symbolic language not only expresses but also shapes "reality" and "the way things are." She shows how images of female saviors such as Isis shaped the perception of reality in the ancient world. However, Paterson Corrington does not apply the same methodological insight to her own assumption of gender reality when she repeatedly asserts that female images reflect actual women and their needs; she does not acknowledge that texts about women are part of the same preconstructed discourse of masculinity and femininity and hence are not a reflection of women's actual lives. Such a rhetorical sliding from "gender role" to "naturalized" gender essence can be illustrated with reference to Paterson Corrington's discussion of the Lukan Mary-Martha story, which she reads as the story of "a woman taking on a male role: the student sitting at the feet of a male rabbi. As in the case of asceticism and martyrdom, women must become men in order to be saved."[43]

This interpretation slides from "male role" to "become men" without critically reflecting on the implication of such a shift in meaning. Paterson Corrington correctly sees that in some early Christian traditions Jesus' saving activity was construed in masculine terms and that these scriptural texts invite wo/men to identify with the masculine-coded Jesus. However, she then goes on to reinscribe such a sex/gender framework by identifying sexuality, motherhood, and bodiliness with women/femaleness/femininity. She does not consider that the reader's identification with cultural-religious "maleness" as divine humanness might have enabled Christian women to evade the impact of cultural feminine gender discourses. As Virginia Burrus has shown, "becoming male" in early Christian discourses did not necessarily express the rejection of self-worth as a woman.[44] Rather it could mean a radical rewriting of cultural femininity and masculinity. Consequently, instead of reading texts in conjunction with the preconstructed frame of the sex/gender system, women readers must question its cultural construction.

This methodological insight cannot be sufficiently stressed when we move to malestream scholarly analyses that claim to advance the cause of women. I want to single out two examples, one *socio-rhetorical* and one *historical-theological,* in order to show how malestream interpretations that posture as "scientific" uncritically reinscribe the kyriarchal sex/gender system as a "scientific fact."

My first example refers to the scientific posture of socio-rhetorical analysis. Such an analysis is not interested in the traditions behind the text. It does not use the text as a window to the historical reality of Jesus but seeks to elaborate the linguistic and symbolic worlds of biblical texts and their structures of meaning. It utilizes divergent methods and approaches such as narratology, structuralism, poststructuralism, anthropology, sociology of knowledge, psychology, folklore, ideological criticism, reader response criticism, and rhetoric to elucidate how the text constructs the literary persona "Jesus Christ" and inscribes it in different ways.[45]

My discussion of this method in action seeks to illustrate how a socio-rhetorical analysis together with a positivist social-scientific approach constructs a "scientific" historical reading in interaction with the preconstructed cultural sex/gender system. I single out this particular socio-rhetorical reading for critical discussion not because I want to suggest that it is more liable to reinscribe the cultural sex/gender system than are other readings. Rather, I want to show how a reading that postures as scientific reinforces the masculine rhetoric of the text's grammatical gender system by constructing a sociocultural sex/gender system and by then going on to "naturalize" it as a scientific historical reading that accurately reflects the "commonplace" ethos of the Mediterranean in antiquity.

Advocating a socio-rhetorical poetics for interpreting the story of the woman who anointed Jesus, Vernon K. Robbins reviews and appraises alternative interpretations. He discusses rhetorical, literary social-science, and ideological interpretations as separate methodological procedures. By positing ideological criticism as one method among others he suggests that only ideological criticism is concerned with and determined by ideology and, moreover, that other approaches do not reproduce the ideological texture of the Markan account. Not surprisingly, Robbins singles out Ched Myers's commentary on Mark and my own interpretation as examples of "ideological criticism." He claims that I and subsequently Ched Myers have removed "the story from the social and cultural value and image systems that pervaded the Mediterranean world in late antiquity" because we allegedly assume a biblical "ghetto culture" and read Mark's text against a "story one regularly studied in Bible study." Robbins asks rhetorically, "Is a reader really to believe that the story of Samuel's anointing of Saul would be the primary semantic framework for understanding this story in the first century?"[46] Yet he conveniently neglects to mention that this story was not as arcane for a Jewish audience in antiquity as it may appear to Christian readers of the twentieth century.[47]

Moreover, Robbins's restrictive literary understanding of socio-rhetorical criticism does not allow him to distinguish a long process of transmission for which I, among others, have argued. Instead, he prefers to read the Markan text against the story of "the Mediterranean

world," which a social science approach in biblical studies continues
to present as a "given scientific fact" and a descriptive account of reality in the first century, although ethnologists have long pointed out
that the "Mediterranean" is a scholarly construct. In Robbins's opinion
this "scientific" account of the ancient world has more social verisimil-
itude than the "Bible land" story of prophetic anointing. He does not
critically reflect on the fact that the "systems and cultural values of
the Mediterranean" are a twentieth-century theoretical fabrication that
needs to be seen as "story" rather than as an objective "social scientific"
description of reality. Finally, Robbins does not question his own reconstructive frame of reference. A kyriocentric framework makes it seem
"common sense" that in "preparation for burial, it would be *appropriate for a woman* [my emphasis] to anoint every part of a man's body
with ointment."[48] Although Robbins ostensibly wants to undermine traditional male culture that shuns the body, he ends up by reinscribing
the malestream sex/gender system that associates body and death with
women but ascribes signifying, naming, and defining activities to men.
He does so not only by eclipsing women's signifying agency but also
by eliminating the methodological significance of a Jewish scriptural
contextualization.

My second example illustrates how historical-critical scholarship
reinscribes the kyriarchal sex/gender system for the sake of doctrinal
interests. Although historical-critical scholarship was originally developed against the authority claims of ecclesiastical doctrine, the various
attempts to historically verify the person and work of Jesus nevertheless
are often constructed to legitimate theological authority claims on scientific grounds. Since today the scholar rather than the churchman has
the function of giving credibility to Christian doctrine, the churchman
assumes the voice of the "detached," unbiased scholar so that his historical reconstruction of Jesus can serve to support theological authority
claims.

This can be illustrated with reference to a recent book by Ben Witherington III, entitled *Women and the Genesis of Christianity*. I single out
this book both because of its popular influence and because it can serve
to highlight the antifeminist politics of scholarship. Witherington's book
is a condensation of his two previous works written for a wider audience. In this book he intends to give an account backed by "detailed
scholarly research." He explicitly introduces his description of "the historical Jesus and women" as a scientific and well-reasoned record that
avoids the forms of "propaganda" allegedly produced by "conservative"
as well as "feminist" bias and "selective hermeneutics." For himself,
he claims scientific objectivities. Yet from the outset he makes it clear

that he is a believing Christian who holds "that the bible is the primary authority of faith and practice" today. While Witherington accuses feminists of bias and "selective hermeneutics," he himself holds to such a biased confessional standard. This standard rejects any criterion "outside the bible" for what is appropriate in matters of faith and practice today.[49] I single out Witherington's apologetic rhetoric here, not because his procedure is singular but because his argument illustrates how such apologetic scholarly rhetoric shapes historical-theological discourses on "Jesus and women."

Christian scholars refer to dogmatic standards as binding and argue that a feminist hermeneutics is "propagandist" in order to establish the theological authority and normativity of their own confessional scholarship on the historical Jesus. At the same time, these scholars claim that in distinction to a "selective" feminist hermeneutics they use scientific methods and critical standards in order to validate their historical reconstructions as "objective" scholarship. This latter claim obscures the fact that the mere attempt to reconstruct the historical Jesus and the origins of Christianity requires a hermeneutical framework.

Witherington does not inform the "general reader" that a historical reconstruction, by its nature, consists of a careful weighing and reordering of biblical texts and materials within a historical model of reconstruction. Nor does he indicate in any way that his latest book utilizes research materials and reconstructive frameworks that I developed, for instance, in my book *In Memory of Her*.[50] In the interest of a Christian apologetics Witherington not only takes over but also seeks to undermine the persuasive impact of such feminist work. Because of his Evangelical theological goals, he is not able to explicate how he modifies my feminist reconstructive model, which underscores the tension and contradiction between egalitarian and patriarchal practices of the early Christian movements. As he himself makes clear, his faith conviction requires taking the *whole* Bible as authoritative, and so he attempts to prove scientifically that, for instance, the so-called household code texts that uphold the kyriarchal family do not stand in tension or conflict with those Gospel texts that require the abandoning of the kyriarchal family as a precondition for following Jesus. Witherington states:

> If we are right that Jesus was attempting to reform, not reject, the patriarchal framework of His [sic] culture, then it is understandable why Paul and other New Testament authors sought to redefine, not reject, the concept of male headship and leadership in light of Christian or biblical ideas.[51]

It is obvious that a particular theological hermeneutics is at work here that ostensibly bases the authority of its narrative for the "lay" person

on historical scholarship in order to give scientific legitimacy to its con-
fessionally based theological historical reconstruction. At stake is the
power of kyriarchal christological discourse; this is apparent in apologetic scholarship on "Jesus and women" in particular as well as in the
general enterprise of historical Jesus scholarship.

Historical Jesus Research and Wo/men

Ecclesiastical and scholarly discussions of the topic "Jesus and women"
often adopt the objectivist postures of historical criticism and the kyriocentric categories of the social sciences to justify the cultural and
ecclesial status quo that marginalizes or excludes women from ecclesial
and academic leadership. Christian assertions that "Jesus was a feminist" must therefore be seen as apologetic attempts to challenge the
dominant reconstructions of Jesus and the movements named after him.
However, these apologetic attempts collude with dominant scholarly reconstructions when they seek to show that Jesus was an exception to the
patriarchal rule. Although such kyriocentric as well as feminist apologetic arguments are today generally formulated in historical terms, they
remain caught up in the doctrinal paradigm of interpretation that utilizes the Scriptures as a store of proof-texts for church teachings or as a
multilayered source for religious-spiritual Christian identity formation.

Insofar as the scientific reconstruction of *the* historical Jesus reduces
the multiple and sometimes contradictory canonical images of Jesus to
a single representation, it provides a presumably reliable scientific criterion and positivist biblical "canon" against which to evaluate all other
representations. Hence, Christian feminists find themselves in a double bind. If they assert the uniqueness of "Jesus the feminist" and his
atypical relations to women, they adopt the arguments of hegemonic
historical scholarship on Jesus, which are imbued with anti-Judaism because doctrinal christology and historical Jesus research have provided
some of the most fertile grounds for Christian anti-Jewish articulations. Since feminist christological assertions about Jesus are formulated
within the preconstructed historical and theological frames of meaning
produced predominantly by Christian male scholars and theologians, it
becomes necessary to examine what kind of christological discourses
foster feminist collusion in the production of Christian anti-Judaism.

Even a cursory review of scholarship on the "Jesus of history" can
show how the various "quests" for the historical Jesus have been caught
up in a similar apologetic-historical dynamics as "Jesus and women"
research insofar as they have created either anti-Jewish feminist for-

mulations or prokyriarchal Christian determinations of the relationship
between Jesus and women. Scholars generally distinguish between four
periods of historical Jesus research.[52] The first, the so-called Old Quest,
which attempted to write the biography of Jesus, was clearly the product of the European Enlightenment. This liberal quest for the life of Jesus
flourished in the nineteenth century and approached its end in 1906 with
the appearance of Albert Schweitzer's book *The Quest for the Historical
Jesus,* which concluded that scholars will inevitably discover a historical Jesus who is fashioned in their own image and likeness. The notion
of Jesus as the exceptional man who as a specially gifted and powerful individual transcends normal boundaries resonates with a masculine
liberal ethos. Jesus as the paradigm of true humanity and individual-
ity becomes the model for the genial or heroic personality that can be
achieved through education and imitation.

Many popular studies on the relation of Jesus to women remain
within the ambiance of the Old Quest if they seek to produce a biography of Jesus. They stress Jesus' intimate relations with women or
elaborate how Jesus develops psychologically in interaction with them.
While Jesus represents the great (male) individual and hero who proves
his capacity for enduring conflict, suffering, and even death, the women
around him — especially Mary of Magdala — are thought to be related
to him either through romance or through obedience. Insofar as Jesus'
behavior is supposed to have been gentle, full of mercy, and always loving, he is seen as encompassing both masculine and feminine qualities.
Rita Nakashima Brock has rightly criticized such feminist christological
discourses for their understanding of Jesus as a hero-savior figure who
defies established authority by obeying his Father's will.[53]

The Old Quest for the historical Jesus was suspended after World
War I and replaced by "kerygmatic theology." This second phase of
historical Jesus research was inaugurated by a book of Martin Kähler
entitled *The So-called Historical [historisch] Jesus and the Historic
[geschichtlich] Biblical Christ,* which appeared in 1892. Kähler distinguished between the historical Jesus of the modern scholar and the living
Christ, i.e., the proclaimed Christ of faith. Such a kerygmatic approach
insists that it is no longer possible to sustain a liberal Jesus-religion
based purely on the historical Jesus freed from apostolic tradition and
church dogma. Rather, historical-critical Jesus research, Kähler argued,
had to relinquish psychological interpretation and study the still extant
sources as witnesses to the faith and theology of the evangelists as well
as of the communities to which they wrote.[54]

When asking about Jesus' relation to women in historical terms and
within the form- and redaction-critical research paradigm, which gen-

erally presupposes such a kerygmatic theology, scholars focus on how the Gospels portray the relationship between Jesus and women theologically.[55] They understand the biblical text as a window to the world of Jesus and the women around him. More recently, the literary dimension of the form- and redaction-critical paradigm has been rediscovered. Literary studies continue to work within this research paradigm as they explore how individual stories or the overall narrative constructions of the Gospels depict Jesus as a literary character in relation to the women characters of the Gospels. They show, for instance, how the androcentric narratives of the Gospels restrict discipleship to male characters while they accord followership to the women characters. They underline that the kyriocentric text centers on Jesus and makes female figures either dependent on or peripheral to this central male character. By adopting linguistic masculine determinism, they reinscribe both kyriarchal and anti-Jewish relations. When such literary readings become historicized in scholarly or popular accounts, they reinscribe into the scholarly reconstructions of the Jesus of history — in a positivistic-literalist fashion — the biblical texts' androcentric construction of women's marginality and Jewish culpability.

The third period in historical Jesus research, termed by James Robinson, the "New Quest," originated primarily in reaction to Rudolf Bultmann and flourished in the 1950s and 1960s. Against scholars who read the Gospels primarily as witnesses of the early church, the New Quest insisted that such an approach does not prohibit us from asking fruitful questions concerning the historical Jesus and his cultural-religious contexts. Although we cannot reconstruct the life of Jesus in developmental, psychological terms, these scholars argue, we are nevertheless able to "extract" or "distill" the Jesus of history from the early Christian witness to the Christ of faith.

The New Quest articulated three criteria of authenticity by which to distinguish material that can be traced back to the historical Jesus from its present theological literary articulations in the Gospels.[56] To be considered authentic, sayings and practices must, first, be recorded in more than one source; second, they cannot be logically derived from Jewish practices; and, third, they cannot reflect the interests of the early church. In other words, the New Quest adopts a reductionist historical method that underscores Jesus' independence from Judaism and the early churches in order to establish his singularity and uniqueness.

Both the Old and New Quests emphasize the exemplary or unique historical figure of Jesus and his radical ethics. This emphasis requires a negative portrayal of Judaism as its foil. Since Jesus is said to have been conscious that his preaching radically undermined the fundamental beliefs of Judaism, he is understood as having gone to Jerusalem in the full awareness that he risked death. In this interpretation Jesus' conflict with the Roman authorities of Palestine results from his basic conflict with ritualistic or legalistic Judaism.

The anti-Jewish framework of this interpretation has influenced many studies on "Jesus and women." Studies that position Jesus the feminist against Judaism argue that Jesus, unlike any other Jewish man or rabbi, treated women as disciples, broke the Sabbath law to heal them, and discarded all levitical ritual taboos in his dealings with women. Such apologetic studies that stress the practice of Jesus in opposition to Jewish ritual and legalism generally do not intend to be anti-Jewish. Rather, they often take Jesus' own religious context as a foil for criticizing contemporary church policies and Christian practices. However, the more that Christian discourses picture Jesus as the liberator of women, the more they tend to make him appear un-Jewish or anti-Jewish. This proclivity tends to reproduce feminist Christian identity as inescapably intertwined with anti-Judaism because it asserts Christian identity as intrinsically bound to the historical man Jesus of Nazareth who acted against the Torah of Moses.

If we focus on the historical figure of Jesus the Jew, we are immediately confronted not only with the Old and the New Quests but also with the "Newest Quest" for the Jesus of history. During the late 1960s and the 1970s the New Quest began to subside, and around 1980 it gave way to the Newest Quest. Since that time an explosion of interest in the Jesus of history has taken place. In distinction to the Old and New Quests this Newest Quest does not seek to reconstruct the Jesus of history against first-century Judaism but decidedly sees him as a part of it. The Newest Quest has been fueled by renewed study of the early Jewish Pseudepigrapha, the Dead Sea Scrolls, and archaeological discoveries. It ostensibly is not "motivated by theological concerns." Rather, "prompted by the *realia* of history," it responds to a variety of intra- and extracanonical stimuli and engages scholars from a broad range of religious perspectives.[57]

Yet our knowledge of women in first-century Judaism is still very limited because of a lack of scholarly interest in the question.[58] For instance, scholars have extensively discussed whether Jesus was a Pharisee, but they have not asked whether women belonged to the Pharisaic movement. For instance, the German translation of *In Memory of Her* suggests that the term "Pharisees" is inclusive of women, because the book of Judith portrays a woman as a paradigmatic Pharisee.[59] However, this suggestion has been severely criticized and rejected by reviewers as unscholarly and biased.[60] Or to give another example, scholars have alternately seen Jesus as an Essene, a Zealot, or a miracle-working charismatic, but have reconstructed these Jewish movements as purely male. Early Judaism like early Christianity has been slandered by pagans as a "religion of women" because its missionary propaganda is said to have especially attracted well-to-do, influential women.[61] Yet historical reconstructions of Judaism generally do not utilize this information or see it as a historical-theological problem that calls for greater study.

As long as critical reconstructions of early Judaism from a Jewish feminist perspective are still scarce,[62] the emphasis of the Newest Quest on Jesus the Jew is bound to see his relation to women in terms of dominant Jewish as well as Greco-Roman malestream reality. By remaining oblivious to the role of Jewish women or marginalizing it as a feminist ideological question, dominant scholarship tends to preclude a re-visioning of the Jesus of history in line with emancipatory tendencies and movements in early Judaism and Greco-Roman cultures and religions.

Since the Newest Quest for the Jesus of history rightly has rejected the reductive criteria of authenticity formulated by the New Quest, it has had to develop a new method for distinguishing the Jesus of history from the rhetorical narratives of the Gospels.[63] To do so the Newest Quest has resorted to polling practices derived from consumer research and political campaigns in order to distill the authentic sayings of the "historical Jesus" from the Gospel texts. Since 1985 a group of distinguished American scholars, known as the "Jesus Seminar,"[64] has come together twice a year not only to discuss the traditions ascribed to Jesus, but also to cast red, pink, gray, and black balls to establish the "data base" for determining who Jesus really was and what he actually said.

> If two-thirds of the total votes cast on any text are red and pink, then that text is included in the Jesus seminar data base.... If two-thirds of the total votes cast on any text are gray and black, then that text is eliminated from the data base.[65]

Such a methodological approach easily degenerates into what Jacob Neusner has facetiously called a "theology of the balls."[66] Moreover, it seems not quite accidental that the negative judgments of the seminar are cast with black balls, a coding that continues the popular language of racism.

One wonders whether it is accidental that this Newest Quest for the Jesus of history exploded during the 1980s, the Reagan and Thatcher years, which coincided with the revival of political conservatism and religious right-wing fundamentalism. The Newest Quest's stance of liberal relativism, its refusal to reflect on its own ideological or theological interests, and its restoration of historical positivism corresponds to political conservatism. Its emphasis on the *"realia"* of history serves to promote scientific fundamentalism since it generally does not acknowledge that historians must select, reject, and interpret archaeological artifacts and textual evidence and simultaneously incorporate them into a scientific model and narrative framework of meaning. As the feminist sociologist Dorothy Smith argues, objectified forms of knowledge structure the knower's relation to the known object, e.g., configuring "Jesus' relation to women" in terms of contemporary social organizations of ruling.

> If a knower's only access to the object of knowledge is through its textual presence, then the shaping of that presence by the social organization of its production is hidden but effective; the knower is related to the object of her knowledge through it.[67]

Although the Newest Quest for the Jesus of history has shown strong interest in the reconstruction of the Jewish world of Jesus and has uncovered much historical information about the Galilean environment at the time of Jesus, it still labors under the compulsion either to set Jesus apart from Judaism or to reconstruct his ministry and message in kyriarchal terms. On the one hand, the historical reconstruction of Jesus as a wandering Cynic philosopher rather than as a Jewish prophet promotes a process of de-Judaization (*Entjudaisierung*).[68] It rests on a positivist confidence that the various levels of Q (a nonextant hypothetical source) can be determined with certainty. Not surprisingly, this positivist method of reconstruction can go hand in hand with a postmodern "agnostic" posture.

On the other hand, its objectified scientific depiction portrays Jesus in terms of Jewish male prerogatives. It thereby produces the kyriarchal construct of Jesus' masculinity as a historical fact. As long as Jesus research remains compelled by the theological assumption that Christian identity must be bound up with a positivist "scientific" reconstruction of the historical fact "Jesus" — the heroic individual — it cannot but produce the historical "fact" of Jesus' "maleness" as an objectified historical-theological given that is constitutive for the faith and identity of Christians in general. Within such a preconstructed "scientific," common-sense frame of meaning, Christian feminist discussions are forced to critically reject the maleness of Jesus as a naturalized historical fact with ultimate theological significance for Christian identity formation.[69]

In short, it seems well documented that a reductionist method, which

abstracts Jesus as a historical artifact from the movement of his followers and separates him from his historical-religious context, cannot
achieve its scientific aim of historical certainty. Neither can polling.
Moreover, the abundance of books and articles on the historical Jesus
proves that the judgment of Albert Schweitzer is still correct; after all,
scholars and writers inescapably fashion the image of Jesus in their own
image and likeness. At best they can glimpse the historical shadow of
Jesus, but how they capture "his picture" will always depend on the
"lens" they use or the reconstructive model they adopt. This also holds
true for the earliest portrayals of Jesus formed in the canonical and
extracanonical early Christian literature. Any presentation of Jesus —
scientific or otherwise — must therefore own that it is a "reconstruction"
and open up its historical models to public reflection and critical inquiry.
Such reconstructive models must be scrutinized not only to determine
how much they can account for our present textual and archaeological
information on the Jesus of history and his sociopolitical context, but
also to evaluate how much they reveal about the rhetorical interests and
theological functions of scholarly and popular knowledge productions.

As I argued in chapter 2, Christian feminist theology must reject
malestream hermeneutical frameworks rather than reinterpret the historical maleness of Jesus in humanist and liberationist terms. For that
reason, it must also question the preconstructed positivist frame of
meaning that the "scientific quests" for the Jesus of history tacitly import. Moreover, a critical feminist theology of liberation has to challenge
the notion that Christian identity must remain contingent upon scientific reconstructions of the historical Jesus as founding father, feminist
hero, or divine man, since such kyriocentric scientific reconstructions
reproduce not only androcentrism but also anti-Judaism in Christian
historical-theological terms. This is not to say, however, that Christian feminist scholars must eschew all attempts to reconstruct their
historical-theological roots.

The Jesus Movement as
a Jewish Emancipatory Movement of Wo/men

My own work has sought to spell out an alternative reconstructive
model that can simultaneously address some of the questions raised by
decades of historical Jesus research and make explicit its own hermeneutical perspective and theological interests. The study of the relations
between "women and Jesus," I have argued, cannot consist simply of an
investigation of texts about women and Jesus or of an exclusive focus

on gender relations. Rather, critical feminist scholarship must conceptualize early Christianity and early Judaism in such a way that it can
make women and marginalized men visible as central agents who shaped
Christian and Jewish beginnings. This requires a reconsideration of the
theological frameworks that here produced Christian anti-Judaism as
the left hand of christology and divine masculinism as its right hand.
Moreover, feminist scholars in religion must articulate a feminist model
of reconstruction that can do justice to our common struggles for
transforming religious patriarchy as well as to our particular historical
struggles and religious identity formations.

In other words, I propose that feminist theological reflection privilege soteriological over christological discourses and social-cultural over
individual-anthropological theological frameworks. A feminist Christian identity must be articulated repeatedly within diverse emancipatory
struggles for the vision of G*d's *basileia*/commonweal that spells well-
being and freedom for all in the global village. Similarly, feminist
Jewish identity needs to be articulated within emancipatory struggles
for the "restoration of the world," of *tikkun* as the social, political,
and religious transformation of patriarchal structures of injustice and
domination.

To illustrate my point: in *In Memory of Her* I sought to articulate
a reconstructive model that can make visible the historical practices
and theo-ethical visions of the Jesus movement as one of several renewal movements in first-century Israel. Since such a model is often read
either in light of the preconstructed meaning frame of positivist historical Jesus research or in terms of the marginalizing frame of the study
about women, I need to repeat its argument here. In order to counteract
the pervasive anti-Jewish "over and against" strategy of reading, I began the chapter on Jesus with a discussion of what we can know about
women in pre-70 C.E. Judaism and pointed to the story of Judith as the
portrayal of a strong and independent leader and Pharisaic paradigm.
Then I named the dominant ethos of Israel in the first-century as that
of a "kingdom of priests and holy nation." Only in a third step did I
discuss the *basileia* vision and practice of the Galilean Jesus movement.
The fourth and fifth sections discuss texts that speak about Divine Wisdom as the G*d proclaimed by the earliest Jesus movement of wo/men
and sketch antipatriarchal visions and structures advocated by those
movements.

Undergirding this argument are four basic assumptions: First, anti-
Judaism is contrary to a Christian feminist theology of liberation
because an anti-Jewish perspective does not recognize that Jesus and
his first followers were *Jewish wo/men*. They were *not Christian* in

our sense of the word. As Galilean wo/men they gathered together for common meals, religious reflection, and healing events. They did so because they had a "dream" and followed a vision of liberation for every wo/man in Israel.

Second, who Jesus was and what he did can be glimpsed only in the interpretation and memory of the Jesus movement probably as one among several first-century Jewish movements. Therefore, the variegated Jesus movement must not be separated methodologically from the other messianic movements in first-century Judaism. Moreover, we must keep in mind that just as there was no unified early Christianity, likewise there was no singular "orthodox" Judaism in the first century C.E. Orthodox Judaism like orthodox Christianity emerged only in subsequent centuries.

Third, this emancipatory movement of Galilean wo/men must be seen as a part of the various *basileia* and holiness movements that in the first century sought the "liberation" of Israel from imperial exploitation. The concrete political referent of these movements was the colonial occupation of Israel by the Romans. It is no accident that the covenant promise of Exodus 19:6 was actualized in such a political context by these movements. Some of them, like the Pharisees and Essenes, stressed the notion of "priesthood and holy nation"; others, like the apocalyptic prophetic movements — among them the Jesus movement — stressed the political notion of the *basileia* (empire) of G*d as a hegemonic vision counter to that of the Roman empire.

Fourth, the emerging Galilean Jesus movement probably understood itself as a prophetic movement of Sophia-Wisdom. That it named itself after Jesus the Christ was probably due to the conviction that had emerged after Jesus' execution that he was the Vindicated or Resurrected One. As I will attempt to show in the next chapter, this conviction had its base in the tradition of the "empty tomb" attributed to women. This tradition centered around the proclamation "that Jesus is *going ahead* of you to Galilee," the site where antimonarchical prophetic traditions of the Northern Kingdom were still alive. In short, building on my argument in *In Memory of Her,* I propose that the self-understanding of the emancipatory Galilean *basileia* (commonweal) of G*d movement had its roots in the vindication tradition of the empty tomb stories, which was attributed primarily to women, rather than in the pre-Pauline (1 Cor. 15:3–7) and Gospel appearance tradition that sought to authorize primarily male apostles. The vindication tradition attributed to women manifests the self-understanding of the Galilean *basileia* of G*d movement as a movement of prophets sent by Divine Wisdom, like Elijah, Miriam, John, and Jesus.[70]

This critical feminist reconstructive model developed in *In Memory of Her* adopted as its frame of meaning a historical model of struggle. Such a model places the beginnings of the Galilean prophetic-Wisdom movement within a broader cross-cultural historical frame of reference that allows us to trace the struggles between emancipatory movements inspired by the democratic logic of equality, on the one hand, and the dominant kyriarchal structures of society and religion, on the other.

Ancient movements and emancipatory struggles against kyriarchal exploitation do not begin with the Jesus movement but rather have a long history in Greek, Roman, Asian, and Jewish cultures. The emancipatory struggles of biblical wo/men must be seen within this wider context of cultural-political struggles. Such a historical model of emancipatory struggles understands the Jesus of history and the movement that has kept alive his memory not over against Judaism, but against kyriarchal structures of domination in antiquity. Such a reconstructive frame of reference is able to conceptualize the emergent Jesus movement and its diverse articulations as participating in popular movements of cultural, political, and religious resistance. To paraphrase Bultmann's well-known scholarly dictum: Jesus did not simply "rise into the kerygma," understood as "dangerous memory." Rather he rose into and is "going ahead" in the struggles for a world of justice and freedom from kyriarchal oppression.

Yet, to speak about the Jesus movement as a Jewish renewal movement still provokes misunderstandings between Jews and Christians. Jacob Neusner has rightly pointed out that the notion of "renewal" still carries traces of supersessionism insofar as it suggests that Christianity is best understood as a "better" form of Judaism. In other words, the notion of a reform movement still can be made to fit into the hegemonic Christian construct of a Judeo-Christian tradition that posits a continuity between Judaism and Christianity. Only if we explicitly acknowledge that Judaism and Christianity are two different religions, which have their roots in the Hebrew Bible and in the pluriform religious matrix of first-century Israel, can we avoid reading "renewal movement" in a supersessionist fashion. As Alan Segal argues: early Judaism and emergent Christianity are Rebecca's children, twin siblings of the same mother.

To speak about the Jesus movement as a Jewish renewal movement of the first century can be and has been further misread as implying that the Jesus movement was the *only* reform movement at the time and that Jewish or Greek wo/men who did not join this movement suffered from a "false consciousness."[71] If read in a preconstructed frame of meaning that maintains the uniqueness of Jesus, the expression "renewal

movement" suggests not only Christian particularity and exceptional-
ity but also superiority. Hence, it cannot be stressed enough that the
Jesus movement must be understood as *one among several prophetic
movements* of Jewish wo/men who struggled for the liberation of Israel.
In order to avoid as much as possible such anti-Jewish misreadings, I
have replaced here the notion of renewal movement with the concept of
emancipatory movement.

The central symbol of this movement, the *basileia tou theou*,[72] expresses a Jewish religious-political vision common to all the movements
in first-century Israel. This central vision spells freedom from domination. The Greek term *basileia* is difficult to translate adequately because
it can either mean kingdom, kingly realm, domain, or empire, or it can
be rendered as monarchy, kingly rule, sovereignty, dominion, or reign.
Since Dalman, who decreed that when applied to G*d *basileia* always
means kingly rule and never has the territorial sense of kingdom, most
exegetical-theological discourses translate *basileia* with "kingly rule or
reign," meaning G*d's all-overpowering initiative and sovereign ruling.[73] Hence, most scholars insist on a kyriarchal meaning of the term.
Moreover, most reviews of scholarship on the meaning of the expression
basileia tou theou do not even discuss its political overtones, which were
apparent in a context in which people thought of the Roman empire
when they heard the word *basileia*.

To lift this very real political meaning into consciousness in my own
writings I have privileged the localized meaning of the term as "empire,"
"domain," or "commonweal." Such a rendering of the word *basileia*
linguistically underscores the character of the empire/commonweal of
G*d as oppositional to that of the Roman empire. Since the translation
of *basileia* does not mark the oppositional sense of the word but rather
ascribes imperial power to G*d, I have tended to use the Greek word
basileia as a tensive symbol that evokes a whole range of theological
meanings and at the same time seeks to foster a critical awareness of the
word's ambiguity. Such a symbolic use of the term seeks to emphasize
the political impact and significance of *basileia* in the first century C.E.
and at the same time to raise the question of its kyriarchal politics of
meaning.

In order to grasp more fully the notion of the Jesus movement in
all its differing forms as one among several Jewish apocalyptic resistance movements organized against Roman imperial domination, we
must shift our attention from the question of *who* crucified Jesus to the
question of *what* killed him. The imperial system that killed Jesus exploited not only the Jews, but all those living under its colonial rule.
This imperial system determined the life of men and had an even greater

impact on women — whether freeborn, impoverished, slave, or freed women, country or city women, widows or virgins, wives or prostitutes. Jesus was not crucified because of his theological teachings but because of their potentially subversive character and the political threat to the imperial colonial system.

The Roman form of imperial domination signified by the term *basileia* ruled the world and experience of all Jewish movements in the first century, including that of Jesus. This Roman form of imperial domination and exploitation is eloquently described by the Jewish scholar Ellis Rivkin:

> The Roman emperor held the life or death of the Jewish people in the palm of his hand; the governor's sword was always at the ready; the high priest's eyes were always penetrating and his ears were always keen; the soldiery was always eager for the slaughter.... The emperor sought to govern an empire; the governor sought to hold anarchy in check; the high priest sought to hold on to his office; the members of the high priest's Sanhedrin sought to spare the people the dangerous consequences of a charismatic's innocent visions of the Kingdom of God, which they themselves believed was not really at hand.... For he had taught and preached that the Kingdom of God was near at hand, a kingdom which were it to come, would displace the kingdom of Rome. By creating the impression that he... would usher in the Kingdom of God... he had readied the people for riotous behavior. The fact that the charismatic of charismatics had taught no violence, had preached no revolution, and lifted up no arms against Rome's authority would have been utterly irrelevant. The High Priest Caiaphas and the Prefector Pontius Pilate cared not a whit how or by whom the Kingdom of God would be ushered in, but only that the Roman Emperor and his instruments would not reign over it.[74]

Jesus and his first followers, women and men, sought the emancipation and well-being of Israel as the people of G*d, a kingdom of priests and a holy nation (Exod. 19:6). They announced the *basileia/* commonweal/empire of G*d as an alternative to that of Rome. The *basileia/*commonweal of G*d was a *tensive* religious symbol of ancestral range[75] proclaiming G*d's power of creation and salvation. It was also a political symbol that appealed to the oppositional imagination of people victimized by an imperial system. It envisioned an alternative world free of hunger, poverty, and domination. This "envisioned" world was already present in the inclusive table community,[76] in healing and liberating practices,[77] and in the domination-free kinship community of the Jesus movement, which found many followers among the poor, the despised, the ill and possessed, the outcast, the prostitutes, and the "sinners" — women and men. Lest I be accused of special pleading, I quote the Jewish scholar Alan F. Segal at length to support my point:

> Like the Sadducees' close association with the traditional priestly aris-
> tocracy and the Pharisees' association with urban tradepersons, the
> association of Christianity [sic] with the deprived or those of ambigu-
> ous status is only a generalization. But the Gospels themselves testify
> that early Christians had less access to the means of salvation than other
> people. For one reason or another they felt alienated from the roles that
> society had defined for them.
>
> Jesus' original support came from the country folk of Galilee, whose
> ways and interests were different from those of the Jerusalemites. He
> appealed to a number of people in the society whose rank was inferior
> but whose economic situation was not hopeless, including prostitutes, tax
> collectors, and others considered disreputable or impure by Sadducees
> or Pharisees, as well as many ordinary Jews, Samaritans and Galileans
> with no specific party affiliation. These people often had some economic
> standing in the community. But their status was relatively low compared
> with their economic attainments.[78]

Although Segal does not specifically mention women, except for prostitutes, his description of "status inconsistency" and his ascription of
"low esteem"[79] to those who joined the Jesus-people is also typical for
wo/men in Greco-Roman cultures.

Finally, the Jesus movement must not be construed as free of conflict and kyriarchal tendencies.[80] From its very beginnings, differences
and conflicts existed, as the diverse if not contradictory theological articulations of the movement indicate. *In Memory of Her,* for instance,
discusses the *basileia* sayings tradition (Mark 10:42–45 and 9:33–37
par.) as an antipatriarchal tradition that contrasts the political structures
of domination with those required among the disciples. Structures of
domination should not be tolerated in the discipleship of equals; those
disciples who would be great or would be first must be slaves and servants of all.[81] While this tradition advocates nonkyriarchal relationships
in the discipleship of equals, its imperative form simultaneously documents that such relationships were not lived by everyone. The would-be
"great" and "first" seem to have been tempted to reassert kyriarchal social and religious status. The argument of the Syrophoenician woman
with Jesus, which gave *But She Said* its title, provides a third example,
since this story criticizes the ethnic bias of Jesus himself.

The story of the Jesus movement as an emancipatory *basileia tou
theou* movement is told in different ways in the canonical and extracanonical Gospel accounts. These accounts have undergone a lengthy
process of rhetorical transmission and theological editing. The Gospel
writers were not concerned with antiquarian historical transcription but

with interpretive remembrance and rhetorical persuasion. They did not want simply to write down what Jesus said and did. Rather, they utilized the Jesus traditions shaped by Jesus' first followers, women and men, for their own rhetorical interests and molded them in light of the political-theological debates of their own day. As a result, what we can learn from the rhetorical process of Gospel transmission and redaction is that Jesus, as we still can know him, must be remembered, contextualized, discussed, interpreted, questioned, or rejected not only within an interreligious debate but also within a political-cultural one.

We must not overlook, however, that all four Gospel accounts reflect not only the controversies with hegemonic forms of Judaism but also the anxieties of separation from them. The Gospels inscribe Christian identity as standing in tension and even in conflict with other forms of Judaism. A good example of this kyriocentric process of anti-Jewish and antiwoman inscription can be found if we trace the transmission history of the story about a woman anointing Jesus as the Christ.[82] The Gospel of Mark places this story at the beginning of her/his narrative about Jesus' execution and resurrection.[83] Mark probably takes up here a traditional story that knows of a woman anointing Jesus' head and thereby naming him as the Christ, the Anointed One. A revelatory word of Jesus links the prophetic sign action of this nameless woman with the proclamation of the gospel throughout the whole world. The community that retells this story after Jesus' execution knows that Jesus is no longer in their midst. They no longer "have" Jesus with them.

Either in the course of the transmission of this historical memory or at the redactional stage, three kyriarchal interpretations of the woman's significant prophetic sign-action are introduced. First, the debate with the male disciples advances a kyriarchal understanding that "the poor" are no longer constitutive members of the community but rather "the others," people who deserve alms. Second, the unnamed woman's sign-action is interpreted in feminine kyriocentric terms: she does what women are supposed to do, prepare the bodies of the dead for burial. Finally, the story is recontextualized in the tradition (cf. Mark and John) as an "example story" that counterposes the action of the woman to that of Judas, the betrayer of Jesus. Insofar as the woman disciple remains unnamed but the male disciple who betrays Jesus is named, the text evokes an androcentric response that, contrary to the word of Jesus, does not comprehend the significance of the woman's prophetic naming. It also suggests an anti-Jewish response by naming the betrayer Judas, a response that is intensified in the course of the passion narrative. Although in itself the name is not suspect, its context here makes it so. "Judas" is

etymologically related to "Jew" (Yĕhūdī; Ioudaios); and thus the one
who gave Jesus over could be regarded by those hostile to him as the
quintessential Jew. Augustine holds that as Peter represents the church,
Judas represents the Jews (Ennarratio in Ps 108, 18, 20...). As Lapide
...documents, this was exploited as antiJewish polemic in dramatic literature and art, e.g., depicting Judas with grossly exaggerated "Semitic"
features and generalizing his love for money.[84]

Moreover, we can also see the Gospels' rhetoric of depoliticization
in the process of reinterpreting the anointing story, which was potentially a politically dangerous story. In the rhetoric of the Gospels, we are
able to trace early Christian apologetic attempts to make the Christian
movement politically safe in the eyes of the Roman empire. This rhetoric of depoliticization engendered anti-Jewish interpretations of Jesus'
suffering and execution[85] and forged Christian political adaptation to
Greco-Roman patriarchal structures of dominance that opened the door
to the imperial Roman co-optation of the gospel.

In conclusion: Since this process of the kyriarchal reinterpretation of
the gospel has produced the preconstructed, by now "common-sense"
frame of meaning that marginalizes women and vilifies Jews, it is necessary to dislodge our readings from such a preconstructed frame of
reference and to reconfigure the Christian Testament discourses about
Jesus not as "scientific" but as rhetorical. The reconstruction of the Jesus
movement as an emancipatory *basileia* movement, I suggest, provides
such a different historical frame of reference. It allows for the articulation of a Christian feminist self-understanding that no longer needs to
be articulated over against Judaism nor remain intertwined with theological masculinism. Such a christological rereading in rhetorical terms
is forced neither to relinquish the quest for its historical Jewish roots nor
to end up in Christian supremacy and exclusivism.

In such a reconstructive rhetorical model, Christian self-identity is
not tied to its previous stages of kyriarchal anti-Jewish formations and
their sociocultural contexts but must be negotiated again and again
for every-body and every wo/man in the global village in light of the
messianic *basileia*/commonweal vision of justice and well-being. Biblical
christology no longer can afford to neglect its participation in cultural and religious identity formation; rather it must continue to reflect
critically on the oppressive or liberating functions of its christological
interpretations and historical reconstructions in diverse sociopolitical
contexts.

Chapter 4

PROCLAIMED BY WOMEN
The Execution of Jesus and the
Theology of the Cross

Why do you seek the living among the dead?

(Luke 24:5)

There were three who always walked with the Lord: Mary, his mother, and her sister and Magdalene, the one who was called his companion. His sister and his mother and his companion were each a Mary.

(Gospel of Philip ii.59, 6–11)[1]

As I now reflect on my grandmother's faith in Christ, I realize that the Christ in her life had to be one who understood more than just what it meant to live in a racist society. My grandmother's Christ was one whom she could talk to about the daily struggles of being poor, Black, and female. So, it is in this regard that I continue to learn from my grandmother's faith. Her faith in Christ's empowering presence suggests, at the very least, a womanist Black Christ. But most importantly, it is in the face of my grandmother, as she struggled to sustain herself and her family, that I can truly see Christ.[2]

The theology of the cross is the third hotly debated critical issue in Christian feminist christological discourses. As feminist discussions have shown, this problem is intrinsically connected with the problem of the "maleness" of Jesus. Traditionally, Christian belief in salvation by a male savior has been intertwined with the belief in redemption from sin—which is said to have been brought into the world by a woman—through the suffering and cross of Jesus. In this chapter I will approach this problem of the theology of the cross, first, by staging a roundtable discussion on the theology of the cross at which different feminist voices will be heard. In a second step I will reconstruct the earliest Christian reflections on the execution of Jesus in order to provide a different—albeit not feminist—frame of meaning. By constructing both discourses as rhetorical and by reading the feminist debates in critical interaction with the reconstructed formulae of the earliest christological confessions, I hope in a third step to place both discourses in the hermeneutical space of the ekklēsia of wo/men.

The Theology of the Cross
in Feminist Perspective

Like the problem of the "maleness of Jesus" so also feminist critiques of the theology of the cross have their roots in nineteenth-century suffragist arguments. As I have pointed out, in the last century suffragists like Elizabeth Cady Stanton and Mathilda Joselyn Gage underscored that both the doctrinal assertion that Eve's sin[3] brought death into the world and the Christian belief in redemption by a male savior are intertwined.

To my knowledge, Mary Daly was the first contemporary theologian to point out the significance of this nineteenth-century suffragist discourse on sin and salvation. Over twenty years ago Daly wrote in *Beyond God the Father:*

> The qualities that Christianity idealizes, especially for women, are also those of the victim: sacrificial love, passive acceptance of suffering, humility, meekness, etc. Since these are the qualities idealized in Jesus "who died for our sins" his functioning as a model reinforces the scapegoat syndrome for women.[4]

This negative evaluation and rejection of the Christian doctrine of atonement and redemption, first articulated by white suffragists in the last century and developed by Daly and others in this century,[5] have been confirmed in recent feminist christological discussions. Their contextualization in the discourse concerning violence against women heightens the problematic character of Christian belief in redemption. The debate has been invigorated by the publication of a collection of feminist essays entitled *Christianity, Patriarchy and Abuse.* In their contribution to this book Joanne Carlson Brown and Rebecca Parker write:

> Christianity has been a primary — in many women's lives *the* primary — force in shaping our acceptance of abuse. The central image of Christ on the cross as the savior of the world communicates the message that suffering is redemptive.... Our suffering for others will save the world. The message is complicated further by the theology that says Christ suffered in obedience to his Father's will. Divine child abuse is paraded as salvific and the child who suffers without even raising a voice is lauded as the hope of the world. Those whose lives have been deeply shaped by

the Christian tradition feel that self-sacrifice and obedience are not only virtues but the definition of a faithful identity. The promise of resurrection persuades us to endure pain, humiliation, and violation of our sacred rights to self determination, wholeness and freedom.[6]

After reviewing the classical doctrines of atonement and discussing modern theologies of suffering and the cross, they conclude:

> Christianity is an abusive theology that glorifies suffering. Is it any wonder that there is so much abuse in modern society when the predominant image or theology of the culture is of "divine child abuse" — God the father, demanding and carrying out the suffering and death of his own son.... This bloodthirsty God is the God of the patriarchy who at the moment controls the whole Judeo-Christian tradition.[7]

In the same volume Sheila Redmond explores Christian attitudes and virtues that foster the sexual abuse of children. Although Christian theology officially condemns sexual violence and abuse, she argues, its doctrinal fund nevertheless reinforces attitudes that lead to the acceptance of such abuse. Recovery from child sexual abuse is hindered by the fact that many victims have internalized questions, images, and values that prevent such recovery, namely, the notions of suffering as good and forgiveness as a virtue, the necessity — especially for little girls — of remaining sexually pure, the need for redemption, and, most importantly, the emphasis on obedience to authority figures.[8] All these beliefs and values reinforce personal guilt and responsibility for the abuse. They make it difficult for sexual abuse victims to resolve the lingering feelings of guilt for the crime that has been perpetrated upon them.

Well aware of this trenchant critique of the theology of the cross, leading feminist theologians, especially in Europe, have sought to reassert its importance for a feminist theology. For instance, the German feminist theologian Elisabeth Moltmann-Wendel argues for a feminist retrieval of the theology of the cross. If the cross remains embedded in the whole life-story of Jesus and his mutuality with women, she maintains, it can become again for women the symbol of life and wholeness, which it was in pre-Christian times.

> In the last analysis, the Cross is a paradoxical symbol. It is not simply the guillotine or the gallows. It is also subconsciously the symbol of wholeness and life and it probably could only survive as a central Christian symbol because of this simultaneous subconscious meaning.[9]

Like Moltmann-Wendel, the British feminist theologian Mary Grey also seeks to "unravel" traditional theologies of atonement and to "reweave" them in a feminist perspective. After a critical review of Greek, Latin, and modern "atonement doctrines," she concludes that a Christian feminist interpretation looks not simply to the cross of Jesus but to

the values it represents.[10] Contradicting Hans Küng, who argues that
"the cross is not only the example and model, but also the ground,
power and norm of Christian faith,"[11] Grey maintains that "it is not
the cross as such, but our inadequate interpretation of it and fixation on death and violence which is the problem."[12] Such a theological
"metaphorization" of the cross allows her to reinterpret atonement as
"at-one-ment" and "redemptive mutuality" and to reimage the cross as
creative "birth giving." Her own proposal for reimaging the cross follows the lead of the apostle Paul[13] and the Jewish philosopher of religion
Carol Ochs:[14]

> Because fear of death haunts most people, they cling to the image of
> Christ on the cross as model of endurance. But suppose there was another
> way to see this which used the images of birth, change, transformation.
> Instead of taking the image of victory over death, the "Christus Victor"
> symbol of Jesus, innocent lamb, delivered up to slaughter as ransom pay-
> ment, suppose we try to see if there are other transformative possibilities,
> based on the image of birth.[15]

In line with liberation theology, Grey insists on an understanding of
"redemptive mutuality" as solidarity in the struggles against oppression; but it seems to me that this new reimaging of the cross in terms
of "at-one-ment" and "birth" is misplaced insofar as it reimages the
cross rather than the resurrection. Such a symbolic misplacement, I fear,
cannot but depoliticize and spiritualize Jesus' execution in "feminine"
terms.

The Swiss theologian Regula Strobel provides a helpful summary not
only of the feminist critique of traditional christologies[16] but also of
feminist attempts to reconstruct the doctrine of redemption positively.[17]
She does so in order to critically evaluate such feminist attempts to re-
vision the theology of the cross according to how they deal with its
sociopolitical functions in kyriarchal systems of oppression. Her review
refers particularly to those criticisms that European German-speaking
and North American feminist theologians have developed.

Strobel delineates the following "pathologies" of hegemonic christologies of the cross as they have been elaborated in feminist critical
theologies: the understanding that G*d is a patriarchal king and ruler as
well as the notion that the atoning death of Jesus was necessary because
of human sin, especially the sin of Eve; the perception of sin as rebellion
and unbridled will to power and knowledge with its pendant in the theology of obedience exemplified in the silent submission of Jesus in his
suffering and death; and finally, the belief that redemption and salvation are wrought through sacrifice, submission, surrender, freely chosen
suffering, scapegoating, and violence against the innocent.

After reviewing key points of the feminist theological critique of male-stream theologies of the cross, Strobel goes on in a second article to develop her own position in dialogue with constructive proposals by other feminist theologians. Whereas post-Christian feminist theologians like Mary Daly and Elga Sorge seek to leave behind the "death-loving," necrophilic culture of Christianity, Strobel points out, liberation theologians like Dorothee Soelle, Carter Heyward, and Luise Schottroff no longer construe "the cross" as an atoning sacrifice. Rather, they seek to understand the cross, not as a religious symbol, but as an actual political means of punishment not restricted to Jesus but suffered by all those who stand up against injustice. She notes that Elisabeth Moltmann-Wendel insists that for women the cross must remain a paradoxical symbol of life.

Further, Strobel refers to attempts to understand the cross in a positive fashion as a cosmic symbol that holds together polar opposites and the four seasons. She also refers to feminist efforts that liken the cross to the vertebral columns or spine (in German *Kreuz* means cross and lower spine), which makes possible bodily movement and erect posture. Finally, Strobel presents feminist theologies that understand the death of Jesus in psychoanalytic terms. They interpret the cross in a matriarchal context as the tree of life and Jesus' death as the death of the divine hero who dies and rises again akin to the myth of the goddess and her consort.

Strobel's own position is close to that of the liberation theologians she discusses. However, in distinction to them, she believes the assumption is too negative that struggle and commitment necessarily lead to suffering and rejection. She underscores the point that traditional theologies of redemption and the cross strengthen kyriarchal societal values and structures of domination and exploitation. Utilizing the work of Judith Plaskow on the theological construction of sin from a male perspective,[18] she contends that the traditional theologies of the cross perceive sin in male terms as arrogance, pride, and hybris. Their call to self-sacrificial love and obedience bolsters the cultural socialization of women and oppressed men to sacrifice and service.

With other feminists she argues that traditional theologies of the cross promote the understanding of G*d as a sadist who demands for his own satisfaction the death of his only child. The notion that human sin can be atoned for only through the bloody sacrifice of G*d's own son serves to support the powerful in a society whose interests in domination and profit demand a multitude of human sacrifices. Most pernicious for women and subordinated men is the notion of redemption as freely chosen obedience and self-giving love. Such a theological belief also supports hierarchical relationships of domination.

Yet despite its perspicacity, Strobel's discourse does not abandon completely the concept of the "innocent victim" that has proven so deleterious for women and other nonpersons. That she unwittingly presupposes this doctrinal notion is apparent in the following rhetorical question — which does not allow for the possibility that in the eyes of the Roman judicial system Jesus might have been guilty of subverting the kyriarchal order: "Are we at all able to interpret the violence against an innocent person — and that was the murder of Jesus on the cross — without falling into the abyss of either Necrophilia . . . or of trivializing this violence?"[19]

The notions of innocent victimhood and redemption as freely chosen suffering enable militarist and capitalist societies to persuade people to accept suffering, war, and death as important ideals for which people have died in the past and for which it is still worthy to die. For women, a theology of the cross as self-giving love is even more detrimental than that of obedience because it colludes with the cultural "feminine" calling to self-sacrificing love for the sake of their families. Thus it renders the exploitation of all women in the name of love and self-sacrifice psychologically acceptable and religiously warranted.

Strobel rightly maintains that to willingly suffer violence always serves kyriarchal interests, even when such suffering is understood as redemptive. Therefore she insists that feminist theologies must distance themselves from an understanding of G*d and human life that is built on sacrifice, obedience, self-giving, and suffering, because these values will always lead to the strengthening of the patriarchal exploitation of all women and oppressed men. With this emphasis she parts company not only with malestream theology but also with Latin American, African, and especially Asian feminist liberation theologies that stress that suffering and death is the fate of those who have committed their lives to struggles for justice and liberation.

In reviewing the christological understandings of Asian women, the Korean feminist theologian Chung Hyun Kyung states from the outset that the central image for the theology of Asian women is that of the suffering servant. She suggests that this image has such power for Asian women because it connects with their "life experience filled with the experiences of suffering. It seems natural for Asian women to meet Jesus through the experience that is most familiar to them."[20] Although Chung recognizes that "making meaning out of suffering is a dangerous business," she goes on to assert:

> Asian women are discovering with much passion and compassion that
> Jesus takes sides with the silenced Asian women in his solidarity with all

oppressed people. This Jesus is Asian women's new lover, comrade and suffering servant.[21]

In a similar fashion the Hong Kong theologian Kwok Pui-lan, who lives and works in the United States, elaborates:

> It is the very person on the Cross that suffers like us, who was rendered as no-body that illuminates the tragic human existence and speaks to countless women in Asia.... We see Jesus as the God who takes the human form and suffers and weeps with us.[22]

New transformative images of Jesus that emerge in a context of suffering are those of Jesus the liberator, political martyr, revolutionary, shaman, worker, grain, mother, and menstruating woman. Chung quotes at length a poem by the Indian theologian Gabriele Dietrich, who makes a connection between the life-giving blood of menstruation and Jesus' sacrificial blood shed on the cross: "Like Jesus, women's blood has been shed from eternity. Women's menstruation is a holy Eucharist through which the renewal of life becomes possible. Jesus joins women in his life-giving bleeding."[23]

The kyriarchal pitfalls of such a "naturalizing" or "biologizing" interpretation of Jesus' death on the cross must not be overlooked, however. Such perils are apparent when one contextualizes such a theology of compassionate suffering and reads it in conjunction with a womanist critique of malestream theologies of redemption, like that elaborated by the womanist theologian Delores S. Williams with reference to African American women's experience of motherhood. She maintains that the specific character of black women's oppression consists in their coerced and voluntary surrogacy roles during slavery and after emancipation. These surrogacy roles, especially those of "mammy" and "sex object," were enforced during slavery. After the American Civil War the same roles of self-sacrificing mammy, sexual temptress, and unpaid homemaker were advocated as "freely" chosen roles. Particularly, the mammy tradition has determined the image of black women "as perpetual mother figures, religious, fat, asexual, loving children better than themselves, self-sacrificing, giving up self-concern for group advancement."[24]

The African American institution of the Mothers of the Church, according to Williams, should also be seen as standing within this mammy tradition insofar as a "mother of the church" develops considerable power if she acts in such a way that her influence does not threaten the male preacher of the church. Williams compares the surrogate status of black women with that of Christ who dies on the cross in order to redeem sinful humanity. Whether Jesus on the cross represents coerced surrogacy (willed by G*d) or freely chosen surrogacy or both, he becomes the ultimate surrogate figure.

> It is therefore altogether fitting and proper for black women to ask whether the image of a surrogate-G*d has salvific power for black women, or whether this image of redemption supports and reinforces the exploitation that has accompanied their experience with surrogate.[25]

Like Carson Brown, Parker, and Strobel, Williams rejects traditional and contemporary theologies of atonement and suffering. These theologies, she argues, must be understood in their own sociohistorical contexts and seen as the attempt of theologians to "make the Christian principle of atonement believable by shaping theories about it in the language and thought that people of a particular time understood and were grounded in."[26]

Williams suggests that womanist theologians must use the language of their own culture to convince black women that G*d did not intend their surrogate roles. Pointing to the Gospel narratives, she contends that humankind is not redeemed through Jesus' death but through his ministry and life. Williams thereby shifts the argument from a doctrinal-apologetic or rejectionist level to a practical theological level. I made a similar theological move in *In Memory of Her,* where I maintained that "the Sophia-God of Jesus does not need atonement or sacrifices. Jesus' death is not willed by God but is the result of his all-inclusive praxis as Sophia's prophet."[27]

I would insist now, however, that such a hermeneutical move must be justified through a critical assessment of the early Christian theological interpretations of Jesus' death. Otherwise such a shift easily lends itself to an apologetic argument or unwittingly imports traditional notions of atonement and redemption into the text since the Gospels narrate Jesus' life in terms of Jesus' death and resurrection. Such a reconstruction of the earliest Christian interpretations of the death of Jesus should not, however, be interpreted as a search for pristine nonkyriarchal origins. Rather, early Christian interpretations of Jesus' execution must be understood as sharing in the kyriarchal framework and androcentric language of their time. Hence, they ought to be critically assessed and rhetorically reconfigured in a different frame of meaning.

Scriptural texts are often read by feminist and other theologians against the preconstructed Anselmian frame of theological meaning. In his work *Cur Deus Homo?* Anselm of Canterbury (1033–1109) sought to show that the salvation of humanity would not have been possible without the incarnation. Drawing on the legal theory of his day, Anselm argued that the incarnation was necessary to repay the debt that re-

sulted from committing an offense against the majesty and dignity of
G*d. Satisfaction and punishment for human sins are required. Since
the offended party is G*d, the debt of sin is infinite and cannot be repaid by a human being because satisfaction offered by a limited being
would always remain finite. However, such debt must be repaid freely
by a member of the human race since G*d respects and does not over-
rule human dignity and freedom. Consequently, the incarnation of G*d's
Son was necessary to achieve the divine purpose in creation.

> Since death is a consequence of sin and Christ is sinless, he did not have
> to die. Nonetheless as a true human being composed of body and soul,
> he was able to die if he freely chose to do so. Because of the dignity of
> his person as true God, his death is of infinite value and constitutes the
> necessary satisfaction for sin. Incarnation is the necessary presupposition
> for a necessary redemption.[28]

Modern theology has severely criticized the satisfaction theology of
Anselm for its focus on suffering and the cross as satisfaction and for
its reliance on legal categories.[29] The critical feminist debate on redemption and salvation is conducted mostly in terms of the Anselmian
interpretation of atonement but does not extend to the canonical Christian Testament itself, although texts that support kyriarchal violence
abound in it. Not only traditional theological discourses but also Christian scriptural texts theologize and christologize kyriarchal suffering and
victimization.

For instance, the Epistle to the Hebrews admonishes Christians to
resist sin to the point of shedding their blood.[30] It points to the example of Jesus, "who for the joy that was set before him endured the
cross, despising the shame." Because they are "sons," Christians have
to expect suffering as disciplining chastisements from God. Just as they
respect their earthly fathers for having punished them at their pleasure,
so believers should subject themselves to "the Father of spirits and life"
who "disciplines us for our good, that we may share his holiness" (Heb.
12:1–11). By pointing to the example of Christ, the first Epistle of Peter,
which also stands in the Pauline tradition, explicitly enjoins slaves to
suffer and to subject themselves to the kyriarchal politics of domination. Servants are admonished to subordinate themselves not only to
kind and gentle masters but also to unjust and overbearing ones. There
is no credit in enduring beatings patiently if one has done wrong. But
if one does right and suffers unjustly, one finds G*d's approval: "For to
this you have been called, because Christ also suffered for you, leaving
you an example, that you should follow in his steps...for he trusted
him who judges justly" (1 Pet. 2:18–23).

This text should give pause to feminist theologians who would claim a theology of suffering and the cross as liberating. Such admonitions are not isolated aberrations in the Christian Testament but go to the heart of Christian faith: trust in God the Father and believe in redemption through the suffering and death of Christ. Such admonitions belong to a preconstructed kyriarchal frame of reference, advocating "freely chosen" suffering.

Feminist theologies have underscored the pernicious impact of a theological and christological symbolic system that stresses that God sacrificed his son for our sins. If one extols the silent and freely chosen suffering of Christ, who was "obedient to death" (Phil. 2:8), as an example to be imitated by all those victimized by patriarchal oppression, particularly by those suffering from domestic and sexual abuse, one not only legitimates but also enables acts of violence against women and children. Rita Nakashima Brock argues that christological discourses articulated within the paradigm of kyriarchal submission "reflect views of divine power that sanction child abuse on a cosmic scale."[31]

Moreover, Christine Gudorf has pointed out that, contrary to René Girard's thesis, the sacrifice of surrogate victims does not contain and interrupt the cycle of violence.[32] Rather, by rechanneling violence, it serves to protect those in power from the violent protest of those whom they oppress. By ritualizing the suffering and death of Jesus and by calling the powerless in society and church to imitate Jesus' perfect obedience and self-sacrifice, Christian ministry and theology do not interrupt but continue to foster the circle of violence engendered by kyriarchal social and ecclesial structures as well as by cultural and political discourses. A theology that is silent about the sociopolitical causes of Jesus' execution and stylizes him as the paradigmatic sacrificial victim whose death was either willed by God or was necessary to propitiate God continues the kyriarchal cycle of violence and victimization instead of empowering believers to resist and transform it.[33]

In the first two chapters of this book I focused on the cultural and political structures in antiquity and modernity that have undergirded this preconstructed doctrinal frame of kyriarchal domination. Brian Wren has explored these sociopolitical underpinnings of christological and theological discourses and their expression in Christian prayer and liturgy. He argues that the metaphorical system that undergirds Christian imagination, worship, and hymnody is that of "KINGAFAP — the King-God-Almighty-Father-All-Powerful-Protector."[34]

In this frame of reference G*d is pictured and worshiped as a powerful king enthroned in splendor who receives homage and atonement for offenses against his majesty, rules by word of command, and stabilizes the cosmic order. This Almighty, All-powerful, and often terrifying King is also called Father. He is the creator, merciful Lord, and Father, who is the sole (male) parent of the crown prince, his Son, Jesus Christ. Since evil enemies have invaded the Father's kingly realm of creation, the crown prince obediently surrenders his royal power and privileges and at his Father's command becomes human. The royal prince is killed by the enemy powers, Sin and Evil, but lifted up to the glorious abode of his Kingly Father. He leaves behind his humble and suffering station as one of humanity and waits on his throne until he can come back in glory to slay his enemies and judge humanity. Meanwhile the Father-King and Son-Prince send their Spirit down to earth to help their followers and to teach only them the revelation of KINGAFAP and the story of the Only Son of G*d, Humiliated Slave but Prince, the enthroned Christ who rules with KINGAFAP.

This Christian symbol system of Kingly Father, Princely Son, and Exclusive Spirit has no room for a female figure, be it mother, consort, sister, or daughter, nor for a female personification like Shekinah or Sophia. It envisions the Divine in terms of control and rule and imagines divine transcendence as absolute, distant, and completely foreign to the world. Hence, this kyriarchal symbolic system cannot but function to bolster kyriarchal society and church. Since it is deeply ingrained in Christian consciousness, it has become "common sense" according to Althusser's understanding of ideology. Consequently, it is very difficult, if not impossible, to reimagine and reconstruct this central Christian myth differently. It claims the authority of orthodoxy although it seems to cohere completely with what we know about the account of the world historically articulated in Gnostic speculation.

The Execution of Jesus and Its Rhetorical Interpretations[35]

Since most of the critical feminist discussions of the theology of the cross either refer to the doctrinal KINGAFAP frame of reference or are heavily influenced by it, their critical evaluation and rejection of the doctrine of atonement and redemption seem to be justified. However, if we can transform a system not by rejecting but only by reconfiguring it in a different frame of meaning, it becomes important to contextualize feminist reflections on Jesus' suffering and cross within a different politics of meaning. Only if we dislocate the doctrinal discourses of redemption and salvation from their preconstructed "common-sense" meanings does it become possible to reconfigure and to transform them.

I will attempt to do so by recontextualizing the discourses on the theology of the cross within the earliest Christian attempts to "make meaning" out of Jesus' suffering and execution. I cannot overly stress, however, that in so doing I do *not* seek to employ form-critical exegetical reconstructions to prove that these earliest christological proclamations are liberating rather than kyriarchal articulations. Such a reconstruction of the earliest Christian interpretations of Jesus' death and of the proclamations of his resurrection must also not be understood as "telling how it actually was" but as an attempt to construct a different politics of meaning.

The early Christian interpretations of Jesus' death are best understood as rhetorical accounts. They were articulated in a sociohistorical situation where the followers of Jesus had to "make sense" out of his brutal death as a condemned criminal. Hence, I seek to dislocate the hegemonic doctrinal discourses on redemption by relocating them within a differently "preconstructed" frame of reference. However, such a critical reconstruction must not be construed as nonkyriocentric. Since the early Christians were limited by the discourses of their environment, they could speak only in the languages of the first century when they expressed their faith in Jesus. To assume otherwise would be to argue that they could not have communicated either with one another or with outsiders.

Rather than searching for nonkyriarchal expressions of Christian redemption that can offer wo/men "a perfect vision of ministerial relation,"[36] feminist theologies might learn from the early Christians, who used a great diversity of formulas to make sense of the cruel death of Jesus. They were forced to do so because Jesus' execution posed for them both a difficult political problem and a great spiritual one as well. I am well aware that such a short review and typology of the earliest interpretations of Jesus' execution enters a minefield of exegetical, historical, and theological problems. We do not know how Jesus himself understood his death, and we have only fragments of the earliest Christian interpretations of this death, which are embedded in later, especially Pauline, writings. Still, even a precarious historically responsible reconstruction allows one to glimpse a different theological frame of reference. The language and the "setting in life" of the early christological narrative interpretations of Jesus' execution and of the earliest confessional formulas tell something about the self-understanding of the early Christians who articulated them. Like these early Christian interpretations, feminist christological discourses are best understood as religious-political rhetorical practices,[37] I suggest, rather than as presentations of historical facts or as doctrinal reflections on redemption and atonement.

The Originating Event:
Jesus' Execution as the "King of the Jews"

Critical biblical scholarship has "unearthed" a host of different interpretations of Jesus' death and resurrection that might or might not have a claim to being "original." While scholars disagree in their historical evaluation of individual texts about Jesus' death, they almost universally agree that these texts were generated by historical "factual events." These "facts" are that Jesus suffered the excruciating death of crucifixion and that he was proclaimed by his followers to have been raised from the dead. However, exegetes disagree, for instance, on whether the Roman or the Jewish authorities were responsible for the crucifixion.[38] They also debate whether Jesus' death was an accident[39] and whether the linkage between his public teaching and his death is simply a Markan "narrative fiction."[40] Finally, it must be noted that even in antiquity some voices, although they seem to have been in the minority, raised the question of whether Jesus actually died on the cross or whether he only appeared to be dead and was resuscitated by his disciples afterward.[41]

The actual form of Jesus' execution is not controverted. Crucifixion was an excruciating form of death not unique to Jesus but suffered by many women and men in the Roman empire who did not comply with imperial policies or were simply accused of wrongdoing or treason.[42] We know from Josephus that the Romans reacted brutally against those suspected of fomenting rebellion.[43] According to him various prophetic figures appeared on the scene of first-century Palestine as messianic would-be deliverers from Roman rule: "Deceivers and impostors under the pretense of divine inspiration fostering revolutionary changes... led them out into the desert under the belief that God would there give them signs of salvation."[44] The Roman imperial police did not hesitate to take harsh measures against such would-be liberators. For instance, the Romans took swift military action against two Jewish prophetic figures, one by the name of Teudas and the other, a nameless "Egyptian Jew," and killed them. In short, the Roman imperial police used the crucifixion as a mode of execution, especially against seditious provincials and rebellious slaves, because of its great deterrent value.[45]

According to all four Gospels, Jesus was charged with a political crime. Pilate had a placard attached to Jesus' cross proclaiming the crime for which he was killed: he was "the King of the Jews."[46] Although scholars do not universally accept that this official interpretation of Jesus' execution is historical,[47] it would be difficult to argue for its later invention since it serves neither Jewish nor Christian political-religious interests. To the contrary, it caused great difficulties for both. In any case, Pilate's public identification of Jesus as "King of the Jews" constitutes a very early explanation of why Jesus was crucified. That the Gospels have the tendency to shift attention from this political reason for Jesus' death to a religious one also speaks to the historicity of this designation. Such a shift in interpretation tends to take away the responsibility for Jesus' execution from the Roman government and to place it increasingly on the Jewish leadership and people.

As I pointed out in chapter 3, the Jewish scholar Ellis Rivkin suggests that to understand the crucifixion of Jesus we have to shift attention from the question of *who* crucified Jesus to the question of *what* killed Jesus. He argues persuasively that Jesus was not crucified because of his religious beliefs and teachings but because of their potential political implications: "It was not the Jewish people who crucified Jesus, and it was not the Roman people — it was the imperial system, a system that victimized the Jews, victimized the Romans, and victimized the Spirit of God."[48] This system of victimization was kyriarchal; its imperial powers affected in various ways all men who had no power and all women even more. The history of resistance against the Roman imperial system of victimization still needs to be written, both as a political history and as a cultural-religious history.

Exegetes debate whether the official inscription on Pilate's placard, or *titulus,* represented a Roman misunderstanding (e.g., Bultmann), whether Jesus actually claimed to be the Davidic Messiah of Israel, or whether his miracle working and preaching led to the charge.[49] They also disagree on what the actual charge brought against Jesus was. Scholars have suggested a variety of reasons for Jesus' execution: that he attempted to overthrow the government in Jerusalem,[50] that he threatened to destroy and replace the temple,[51] that he was considered a dangerous charismatic preacher,[52] or that he was accused of being a "deceiver of the people."[53]

Although exegetes disagree on the actual charge against Jesus and whether he had a messianic self-consciousness, they generally do agree that the center of his message was the *basileia,* i.e., the reign, realm, or commonweal of G*d.[54] *Basileia* is the Greek word referring to the Roman empire. Hence, Jesus' message about the *basileia* was both *political* and *religious.* Jesus' announcement of the *basileia* must be understood in religio-political and social terms.[55] The tensive symbol "*basileia* of G*d" was an ancestral symbol that referred to G*d's covenant with Israel as the people of G*d. It was also a cosmic symbol that invoked creation and the eschatological "new creation."[56] *Basileia* conjures up the image of and hope for G*d's renewed and different world, a world free from suffering and death. Exegetes tend to agree that Jesus announced the *basileia* not simply in apocalyptic language as a future hope, but spoke of it also in sapiential language as a present reality. Like leaven the *basileia* was already present in the Jesus movement's own table community and healing activity.[57] It is because of this vision and practice of the *basileia* that Jesus was executed by the Romans as "the King of the Jews."

Whatever explanation we accept, the execution of Jesus raised the difficult theological problem for his followers of whether he and his message were wrong because they were not confirmed by G*d. It also created the need for a political apologetics capable of showing that the early Christians were not seditious enemies of the Roman order. Such a political apologetics had to shift theological attention away from the political character of the death of Jesus to a religious symbolic interpretation of the cross and away from the culpability of the Roman imperial administration to that of the Jewish leadership and people. Since this shift had already been accomplished by the time our canonical Gospels were written, it is important to trace the pre-Gospel reflections on the execution of Jesus with the help of form-critical analysis.[58]

Early Christian Theological Interpretations of Jesus' Execution

Form-critical analyses have reconstructed early Christian attempts to make sense out of the brutal execution of Jesus.[59] In the following sections I single out six interpretive strategies that can be reconstructed from this rhetorical tradition embedded in the Pauline literature.[60] Yet, I do not want to suggest that such a delineation is comprehensive. Instead I want to show how early Christian "meaning-making" was put into practice. Probably one of the first Christian interpretations of the execution of Jesus that a form-critical analysis can disentomb,[61] is the confessional formula "G*d raised him from the dead," or "he was raised" (passive voice).[62] This formula seems to be structurally patterned after the central Israelite confession "G*d brought Israel out of Egypt."[63] Only at a later stage and probably in a context of the mystery religions,[64] which proclaimed a dying and rising God, did Christians begin to use the active form "Jesus rose from the dead." This formula asserts: G*d's saving activity is manifested in the vindication of Jesus, who is now the Resurrected One. Such an articulation of vindication proclaims the discredited and dehumanized Jesus who was executed, and "not an other-worldly Jesus, . . . as the criterion for discerning God's true intentions."[65] This attempt of theological "sense-making" of Jesus' execution speaks of G*d as having brought about Jesus' resurrection. It thereby clearly stands within the language world of apocalyptic Judaism, where this belief is connected with the notion of exaltation and vindication.

For instance, Daniel says that in his night visions he saw someone like a human one (son of man) who came on the clouds of heaven and was presented before the Ancient One to receive the dominion and glory of the *basileia* (Dan. 7:13–14). According to the interpretation given to Daniel, this figure of someone "like a human being" signifies Israel, the holy ones of the Most High who are now oppressed by worldly powers but will receive the *basileia* forever (7:18). In a similar fashion, Daniel 12:1–3 states that G*d will bring about a turn in the life of Israel through Michael:

> Then those who have endured the test and whose names are written in the "book of life" will be delivered. Many of those who sleep in the dust of the earth shall wake — some to everlasting life and some to shame and everlasting contempt.

Such language of vindication is, however, found not only in Apocalyptic literature but also in Hellenistic Wisdom literature. Wisdom of Solomon 2:13–20 asserts that the righteous one will be numbered among the children of G*d and not be put to shame. The righteous one will be saved by G*d and exalted to glory as a witness to G*d's help for those who are truly righteous.[66] Thus the first early Christian formulaic interpretation of the death of Jesus stands within the thought world of both Apocalyptic and sapiential Judaism when it asserts that "G*d raised Jesus" and thereby expresses the conviction that Jesus' message and person were vindicated despite all evidence to the contrary.[67] Jesus' resurrection is here understood as the *vindication* of the righteous one.[68]

In 2 Maccabees 7 a moving statement is ascribed to a woman. This text narrates the martyrdom of seven young men and their mother.[69] During cruel torture one after another they confess their hope of resurrection. These young Jews are portrayed as the suffering servants of YAHWEH whose lives and deaths will be vindicated. Watching her sons die, the mother

> . . . encouraged each of them in the language of their ancestors. Filled with a noble spirit, she reinforced her woman's reasoning with a man's courage, and said to them, "I do not know how you came into being in my womb. It was not I who gave you life and breath, nor I who set in order the elements within each of you. Therefore the Creator of the world, who shaped the beginning of humankind and devised the origin of

all things, will in his mercy give life and breath back to you again, since you now forget yourselves for the sake of his laws." (2 Macc. 7:21–23, NRSV)

This woman expresses the same conviction as does the early Christian confessional formula: G*d did not leave Jesus in death but raised and made him alive again.

Second, the statement "G*d raised Jesus from the dead" was soon combined with the confessional formula "Christ died for us"[70] or "Christ died for our sins" (1 Cor. 15:3–4), which is found more often as an independent statement. This independent formula "Christ died [was crucified] for" is quoted often in Pauline literature.[71] The most concise combination of both statements is given in Romans 8:34: "It is Christ Jesus who died, who was raised."

Hellenistic Jewish ideas affected the theological understanding of the "Christ died for" formula. According to classical Greek tradition friends died for their friends, soldiers for their nation, and lovers for each other. Josephus reports that the Jewish leader Judas died for the people and that subsequently his brother Jonathan was exhorted to imitate him who "died for the freedom of all" (Jos. *Ant.* 13.5) This formula "Christ died for" underscores the great value and high appreciation for people that is expressed in the messianic death of Jesus. By likening Jesus to a friend giving his life for his friends — an interpretation explicitly given in the Fourth Gospel — this christological formula understands Jesus' execution as a death for his "friends."[72]

The formula "my blood of the covenant which is poured out for many," which is associated with the Eucharist, belongs to the same Hellenistic Jewish context of meaning. Since biblical writers understand blood as the seat of life's power, blood can become a potent and effective agent. The "blood of the covenant"[73] refers to the blood on the doorpost of Hebrew houses, which inaugurated the Exodus from Egypt (Exod. 12:7). This expression refers to the deliverance of Israel from the slavery of Egypt. To shed one's blood and to give one's life for others is a part of the practice of solidarity in the covenant community. According to Exodus 32:30, Moses' intercession for his people communicated his willingness to share their fate. However, it must be stressed that the confession "Christ died for" should be distinguished from the statement "Christ died for our sins" an expression that derives from a different linguistic and theological context of meaning.

Third, although the formula "Christ died for our sins" is interconnected with the preceding one, it must be clearly differentiated from it. This expression is at home in three different contexts of meaning of

early Judaism: the reflection on the death of the martyr, the cultic language of atonement, and the practice of reconciling two parties alienated
from each other.[74]

1. The death of the martyrs is interpreted as a means to end G*d's
wrath and punishment of Israel. What it meant "to die for others" is
expressed in 4 Maccabees. Here the story is told of martyrs prepared
to give their lives as a satisfaction on behalf of their people and their
country. Since they are in complete solidarity with the community to
which they belong, their deaths will purify the covenantal relationship
between G*d and G*d's people Israel. In 4 Maccabees 6:27–29 Eleazar,
on the point of dying, prays to G*d:

> You know, God, I could have saved myself. I am dying in these fiery
> torments for the sake of the law. Be merciful to our people and let
> our punishment be a satisfaction in their behalf. Make my blood their
> purification and take my life as a ransom for theirs.

The same conviction is articulated in 4 Maccabees 17:21–22, which
asserts that through the blood of the righteous ones and through the
propitiation of their death G*d punished the tyrant and rescued the
people of Israel who had been treated shamefully. The interpretation of
the martyrdom of the innocent and righteous Israelites in the times of
the Maccabees thus could provide a significant rhetorical model for the
interpretation of the death of Jesus, who is now said to have died for our
sins. Romans 3:25 understands the death of Jesus in a similar fashion,
although it utilizes cultic language for expressing it.

2. For most ancients violation of the world order meant the offense
of divine powers and consequent punishment by them. Only satisfac-
tory atonement could prevent or end such punishment. In Israel G*d
had again and again provided the means for restoring the covenant
relationship violated by transgressions. Rituals of atonement therefore
had the power to remove the sinful actions that violated the covenantal relationship. Such a covenant renewal was connected to the "Day of
Atonement" (Lev. 23:27–32) when the sins of the people were symbolically placed on the "scapegoat," which was driven into the wilderness.
In this Jewish cultic context of meaning the formula "Christ died for our
sins" cannot but have cultic overtones. Such explicitly cultic language is
found in Romans 3:24–25:

> they are now justified by his grace as a gift, through the redemption that
> is in Christ Jesus, whom God put forward as a sacrifice of atonement
> [*hilastērion*] by his blood, effective through faith.

Yet it must not be overlooked that such cultic language, which has its
roots in the sacrificial temple cult of Jerusalem, had already been ethi-

cized and individualized in Jewish theological reflections of the time. Such moralizing interpretation understands good deeds, fasting, religious devotion, and loving-kindness as effective means to atone for sins. Hence, Paul can use this cultic notion to characterize the new status of Christians brought about by the grace of God and the redemption in Christ.

3. The notion of atonement is to be carefully distinguished from the notions of reconciliation and justification. Reconciliation signifies the repair of a disturbed relationship between G*d and Israel. It must be stressed that in the language world of Israel this fractured relationship was not blamed on Eve's sin but rather connected with the offenses against the covenantal relationship with G*d. Israel's G*d, who made a covenant with the people, had always been and continued to be faithful to this covenantal agreement. The people, on the other hand, had not always remained faithful and again and again had "sinned" and broken their covenantal commitment to G*d, either individually or corporately, morally or ritually. Paul speaks in such terms of reconciliation through Christ, for example, in 2 Corinthians 5:19: "that is, in Christ God was reconciling the world to himself, not counting their trespasses against them, and entrusting the message of reconciliation to us" (NRSV). G*d's reconciling grace manifested in the Christ includes the whole world. It marks "a new life, a new creation, and a different way of perceiving the world and one's relationships."[75]

4. A fourth interpretation of Jesus' death is expressed in Mark 10:45, which stresses that Jesus came to serve and to give up his life as a ransom for many.[76] This text is usually understood in terms of atonement from sin. However, such an explanation overlooks the economic context of the formula's meaning. While the meaning of this expression in the Hebrew Bible can gravitate toward "atonement," its primary sense derives from practices of economic transaction. "Ransom" can refer to the redemption of an inheritance, to the rescuing of family members from servitude or from other difficulties, to the redemption of the firstborn among male children from being sacrificed, or to buying the freedom of slaves.

The image evoked in Mark 10:45 is not that of atonement but rather that of the ransoming of a people living under slavery or that of captives of war set free by the death of Christ. Jesus is understood here as an envoy who, so to speak, used his life as a payment for setting people free from bondage and oppression. Such a meaning is derived from an apocalyptic mythological context that understands the present situation of suffering and persecution as enslavement and bondage.[77] This world view is apparent especially in the Book of Revelation.[78] It is already found in the Pauline letters, where Sin and Death are personified and understood as cosmic powers that keep humans in bondage and exploitation. Death, like Sin, is a demonic power that "reigns" (*basileuein*) in this age (Rom. 5:14, 17) in distinction to "the age to come" (Rom. 8:38; 1 Cor. 3:22). The present world is captive to evil powers. They are alien to the creative and redemptive power of G*d, "which summons into being things that are not" and makes the dead come alive (Rom. 4:17).

G*d's salvific power is manifest in the death and resurrection of Christ (Gal. 1:3–4), who at the end yields the reign to G*d (1 Cor. 15:24). G*d's power for life is expressed especially in resurrection, first in the resurrection of Christ and then through him in the resurrection of all those who believe in him (Phil. 3:13). According to 1 Corinthians 15:43, to be raised in "glory" means to be raised "in power." In this apocalyptic context of meaning the death and resurrection of Jesus become a means to set people free and to inaugurate the "new creation." Accordingly, Jesus Christ is the firstborn of the dead, the "down payment" of the renewed creation.

5. A fifth interpretation is indicated by the expression "G*d gave up the son." Romans 8:32 explicitly states: "G*d who did not spare G*d's own son, but gave him up for us all." This statement could allude to Genesis 22, the story of Abraham's sacrifice of his son.[79] But it is not clear why Paul used a phrase drawn from the story of Abraham's sacrifice to speak about the death of Christ. It is more likely that the formulation of Romans 8:32 is not a direct reference to Genesis 22, but rather draws on a midrashic interpretation of Genesis 22. We must also ask how the accord between this formula and the Akedah, or binding of Isaac, is to be understood. Traditionally, exegetes have construed a typological relationship between the binding of Isaac and the death of Christ to mean: just as Abraham did not spare his son, so G*d did not spare G*d's own son. However, as Niels Dahl has observed, the statement in Romans 8:32 does not relate to the suffering of Isaac but to the conduct of Abraham. Hence, he concludes, "it is unlikely that Abraham's act of obedience was ever considered a typological prefiguration of God's act of love."[80]

According to Dahl, the text of Genesis 22:16–17 instead suggests a different kind of correspondence: that of *act and reward*. In a Jewish-Christian homiletic context Christians might have interpreted the death of Jesus on the cross as fulfilling the promise that G*d had given to Abraham by oath. Since Abraham had not withheld his son, G*d has kept the divine promise and did not spare G*d's son, but gave him up for Isaac's descendants. Christ's death is then understood here as a reward for the Akedah and as a divine blessing for the descendants of Abraham. As Dahl states: "Vicariously, Jesus was made a curse to redeem them from the curse, caused by their transgressions of the law so that even the Gentile nations might be blessed in the offspring of Abraham, the crucified Messiah, Jesus."[81]

6. A sixth theological interpretation of the execution of Jesus is closely connected with the formula "G*d sent G*d's son." The formula "G*d sent me" is found in the early traditions and may go back to the historical Jesus.[82]

> There was a pre-Q, pre-Markan, and pre-Johannine logion that spoke of Jesus coming to us in the "little ones" (disciples or children in need) and probably from the beginning, also of God "who sent" Jesus and comes to us in him. In any case, the definition of Jesus as the one sent by God is rooted firmly in the tradition.[83]

This sixth interpretation is developed in three ways: in the formulation of a prophetic christology, in the identification of Jesus the prophet with Divine Wisdom herself, and in the stress on the perfect obedience of the son.

First, a christology that understands Jesus as a prophet and sees his death as the outcome of his prophetic actions can be found in the hypothetical Sayings Source called Q. It sees Jesus together with John the Baptizer as standing in a long line of prophets sent to Israel and conceives of Jesus' death as similar to the fate of the prophets of old who were also rejected and killed. This christological interpretation understands the execution of Jesus as the total outcome of his prophetic practice.[84] Wisdom's lament over Jerusalem articulates this understanding of the Q community: Wisdom sent her prophets and messengers to call Israel to repentance but they were rejected and killed by their own people.

A similar christological interpretation is expressed in the parable found in Mark 12:1–9, where the owner of the vineyard dispatches several messengers and finally sends his own son and heir (v. 6): "He had still one other beloved son. Finally he sent him to them." It is clear that the owner of the vineyard here stands for G*d, whereas the "son" signifies the fate of Jesus.[85] This pattern of sending is also found in Galatians 4:4, where Paul says that G*d sent forth G*d's son, "born of a woman, born under the law to redeem those who were under the law so that we receive adoption as sons."

Second, in this text we can observe the beginnings of the interpretation that connects a prophetic christology with a "son" christology. Mussner has shown that such a replacement of prophetic christology, which has a broad basis in the Christian Testament, was made possible

through the development of the "son" christology.[86] This "son" christology seems also to provide a reason why the way and fate of the son,
who was sent, soon became identified with that of Divine Wisdom. Just
as Sophia did not find a resting place and returned to the heavenly realm,
so also Jesus Christ did not receive a welcoming reception among her/his
people and hence returned to heaven (see 1 Enoch 42). Like that of Wisdom, the fate of Jesus as the "son" is conceptualized as humiliation and
exaltation or as descending from and ascending to the world of G*d.
Jesus Christ is perceived as a heavenly being who gave up his divine
status, humiliated himself, died on the cross, was exalted as the *kyrios*,
and was given the name of cosmic Lord. This manner of speaking is
found in the early Christian hymns, particularly Philippians 2:6–11,[87]
and provides the pattern for the narrative of the Fourth Gospel. Since
this interpretation of Jesus' fate is modeled on the Jewish theological discourse about the way of Divine Wisdom, I will discuss this christological
pattern more extensively in the next chapter.

Both of these interpretations of Jesus' execution shift the responsibility for Jesus' death from the Romans to Jerusalem and Israel. This
shift determined the accounts in the Synoptic Gospels, which have been
dubbed "extended" passion narratives. Jesus' suffering and death are
understood not only as the outcome of his life-praxis, of his preaching, healing, and ministry, but also as the responsibility of the Jewish
people. However, this early Jewish (Christian) interpretation of the execution of Jesus in terms of the fate of Israel's prophets and the "sending
of the son" who was killed perpetrates anti-Jewish sentiments when it
is no longer spoken to Israel but taken out of its original Jewish context. In all four Gospels it functions both to draw the boundaries of the
Christian community against Judaism and to shift the blame for Jesus'
crucifixion from the oppressive Roman patriarchal power to the Jewish
people and their leaders.

Third, this reading gives as a theological rationale for the suffering
and death of Jesus that it was the will and decree of G*d. Apocalyptic theology explains suffering and evil with the "divine must" in order
to assert that despite all appearances to the contrary G*d is in control
of the world. Hence, the suffering and execution of Jesus can only be
understood as willed by G*d; Jesus died in radical obedience to the will
of an almighty G*d who is the sole ruler of the universe.

Such a theological interpretation of suffering is typical of apocalypticism. This interpretation is given in the passion narratives of all four
Gospels[88] and is often connected with a "proof" from Scripture. That
the death of Jesus happened according to G*d's will seems to be spelled
out in Matthew 26:53–54, which argues: If Jesus had wanted, the Father

could have sent an army of angels to defend him. However, G*d did not do so in order that the Scriptures might be fulfilled. The reference to the "will of G*d" or to the "plan of G*d" is given as theological justifications for Jesus' suffering and execution. This apocalyptic interpretation of Jesus' execution clearly expresses a kyriocentric world view, since it defines sonship in terms of perfect obedience and fatherhood in terms of perfect control.

In conclusion: these various rhetorical interpretations of the death of Jesus could be multiplied if we were to add here a critical study of christological titles, almost all of which were ascribed to Jesus after his death and resurrection.[89] These titles are not definitions of the true being or nature of Jesus. Rather they are best understood as language models and metaphors that seek to "make sense" out of the terrible fate of Jesus. By giving dignity and value to the one who in his execution became a dehumanized nonperson, these titles seek to exonerate him. We also could multiply instances of such "naming" and "meaning-making" rhetorical gestures by looking closely at how the oldest narrative traditions characterize Jesus. Even though I am not able to discuss here all the early Christian rhetorical attempts of "making sense" out of the cruel death of Jesus, I hope that I have indicated that, by borrowing from various contexts of meaning, early Christian wo/men in many different ways attempted to reflect upon the terrible experience of the execution of their friend. Instead of extending the discussion of christological interpretations embedded in the Christian Testament, I will place alongside each other those early Christian discourses that seek to "make meaning" of the execution of Jesus, on the one hand, and contemporary feminist christological discourses, on the other, to discuss them within the frame of meaning constituted by the ekklēsia of wo/men.

Named and Proclaimed by Wo/men

Understanding both discourses — the critical feminist discussions on the theology of the cross and the early Christian rhetorical attempts at "meaning-making" in the face of disaster — as rhetorical discourses allows one to read them in conjunction with and against each other. In the following discussion I will attempt to read these discourses, first, in conjunction with each other; then in a second and third step I will discuss them as discursive formations that mutually correct and enhance each other. Although these discourses deploy various interpretive strategies, such a critical reading is possible if one construes them as arguments around the same Wisdom table.

First, one can observe several structural and methodological similarities between feminist liberationist and early Christian "naming" processes.

1. Feminist critical assessments of the theology of the cross are not purely theoretical ruminations but rather must be understood as generated by the experience, in particular, of violence against wo/men, and, in general, of the oppression of wo/men. Similarly, the early Christian attempts of meaning-making in the face of the devastating execution of Jesus should not be conceptualized merely in terms of the history of ideas. Nor should they be understood primarily as responses to and affirmations of Jesus' resurrection. Rather, we must read these early Christian attempts of theological meaning-making as critical arguments that begin with the very real experience of Jesus' dehumanization and crucifixion as a political criminal. According to such a reading both discourses, the feminist discourse on the theology of the cross and the early Christian interpretations of the cross, have the same starting point. They begin with the historical "fact" of unjust oppression, the experience of struggle for a different world, and an encounter with the victimization and death of the dehumanized person. Thus both discourses seek to make meaning in the context of unjust suffering. In doing so, they claim the historical agency of the oppressed and disenfranchised to define and change death-dealing situations of dehumanization.

2. Both discourses utilize the language world of their own times for such meaning-making. Whereas contemporary feminist discourses on the meaning of the cross operate within the problematics of modernity and/or national liberation struggles, the early Christian formulaic interpretations are at home in the Jewish and Greco-Roman language worlds of the first century. These respective language worlds are not simply a form of expression but rather constitute meaning. Early Christians utilized Israel's sacred Scriptures and traditional reflections on the suffering of the righteous people for making meaning of the death of Jesus and their own situation; to articulate and authorize their politics of meaning feminist liberation discourses today utilize not only biblical languages and images about Jesus the Christ, but also systemic analyses of oppression.

3. Both discourses evoke a multiplicity of images and articulate diverse, even contradictory, insights into the process of meaning-making. However, insofar as their interest is in liberation and salvation, neither a feminist liberationist nor a biblical-exegetical discourse of meaning can rest with the play of multiple meanings, languages, and images. Rather their interest in survival and liberation compels both discourses to evaluate critically the play of images and meanings and their pre-

constructed kyriarchal frame of reference that generates and orders multiple meaning possibilities and in turn is sustained by them. A critical interpretation for liberation cannot eschew critical evaluation of discourses and refrain from ethical judgment on cultural-religious meanings and their productions if it wants to produce change and transformation.

4. Both discourses — early Christian and contemporary feminist — insist that resurrection is a symbolic yet "real" justification for Jesus and all those "little ones" or "nobodies" who struggle for survival, human dignity, and liberation from oppression. Faith in resurrection and hope in the overcoming of brutal suffering and execution celebrates "the Living Ones." It does so with ever new names and images that reconstitute the human dignity, agency, and memory of those killed. Both discourses enable us to understand the meaning of resurrection as a political, "real" vindication of struggle for a world free from hunger, abuse, and injustice. Resurrection does not simply spell the survival of the soul but requires the transformation of the world as we know it. Hence, we are justified in positioning both christological discourses within the hermeneutical space of the ekklēsia of wo/men, the discipleship community of equals that struggles for liberation and well-being for all.

Second, since feminist discussions of the theology of the cross explicitly claim women's experience and authority for assessing and rearticulating malestream theological meaning-making, they force us to ask *who* the agents of such christological meaning-making processes might have been. If one reads the earliest Christian attempts of christological meaning-making in light of feminist theological critiques of the traditional malestream theologies of the cross, one is struck by the fact that form-critical reconstructions of these attempts of meaning-making generally do not name the subjects who articulated these early Christian confessions.

To the contrary, the method of form criticism does not allow us to ask this question but only to inquire into the typical *Sitz im Leben* (setting in life) that generated such early Christian confessions. One must keep in mind, however, that the form-critical concept of *Sitz im Leben* spells out not the particular sociohistorical location of the text but rather the typical generative matrix of formulaic statements. Two "doctrinal locations" are generally proposed as settings for the articulation of the early Christian christological "confessions": teaching and/or catechesis on the one hand and baptismal and/or eucharistic liturgy on the other. But both of these "typical" settings were traditionally reserved to men. Hence, this historical method tacitly assumes as a "common-sense" frame of reference that the earliest theological interpretations of the death and resurrection of Jesus, which scholars call the kerygma, were articulated by leading men.

To challenge this "common-sense" assumption of exegetical scholarship, I have argued that students of early Christianity — or of any other cultural-religious group — must begin their investigations with the assumption that women actively shaped cultural traditions in general and the early Christian traditions in particular, unless scholars can prove otherwise. If we look at historical source-texts in light of this methodological principle, it is striking that the narrative presentations of Jesus' suffering, death, and resurrection ascribe to women a leading role in these events.[90] All Gospels mention Mary of Magdala as the primary witness to the resurrection,[91] and some refer to other women as well. These women are said to be the first proclaimers of Jesus' resurrection and are also characterized as the primary witnesses to his execution and burial. No human being is reported, however, to have witnessed the resurrection event itself!

In contrast, the "confessional formula" quoted by Paul in 1 Corinthians 15:3–6 does not mention women at all but gives the place of eminence to Peter and the twelve. It is debated whether the earliest Christian confessional formula of Romans 8:34, which reads, "Christ Jesus who died but who was raised" (*Christos Iēsous ho apothanōn, de egertheis*) was enlarged by Paul or already existed in the received tradition:

> For I handed on to you as of first importance what I in turn had received: that Christ died for our sins in accordance with the scriptures, and that he was buried, and that he was raised on the third day in accordance with the scriptures, and that he appeared to Cephas, then to the twelve. Then he appeared to more than five hundred brothers at one time, most of whom are still alive, though some have died. Then he appeared to James, then to all the apostles. Last of all, as to one untimely born, he appeared also to me. (1 Cor. 15:3–8, NRSV)

Most scholars would agree, however, that the original confessional formula "that Christ died, and that he was buried, and that he was raised" (*hoti Christos apethanen kai hoti etaphē, kai hoti egēgertai*), is embedded in this text. But they would ascribe accretions to this formula differently. It seems that elements such as the proof from Scripture, the interpretation of Jesus' death "for our sins," or the temporal location of the resurrection on "the third day" are later accretions to the basic kerygmatic formula. The same also appears to hold true for the reference to the various appearances of the Resurrected One, which legitimate a male chain of authority — Peter, the twelve, five hundred brethren, James, the apostles, and Paul. In any case, Paul quotes this tradition here because he wants to justify his own apostolic authority by asserting that he has seen the resurrected Christ, since Paul could not claim to have known Jesus himself.

This early Christian kerygmatic formula was embedded in the Gospel narratives about the passion and resurrection of Jesus of Nazareth in a different manner. These narratives are basically structured in the same way as the nucleus of 1 Corinthians 15:3–5. However, the resurrection proclamation in the pre-Gospel Easter stories differs from the early Christian kerygmatic formula in three important ways. First, the Easter message is given first to Mary of Magdala and to the other women who went to the grave site.[92] Second, the kerygmatic formula proclaimed in Mark 16:6 and stylized in Matthew 28:5–6 mentions the death of Jesus not in general terms but specifically as a crucifixion. Moreover, the middle term of the kerygmatic formula "he was buried" is stated in the resurrection stories as "he is not here," i.e., in the place where Jesus was buried, and the proclamation "he was raised" is the "proof" for it.[93] Third, the Easter message is a proclamation that requires action rather than confession. It is future-oriented rather than backward-looking: the women "seek" Jesus among the dead but are told that the tomb is empty. We must be careful, however, not to read the "empty tomb" and Easter message in light of the later account of the Fourth Gospel or of Luke's account of ascension, according to which Jesus returns to the father, going from earth to heaven. Instead the proclamation of the empty tomb locates the Resurrected One on earth, in Galilee. Resurrection means that Jesus, the Living One, goes ahead of us.

In sum, the imaginative space of the "empty tomb" leads to the proclamation of Jesus as the Resurrected One who has been vindicated. The Living One can be found only when we experience that he "is ahead of us" and that he opens up a future for us. Christian Testament sources ascribe the proclamation of this "revelatory" experience and of the future-oriented empty tomb message primarily to women, whereas they associate primarily with men the confessional articulation of resurrection that served as a visionary legitimation of authority. The Gospel attributed to "Matthew" combines both traditions, that of the empty tomb narrative and that of the legitimating claim of "having seen the Resurrected One," but still gives primary place to the women witnesses.[94] The author of Matthew probably wants to make sure that resurrection is not misread in a platonic fashion to mean simply a vision of the Living One. In this way s/he attempts to safeguard the experience of the women that "Jesus was vindicated and not left in death" against a platonic or docetic "supernatural" misreading. The text does so by connecting the visionary experience of the Resurrected One with the

"open space" of the empty tomb and the "open road" pointing ahead to
Galilee. It also entrusts the resurrection proclamation to the witness of
women. It insists on the bodily materiality of resurrection and the vindication of unjust suffering and death with the assertion that the tomb
is "empty."

Such a reading of the Gospel stories deviates significantly from "established" malestream interpretations. On the one hand, against the
overwhelming consensus produced as "common sense" by modern critical scholarship, this reading does not consider the empty tomb stories
to be secondary legends or hold that the "appearances" were primary.
On the other hand, it is exceptional in that it orders source texts and
exegetical interpretations in terms of a "male and female" or "Peter
and Mary Magdalene" tradition. The Jesuit scholars Gerald Collins
and Daniel Kendall have chastised me for not following in *In Memory
of Her* the commonly accepted scholarly practice of distinguishing between a Jerusalem tradition and a Galilee tradition of resurrection but
instead classifying early Christian canonical and extracanonical texts
in terms of male and female witness traditions of the resurrection.[95]
This criticism implicitly acknowledges that all scholarly classifications
are preconstructed typologies that produce "common-sense" meanings
by hiding their constructedness, but criticizes me for not accepting the
preconstructed malestream frame of meaning.

Although Collins and Kendall insist that one has to use the geo-
graphical "Jerusalem–Galilee" ordering schemes and may not stratify
the textual material along gender lines, they then go on to do exactly
that when they stress that the interpretation given in the exclusively male
tradition of 1 Corinthians 15:3–5 has priority over the "empty tomb
tradition" ascribed to women. While they ostensibly seek to strengthen
the feminist historical rediscovery of Mary of Magdala as the primary
witness of the resurrection, their overall rhetoric reveals that they are
actually interested in relativizing this tradition because of its threat to
the primacy of the visionary tradition that supposedly authorizes males
only. Hence, they argue against my proposal that the conflict of the
"Mary of Magdala tradition" with the "Petrine tradition" is transmitted in extracanonical writings but not by the "Fathers."[96] In short, a
"symptomatic" reading, i.e., a careful attention to traces and tensions
inscribed in the text, that examines the rhetorical interests inscribed in
their argument "reveals" what is at stake for them in their defense of
the primacy of the male confessional tradition.

Third, positioning contemporary feminist discourses on the theology
of the cross within the rhetorical space of the "empty tomb" as an
ambiguous "open space" allows us to reclaim this space of resurrec-

tion for women's meaning-making today in the face of dehumanization and oppression. Feminist christological discourses can take seriously the spaces of the brutal victimization of women and other nonpersons and at the same time claim wo/men's agency in either collaborating with or transforming such spaces of death. Accordingly, it becomes important to explore the "resurrection reality" inscribed in the empty tomb discourse associated with women. I am not interested here in reconstructing a gender discourse or a "feminine space." Rather, I seek to explore the experiential theological "reality" inscribed in the narrative textualization of the empty tomb as a space of resurrection, as a space for affirming the vindication of the Crucified Ones and their agency of possibility for becoming the Living Ones.

It is difficult to prove which tradition was primary, that of the "empty tomb" associated with women or that of the "visionary experience" authorizing men.[97] It is equally difficult to ascertain whether the empty tomb tradition and the narrative account of Jesus' death, burial, and resurrection were first articulated and transmitted by women. Whatever the case might have been historically, the privileging of the "women's tradition" can function as a heuristic means to develop and adjudicate our own christological meaning-making in the face of violence and killing today. By privileging the empty tomb as the originating space for the proclamations that Jesus of Nazareth, the Crucified One, has been vindicated, the announcement of this "resurrection reality" opens up a road ahead into the messianic future.

If we place the texts about the empty tomb and the visionary authorization experiences of resurrection alongside each other for comparative purposes, we can construct a theological grid or frame of reference in which to position feminist discourses about the theology of the cross. The texts of the empty tomb tradition take suffering and death seriously but do not see them as having the "last word" or a religious-theological value in themselves. Since G*d was absent in the execution of the Just One, the women's presence under the cross is a witness to this absence. The tomb is the brutal final reality that eclipses G*d and vitiates all possibilities for the future. But the "tomb is empty!"

Hence, the textualizations of the empty tomb are ambiguous insofar as they leave open what actually happened to the body of Jesus. Their narrative valorizes a compassionate practice of honoring those unjustly killed. It celebrates women as faithful witnesses who do not relinquish their commitment and solidarity with those who fall victim in the struggle against dehumanizing powers. Most importantly, it affirms that Jesus' struggle did not end with execution and death. The tomb is

empty! But the Living One is not going "away," not leaving us to struggle on our own while he is "ascending to the Father" to live in heavenly
glory.

The empty tomb does not signify absence but presence: it announces
the Resurrected One's presence on the road ahead, in a particular space
of struggle and recognition such as Galilee. The Resurrected One is
present in the "little ones," in the struggles for survival of those impoverished, hungry, imprisoned, tortured, and killed, in the wretched
of the earth. The empty tomb proclaims the Living One's presence in
the ekklēsia of wo/men gathered in Jesus' name, in the faces of our
grandmothers who have struggled for survival and dignity. Jesus is going ahead — not going away: so the women in the Gospels, and we with
them, are told.

In contrast, the visionary appearance tradition of the confessional
formula transmitted in 1 Corinthians 15:3–8 claims individual male religious experience as authorizing experience. Jesus is "absent"; he has
gone back to heaven, where he sits at the right hand of G*d the Father. His presence is available only in visionary form and only to a
few: to apostles, prophets, and specially gifted "spiritual" people. His
death is no longer an execution, but a "sacrificial atonement," no longer
a violent dehumanization, but an obedient self-immolation, no longer
an encounter with brutal force, but a willingly accepted victimization.
Suffering becomes revelatory of a more important religious reality. The
brutal torture of crucifixion no longer bespeaks the political reality
of kyriarchal power and systemic victimization but rather becomes a
religious symbol. Its "revelation" does not authorize everybody, even
women, to "go and tell" but rather circulates within the power struggles
of those who claim to be "in authority." It no longer authenticates itself
but rather needs proof from Scripture and tradition.

Such a malestream christological discourse, which sees death as the
culmination of Jesus' life, finds exemplary expression in the following
well-intentioned apologetic statement:

> Atonement is not, then, appeasement of God, nor propitiating God for
> sin by the death of a penal substitute. When Christ's death is described
> as a sacrifice, it does not mean that he instead of us is punished by
> death in order to satisfy God's justice. Rather, it means that Christ's
> death is his perfect offering of his life to God, an expression of perfect
> obedience or perfect unity of wills, which as representative for all hu-
> manity enables us to move out of sin and alienation into renewed unity
> with God.[98]

If we locate the feminist critiques of the theology of the cross discussed in the first section of this chapter within such a preconstructed

malestream frame of meaning, then feminist theological rejections of the understanding of Jesus' death as self-sacrifice, radical obedience, and atonement becomes fully understandable. Theological discourses that give an intrinsic religious value to suffering and death must be dislodged from their preconstructed Pauline, Augustinian, Anselmian, Lutheran, or modern Neo-orthodox frames of meaning. Moreover, if feminist discourses on suffering and the cross do not position themselves within the open space of the empty tomb but remain within the dominant theological frame of meaning, then even feminists will continue to speak of Jesus as the innocent victim or as the perfect liberator who gives meaning to brutalization, suffering, and murder. Only if one positions feminist christological articulations within the ambiguous open space of the "empty tomb" and the open-ended "road to Galilee" can we evaluate critically those feminist discourses that understand G*d or Christ as present in the suffering and victimization of wo/men. Positioned within this ambiguous open space, we can reject all those "platonic," "spiritualized" readings that understand suffering and victimization as "revelatory" of a higher, more important reality, a greater and more valuable life than the lives of those who are "crucified" daily.

A critical feminist discourse of liberation that positions itself within the space of the empty tomb is able to insist that G*d and the Resurrected One can be found only among the Living Ones. S/he is not to be searched for and found among the dead. Summarizing the statement of an Indian woman from a famine-stricken area, Chung Hyun Kyung powerfully articulates such a reconfiguration of the Johannine saying that out of love for the world G*d gave away G*d's beloved child (John 3:16). This Gospel saying, which has been severely criticized in North American feminist theological discourses, is here recontextualized and reconfigured in a sociopolitical context of starvation:

> Without food, there is no life. When starving people eat food, they experience God "in every grain." They "know" and "taste" God when they chew each grain. Food makes them alive. The greatest love of God for the starving people is food. When the grain from the earth sustains their life, they discover the meaning of the phrase, "For God so loves this world that He gives His beloved Son." When God gives them food through other concerned human beings, God gives them God's "beloved Son," Jesus Christ.[99]

The authorization of such theological discourse about Jesus, who was executed as the Christ, who was vindicated by G*d as the Living One, and who is always ahead of us, does not derive its authority from "revelatory," "feminine," "spiritual" experiences. Rather it must be articulated and proven "right" again and again within the continuing struggles for survival, justice, and well-being. Such a discourse derives its life-enhancing powers from its critical articulation and practices of struggle positioned within the open space of the empty tomb experiences and the traditions of the ekklēsia of wo/men gathered around the table of Divine Wisdom.

Part 3

The Power of Wisdom

Chapter 5

PROPHETS OF SOPHIA
Searching for Divine Wisdom

Yet Sophia is justified by all her children.
(Luke 7:35)

You are the Bread, and You the Table, the Love
Who serves at our feast. You are the Leaven of
promise among us, the Life in every seed.
God of the galaxies, of time and space,
Wisdom at play in our world,
bear our fragile, living earth
upon Your wings of peace.
(Monks of Weston Priory, Vermont)

In dialogue with Judith Plaskow I attempted to show in chapter 3 that the "uniqueness" of Jesus and the Jesus movement can be reconstructed as a particular form of the diverse *basileia tou theou* (commonweal of G*d) movement in Second Temple Judaism. In this chapter I will return to this problem but approach the question of Jesus' uniqueness by asking whether early Christian Wisdom discourses spelled out his uniqueness not in terms of particularity and distinctness but rather in terms of exclusivity, privilege, and superiority. Hence, in this chapter I will focus on historical theological discourses that seek to articulate the significance of Jesus with the help of the traditions of Divine Wisdom (Sophia). I will do so because interreligious dialogues have raised the question of both christological exclusivity and the exclusivity of the Wisdom discourses. Moreover, recent feminist work has recovered and rediscovered the submerged early Christian tradition of Wisdom-Sophia, which has been almost completely erased from the memory of Western Christianity.[1]

My argument will proceed on two levels. First I will attempt a critical rereading of my own reconstructive proposal regarding the early Chris-

tian "meaning-making" about Jesus as Divine Sophia.[2] In this chapter
I want to trace the "footprints" of Divine Sophia, not as a logical
or theological progression from one level or stage to the next but as
different "nodal points" or discursive sites in which strands of this submerged tradition have resurfaced. Then in a concluding section I will
discuss various feminist theological receptions and interpretations of
historical-critical work on Divine Wisdom.

In her poem "Natural Resources" Adrienne Rich compares feminist
work with the work of miners: miners dig up and bring to light the
hidden treasures of the earth.[3] Like miners, she suggests, feminists must
seek to unearth the buried treasures of cultural traditions in order to
reconstitute their world. Similarly, feminist scholars in religion labor be-
neath the headlamp to mine religious traditions for the "emerald lying
against the silver vein waiting for the light to reach it."[4] If I attempt
to trace the "silver vein" of Chokmah-Sophia-Wisdom[5] traditions, then
this must not be misunderstood as a search for a feminist remnant tradition that has the liberating power to become the essential feminist
tradition of Christianity. Rather I want to offer an example of how
feminist historical reconstruction works and proceeds.

To try to reconstitute these buried early Christian sapiential treasures
that are unfamiliar to popular Christian devotion is not to say that such
a reconstruction necessarily provides a tradition usable by feminists or
liberationists. Nor do I want to single out this tradition as the sole biblical tradition that is helpful to feminist Christian discourses about G*d
and Christ. Rather, I want to explore how feminist critical interpretations challenge the whole Christian community to engage in theological
struggles to find appropriate language about the Divine.

In their search for the tread marks of Sophia in Christian writings,
feminist scholars immediately encounter several problems: the references
to Divine Wisdom are embedded in masculine-determined christological
traditions and must be traced and reconstituted in a critical exegetical
process. Moreover, sophialogical teachings permeate the texture of the
Christian Testament,[6] although Divine Sophia herself emerges only on
the margins of early Christian literature. In contrast, the magnificent female divine figure of Wisdom openly appears in Jewish discourse, albeit
"clothed" or "actualized and incarnated" in kyriocentric language. She
does so for the most part in a body of literature articulated either in the
form of instructions of a father for his son[7] or as a fictive address to a
young king. Hence, it is safe to assume that Jewish Wisdom literature
was shaped to serve the kyriarchal interests of elite men.[8] Nevertheless,
this literature also expresses the need of wo/men for a powerful divine
savior figure.

In light of the overwhelming androcentric shape and kyriocentric framework of the texts that speak of Divine Wisdom, we must ask whether it is possible in a feminist exegetical-theological "alchemy" to transform such a figure clothed in kyriocentric language in a way that she can once again not only develop her freeing power in feminist theologies but also have a liberating function in emancipatory struggles for a more just world. How can we trace the submerged spoor of Divine Sophia in biblical writings in such a way that the theological possibilities offered by Wisdom, the Divine Woman of Justice, but never quite realized in history, can be realized? How can we reconstitute this tradition in such a way that the rich table of Sophia can provide food and drink, nourishment and strength in the struggles for transforming kyriarchy?

To address these questions, I will attempt to trace first the Jewish and then the early Christian discourses about Divine Wisdom and so to sketch the difficult problems encountered when we attempt to track the Sophia traditions and their various contextualizations. I will thereby pay particular attention to whether inclusive or exclusive arguments are inscribed in such discourses about Divine Wisdom. In a concluding section, in dialogue with other feminist proposals I will try to assess and evaluate the significance of Divine Wisdom for a critical feminist theology of liberation.

Early Jewish Wisdom Theology

To understand the submerged early Christian traditions of Divine Wisdom, it is first necessary to trace their roots in Jewish Scriptures and theology.[9] Wisdom's theological roots are found not only in postexilic Jewish circles, especially in Egypt, but also in Apocalyptic literature and in the writings of Qumran. Hence, it is methodologically no longer feasible sharply to divide Wisdom and Apocalyptic traditions and to play out the Wisdom tradition as a tradition of male elites against the Apocalyptic tradition as that of poor and oppressed people.[10]

Women and Wisdom

Recent studies have shown that we are no longer justified in seeing the Wisdom tradition simply as a purely kyriarchal tradition that does not tell us much about women. Claudia Camp has pointed out that in the Book of Proverbs "Woman Wisdom" plays a mediating role between YHWH and Israel — a role that the king had in Israel before the exile.[11] The female figure of Wisdom is determined not only by the grammatical feminine gender of the Hebrew (*Chokmah*) and Greek (*Sophia*) terms for Wisdom but also by sociological changes that had theological consequences. After the exile, Israelite society had to theologically work through the loss of the monarchy. The change from a monarchic, centrally administrated society to a society oriented toward the needs and interests of families and extended households was positively expressed in the image of the ideal Israelite woman in Proverbs 31 and in the praise of Woman Wisdom who builds her cosmic house (Prov. 9).[12] The role of the king as proclaimer of G*d's will, administrator of divine justice, representative of G*d's universal reign, authoritative counselor, and guarantor of cosmic order is now exercised by Divine Woman Wisdom.

Silvia Schroer proposes that the Wisdom mythology of the earliest postexilic period patterned its understanding of YHWH after actual women.[13] She argues that the discourse on personified Wisdom seeks to integrate masculine and feminine elements into the image of G*d and to connect such an "inclusive monotheism" with the experience of women in Israel. She locates such reflective Wisdom theology in the social situation after the Exile in which women appear as religious subjects. Proverbs 1:8 and 6:20 admonish readers to keep their father's instruction and their mother's teaching: it is women who transmit religious traditions.

Women prophets such as No-adi'ah (Neh. 6:14) actively participated in the religious politics of the day. The wife of Job advocates a religious position just as his friends do (Job 2:9f.), and like his sons the daughters of Job become his heirs (Job 43:13–15). The assembly before which Ezra proclaimed the Torah of Moses consisted of men and women (Neh. 8:3f.); sons and daughters promised to "walk in G*d's law which was given by Moses, the servant of G*d" (Neh. 10:29). Particularly, the deutero- and trito-Isaianic traditions exhibit an integrative form of monotheism that can speak of G*d as consoling mother (Isa. 49:15; 42:14) and refer not only to Abraham as forefather of Israel but also to Sarah as foremother (Isa. 51:2). Schroer argues, however, that these attempts to articulate a more inclusive and open YHWH theology — which relates to family and home rather than to temple and cult and in which women could participate as religious subjects — were soon replaced by a new alliance of temple, priesthood, and law that in its effects was less open to women.[14] In her opinion later Wisdom theology once again takes on a more negative valence with regard to women.

Dieter Georgi, however, has suggested that the communities in which the Wisdom of Solomon was at home consisted of women and men. He argues that the book served dramatic-liturgical purposes and was composed by a group of male and female worshipers.[15] For support of his thesis Georgi points to Philo's portrayal of the Therapeutae as an example of such a Wisdom community of women and men. In *De Vita Contemplativa* Philo, who lived in the first century C.E. in Alexandria (ca. 25 B.C.E.–ca. 40 C.E.), describes an ascetic group of women and men who weekly gather around the table of Divine Wisdom to feast on her teaching as a kind of heavenly food.[16] Feminist research on Egypt has pointed out that women were independent and powerful in Egyptian culture.[17] There is no reason not to assume the same for Jewish women. Philo's polemical arguments and negative portrayal of the feminine might be directed against influential women in the Jewish community[18] in Egypt and could have their rhetorical roots in such a polemic.[19]

Discursive Construction of Divine Wisdom

On the whole Jewish Wisdom theology celebrated G*d's grace and benevolence as effective in the creation of the world. Israel is the chosen people among whom G*d is present in the female personification of Divine Wisdom. Woman Wisdom is leader on the way, preacher in Israel, architect of the world. She is called sister, spouse, mother, beloved, and teacher. She searches the streets for people, finds them, and invites them to her festive table. She offers life, knowledge, rest, and salvation to all those who will accept her. She has a permanent residence in Israel, which is her very special people (Bar. 4:1–4). She celebrates festive liturgies in the temple of Jerusalem, sends prophets, apostles, and wise people, and makes those who follow her friends of G*d. Moreover, Apocalyptic-Wisdom theology knows also that Divine Woman Wisdom has sought a resting place among her people, but has not found one. Therefore, she has returned to heaven and taken her seat among the angels (1 Enoch 42:1f.).

Even a cursory reading of the biblical discourses on Divine Wisdom shows how this tradition struggles to characterize Woman Wisdom as an all-powerful divine figure without falling into ditheism, i.e., belief in two gods. This struggle bespeaks the possibility that Divine Wisdom might have been worshiped by Jewish wo/men and men. This comes to the fore especially in the depiction of Divine Sophia in the Wisdom of Solomon:[20] Divine Sophia has her residence in heaven. She is the glory of G*d (Wisd. 7:25–26), mediator of creation (Wisd. 8:5–6), and shares the throne of G*d (Wisd. 9:3).[21] She rules over kings and is herself all powerful. She makes everything, renews everything, and permeates the cosmos (Wisd. 7:23, 27; 8:1, 5). "She is but one, yet can do everything; herself unchanging, she makes all things new" (Wisd. 7:27). She is "intelligent and holy, free moving, clear, loving what is good, eager, beneficent, unique in her Way" (Wisd. 7:22). She is a people-loving spirit (Wisd. 1:6) who shares in the throne of G*d and in the ruling power of G*d (Wisd. 9:10). She is an initiate into the knowledge of G*d, collaborator in G*d's work, the brightness that streams from everlasting light, a pure effervescence of divine glory, and the image of G*d's goodness. In short, Divine Wisdom lives symbiotically with G*d (Wisd. 8:3f.; 7:26). Kinship with Wisdom brings immortality and friendship with her, resulting in pure delight (Wisd. 10:17).

Several scholars have suggested that Hellenistic Jewish wo/men in Egypt conceived of Divine Wisdom as prefigured in the language and image of G*ddesses like Isis,[22] Athena, or Dike.[23] Like the G*ddess Isis, Divine Wisdom uses the proclamatory "I am" style for proclaiming her universal message of salvation. According to a very well known Isis prayer, all the different nations and people use divine titles derived from their own local mythologies when they call on the G*ddess Isis. They do so in the full knowledge that Isis is one but encompasses all. Hence the various Wisdom discourses of Hellenistic Jewish wo/men are able to hold belief in the "one" G*d together with a cosmopolitan ethos that respects local particularities without giving up claims to universality.

Like Isis, Sophia is especially called upon as Divine Savior. Isis is called *pansōteira, sōteira,* and *sōtēr,* and countless inscriptions praise her as benefactor. According to Apuleius, Lucius prays to her:

> Holy and eternal savior of the human race,
> ever beneficent in cherishing mortals,
> You indeed bestow the sweet affection of a mother
> upon the tribulations of the unfortunate.[24]

Like Isis, Sophia is a divine savior figure who promises universal salvation. The encomium of Wisdom 9:18–10:21 begins with the statement that people were saved by Sophia and summarizes her saving activity in 10:9: "Sophia rescued from troubles those who served her." Kloppenborg points to three commonalties between Isis and Sophia in this text:

> 1. The *saving role* of Sophia, corresponding to Isis' major function;
> 2. The *selection of events* which the author used as examples of this role; and 3. The *allusive re-telling* of these events in such a way that they resonate with the *mythic pattern* characteristic of the Isis-Horus cycle. The biblical account is thereby allowed to participate in the *mythic power* of the symbol of a savior deity, but without acquiring the explicit aspects of the Egyptian myth. The perspective remains biblical.[25]

In contrast to the classical prophets with their harsh polemics against G*ddess worship (see, e.g., Hos. 1–3 or Jer. 44),[26] Wisdom theology with its inclusive language about the Divine seems intent on using female G*d-language for its own theological purposes. The theological discourses on Sophia speak positively about Israel's G*d in the language of their own Egyptian-Hellenistic culture. They use mythological elements from the international G*ddess cults, especially the Isis cult, and integrate them into Jewish monotheistic theology. Following Hans Conzelmann's pathbreaking study, which appeared thirty years ago in German, several scholars have suggested that such Wisdom theology is best understood as reflective mythology.[27] This is a type of theology that uses elements from G*ddess language and cult to speak about the loving care of G*d for her people Israel as well as for all of creation. Chokmah/ Sophia is the personification of G*d's saving activity in the world, of Israel's election, and of the salvation of all peoples. This becomes particularly clear in the fact that Wisdom's salvific actions are identified with the actions of YHWH in Israel's salvation history.

One must not overlook, however, that later Jewish Wisdom and Apocalyptic speculation often combine this positive understanding of the divine female figure of Wisdom with a negative understanding of actual historical women. Such androcentric gender dualism, which understands masculinity positively and evaluates femininity negatively, determines especially the theological work of the Jewish philosopher and theologian Philo.[28] According to him "femaleness" is "weak, easily deceived, the cause of sin, lifeless, diseased, enslaved, unmanly, nerveless, mean, slavish, sluggish."[29] With Aristotle he holds that the human male is perfect and that the human female is nothing but an imperfect male. Masculinity and maleness, but not femininity and femaleness, are qualities that can express the Divine.

In *De fuga* Philo speaks of Wisdom as the daughter of G*d. He explains that she is imaged as a female figure only to give first place to the Creator G*d, who must be understood as masculine. Masculinity has priority over femininity, and femininity is always less than masculinity. In reality, however, Wisdom is masculine (*arsen*). Therefore, Philo argues, one should not attribute any significance to the grammatical gender of Wisdom.

Within Philo's philosophical framework, only maleness and masculinity can signify preeminence, whereas femaleness and femininity are always secondary and defective. Philo is thus forced to stress that Sophia, the daughter of G*d, is not only masculine but also must be called "father." She is a father who sows and begets in human souls learning, education, knowledge, and insight as well as good and laudable deeds.[30] This text documents that the ancients were well aware of the grammatical rule that so-called grammatical gender was not identi-

cal with so-called natural gender. Hence, the suggestion of Dieter Georgi
that Philo introduces a theological "sex change" seems somewhat off the
mark.[31] Philo's gender system requires a theological change of grammatical gender since in it femaleness cannot signify a position of eminence.
Georgi might be right, however, in his suggestion that such a grammatical change was also a response to an existing Wisdom tradition that
saw Divine Sophia as a female figure who had great attraction for many
Jews, especially for women.

Philo draws out his theological system of asymmetric gender dualism
into a system of cosmological dualism. This theoretical move enables
him to transfer the attributes of Woman Wisdom onto the Logos who,
in Wisdom 18:14–19, is still subordinate to Sophia. According to Philo,
two worlds exist: Sophia's heavenly world of life and salvation and our
earthly world of mortality and struggle. Whereas Divine Wisdom is in
the heavenly world of G*d, her son, the Logos (the Word), lives in the
historical world in order to clear a path for the soul to return to heaven.
Insofar as Philo restricts the sphere of Divine Wisdom to the heavenly
world, he vacates her place as mediator of salvation and as people's advocate in a historical world so that her son, the Logos, can take over her
functions and titles. On a first level, Philo applies to the Logos similar titles: "son of G*d," the "oldest," the "beginning," and the "firstborn of
G*d" — just as he applies to Divine Sophia the names and predicates of
Isis — "firstborn daughter of G*d," the "oldest," the "first fruit," and
the "beginning."

On a second level of theological reflection or reflective mythology
Philo identifies the Logos with Divine Wisdom. The Logos, as the son of
G*d and of Sophia (De fuga 109), is at the same time the Eikon, i.e., the
image and essence of G*d. This identification opens the way for Philo
to telescope Sophia-Eikon and Logos-Eikon together. Burton Mack suggests that Philo replaced Divine Wisdom with the Logos because of the
association of Logos with Israel.[32] This association is rooted in Philo's
theological reflection on Israel's essence and fate that identified Israel
with the Logos. Logos-Israel is then further figured in terms of Israel's
representative heroes, e.g., the patriarchs, the high priest, and Moses.
Logos-Israel is understood in cosmic dimensions as the wise king, the
just one.

This replacement of Sophia with Logos-Israel produced the mascu-
line linguistic sequence Father–Son of G*d–Sons of the Son of G*d.
One must not overlook, however, that Philo uses such cosmological lan-
guage and mythological imagery, which is probably derived from the
Isis-Osiris cycle, to express the psychological realities of the human soul.
The Logos as the priest and king of the cosmos becomes the priest

and king of the soul. Historical figures like Moses and Isaac become symbols representing virtues of the individual soul and psychological archetypes. Israel's history is transformed into a psychological mythic drama that takes place in the soul. Although early Christian discourses are not concerned with interior, psychological reality, Philo's theologizing, nevertheless, turned out to become very important for Christian meaning-making with regard to Jesus of Nazareth.

Early Christian Wisdom Theologies

When one moves from Jewish Wisdom literature to early Christian writings the figure of Divine Wisdom seems to disappear. Yet a symptomatic reading, which attends to traces and tensions inscribed in the text, can show that a submerged theology of Wisdom, or sophialogy, permeates all of Christian Scriptures. Early Jewish discourses on Divine Wisdom provided a theological linguistic matrix that was activated by early Christian communities. Early Christian theological discourses could thus use the traditions of Divine Wisdom together with other early Jewish traditions to elaborate the theological significance of Jesus.

Christian Testament studies largely agree that, just as in the work of Philo, two levels of reflection can be distinguished in early Christian theological discourses on Sophia. The first level, which may go back to the historical Jesus himself but is barely traceable any longer, understands Jesus as messenger and prophet of Sophia. The second level of theological reflection identifies Jesus with Divine Wisdom. Jesus, however, is not called "Sophia" but receives "male" christological titles such as *kyrios* and *sōtēr*, which also were titles of Isis-Sophia. Just as in Philo so also in early Christian discourses we find a middle stage where the attributes of Divine Wisdom are applied to the Logos. Early Christian sophialogical reflection also knows a transitional stage in which attributes of Sophia were given to Jesus. For instance, it is debated whether the pre-Pauline hymns or the Fourth Gospel already identify Sophia and Christ or whether they see Jesus and his work only as a paradigm that interprets Jesus in analogy to Divine Wisdom.

The Sayings Source Q

The Sophia-G*d of Jesus: Martin Hengel has argued persuasively that the diversity of christological discourses that developed in a time span as short as twenty years after Jesus' death can be plausibly explained if we assume Jewish Wisdom theology as the generative matrix.[33] The tradition of Jesus, the Galilean preacher and representative of Divine Wisdom, Hengel has suggested, can bridge the chasm between the actual person Jesus of Nazareth, who was executed as the "king of the Jews," and Jesus Christ, who was proclaimed powerful Lord, preexistent son of G*d, and Mediator of creation. Jewish Sophia theology provides the language world and mythological frame of reference that can explain the earliest attempts to make meaning out of the ministry and execution of Jesus as well as the meaning-making of the later christological developments in the early church.

Some of the earliest traditions of the Jesus movement understood the mission of Jesus as that of a prophet of Sophia sent to proclaim that the Sophia-G*d of Jesus is the G*d of the poor, the outcasts, and all those suffering from injustice. It is likely that these early Jesus traditions interpreted the Galilean mission of Jesus as that of Divine Sophia because Jesus of Nazareth understood himself as messenger and child of Sophia. The G*d of Jesus is Israel's G*d in the Gestalt and the figure of Divine Woman Wisdom.

As Sophia's messenger and prophet Jesus not only proclaimed the *basileia* of G*d to the poor, the hungry, and the excluded of Israel but also made it experientially available to all in his miracles and ministry. One of the oldest Jesus sayings states that "Sophia is justified by her children" (QLk 7:35). This saying most likely has its "setting in life" in the inclusive table community of Jesus with sinners, tax collectors, and prostitutes. The Sophia-G*d of Jesus recognizes all Israelites as her children. She is justified, "made just," in and by all of them. Hence, it is plausible to suggest that the open-ended empty tomb tradition associated with women may have had its matrix in such an understanding of Jesus as Sophia's prophet.

The oracles in which Sophia probably speaks directly imply that the fate of Jesus was that of a prophetic messenger of Sophia:

> Therefore also the Wisdom of God said, "I will send them prophets and apostles, some of whom they will kill and persecute." (Luke 11:49, RSV)

The same interpretation is expressed in the lament over Jerusalem:

> O Jerusalem, Jerusalem, killing the prophets and stoning those who are sent to you! How often would I have gathered your children together as a hen gathers her brood under her wings, and you would not! (Luke 13:34, RSV)

Finally, the following statement, found only in Matthew and there placed in the mouth of Jesus, must originally have been an invitation by Sophia herself:

> Come to me, all who labor and are heavy laden, and I will give you rest.
> Take my yoke upon you, and learn from me; for I am gentle and lowly
> in heart, and you will find rest for your souls. For my yoke is easy, and
> my burden is light. (Matt. 11:28–30, RSV)

As far as we are still able to see, the first christological reflection theology was *sophialogy.* Hence, the Sayings Tradition, which was called
by James Robinson *logoi sophōn* (words of the sages),[34] might better be
termed *logoi sophias* (words of Sophia).

The Prophet of Sophia: The reconstruction and social-historical contextualization of the Sayings Source Q, a hypothetical collection that
probably had undergone some revisions before it disappeared from the
historical scene, is very controverted.[35] Leading scholars in the field have
proposed that three redactional stages of Q can be distinguished. The
first stage speaks of Jesus as a Cynic sage who addresses individuals.
Only at a second stage are the above sayings of conflict between Sophia
and Israel introduced. However, Richard Horsley in my opinion argues
correctly that such a reconstruction of the development of Q does not
account for the crisis introduced by the suffering and execution of Jesus.
To argue that the Q community was not concerned with Jesus' violent
fate does not take into account the historical fact that Jesus was crucified
as a criminal.

Nonetheless, it is clear that the Jesus people of Q understand Jesus as
a prophet and messenger of Sophia. As Sophia's messenger, Jesus calls all
the nobodies who are heavy laden and promises them rest and shalom.
The yoke of Sophia is not heavy but light (QMt 11:28–30). However,
Q ascribes to Jesus and John an eminence and excess of meaning that
heightens the significance of their work and fate. It emphasizes that the
most prominent among the children of Sophia are John the Baptist and
especially Jesus, whose work continues in the communities of Q. This
theological "more" is expressed in the following saying about the queen
of Sheba:

> The queen of the South will arise at the judgment with the men of this
> generation and condemn them; for she came from the ends of the earth
> to hear the wisdom of Solomon, and behold, something greater than
> Solomon is here. (QLk 11:31, RSV)

Jesus' ministry and teaching are here seen as greater than those of the
great Wisdom teacher Solomon and as excelling those of the prophet
Jonas. Such a sophialogical context also makes comprehensible the very
difficult saying in Matthew 12:32 ‖ Luke 12:10, which states that the
blasphemy against Jesus, the "Human One" or the "Offspring of Hu-

manity," will be forgiven whereas blasphemy against Spirit-Sophia is unforgivable.

However, against what seems to be the consensus of exegetes, I would like to stress that this "more" of the comparative should not be misread in an exclusive sense as a superlative, as is often done. Even Horsley, who is concerned with the preconstructed assumptions affecting the reconstruction of Q and Jesus, feels compelled to stress that Jesus is the one of utmost historical significance: "That Jesus, while obviously a prophet, far transcends the significance of any ordinary prophet for the Q people, can be seen most directly in the next set of sayings regarding John's significance (QLk 7:24–28)."[36] Although Horsley recognizes that the "least in the kingdom of God" — and not Jesus — is compared with John, he nevertheless concludes:

> Implicit, of course, is that if John was more than a prophet, how much more extraordinary is Jesus.... Q apparently understands Jesus as the climactic figure in the long line of Israelite prophets. *That is never articulated directly* [emphasis added] but it is implied in the insertion of 11:49–51 into the woes against the Pharisees.[37]

I want to argue, to the contrary, that for the Q people this prophetic tradition is an open, ongoing tradition. Jesus of Nazareth, whom they understood as an eminent prophet of Sophia, does not close this tradition but activates it. As the child of Sophia-G*d, Jesus stands in a long succession of prophets who seek to gather together the children of Israel to their gracious Sophia-G*d. Like some of the other prophets, both women and men, who had gone before them, John the Baptizer and Jesus were persecuted and killed as the emissaries of Divine Wisdom.

In the "lament over Jerusalem" Sophia mourns the murder of her messengers (QLk 13:34). This lament compares the work of Divine Sophia with the care of a mother bird for her young. If this moving statement of Sophia's gracious care and invitation is taken out of its original Galilean historical context and universalized in a Christian reading, it becomes a statement rife with anti-Jewish meaning. Richard Horsley correctly warns Christian readers not to misread this lament as an anti-Jewish statement. Rather it expresses the sentiment of the Galilean people against the governing authorities whose center is Jerusalem.[38] This Sophia lament is not directed against all of Israel or Judaism as a whole but only against the governing authorities in the capital. Early Christian sophialogy thus understands the execution of Jesus, like that of John and other prophets, both women and men, as the outcome of his mission as messenger of Divine Sophia. Jesus, who opens up a future for the poor and oppressed in Israel and promises salvation and well-being without exception to all the children of Israel, was one of Sophia's children who vindicated her. Jesus' execution was not intended or willed by Sophia-G*d but is rather the outcome of his prophetic ministry and mission.

Such a prophetic sophialogical understanding of the death of Jesus is also expressed in the following very difficult Q saying: "Since the days of John the Baptist until today the *basileia* of G*d suffers violence and is hindered by those who are violent" (QMt 11:12). If understood in this way, this saying brings the Sophia and *basileia* traditions together. It also knows of the violence encountered by those who struggle for the *basileia* of the Sophia-G*d of Jesus. In short, the inclusive early sophialogical Jesus traditions speak of Jesus as standing in a succession of Sophia's prophets and messengers, both women and men, a succession continued by the Q community.

Father-Son: The prophetic Sophia sayings in Q, like the proclamation of the empty tomb associated with Galilean women, reflect an understanding of community as an open-ended movement. The following "father-son" Wisdom saying, however, seems to echo the exclusivist resurrection-appearance proclamation that the tradition has associated with men. It is debated whether the final redaction of Q already identified Jesus with Divine Sophia or whether such an identification happened only later. In any case, the so-called Johannine saying of Jesus (QMt 11:25–27) not only seems to understand Jesus in terms of Divine Sophia but also emphatically identifies him as *the son of the father* who mediates exclusive revelation:

> [25]I thank you, Father, Lord of heaven and earth, because you have hidden these things from the wise and the intelligent and have revealed them to infants; [26]yes, Father, for such was your gracious will. [27]All things have been handed over to me by my Father; and no one knows the Son except the Father, and no one knows the Father except the Son and anyone to whom the Son chooses to reveal him. (Matt. 11:25–27, NRSV)

It is debated whether Matthew 11:25 was originally an independent saying or whether it was from the beginning a part of the thanksgiving prayer. In any case in its present context verse 25 shares the exclusionary meaning of verse 27. Every feature of this exclusivist Jesus saying (11:27) can be traced back to Jewish Wisdom traditions. Just as Wisdom has received everything from G*d, so Jesus has received everything from G*d (v. 27a). Just as Wisdom is only known by G*d and is the only one who knows G*d, so Jesus has all Wisdom; he is even Wisdom herself (v. 27bc). Just as Divine Sophia gives her Wisdom as a gift, so also Jesus reveals Wisdom to all those to whom he wants to reveal himself

(v. 27d).[39] Hence it could be concluded that here Jesus replaces Sophia. However, Kloppenborg has drawn attention to the fact that:

> nowhere in the Wisdom tradition is it stated that Sophia has *received* either knowledge or power from God. Sophia indeed has knowledge of all things (Wisd. 7:18–21; 8:8) and *exousia* in Jerusalem (Sir. 24:11b) but these derive from the fact that She was present with God at the creation and is the instrument of creation.[40]

Kloppenborg concludes that the Philonic Logos tradition, which understands the Logos to be the firstborn son of Wisdom and also of G*d, has determined the theological reflection of QMt 11:25–27. Such a shift from Sophia-prophets to Father-Son-Logos indicates either a shift in the self-understanding of Q or a different understanding within the Q community. The "father-son" language documents that now the "father-son" relationship both of the patriarchal household and of the Wisdom school is operative.

This shift in social location constitutes not only a linguistic shift but also a theological shift in the Jesus traditions. As Carol Newsome has pointed out, when reading such texts or praying such prayers:

> the male subject is to a certain degree apportioned between father and son. One is always a subordinate son to the collective authority of the symbolic order. But its transcending father status is what underwrites the father-status of those who occupy positions of authority within it.[41]

The Q people (men?) who articulated this saying replaced the inclusive sophialogy of the earliest Jesus traditions with an exclusive understanding of revelation.

In short, the introduction of father-son language into early Christian sophialogy is intrinsically bound up with a theological exclusivity that reserves revelation for the elect few and draws the boundaries of communal identity between insiders and outsiders.[42] Like the revelatory resurrection formula it seeks to bolster the authority of those in power who are the chosen mediators of G*d's revelation. Thus verse 11:27 either theologically contradicts the assertion of 11:25 that Sophia has revealed herself to the "babies," the little ones, and hidden "these things" from the wise and powerful, or this saying subsumes 11:25f. and thereby marks verse 27 as an assertion of the authority of marginal and powerless men. It would need another study to investigate whether the language world of the numerous early Christian sapiential abba/father sayings is open to wo/men. And it would also be interesting to determine which sayings should be translated in inclusive terms and which, like QMt 11:27, assert a restrictive "father-son" relationship.

The Pre-Markan Tradition

The Baptism of Jesus: Silvia Schroer has unearthed some traces of the early inclusive Christian Sophia theology that also appears in the pre-Markan tradition. At the baptism of Jesus by John in all four Gospels the Spirit comes down on Jesus in the figure of a dove accompanied by a voice saying, "You are my beloved son, in whom I have delight" (Mark 1:11). Schroer's sorting out of the history of religions material indicates that the dove is the messenger bird of the Near Eastern Love G*ddess. She points out that Philo distinguishes between the turtle dove as the symbol of the transcendent Sophia and the gray dove as the symbol of the immanent Sophia.[43] Schroer therefore concludes:

> The baptism event reveals that Jesus is the Human One in whom and upon whom the Wisdom-Spirit finds rest. The voice from heaven is the voice of Divine Sophia who has found Her elect one. As a symbol of Sophia, as a messenger of Her love and as a sign of Her presence the dove of the G*ddess Sophia-Pneuma comes upon Jesus.[44]

According to Schroer, this Markan baptismal text understands Jesus not only as the Spirit-filled prophet of Divine Wisdom but also as Her incarnation, since this text identifies Wisdom and Spirit. One can also read this text, however, as marking the empowerment of Jesus by the Spirit and as referring to him as the messenger and elect one of Sophia. Such a reading is in accord with the traces of Wisdom theology that are still accessible in the Christian Testament and that reflect on the special status of Jesus as the prophet, the suffering servant, and the child of Sophia who stands within Israel's history with YHWH.

Divine Wisdom and Spirit: This line of argument can be strengthened by referring to Martin Hengel's discussion of the interrelationship between Divine Wisdom and Spirit. Hengel traces the messianic traditions about the Wisdom teacher endowed with the Holy Spirit through the Hebrew Bible and other Jewish texts and argues that Isaiah 11:2 was the generative scriptural text that has determined Jewish messianic expectations:

> A shoot shall come out from the stump of Jesse,
>   and a branch shall grow out of his roots.
> The spirit of the LORD shall rest on him,
>   the spirit of wisdom and understanding,
>   the spirit of counsel and might,
>   the spirit of knowledge and the fear of the LORD.
> His delight shall be in the fear of the LORD.
> He shall not judge by what his eyes see,
>   or decide by what his ears hear;

> but with righteousness he shall judge the poor,
>   and decide with equity for the meek of the earth;
>   (Isa. 11:1–4, NRSV)

The complete unity between Sophia and the Spirit is expressed in Wisdom 7:22–23, 27:

> There is in her a spirit that is intelligent, holy,
> unique, manifold, subtle,
> mobile, clear, unpolluted,
> distinct, invulnerable, loving the good, keen,
> irresistible, beneficent, humane,
> steadfast, sure, free from anxiety,
> all-powerful, overseeing all....
>
> Although she is but one, she can do all things,
> and while remaining in herself, she renews all things;
> in every generation she passes into holy souls
> and makes them friends of God, and prophets. (NRSV)

Since Sophia has here assumed the functions of the Spirit, it can be said that she, like the Spirit, can be sent by G*d. Hence the "fictional" Solomon calls unto G*d to send her down to earth:

> With you is Sophia, she who knows your works
> and was present when you made the world;
> she understands what is pleasing in your sight
> and what is right according to your commandments.
>
> Send her forth from the holy heavens,
> and from the throne of your glory send her,
> that she may labor at my side,
> and that I may learn what is pleasing to you.
>
> For she knows and understands all things,
> and she will guide me wisely in my actions
> and guard me with her glory. (Wisd. 9:9–11, NRSV)

One can conclude with Hengel that a broad-based sophialogy can be traced in early Christian discourses, even if one cannot be as certain as Hengel that the tradition goes back to the historical Jesus himself.

> If we search for a pre-Christian Jewish key to understand post-Easter christology, we will find this key in the Wisdom of Solomon, in which Palestinian traditions of Apocalyptic and sapiential background are combined with Hellenistic vocabulary in a unique way. The presupposition for the influence of the Wisdom and Spirit teachings upon christology, however, are not first given in the primitive post-Easter community and its exaltation christology. Rather — as I have attempted to show in the first part of the article — they go back to the ministry of Jesus as messianic teacher and Spirit-endowed charismatic.[45]

However, one must not overlook that early Christian articulations of sophialogy were not derived from the rarefied atmosphere of elite Wisdom scholars but rather were forged in the meaning-making process that took place after the execution of Jesus in the everyday life of Galilean villagers and townspeople. Jesus, who like many of these Galilean wo/men had no place to go and had to sustain himself on what was offered to him, was remembered as one of the prophets who was sent by Divine Sophia, who was executed, and who was proclaimed as the Living One by Galilean wo/men.

The Pre-Pauline and Pauline Traditions

The Sophia-Jesus identification appears in a milieu quite different from that of Palestine in hymns and prayers embedded in the epistolary literature of the Christian Testament. These hymns and prayers emerge not only in a different cultural-religious context but also in a different form. They are articulated not as sayings of Jesus but as hymnic praise.

Sophia-Christ: Form-critical research has traced such a sophialogical form of praise in the so-called pre-Pauline hymns that scholars have reconstructed.[46] These hymns are widely regarded as employing elements of a mythological pattern developed with reference to Sophia. Since these texts do not mention the subject of their praise directly but only introduce him or her with the relative masculine pronoun *"hos,"* it is possible that they were patterned after songs to Sophia or after hymns to a G*ddess like Isis. These reconstructed "pre-Pauline" hymns proclaim the universality of salvation in Jesus Christ in a language derived from Jewish Hellenistic Wisdom theology and rooted in the language of the mystery religions.[47] The mission and meaning of Christ the "Lord" are understood, for instance, in Philippians 2:6–11 in terms of Wisdom-Isis theology.

The way of Jesus Christ was the same as the way of Sophia-Isis.[48] According to Jewish apocalyptic theological reflection, Wisdom was sent or came down to earth. She found no place where she could dwell. Hence, a dwelling place was given to her in the heavens:

> Wisdom went forth
> to make her dwelling among the children of humanity,
> but she found no dwelling place.
> Therefore Wisdom returned to her place
> and took her seat among the angels.
>
> (1 Enoch 42, 1–2 vgl. Sir., 24, 3–7)

In a similar fashion, through his/her exaltation and enthronement, Christ-Sophia assumed rulership over the whole cosmos, over heavenly and earthly powers. This is proclaimed in Philippians 2:6–11 in language alluding to Isaiah 45:23 and to the contemporary Isis cult. Like Isis, Christ-Sophia is worshiped by all the cosmic powers and given a name "which is above all names." Just as the acclamation of the G*ddess Isis gives to Isis the masculine title "Lord," so the true Christian acclamation is "Jesus Christ is the Lord."[49]

This proclamation of the universal vindication of Jesus-Sophia and his/her "lordship" is addressed to peoples of the Hellenistic world who believed the world to be ruled by merciless powers and, above all, by blind fate. This sophialogical hymnody expresses the longings of Hellenistic people who hope for liberation from the cruel powers of this world and desire participation in the heavenly divine world. A similar cosmological understanding is expressed in the christological hymns of Hebrews 1:3 and Colossians 1:15–20, texts that transfer names and predicates of Sophia "onto Christ in order to stress his or her cosmic power."[50]

In this religious milieu of the mystery religions, Christians proclaim that, like Isis, Jesus-Sophia is now the ruler of the principalities and powers that have previously enslaved the world. In a milieu in which the hymns and aretalogies, i.e. the praise of the great deeds, of Isis and other G*ds and G*ddesses are sung, the Christian community chants hymns in praise of Jesus Christ, the Sophia of G*d who appeared on earth and who is now exalted as *Kyrios* over the whole world. These Christians believe that they are freed from their bondage to death and liberated from the powers of cosmic principalities. They believe that they already participate in the power and "energy field" of Christ-Sophia, that they represent the renewed creation because in baptism they have entered into the life-giving power and sphere of Spirit-Sophia.

This early Christian "reflective mythology," which uses mythological elements to speak of Jesus Christ as the Divine Sophia and cosmic *Kyrios,* came to function in the Christian community as a foundational myth that created its own cult. Christ's exaltation and enthronement in cosmic reconciliation and sovereignty are the central symbols of this myth. The understanding of Christ in terms of Sophia as the mediator of the first creation and as the power of the new, qualitatively different creation underlines the cosmic significance of Christian faith. It also retains the knowledge that their cosmic *Kyrios* is the same Jew, Jesus, who sought a resting place in Israel. This knowledge is expressed in the categories of humiliation, incarnation, and death. The mythological features of these early Christian hymns are so strong, however, that their cosmic imagination threatens to absorb the knowledge about the human life of Jesus, the prophet from Galilee.

This danger of spiritualizing and psychologizing Jesus Christ is apparent not only in later Christian Gnosticism[51] but in orthodox spirituality as well. Its danger can already be sensed in the pre-Pauline christological hymns themselves. However, one cannot overemphasize that this theological danger consisted not in the adoption of female language and G*ddess symbolism for G*d. Rather, it was that Jesus, who was a historical being, was now proclaimed in masculine mythological terms as a divine being and that the Galilean prophet and emissary of Sophia was now envisioned in kyriarchal terms as cosmic lord/master and sovereign comparable to Isis in universal power and world dominion. While such a mythologization and kyriarchalization may or may not have served to hold together and strengthen the identity of the Christian community consisting of Jews and Gentiles, such kyriarchal christology lends itself in the long run to legitimize Christian domination in christological terms.

Christ, Spirit, and Sophia: That women were actively involved in the articulation of sophialogical discourses about Jesus is evident from the first four chapters of Paul's first letter to the Corinthians, where most of the references to "wisdom"/"wise" in the Pauline literature appear.[52] The sophialogical traces embedded in Paul's letter to the Corinthian community, in which women were leaders and active as prophets, recognize the Resurrected One as identical not only with the Spirit of G*d but also with Divine Sophia. This was possible because in Hebrew and Aramaic both terms, "Spirit" and "Wisdom," are grammatically feminine. Therefore they can be used interchangeably not only with each other, but also with the Hebrew notion of the *Shekinah,* i.e., the Divine Presence. Such an interchangeable usage was rooted in christological reflections on Jesus and his fate similar to those at the final stage of the development of Q, which also telescoped Sophia and Jesus.

Although the polemical rhetoric of Paul in 1 Corinthians misconstrues the arguments and beliefs of the Corinthian wo/men, it nevertheless indicates that the early Christian missionary movements in urban centers of the Greco-Roman world understood Jesus in terms of Sophia-Spirit. The meaning of the "Wisdom" against which Paul polemicizes is probably expressed in the traditional christological formula of 1 Corinthians 1:24, which confesses Christ as G*d's Power and Sophia. The Resurrected One is seen in 1 Corinthians as Divine Sophia who led Israel on the Exodus out of Egypt (1 Cor. 10). Such an early sophialogical theology might also be expressed in the characterization of Jesus Christ

in 1 Corinthians 1:30, which probably refers to baptism[53]: "You, however, are in Christ Jesus who has become for us Sophia from G*d; not
only justice but also sanctification and liberation." Christ is the Divine
Sophia, secret and hidden (1 Cor. 2:7) but revealed to the initiates of
Sophia.

It is widely debated whether the Corinthians, under the leadership
of Apollos, cultivated a rarefied (Gnostic) spirituality of eloquence and
wisdom, as Paul claims. In this view it is Paul who, against such an
"otherworldly" enthusiasm, insists on the proclamation of Christ Crucified in the everyday realities of life. The opposite view has been
underscored by recent feminist work.[54] It holds that the Corinthian
wo/men prophets understood themselves and other apostles as standing
in a long line of Sophia's emissaries. Moreover, they interpreted baptism
as the inauguration into a "new creation" in which status differences
and divisions were abolished (Gal. 3:28). They believed that the crucifixion was a violent act of the kyriarchal powers of this world and
that they had direct access to the Resurrected One's life in the Spirit of
Sophia, whose life-giving power was with them in their struggles.

In this latter view Paul insists on Christ's death as a model whose
downward path unto death and subordination to G*d must be imitated.
It is Paul who asserts the revelatory authority of a few — and especially
of himself — as the only "father" of the community. His rhetoric of ca-
joling and threat bespeaks his own tenuous status in the community of
Sophia and not his actual kyriarchal power. Such kyriocentric rhetoric,
however, paved the way for the transformation of the radical democratic ekklēsia of Sophia-Spirit into a "school of the wise" built on the
exclusivist revelatory discourses between "father(s) and son(s)."

The Gospel Traditions: Matthew and John

It is not clear whether the "pre-Pauline" tradition understood Jesus the
Christ as *identical* with Sophia or whether it simply interpreted his life
and work with reference to Divine Wisdom. In the latter view, Jesus the
Christ was the representative and embodiment of Sophia, who manifested herself in his life, death, and exaltation. Similarly, it is debated
whether Matthew understands Jesus and Sophia in terms of essential
identity or whether "s/he" interprets Jesus' work and preaching as making present or exemplifying the way and work of Divine Wisdom among
her friends and in the world. Likewise, the Fourth Gospel presents Jesus
of Nazareth as the personified Logos, but it is not clear whether Jesus
is called the Logos and thereby characterized as the Son of Sophia or
whether he replaces her.[55] The sophialogical characterization of Jesus in

the Fourth Gospel narrative suggests that he represents her as the One who came to live among her children, whereas the exclusive "father-son" language of the Gospel narrative seems to eclipse her presence totally. Hence it is important to critically evaluate the inclusive/exclusive nature of such sophialogical discourses.

Jesus-Sophia: The representation of Jesus as Divine Sophia in the Gospel of Matthew[56] serves interests quite different from those in the pre-Pauline hymns. This representation further develops the sophialogical interpretation of Q (QLk 7:37). "Wisdom is justified *by her children*" becomes in the redaction of Matthew 11:19c "Wisdom is justified *by her works.*" This change relates Jesus' words in v. 11:19c directly to the question of John the Baptist in Matthew 11:26:

> When John heard in prison what the Messiah was doing, he sent word by his disciples and said to him, "Are you the one who is to come, or are we to wait for another?" Jesus answered them, "Go and tell John what you hear and see: the blind receive their sight, the lame walk, the lepers are cleansed, the deaf hear, the dead are raised, and the poor have good news brought to them. And blessed is anyone who takes no offense at me." (Matt. 11:2–6, NRSV)

The messianic work of Jesus and that of Divine Sophia are seen as identical. Moreover, Matthew puts the logion of Sophia (QLk 11:49) directly into the mouth of Jesus (Matt. 23:34). The speaker is no longer Sophia, but Jesus. By putting the Sophia oracle that speaks of a future mission into the mouth of Jesus, Matthew characterizes Jesus as Sophia herself, who sends her disciples to Israel. Jesus does what Wisdom does. Thus Matthew seems to heighten the identification of Sophia with Jesus.

Insofar as Matthew incorporates this oracle into his diatribe against the Pharisees and Scribes and at the same time connects it with the lament over Jerusalem (Matt. 23:37–39), s/he intensifies the exclusivist, anti-Jewish rhetoric of this Gospel saying. Jesus seems to be identified with Divine Wisdom in order to elaborate theologically his rejection by his own people. Moreover, the occupation and destruction of Jerusalem by the Romans are depicted as the consequence of the execution of Jesus/Sophia. Jesus/Sophia looked in vain for a dwelling place in Israel, his/her own people, but s/he was rejected. Therefore s/he has withdrawn until s/he returns in glory (Matt. 23:39).[57]

We have seen that because of their universal religious interests, the sophialogical reflections of the early missionary movements in the Greco-Roman cities celebrated the Risen Jesus and cosmic *Kyrios* in the language of the mystery religions, particularly in the image of the divine cosmological "Lord" Isis. In contrast, the Matthean identification of Jesus with Divine Sophia is rooted in the conflict between the community of Matthew, which is probably still Jewish,[58] and the rival Jewish schools of the Scribes and Pharisees.[59] It seems that Matthew portrays Jesus as Divine Wisdom in order to authorize the disciples who are described in school language[60] as Sophia's envoys. Celia Deutsch suggests that the identification of Jesus with Sophia in Matthew reflects school competition and legitimates a male teaching class.[61] However, the portrayal of Jesus as Sophia, who calls the heavy-laden and oppressed and announces the Human One ("son of man") who will return for judgment, seems to have its roots in such a religious community conflict[62] and to be shaped more by it than by school competition. In any case, we cannot simply take Matthew's conventional androcentric language at face value and assume that Matthew's Sophia envoys were all male.[63]

Logos-Sophia/Father-Son: The christology of the Fourth Gospel appears to integrate the hymnic and narrative traditions that see Jesus as a paradigmatic representative of Divine Wisdom. The Fourth Gospel seems to develop this tradition further by taking over the cosmic-journey aspects of the pre-Pauline hymns[64] and by combining them with the kind of Sophia reflection found in Matthew's Gospel. Most importantly, the Fourth Gospel makes central to its reflections the exclusivist "father-son" language[65] that we have already encountered in the Q tradition.

It is debated whether according to the Fourth Gospel Jesus is Wisdom Incarnate[66] or whether he replaces her. The narrative characterization of Jesus seems to speak for the first. Like Sophia-Isis, Jesus speaks in the revelatory "I am"-style, and with the symbolism of bread, wine, and living water s/he invites people to eat and drink. Like Sophia, Jesus proclaims his/her message aloud in public places. Like Sophia, Jesus is the light and life of the world. To those who seek and find her/him Sophia-Jesus promises that they will live and never die. Like Sophia, Jesus calls people and makes them his/her children and friends.

As the logos-son of Sophia Jesus could be seen as following the way of Sophia. The mission and rejection of Divine Wisdom seems to provide the pattern for narrating the life and mission of Jesus. Like Sophia, Jesus was sent. Jesus-Sophia came into his/her own but was not received by his/her own people and therefore has returned through his/her exaltation to the world of G*d. Wisdom mythology seems all-important for understanding the life and fate of Jesus. The logos title of the prologue, therefore, seems not to lessen but to increase the possibility that the Fourth Gospel understands Jesus as making Sophia present in and through her/his work.

Unfortunately, this Wisdom matrix of the Fourth Gospel remains almost completely hidden in a cursory reading of the text because the narrative does not introduce Jesus as the Son of Divine Sophia but as the only begotten Son of the Father. In 1:14–18 it is said that the glory of the Logos that became flesh was the "glory of the only Son from the Father." The prologue ends with the assertion that "no one has ever seen God; the only Son, who is in the bosom of the Father, he has made him known (John 1:18, RSV). The "son" does not reveal G*d as Sophia but as Father, "although the Sophia tradition knows of both a mother/child system and a father/son system."

> John's story about Jesus is in the final analysis doubly anti-structural, for on the one hand it is a reaction to the story of Moses by which his opponents lived, while on the other hand it is a reaction to the story of Sophia which was itself a revision of the story of Moses.[67]

By introducing the "father-son" language in the very beginning and using it throughout the Gospel, the whole book reinscribes the metaphorical grammatical masculinity of the expressions "logos" and "son" as congruent with the biological masculine sex of the historic person of Jesus of Nazareth. The Fourth Gospel thereby not only dissolves the tension between the grammatical feminine gender of Sophia and the "naturalized" gender of Jesus but also marginalizes and "silences" the traditions of G*d as represented by Divine Woman Wisdom. In so doing, the christological language of the Gospel opens the door to a kind of philosophical/ontological theological reflection that is now able to merge the *biological* masculine gender of Jesus and the *grammatical* masculine gender of Logos, Son and Father. It thereby not only naturalizes grammatical gender, which is not identical with biological gender, but also theologizes it.

The Fourth Gospel does not simply introduce the Logos title. Instead, to interpret the revelation of G*d in Jesus it prefers the "father-son" language also derived from Wisdom literature. It thereby likens the relationship between Jesus and G*d to that of the father-son relationship in the patri-kyriarchal household or Wisdom school. As on the last level of Q, this father-son language is interconnected with an exclusivist understanding of revelation, and as in the Gospel of Matthew it serves apologetic interests, so also in the Fourth Gospel it serves to articulate defensive boundaries vis-à-vis the Jewish context of the Johannine community.

The christological discourses of both Matthew and John that identify the mission and life of Jesus with Divine Sophia seem to have their "setting in life" in a rhetorical situation in which the Christian community no longer understands itself in continuity with Israel but rather defines its identity in opposition to its Jewish roots. The Johannine community's attempt to draw its boundaries in terms of Wisdom christology has been inscribed in the Fourth Gospel and perpetuated by its canonization. Hence, the Fourth Gospel has occasioned anti-Judaism and anti-Semitism through the centuries and still does so today.

It is important to note that this process of christological genderization also has deeply affected the meaning of the name "father" for G*d in the Gospels. The loving attention and divine care for the world that shaped the meaning of "father" language and imagery in earliest Christian theological reflection was seen in Jewish Wisdom literature as *embodied and made present* in the figure of Divine Sophia. This sophialogical determination and qualification of the "father" title for G*d has been almost completely lost in Christian consciousness. Instead, the kyriarchal and theological understanding of Philo, John, and other Jewish and early Christian writers has determined the meaning of "father."

The canonical processes and kyriarchal "strategies" that have marginalized or eliminated sophialogy — and not later Gnosticizing mythologizations of Sophia, as some have argued — have had far-reaching consequences for christological articulations and Christian self-understandings. In this process, early Christian sophialogical reflection not only has become intertwined with anti-Judaism but also has been erased from Christian "orthodox" consciousness. However, the kyriocentric framework of masculine-feminine gender dualism, which has shaped the Wisdom traditions, has not been eliminated but rather strengthened by this process. By "naturalizing" the *grammatical masculine* gender of Logos, Son, and Father, Christians have forgotten that such conventional masculine gender language is as metaphoric as the grammatical feminine gender language is for Sophia.

This overt masculinization and covert genderization of Christian theology has determined the theological articulations of pneumatology, mariology, and spiritual experience that understand Woman, Wisdom, or Mary as the representative of humanity or the soul. Feminist discourses have tended to follow this logic of the canonical exclusion of Divine Sophia and to reinstitute Sophia rather than to challenge the overall masculine/feminine kyriocentric framework of the malestream orthodox tradition. The concluding section of this chapter will explore these feminist attempts to recuperate the Sophia traditions.

Feminist Theological Reflection

As we have seen, in contrast to Jewish and Gnostic Wisdom literature only a very few direct traces of Divine Wisdom are found in Christian canonical writings. This explains why the early Christian imagination of Israel's G*d within the Gestalt of the G*ddess as Divine Sophia is almost completely lost and forgotten in the self-understanding of the Western churches. Early Christian reflective mythology has either absorbed those "female" elements derived from Wisdom theology or G*ddess symbolism through the grammatical masculine term "Logos," or it has transferred them to Mary the mother of Jesus, a process that I will seek to trace in the next chapter.

Given such a "selective memory" of the Christian tradition, feminist theology has evaluated the remnants of early Christian Wisdom traditions and sophialogical reflection in various ways. Four feminist directions in interpretation can be distinguished. On feminist-exegetical grounds, the first approach objects to a historical-theological retrieval of the Sophia traditions and discourses. The next two interpretational approaches work either with the psychoanalytic terms "repression" and "archetype" or with the notion of theological appropriation in terms of incarnation and androgyny, concepts that allude to Chalcedon. Finally, my own approach to the problem works with a sociocultural theory of language that does not subscribe to linguistic determinism but, on the contrary, sees language-users "as creating meaning in specific contexts, negotiating where necessary in order to achieve as fully as possible their communicational aims."[68]

First, Luise Schottroff has raised serious historical and theological objections to the feminist recovery of early Christian Sophia discourses.[69] She argues that the fascination of feminist theologians with Sophia christology is misplaced. Wisdom speculation is at home in Israel's elite male circles and bespeaks their interests. Wisdom literature seeks to give instruction to the *pater familias* of upper-class standing. To privilege the early Christian Sophia traditions in feminist theology would mean to eclipse the "gospel of the poor" (*Armenevangelium*) that is at the heart of Jesus' preaching. This *Armenevangelium* is completely determined and shaped by the prophetic tradition. Texts such as Matthew 11:25 and 11:28–30 are not to be considered as Wisdom texts but rather are sapiential elements that have been integrated into the *Armenevangelium*. The rejection of the messengers of Sophia is not comparable to the rejection of Sophia since she is not killed but withdraws unharmed to heaven.

The references to Sophia, therefore, ought not to be the starting point of feminist liberation theology. Rather, it must begin with the fact that the *Armenevangelium,* the revelation of G*d to the *nēpioi,* the babes, the uneducated, or the nobodies, is a women's gospel (*Frauenevangelium*) since more women than men are to be counted among this group. God's election of the "babes," the unemancipated and uneducated, the poor and the children, entails becoming aware of the plight of women in the praxis of a generally androcentric Jesus movement. It means encouraging women to independent action in the consciousness of being a daughter of God. Schottroff concludes that Sophia christology must be rejected on historical and theological grounds. The historical reason is given in Schottroff's negative evaluation of the Wisdom tradition, which in her estimation is not at all oriented toward the G*d of all-encompassing justice but instead preserves the interests of elite males. The theological reason consists in the very important connection between the *Armenevangelium,* which spells justice for women, and women's liberation in the past and present.

In a similar fashion but on quite different grounds Amy Jill Levine questions whether the Q traditions are positive with regard to women.[70] She adopts the distinction between an earlier and later edition of Q and argues that we have no direct evidence that women were addressed or incorporated into the Cynic-like lifestyle of the mendicant preachers in the first layer. Building on this argument Mary Rose D'Angelo points out that "it is particularly noteworthy that all the references to God as father occur in units assigned to Q1, and the references to Sophia occur in units assigned to Q2."[71] This argument does not, however, address the preconstructed androcentric framework and historical-theological assumptions undergirding the stratiographic arguments of Q scholarship. Neither Levine nor D'Angelo take into account the challenges of Stegemann, Horsley, and others, who question the reconstruction of the first layer of Q. It is difficult to see how the first layer of Q teachings could have pertained to a radically individualistic ethic of voluntary homelessness or to conclude that the historical traditions of Jesus' execution were utterly unrelated to the original sayings of Q.

Schottroff's objections seem to have more historical and theological weight than those of Levine and D'Angelo. Schottroff, however, seems to assume that we are able to definitely identify the *Armenevangelium* as the liberating early Christian tradition for women and that it can be separated from the Wisdom tradition. She conjectures that prophetic-Apocalyptic and Wisdom traditions were clearly separated in first-century theological discourses. She does not consider the transformation of Wisdom traditions in and by the *basileia* proclamation of the Jesus movements, which I have proposed in my own work. Instead

Schottroff insists that the Sophia tradition is permanently suspect as an elite male kyriocentric tradition not concerned with justice at all.

Silvia Schroer rightly objects to such a history-of-religions classification of the Wisdom traditions.[72] She points out that Wisdom discourses are permeated with the teachings of Woman Justice and also that in the first-century prophetic-Apocalyptic and sapiential traditions were intertwined, integrated, and changed. Finally, with others she points out that the Wisdom traditions had been democratized in the first century and that much of the sapiential tradition of the Gospels reflects folk wisdom that could very well have been articulated by and for women.

To these historical arguments I would like to add a methodological-theological observation. In my own work I have elaborated the Sophia traditions as one but *not the only* early Christian discourse that might open up unfulfilled possibilities for feminist liberation theology. The *Armenevangelium* seems to me closely related if not totally integrated with those open-ended Q traditions that understand Jesus and Jonah as the messengers of Sophia who continue but do not close off a long line of prophets. Such a historical-theological argument radically challenges the assumption of Q scholarship that the earliest layer of the Sayings Source portrays Jesus as a wandering Cynic-like philosopher.

As I have argued throughout this chapter, I find the early "Jesus messenger of Sophia" traditions theologically significant because they assert the unique particularity of Jesus without having to resort to exclusivity and superiority. In contrast to Jewish and Christian Apocalyptic traditions, the Wisdom tradition values life, creativity, and well-being in the midst of struggle. These elements — open-endedness, inclusivity, cosmopolitan emphasis on creation spirituality, and practical insight — have been especially attractive not only to feminists but also to Asians engaged in christological reflection.

Jesus as sage and prophet of Sophia provides us with two christological images. One presents Jesus as a wise teacher, who in his concrete life relates to our ongoing quest for a gracious G*d. The Sophia-G*d of Jesus loves all humanity irrespective of ethnic and social links and shows concern for liberation and empowerment of the underprivileged. The other insight is that Jesus' teaching is meant not only for hearing but also for being acted upon. In Q we find the earliest christological instance that presents Jesus as a spokesperson for Wisdom. In him we find a way to respond to religious pluralism and the greater problem of suffering and injustice.[73] Nothing stops feminist theologians from critically assessing the kyriocentric framework of the Wisdom tradition (and all other biblical traditions) in order to rearticulate some of its discourses in such a way that wo/men can theologically claim it. We must, however, shape this discourse in such a way that it does not reinscribe the preconstructed elite male kyriocentric framework of meaning of Western culture and Christian religion.[74]

The second feminist discourse on Divine Wisdom welcomes the rediscovery of the biblical Sophia traditions. It seeks, however, to explain the fact that the early Christian language and tradition about Divine Sophia are almost totally lost and can be "excavated" only through hard exegetical labor with the help of the psychoanalytical notion of repression. Joan Chamberlain Engelsman uses Carl Jung's theory of archetype and Freud's concept of repression to illuminate why Divine Wisdom, whose power equals that of any Hellenistic G*ddess and rivals that of YHWH, does not appear openly in Jewish and Christian theology.[75] In the theology of Philo and early Christian canonical writers, she argues, Divine Wisdom became a patriarchal victim, insofar as her predicates and functions were transferred to the masculine Logos — Christ. The final repression of Sophia is accomplished in the trinitarian and christological doctrinal disputes of the early church. Hence, in the history of Christianity these repressed feminine dimensions of the Divine return again and again in masked and destructive ways.

However, such an interpretation, which understands Divine Wisdom with the help of the psychological-cultural archetypes of femininity and masculinity, cannot but reinscribe the basic terms of the Western patriarchal sex/gender system. One finds such a kyriocentric symbol system fully developed in the theology of Philo and partially articulated in Christian Gnostic and patristic writings. However, as I have tried to show, it is not evident that the earliest Christian sophialogical reflection works with such a masculine-feminine gender dualism, since it does not reflect on the masculinity of Jesus. Rather its sophialogical language seeks to understand the historical mission and fate of Jesus of Nazareth in theological terms.

One could counter such an argument with the observation that early Christian discourses simply presuppose the masculinity of Jesus but do not address it. But such a counterargument overlooks that early Christian discourses, like their modern counterparts, were aware of gender dualism and its theological implications. For instance, the apocryphal Gospel of Thomas collected probably at an early time the sayings of Jesus, the Living One, who speaks as Divine Wisdom.[76] This gospel has an interesting saying that seems to deal with gender dualism with reference to baptism:

> Jesus saw children being suckled. He said to his disciples, "These children who are being suckled are like those who enter the Kingdom." They said to him, "We are children, shall we enter the Kingdom?" Jesus said to

them, "When you make the two one, and when you make the inner as
the outer and the outer as the inner and the upper as the lower, so that
you will make the male and the female into a single one, so that the male
will not be male and the female (not) be female, when you make eyes in
the place of an eye, and a hand in place of a hand, and a foot in place
of a foot, (and) an image in place of an image, then you shall enter [the
Kingdom]. (Logion 22)

Davies concludes his discussion of his logion:

> Thomas Logion 22 does not speak of baptism into Christ. Rather, one
> enters into the Kingdom through baptism or reunification. It is very likely
> that baptism into the *basileia* (commonweal) is a more primitive idea
> than the idea of baptism into Christ. It accords much more closely with
> the idea of proselyte baptism in Judaism and with the implications of the
> baptism of John than does Paul's idea of baptism into Christ.[77]

Thomas Logion 22 thus asserts that baptism into the kingdom meant
the abolition of sex/gender differences. This new state is not seen as androgynous nor as masculinized but as gender free. Hence, Logion 22
may not be read in light of Logion 114, which is often quoted here:

> Simon Peter said to them, "Let Mary leave us, because women are not
> worthy of the Life." Jesus said, "Look, I shall guide her so that I will
> make her male, in order that she also may become a living spirit, being
> like you males. For every woman who makes herself male will enter the
> Kingdom of Heaven."[78]

In his critical review of this embarrassing saying, in which he contextualizes it within Gnostic thought, Marvin Meyer has gone out of his
way to prove that it is not a later addition to the Gospel of Thomas but
indispensable to its theology. However, in order to make his point, he
has to assume that the Gospel of Thomas in "its present form belongs
at least on the periphery of Christian Gnosticism."[79] Such a circular argument makes it likely that Davies is more correct when he concludes:
"There are, however, too many unique and anomalous uses in 114 to
allow us to consider it part of the original Gospel of Thomas."[80] In any
case, a comparison of the two logia shows that sex/gender was not taken
for granted but rather addressed directly in early Christian discourse.

In her book *Sexism and God-Talk* Rosemary Radford Ruether develops a third way of approaching the problem of Sophia's absence in
canonical Christian writings. She accepts Chamberlain Engelsman's repression theory and argues that Sophia was never developed fully in
the Scriptures as a female divine figure. Although Radford Ruether acknowledges the co-optation of the Goddess in Jewish and Christian
monotheism, she is troubled by its theological importation of femininity.
Yet, in spite of the adoption of Logos imagery, she argues, theological

reflection on the female side of G*d was not completely cut off in Christianity. Many of the Jewish and early Christian traditions about Divine Sophia are picked up in Christian discourse and transferred to the figure of the Holy Spirit. Hence, Radford Ruether cautions feminists that too eagerly to "appropriate the 'feminine' side of God within this patriarchal gender hierarchy would simply mean to reinforce the problem of gender stereotyping on the level of G*d-language."[81]

Positively, Radford Ruether argues that male language for the Divine must lose its privileged place in Christian discourses. She goes on to understand Christ as "the liberated humanity." As such he/it is not to be confined to the historical Jesus. "Rather redemptive humanity goes ahead of us, calling us to yet uncompleted dimensions of human liberation."[82] I agree with her attempt to shift the debate to a discussion of language usage. Nonetheless, I wonder whether her positive articulation of Christ as "liberated humanity" merely shifts the problem from masculine language for G*d and Christ to a masculine/male-defined notion of humanity. As the above quotation of Logion 114 of the Gospel of Thomas illustrates, in Western tradition "humanness" and "humanity" have consistently been identified as male/masculinity.[83] Thus, a shift from G*d-language to so-called human language does not deconstruct the Western cultural and religious frame of reference but rather reinscribes it.

In like manner, a feminist theological discussion of the sophialogical traces in Christian Scriptures that does not at the same time critically evaluate femininity reinscribes the Western sex/gender system. By reading the early Christian footprints of Sophia in terms of christological doctrine, such as approach seeks to understand Jesus as true goddess and true man.[84] In Jesus as the incarnation of Sophia, divine feminine and human masculine nature are integrated. Unlike the hegemonic Western tradition, this interpretation does not conceive of the feminine negatively. It does not consider masculinity as paradigmatic humanness nor understand the divine nature of Christ in terms of kyriarchal gender dualism, which construes femininity as an inferior model or type. Instead, this interpretation is in danger of succumbing to a "romantic" dualistic understanding of gender that idealizes femininity as representing superior transcendent and salvific qualities.

In extolling femininity and the female nature of Christ as divine, this feminist interpretation cannot but reinscribe the Western cultural sex/gender system in theological terms. It does so insofar as it divinizes the sociocultural patriarchal gender notions of femininity and construes femininity and masculinity after the christological doctrinal model of Chalcedon. Whenever theology in general and Wisdom christology in particular is positioned within a framework of essential gender dualism, it cannot but reproduce patri-kyriarchal theological interests.[85]

Building on these feminist discussions I have suggested a *fourth* way in which feminist theological reflection can approach the remnant discourse on Divine Wisdom in Christian Scriptures. Such an approach shifts the discussion on the female figure of Wisdom from the psychological-ontological-christological level to a linguistic-symbolic level of reflection. Such a shift is justified insofar as Wisdom theology is best understood not as producing a unified sophialogical discourse but as a variegated reflective mythology. As I have tried to show in this chapter, the grammatically masculine language of Wisdom theology has a difficult time speaking adequately of Divine Wisdom in the preconstructed kyriocentric framework of Jewish and Christian monotheism. Insofar as this language struggles to avoid turning Divine Wisdom into a second feminine deity subordinate to the masculine deity, it also struggles against the theological reification of monotheism in terms of the sex/gender system.

Biblical discourses on G*d have not always succeeded in avoiding this danger since they have used predominantly masculine language, metaphors, and images for speaking of the Divine. Moreover, biblical interpretation reinscribes such kyriocentric G*d-language when it understands the discourse on divine Woman Wisdom in metaphorical terms while at the same time it construes the masculine discourse on G*d, the Father and Lord, as descriptive theological language that adequately expresses G*d's nature and being. Such language use obscures that according to Jewish and Christian tradition human language about G*d must always be understood as metaphorical. G*d-language is symbolic, metaphoric, and analogous because human language can never speak adequately about divine reality.

Feminist theological reflection on the biblical sophialogical tradition, I argue, must therefore adopt a theory of language that does not subscribe to linguistic determinism. Kyriocentric language is often understood as "natural" language that describes and reflects reality rather than as a grammatical classification system that constructs reality in androcentric kyriarchal terms. Conventional androcentric language is produced, regulated, and perpetrated in the interests of kyriarchal society and culture. If language is not a reflection of reality but rather a sociocultural linguistic system, then the relationship between language and reality is not an essential "given" but is constructed in discourse. This is especially true when language speaks about divine reality since divine reality cannot be comprehended in human language. The inability to comprehend and express who G*d is prohibits any absolutizing of symbols, images, or names for G*d, be they grammatically masculine, feminine, or neuter. Such an absolute relativity of theological G*d-language demands, to the contrary, a proliferation of symbols, images, and names to express a humanly incomprehensible divine reality.

If language is a sociocultural convention and not a reflection of reality, then one must theologically reject the ontological identification of grammatical gender and divine reality as well as grammatical gender and human reality. Not all languages are gendered or have three grammatical genders or identify natural gender with grammatical gender. Masculine or feminine identity is not defined by biological gender but is constructed through social, cultural, religious, and ethnic conventions. Biological womanhood and cultural femininity had quite different meanings, for instance, for a freeborn woman and a slave woman in ancient Athens, for a queen and her serfs in medieval Europe, and for the white lady of a plantation and her black slave woman in North America.[86] Feminist theology tends to continue the understanding of femininity in racist, bourgeois terms. Although it has raised the critical issue of the "feminine" dimension of the Divine,[87] it has not sufficiently dealt with the fact that, for instance, Egyptian Wisdom theology imaged Isis-Sophia in the Gestalt of a *black* Divine Woman nor reflected on the implications of this for Christian sophialogy and self-understanding.[88]

In short, the rediscovery of Wisdom theology and christology inscribed in biblical writings requires that feminist theologians reflect on the inadequacy of andro-kyriocentric language and critically assess its function in Christian theological discourse. A rediscovery of Wisdom traditions does not invite us to repeat the language of early Jewish-Christian Wisdom theology. Rather it compels us to continue the struggle with conventional masculine language for G*d and the exclusivist authoritarian functions and implications of such language. Feminist theology must rearticulate the symbols, images, and names of Divine Sophia in the context of our own experiences and theological struggles in such a way that the ossified and absolutized masculine language about G*d and Christ is radically questioned and undermined and the Western cultural sex/gender system is radically deconstructed. A feminist exegetical attempt to reconstruct the traces of Sophia as emancipatory christology invites us to develop a critical praxis of reflective sophialogy. Such a critical feminist practice has to sort out and evaluate those traces of emancipatory christology in general and biblical Wisdom theology in particular that open up possibilities of liberation and well-being but have not yet been fully realized in history.[89]

Chapter 6

IN HER IMAGE AND LIKENESS
Women of Wisdom

> Surely, from now on all generations will call me blessed;
> for the Mighty One has done great things for me,
> and holy is G*d's name. (Luke 1:48–49)

> Rejoice, vessel of the wisdom of G*d,
> storehouse of G*d's providence.
> Rejoice, for philosophers are revealed as fools,
> the logic of logicians is dislodged.
> Rejoice, for keen disputants grow dull,
> the makers of myth run dry.
> Rejoice, for you break the Athenians' web,
> and fill full the nets of those fishing.
> Rejoice, for you draw souls from the depth of unknowing
> and bathe them in light that contains all knowledge.[1]

> The fact that the blessed Virgin Mary, Mother of God and Mother of
> the Church, received neither the mission proper to the Apostles nor the
> ministerial priesthood clearly shows that the non-admission of women to
> priestly ordination cannot mean that women are of lesser dignity, nor can
> it be construed as discrimination against them. Rather, it is to be seen
> as the faithful observance of a plan to be ascribed to the wisdom of the
> Lord of the Universe.[2]

In this last chapter I would like to focus on the figure of Mary of
Nazareth, who has been "mythologized" far beyond any historical re-
semblance. Not only is a deconstructive approach to the figure of Mary
more acceptable to Protestant theology than taking such an approach to
the figure of Jesus. It also can be shown that the mythologizing of Mary
progressed in ways very similar to that of Jesus. Such a deconstructive
approach to Mary causes greater emotional upheaval, however, among
Roman Catholics, who have cultivated mariology and the Marian devotion for centuries. Nevertheless, a deconstructive approach is necessary

if the images and titles of Marian cult and devotion are to be integrated
into G*d-language, where they have their proper place. Moreover, the
Catholic tradition provides a rich resource for envisioning G*d as manifest in a woman's Gestalt and for speaking about the Divine in female
language and symbolic imagery since it is funded by ancient G*ddess-
traditions. Theology will be able to catch a glimpse of the historical
woman Mary of Nazareth, who visited Elizabeth in the hill country of
Ain Karim, only if it displaces the images and icons of Mary. It will be
able to name the Divine in inclusive terms only if it reintegrates into
theological discourse proper the language and images of the G*ddess
in general and Divine Wisdom in particular, traditions that have been
transferred first to Jesus and then to Mary of Nazareth.

The Beloved Daughter of the Father(s)[3]

Feminist theologians largely agree in their criticism of the malestream
image of Mary and of patriarchal mariology. This criticism has un-
masked the images and symbols of hegemonic mariology as the religious
projection of a celibate male priestly hierarchy — a projection that has
ideologically legitimized male domination in church and society. Malestream mariology has done so in the past and still continues to do so
today, as documented by the statement of John Paul II in the epigraph
above. In holding up to women the image of the perpetual virgin and
sorrowful mother Mary, churchmen preach a model of femininity that
ordinary women cannot imitate. Mary, as the completely desexualized
"plaster being from the grotto of Lourdes"[4] and the symbol of humble
obedience, serves to religiously inculcate normal women with depen-
dency, subordination, and inferiority. Many Roman Catholic women
share the experience of the American writer Mary Gordon:

> In my day, Mary was a stick to beat smart girls with. Her example
> was held up constantly: an example of silence, of subordination, of the
> pleasure of taking the back seat.
>   ...For women like me, it was necessary to reject that image of Mary
> in order to hold onto the fragile hope of intellectual achievement, inde-
> pendence of identity, sexual fulfillment. Yet we were offered no alternative
> to this Marian image; hence, we were denied a potent female image
> whose application was universal.[5]

Malestream mariology and cult of Mary, feminist theologians point
out, devalue women in three ways: first, by emphasizing virginity to the
detriment of sexuality; second, by unilaterally associating the ideal of

"true womanhood" with motherhood; and, third, by religiously valoriz-
ing obedience, humility, passivity, and submission as the cardinal virtues
of women.[6] Mary, the pure, self-sacrificing, humble handmaiden of the
Lord and patient mother full of sorrows is preached to women as the
model that must be imitated but can never quite be reached. Moreover, Mary, the beautiful virgin and merciful mother, is an expression
of modern masculine desire for the eternal feminine which is projected
into heaven. Finally, Mary, the powerful Queen of Heaven and Earth,
expresses modern nationalist desires of hegemony, although her images
and titles are rooted in medieval feudal society. The image of the servile,
obedient, self-sacrificing, and sexually inexperienced "handmaiden of
the Lord," projected into heaven as the eternal feminine, cannot but
serve kyriarchal interests. In short, malestream mariology continues to
inscribe the sociocultural image of the feminine that sanctifies the marginalization and exploitation of women. Such a Mary cannot be an
inspiring and liberatory model for women either as the feminine yet
subordinate human being[7] or as the divinized — but not quite divine —
Madonna.

These ideologizing and mythologizing forms of malestream mariology
often go hand in hand with a conservative politics of ecclesiastical and
societal restoration. It is no accident that the classic mariological dogmas were articulated at a time when the Greco-Roman imperial form of
Christianity became institutionalized and historically operative:

> The images of heavenly rulers developed parallel to secular imperial
> iconography. The imperial Christ, already the norm in the time of Con-
> stantine, was followed after the Council of Ephesus in 431 by the
> empress-like Mary.[8]

Imperial, feudal, and bourgeois social conditions were the root and
horizon of medieval mariology and cult.[9] Such politically conservative
tendencies have also influenced the articulation of mariology in modern times. Barbara Corrado Pope, for instance, has documented that the
"century of Mary," which opened in 1854 with the dogma of Mary's
immaculate conception and climaxed in 1950 with Pius XII's dogmatic
proclamation of Mary's assumption into heaven, propagated a defensive antimodernist attitude. Its conservative, backward-looking nostalgic
politics yearned for the traditional order of monarchy and was afraid of
social upheavals.[10]

In our century, mythologizing tendencies in mariology have fostered
a conservative-restorative and aggressive anticommunist politics. Just as
in the sixteenth century, when the rosary was prayed against the Turks,
and in the nineteenth century, when it was prayed against the atheists, so

too during the days of the "cold war" it was recited for the conversion of Russia. A similar socially and ecclesiastically reactionary political tendency is apparent in the present post–Vatican II restoration of kyriarchal church structures.

In the past decade, in which the "new cult of femininity" has once again been socially promulgated in order to relegate women to low-paying jobs or to push them back into the home altogether, a reactionary politics in the church has gone hand in hand with many reported apparitions of Mary, the increase of capitalist right-wing religious groups, and the exclusion of women from ordination and church leadership.[11] Feminist attempts to revise malestream mariology and to rearticulate mariology as liberating for women must not only scrutinize doctrinal language and cultic imagery. They must also confront their socio-historical context[12] and its politically conservative dominant mariology if they do not want to contribute to the further marginalization and exploitation of women.

Elisabeth Gössmann has criticized feminist theology for too one-sidedly focusing on hegemonic kyriarchal mariology and not paying sufficient attention to the long tradition of women's theological reflection on Mary and the religious veneration of her.[13] Gössmann's work has documented that women have articulated an understanding different from that of malestream mariology and have developed a very positive image of Mary through the centuries. For instance, whereas malestream mariology has underscored the opposition between Mary and Eve, women's mariological reflections have sought to establish a relation between both representations by seeing Mary as Eve's daughter.[14] Any feminist theology, Gössmann argues, that does not take into account that women have articulated a different tradition of mariology is guilty of the same theological oversight and forgetfulness which determines the knowledge production of malestream theology.

Those mariological women's traditions still accessible to us must be critically interrogated to determine whether and how much they dare to allow us to move beyond doctrinally and/or culturally set limits.[15] Like hegemonic mariology,[16] feminist mariological reflection continues to circle around two problem complexes: on the one hand, Mary of Nazareth and her ideal-typological meaning and, on the other, mariological doctrine and cultic veneration.[17] I cannot concur with Gössmann's judgment, however, that contemporary feminist mariology has concentrated too much on remythologization and depth-psychological interpretation and has shown too little interest in the history of dogma and doctrinal belief systems. To the contrary, feminist mariology is limited precisely, I argue, because it has too often confined itself to a "history of ideas" approach that relies on the mariological history of dogma.[18] For that reason feminist theology has tended to neglect a socio-historical approach and critical re-vision of mariology, as, for instance, the book of Marina Warner had begun to do.[19] Feminist theological discourses, I submit, have not critically analyzed how much their theological reflections on Mary remain within the religious-doctrinal and cultural-symbolic limits that malestream theology and ecclesiastical doctrine have set. Feminist attempts at remythologization also suffer from these kyriarchal limitations.

As feminists attempt to rearticulate mariology *differently,* I suggest, we can gain more than simply information from the women's mariological tradition. By studying this tradition we can become conscious of our own epistemological limitations as well as political determinations by kyriarchal power structures. Such consciousness-raising is necessary, because even feminist studies remain caught up in the kyriocentric horizon and preconstructed frame of meaning determined by hegemonic cultural and religious notions of femininity. Feminists today, like their foresisters, remain enmeshed in kyriarchal constraints set by societal and ecclesiastical structures of domination. Any mariology formulated from the perspective of women, therefore, must with the help of systemic feminist analysis consciously seek to explore its entanglement with kyriarchal structures and kyriocentric ideologies to avoid reproducing them unconsciously. Even an astute theologian such as Leonardo Boff, one of the leading liberation theologians in Latin America, does not escape, but theologically reinscribes the bourgeois-romantic and cultural-archetypal myth of femininity.[20] In modern times, this myth has legitimated not only the otherness, inferiority, deficiency, and second-class status of all women but also that of oppressed men, who are categorized as "feminine."

Mariological discourses that understand themselves as feminist must again and again critically scrutinize the sociopolitical location of their theological reflection. As far as I can see, one can distinguish four approaches in malestream mariology, which also tend to surface in feminist reconstructions: the *Reformation approach* seeks to cut back mariological excesses; the *ideal-typical approach* understands Mary as the representative of a new church and humanity; the *doctrinal-mythologizing approach* attempts to integrate Mary "the divine mother and goddess" into the dogmatic system of the church; the *cultic-spiritual approach* celebrates Mary as quasi-G*ddess.

Again it must be stressed that these four approaches are conditioned by political-cultural forces and religious-institutional pressures that a feminist theological reconstruction may not bypass without detrimental consequences. Whereas the Reformation and ideal-typical approaches tend to further masculinize Christianity, the mythologizing and cultic approaches wind up theologically expanding the cultural-kyriocentric feminine construct of the Western sex/gender system. Malestream mariology "from below" as well as "from above" continues to serve kyriarchal interests.

Mariology "From Below"

Discourses that seek to articulate a "mariology from below" focus on the human being Mary of Nazareth by demythologizing her image.

1. *The historizing approach of Reformation theology* insists on a return to the sources of Holy Scripture and emphasizes the centrality of christology.[21] This emphasis occasioned a thorough criticism of the church's mariological cult in the time of the Protestant Reformation:

> It was the wrong focus, namely, on Mary instead of on Christ, which had disastrous consequences. Hence, *the discovery of the Reformation and the execution of the Reformation theological programs consists in a formal correction of mariological doctrine.* (emphasis in the original)[22]

Protestant criticism of mariology has insisted through the centuries that mariology — if it is to exist at all — must be positioned within anthropology or ecclesiology but not within theology proper or soteriology.

Criticism of mariology went hand in hand with the abolition of the ideal of virginity and its monastic institutionalization. Protestant rejection of mariology tended to further the patriarchalization of theology and church, insofar as the Reformation did not critically challenge either patriarchal marriage and views on sexuality or the position of women in the ministry of the church. The elimination of Mary and the saints from the spiritual cosmos of theology and church had as a consequence — probably unintended — that women no longer appeared in the religious symbolic cosmos nor in the public of theology and church at all. This concentration upon a male-determined christology threatened to turn Protestantism into a purely masculine religion without any symbolic heavenly representation of women.[23] Such religious kyriocentrism not only produced the emotional poverty of Reformation spirituality but also determined the religious experience and questions of many Christian feminists.[24]

Feminist proposals that adopt this Reformation approach also turn back to the Bible to develop a liberating mariology from below. The "Summary Statement on Mariology" of the Consultation of Asian Theology, which took place in 1987 in Singapore, defines the task of

feminist theology in a double manner: First, Asian women must name
the destructive formulations of the two-thousand-year-old malestream
interpretations of Mary in order to become free of them. In a second
step, women read Scripture *as women* within their own cultural contexts
in order to rediscover the liberated and liberating woman, Mary.[25] Like
Asian women, other feminist liberation theologians picture Mary as the
exemplary disciple, the poor woman of the people, the prophetic proclaimer of justice, the motherly sister, or the sorrowful mother. Women,
they argue, have no difficulty identifying with Mary as a historical paradigm. Women understand a Mary who had problems with her difficult
son associating with disreputable people.[26] They sympathize with Mary,
who is said to have cut the shirt of her child so big that it could be
lengthened again and again (Mechthild von Magdeburg).[27] They admire
a Mary who stood by her arrested and tortured child and mourned her
executed son. With reference to Scripture,[28] and especially the Lukan infancy stories, Christian liberation theologians picture Mary as the poor
village girl from Nazareth who has made possible salvation through her
freely given consent. They see her as the perfect disciple who fulfills
G*d's liberating intention. They portray her as the spirit-filled mother
who was the gathering agent of the new community.[29]

Because the biblical references to Mary are spotty at best, the "historical Mary" remains even more illusive than the "historical Jesus." This
results in pressure to fill in features of the historical Mary in an idealistic
fashion; idealistic elaboration, however, tends to resort to cultural feminine patterns of the preconstructed sex/gender system. Moreover, the
attempt to see Mary positively as an exceptional Jewish woman tends to
reinscribe the Christian theological anti-Judaism that it seeks to avoid.[30]
Since biblical texts on Mary contradict each other, a historicizing feminist mariology for the most part has privileged the idealizing texts of
the Gospels of Luke and John, without critically scrutinizing their dualistic anti-Jewish frame of meaning. It continues to do so, although in the
meantime feminist biblical scholarship has on exegetical grounds raised
the question of whether the Lukan work is positive for women.[31]

This historicizing and idealizing tendency in biblical interpretation
of texts on Mary almost never transgresses the boundaries set by
church doctrine. For instance, I do not know of any feminist mariological reflection that theologically connects the "free choice" of Mary
with a woman's sexual "right to choose." Equally, the research hy-
pothesis of biblical scholars like Jane Schaberg that Mary might have
been raped[32] has not inspired systematic feminist elaboration. In my
opinion a recourse to the historical Mary can be set free to develop
feminist liberationist possibilities only if it is combined with a critical

feminist hermeneutics,[33] — a hermeneutics able to embed the story of Mary of Nazareth in a critical reconstruction of a feminist liberationist and emancipatory history as well as in the solidarity of the *basileia* movement.

2. *The ideal-typical ecclesiological approach* is inspired by biblical scholarship. Since the beginning of this century Roman Catholic biblical scholarship has pointed out that an almost unbridgeable chasm exists between the historical figure Mary of Nazareth and the queen of heaven and mother of G*d celebrated in the cult of Mary. Although scholastic theology has always distinguished between the veneration of Mary and the adoration of G*d, the impression rightly exists that the Catholic cult of Mary loves and worships Mary like a divine being. The cult of Mary with its candles, flowers, hymns, feast days, and pilgrimages has developed a much richer tapestry of devotion and emotional fund of values than the theology of the word or a catechetical dogmatics has ever been able to do.[34]

Accepting Protestant theological challenges to the cult of Mary, the Second Vatican Council attempted to cut back the excesses of Marian piety in order to connect the Catholic Marian cult more strongly with Scripture and to place christology once more at the center of theological reflection. In the decrees of the council, the Protestant christocentric emphasis thus became an essential part of Catholic theology. For that reason, Vatican II did not confirm Mary as mediatrix of all grace or as co-redemptrix with Christ, but instead proclaimed her as the ideal representative and central symbol of a more human church oriented toward the world. In the theology of the Council Fathers Mary became the symbol of "the new humanity" and hence a paradigm for both women and men.[35]

Like the Reformation, the Second Vatican Council did not address the question of the marginal ecclesial position of women and the kyriarchal church structures that undergird it. Hence, this new "Protestant"-inspired formulation of mariology was not able to develop an impetus for ecclesial change. Rather, Vatican II ended up further masculinizing theology and church because it repressed the almost divine female symbol of Mary in Catholic life and piety.[36] Although Mary was proclaimed as archetype and mother of the church, on grounds of their sex women remained and remain second-class citizens in the Roman Church insofar as they are not permitted to represent Christ and the church as ordained officials.

Admittedly, Vatican II attempted to correct hierarchical church structures of domination. Nevertheless, it was not able to do so because in its search for "brotherhood"[37] it did not touch the status of women in the church. The "opening to the world" and the "democratization" of the church were bound to fail. The exclusion of women from the ordained leadership of the church resulted in a new emphasis on the scriptural patriarchal-theological "bride-mysticism" in which Mary as the bridal representative of church and world remains subordinated to Christ, her head, just as wives are subordinated to their husbands (see Eph. 5:21–33). Whereas the hierarchy is said to represent Christ's masculinity and God's father power, all so-called lay Christians, men and women, are exhorted to imitate Mary, who perfectly represents the feminine qualities of receptivity, subordination, humility, malleability, obedience, and passivity.

It seems that even feminist liberation theologians' attempts at mariological reflection remain within the sex/gender framework of such an ideal-typical approach. True, they seek to place Mary, the historical woman of Nazareth, at the center of attention. Nevertheless, they tend to universalize her as the ideal type of being woman and the paradigmatic model of submission in faith.[38] Rosemary Radford Ruether was among the first to articulate such an ideal-typical understanding of liberation mariology. According to her book *Mary, the Feminine Face of the Church,* which appeared in 1977, Mary mirrors liberated humanity:

> Mary represents the *person of the church* from the perspective of the conversion that has to go on in history, and between people, to overcome the dehumanizing power and suppressed personhood.... [Like Mary, women] as the church represent that whole of redeemed humankind which can only then be liberated and reconciled when the victims have been empowered to be persons and when power itself has been transformed.[39]

In her later book *Sexism and Gold-Talk,* Radford Ruether develops this approach further. According to her, the figure of the church, which is portrayed as feminine, is represented in Mary. Radford Ruether asks whether an alternative mariology that does not reinscribe masculine/feminine relations is at all possible, and she answers in the affirmative by theologically elaborating Luke's infancy account. Mary, as the female personification of the church, in her view represents liberated humanity redeemed from sexism and hence she also represents the liberation of women.[40] Radford Ruether joins other feminist liberation theologians when she insists that the liberation of women as the poorest of the poor "can become the model of faith." She joins me in insisting that their liberation becomes a special theological "locus." However, whereas I have argued that the struggle for survival and liberation of women suffering from multiplicative oppressions is the "locus" of revelation, Radford Ruether sees as such a "locus" the "believing and liberated community."[41] Mary becomes a symbol of the church, Radford Ruether argues, because according to Luke her free act of faith, her co-creatorship, and her responsiveness in faith have made it possible for G*d to enter history in the person of Christ in order "to effect a liberating revolution in human relationships. Mary is exalted because through her God will work this revolution in history."[42] In Luke's "liberation language," which is expressly economic and political, Mary is simultaneously portrayed as subject and object. She makes possible G*d's liberating action, and G*d's redemptive action liberates her.

In this view Mary embodies and personifies those oppressed people who are being liberated: the hungry, who are being fed; the lowly, who are lifted up; the weeping and mourning who receive consolation. In a similar manner, Ivone Gebara and Clara Maria Bingemer understand Mary as the

> image of the people made fruitful by the Spirit of God, from whom is born the new humankind, which will be woven out of all the nations of the earth. Mary is symbol of the people that she begets from God, and Jesus is symbol of the new people begotten of God.[43]

In Latin America, Mary as the representative figure of the church always represents the church of the poor "of which the base communities are a new and outstanding embodiment."[44] As "Our Lady of Latin America" she is invoked as "Mother of the Oppressed" and "Mother of the Forgotten," the "Companion of the People" on their arduous life journeys who sing:

> Oh, come walking along with us,
> Holy Mary, come.
> Oh, come walking along with us,
> Holy Mary, come.[45]

However, this ideal-typical approach of feminist liberation mariology is, I suggest, not able to overcome the kyriarchal-theological dynamics of the preconstructed cultural sex/gender system and symbolic frame of meaning. In conceptualizing Mary as the symbolic representative of the church, even the church of the poor, or of the "new humanity," this approach does one of two things. It either reinscribes the secondary status of women and the feminine insofar as Mary as the representative of the church or of the new humanity clearly remains subordinated to G*d. Or it submerges the poor woman Mary of Nazareth and hence sublates the mariological female symbol into the notion of the poor and subjugated people. Moreover, its stress on the church as the "new people" of G*d unwillingly reproduces the anti-Jewish tendencies associated with this expression since the beginnings of Christianity.

Mariology "From Above"

In contrast to mariological articulations "from below," hegemonic mariology favors the approach "from above," which positions Mary in the heavenly realm and comes close to divinizing her.

1. *The mythologizing dogmatic approach:* It is not necessary to discuss here the classic doctrinal statements about Mary to prove their kyriocentric character. Without question, hegemonic mariology owes its existence and propagation to malestream theology and the patriarchal church. Nevertheless feminist reconstructions of mariology assume that a discourse on mariological dogmas from the perspective of women is not only possible but also necessary since otherwise women would have to relinquish the mariological heritage of women's devotion to Mary that has been accumulated over centuries.[46]

Such a feminist reconstruction of mariological doctrines has been made thinkable and possible through an argument first made by Mary Daly.[47] After a trenchant criticism of the intertwined subordination of malestream mariology to christology, Daly points out that the symbol of Mary communicates a "double message" that has functioned like a double-edged sword. Because of this "double-edged character,"[48] mariology can be heard selectively and understood differently in different contexts. If mariological dogmas can be liberated from their christological entanglement and again be understood as freewheeling symbols, they can be read in a fruitful feminist way.

Such a feminist approach to mariological discourse, which is often combined with a biblical perspective, places Mary, the woman, at the center of attention.[49] The dogma of the perpetual virginity of Mary is then understood as a symbol for the autonomy, integrity, independence, and self-determination of woman whose identity is no longer defined with reference to a man. In this feminist view, Mary the mother of G*d no longer represents middle-class motherhood oriented toward husband and son, but the creative power of women and their redeeming qualities. The dogma of Mary's immaculate conception in this interpretation communicates that women do not need to be redeemed from sin. Womanhood has not been corrupted by sin but remains a source of power and attraction. The bodily assumption of Mary into heaven, this feminist reading asserts, means that sexuality and bodily femaleness have been assumed into the divine realm and that women's struggle against patriarchal oppression as well as the ultimate realization of women's liberation are an important part of eschatological perfection.

Against such a revisionist interpretation it needs to be pointed out that in kyriarchal situations even the image and cult of a woman who is worshiped by women can cement structures of oppression. Insofar as the mariological dogmas tend to make Mary the great exception among women, they reinforce kyriocentric attitudes and structures. Moreover, feminist arguments that seek to understand mariological dogmas as symbols of women's power and as expressions of female salvation have an idealistic-apologetic tinge. As long as the ecclesial structures of oppression and the kyriocentric theologies that have determined the official articulation of dogmatic mariology continue to exert their power, feminist theological reinterpretation cannot develop transformative power.[50] As long as the sexuality of ordinary Catholic women remains feared and controlled, as long as the vocation and true being of women is reduced to corporeal or spiritual motherhood, or as long as Catholic women are divided into two religious classes, nun- and lay-women,[51] the symbol of the perpetual virgin and mother Mary can only be oppressive and cannot be a transforming power for women's liberation.

As long as women do not have the theological authority to responsibly determine their own sexuality and decide whether to become pregnant, as long as women are not allowed to stand as priests at the altar, and as long as women remain second-class Christians, the exaltation of a woman into heaven can only serve to reinforce the kyriarchal oppression of women on earth. Whether mariological dogmas can be reformulated in a feminist way cannot be decided at academic desks or intellectual panel discussions about Mary. Only when Mary is no longer the exception but rather has become the rule for the socioecclesial status of women can her cult be credible and her image develop transformative power for solidarity, justice, and liberation.

2. In distinction to dogmatics, *the "popular religion" approach* does not appeal to reason and rationality so much as to the emotions, to the desire for security and the direct experience of divine presence.[52] The songs, pictures, visions, processions, feast days, altars, candles, flowers, and incense of popular piety celebrate Mary as the mother of all grace, as "our Lady" who is worshiped in countless pilgrimage sites and holy places. Just as Isis was praised with numerous titles of ancient divinities, so through the centuries Mary has been pictured in "a thousand images" and praised in varied rituals and artistic ways. Devotion to Mary celebrates something greater than the human being called Mary. "Our Lady," the "Queen of Heaven," is the revelation of divine goodness and the manifestation of redemptive power. Her cult has attracted a rich heritage of Goddess images and figures celebrated in different times and cultures. Quoting the famous *Mariengedicht*[53] of the German romantic poet Novalis, the Jewish scholar Schalom Ben Chorin observes:

Mary has indeed been represented in many ways but not as the young oriental Jewish woman. But this is the way in which I as a Jewish author writing from Jerusalem, saw her.[54]

Although mariological doctrine has always insisted on the theological subordination of Mary, popular piety and devotion has rendered quasi-divine honors to the mother of G*d. The more G*d became the patriarchal Father-Son-God and all-powerful punishing judge in the eyes of many people, the more popular devotion to Mary increased. In Mary people worshiped the "gracious goodness" of the "anonymous G*ddess," the Mediatrix of all Grace, and the Mother of Mercy. Just as in the patriarchal family, the mother often mediates between father and sons, so also Mary is said to act as mediatrix between a vengeful Father-God and his ecclesiastical sons. In short, mariological research has repeatedly documented that belief in the kyriarchal God of domination and the mariological cult of motherhood and femininity go hand in hand and reenforce each other.

It is widely recognized that wherever it took hold, Catholic Christianity replaced the holy places, temples, shrines, pictures, attributes, and functions of local G*ddesses and appropriated them for Mary.[55] In the multifaceted symbol "Mary" many images of female divinities and ancient features of female power live on. In the cult and symbol of Mary the mother of G*d, the countless names and images of the G*ddess have survived through the centuries. Artists and common people have always celebrated in Mary the "hidden Goddess of Christianity" who transcends all dogmatics. Malestream theology has widely recognized this but has insisted that the cult of Mary and devotion to her be pruned of their "pagan elements" and be "baptized" in Christ.[56] Nevertheless, people in medieval and modern times have tended to divinize Mary and to apply to her the functions of G*d and Christ.[57]

Especially those feminist theologians who seek to rescue androcentric femininity in order to determine it anew in a feminist way have elaborated this "divinizing" tendency of the Marian cult. These attempts remain within the preconstructed dogmatic frame of reference when they seek to show that through mariological doctrine and devotion the Feminine Divine has remained alive in Christianity. Nevertheless, insofar as these feminist articulations are not interested in the integration of feminine-divine elements with androcentric mariological discourses, they evoke much anxiety and even aggressivity among Christian wo/men.

It is not surprising that in Germany — but not only there — a bitter "debate among sisters" (*Schwesternstreit*) has erupted between the representatives of "radical" or "Goddess" feminism[58] and those of Christian liberationist feminism.[59] Although this debate crosses confessional lines, it is in danger of perpetrating kyriarchal divisions and demonizations among feminists. With the help of the history of religions, depth psychology, or metaphysics, the former direction celebrates the return of the Great Goddess or the Divine Couple as liberation from the distortions of malestream theology and mariology. In contrast, the latter direction tends to insist that Christian feminist mariological discourses must remain within the limits set by hegemonic christology and Marian history.[60]

This dualistic either-or alternative of feminist theology is the more surprising if one realizes that for a long time — and not just in the past fifteen years — malestream theology has advocated the integration of feminine symbols into kyriarchally defined Christian discourses about G*d. Systematic theologians who have recognized that it is important to integrate the "feminine" into a one-sidedly conceived masculine image of G*d have attempted to unearth submerged G*ddess traditions[61] and to harvest the forgotten traditions about Divine Wisdom for theological discourse about G*d, Christ, the Holy Spirit,[62] or Mary.[63] In so doing, they have shown that in mediaeval theology mariology replaced the underdeveloped discourse about the Holy Spirit.[64]

Since symbolic formations do not derive from logic or rationalist theological arguments, female symbols for G*d cannot simply be invented from scratch. For that reason the Marian cult and imagery have a very important function in correcting the one-sidedly masculine theological discourses about G*d, since the cult of Mary offers images and symbols for the renewal of G*d-language. As early as 1954 Edward Schillebeeckx argued that the love of G*d is not only like that of a father but also like that of a mother. Since in his opinion Jesus cannot express the motherly side of G*d because of his masculinity, he needs Mary as his symbolic partner: "Mary is the translation and effective expression of the motherly aspect of God's mercy, grace, and redemptive love, which has manifested itself in visible and touchable form in the person of Christ, our savior."[65]

In a similar fashion, the Mexican American theologian Virgil Elizondo argues that through the appearance of Our Lady of Guadalupe on the Tepeyac hill, "where the ancient sanctuary of the motherly aspect of God under the name of Tonantzin stood," the creative and mutual permeation of Christianity and the religion of the Nahuatl was achieved.

In essence her message is, "Know and understand that I am the ever-Virgin Holy Mary, Mother of the true God through whom one lives: the

Creator, the Lord of the Near and the Togetherness, the Lord of Heaven and Earth." In the original Nahuatl narrative it is immediately evident that there is a new discourse about God which *unites not just the Spanish and the Nahuatl languages but equally the Nahuatl understanding of God with the Spanish one.* The very expression of God which the missioners had tried desperately to wipe out as diabolical is now combined with Spanish expressions of God which the Indians had found incomprehensible.... The results of the new expressions of God and of the Mother of God are an amazing enrichment of the very understanding of the selfhood of God. *It is no longer the European expression of God nor the Nahuatl expression of God but a new mestizo expression* which is mutually interpretive and enriching.[66]

Elizondo concludes his argument asserting that the appearance of Our Lady of Guadalupe added a female aspect to the G*d of Christians and gave a personal aspect to the G*d of the Indios. As feminist theologians have pointed out, however, it is far from certain that the cult of Our Lady of Guadalupe has had positive effects for women.[67]

Finally, with the help of the depth-psychological categories of Carl G. Jung, theologians like Leonardo Boff and Andrew Greeley go even further theologically when they understand Mary as "hypostatically unified with the third person of the trinity"[68] or as the passionate, enticing, attractive, irresistible, inspiring, graceful and healing "feminine dimension" of G*d.[69] Gerda Weiler's cultural-historical symbolic interpretation[70] and Christa Mulack's feminist reinterpretation of the mariological dogmas[71] point in the same theological direction. These examples also suggest that the "debate among sisters" is not actually a theological debate in the strict sense but rather concerns psychological-philosophical frameworks of femininity.[72]

The "debate among sisters" centers on the question of whether femininity and feminine essence or gender difference and gender complementarity are physical-metaphysical and religious-psychological *givens* or whether, to the contrary, the preconstructed cultural sex/gender system is a product of kyriarchal structures of domination.[73] In the latter case, femininity, even if it is projected into heaven, remains determined by kyriarchal interests. As long as church and theology insist upon masculine language, patriarchal images and kyriocentric discourses about the heavenly Queen Mary as well as the kyriarchal Father-Son-God they will continue to inculcate the subordination and secondary status of women. This is the case especially when the femininity of the G*ddess is seen as a complementary aspect of the masculine Divine.

Female Symbolism and
Theological Discourses about G*d

A critical feminist liberation theology does not take its cues from established psychology, popular religion, or dogmatics but begins with
a feminist reflection on the particular experiences of women. Hence it
attempts to name and to reflect critically upon both the negative and
positive mariological experiences of women. To do so, it develops a permanent feminist critique that rejects Mary as an ideal type of femininity
and does not project her as such into heaven; at the same time it insists
that Christian theology and piety should not continue to name the heavenly world and the Divine with purely masculine-patriarchal language
and images that are exclusive of women. As Judith Plaskow demands
for Jewish theology, Christian feminists must argue that theology overcome its "fear of the Goddess."[74] G*ddess cults are no longer a threat
to Christian faith today since the worship of the G*ddess holds sway
only over a tiny minority group with little political power.[75] The threat
to Jewish and Christian monotheism consists much more in the misuse of monotheism for religiously legitimating patriarchal domination.
This domination has sanctified the exploitation of women, the poor, and
subjected races and religions. The salvific power of the biblical G*d of
justice and love is not endangered by G*ddess cults but by the (ab)use
of G*d as an idol for inculcating kyriarchal interests.[76]

But how is it possible at all to name the Divine differently in a kyriarchal culture?[77] How can we speak of G*d in a way that the theological
symbols for G*d as well as the images of Mary no longer legitimate
kyriarchal relations of domination nor continue to inculcate the cultural
myth of the Masculine and Feminine in theological terms? How can
we correct the Reformation's focus on Christ the Man and the Catholic glorification of Mary as the symbol of the eternal feminine in such
a way that Jesus and Mary can be seen theologically as concrete historical persons and paradigmatic manifestations of the divine image? In
short, how can we undo the soteriological valorization of the cultural
Masculine and Feminine constructs in Christian-theology? It is neither
patriarchal God nor matriarchal Goddess, neither the Masculine nor the
Feminine, neither divine Fatherhood nor complementary Motherhood
that redeems and saves. Rather all kyriarchal symbols — masculinity
and femininity, pale skin and dark skin, domination and subordination, wealth and exploitation, nationalism and colonialism — must be
carefully tested out in an ongoing feminist ideology critique.

Only a theological strategy that approaches classic discourses about

G*d with a method of deconstruction and proliferation, of symbolic critique and amplification,[78] I suggest, is able to develop a feminist, liberating way for employing Marian language, symbols, and images to speak about the Divine. Here I will consider four such strategies: the *via negativa,* the *via affirmativa,* the *via eminentia,* and the *via practica.*

1. Since G*d radically transcends human experience, no human language, not even that of the Bible, can speak adequately about the Divine. The *via negativa* of classic theology stressed that we are not able to say properly who G*d is but must say again and again who G*d is *not.* God is *not* man, *not* white, *not* father, *not* king, *not* ruler, *not* Lord. She is also *not* woman, *not* mother, *not* queen, *not* Lady. Since, however, Christian tradition and theology for the most part use masculine language for the Divine, theology must focus on the inadequacy of such masculine language, imagery, and titles and reject their exclusive use for speaking about G*d. The same applies to Marian symbolic language and images that identify Mary of Nazareth with the eternal feminine[79] or eternal otherness.[80] Such a critical rejection and deconstruction of kyriocentric masculinity and femininity as determinative for the language about G*d is one of the most important tasks not only of feminist theology but of all Christian theology.

2. Since G*d is the G*d of liberation and well-being, an affirmative theological strategy (*via affirmativa*) can positively ascribe to G*d all the utopian desires of liberation and well-being of which countless people dream and hope. Such an affirmative discourse about G*d should, however, not restrict itself to anthropological individualism but rather must remain oriented toward the reality and vision of the *basileia* of G*d. Moreover, affirmative discourses about G*d must always be conscious that their language is only analogical since G*d always transcends human desires for liberation and our images of salvation.

Since the Christian G*d tends to be understood mostly in masculine terms as father and son, this affirmative strategy of speaking about G*d has the special task of introducing new female symbols and images of wo/men into the language about G*d. Women as well as men, blacks as well as whites, young as well as old, poor as well as rich, Asians as well as Europeans, Christians as well as Jews, Hindus as well as Muslims are the images of G*d. As long as theology remains conscious of the analogical character of G*d-language, it will be able to critically introduce into Christian G*d-language the symbols and names of the G*ddess that have been transmitted through mariology. Images of the "black" or "brown" Madonna are especially important for avoiding G*d-language that reproduces the romantic-colonial image of the "white lady" who signifies the eternal feminine.

However, such images must not be reduced to abstract principles or restricted to the eternal feminine. They are not to be seen as feminine aspects or attributes of a masculine God or applied to only one person of the Trinity. Instead, many different images of women and variegated symbols of the G*ddess must be applied to G*d generally as well as to all three persons of the Trinity equally. Just as language about Jesus Christ does not introduce a masculine element into the Trinity, Marian symbolic language must not be used to ascribe femininity or motherhood to a G*d whose essence is defined as masculine. Just as references to the lamb of G*d do not introduce animalistic features or speaking of G*d as light does not suggest an astral element, so also anthropomorphic G*d-language must not be misunderstood as maintaining femininity or masculinity as an attribute of the Divine. Such a critical-affirmative integration of Marian symbols and G*ddess-images into Christian discourses about G*d would make it possible for theology to return Mary to earth. It would allow for her integration into the *basileia* movement of equals as a part of the struggling, suffering, and victorious *ekklēsia* of women.[81] At the same time it would make it clear that women as well as men are images and representatives of G*d.

3. The third strategy of classic theological reflection, the *via eminentia,* presupposes the first two strategies but stresses that neither the rejection of masculine G*d-language nor speaking about G*d positively as G*ddess suffices. Divinity is always greater and always more than human language and experience can express. This "excess" of the Divine calls for a conscious proliferation and amplification of images and symbols for G*d derived not only from human life but also from nature and cosmological realities.[82]

The *via eminentia* is able to retrieve and reconstruct for theological discourses about the Divine a rich treasure of symbols and metaphors from the manifold G*ddess images and traditions preserved and transmitted in the cult of Mary. One might object that such a proliferation and amplification of G*ddess images would mean a remythologization of the Divine. But such an objection overlooks that all language about the Divine utilizes mythic images and symbols. A strategy of mythologization necessarily leads into a multiplicity of myths and mythologies, but it need not result in polytheism as long as it remains within the boundaries set by the *via negativa* and *via analogica.* Such a strategy of retrieving the cultural-religious images of the G*ddess living on in the cult of Mary and reconstructing or reintegrating them into G*d-language instead would lead to an effective demythologization of Jesus and Mary of Nazareth.

4. The last theological strategy, the *via practica,*[83] attempts to derive

G*d-language[84] and Marian symbolism from the praxis and solidarity of antipatriarchal liberation movements in both church and society. The creativity and emotion of popular piety must be integrated into the discourses of these liberation movements in order that they not be misused in a reactionary kyriarchal way. As liberation theologies of all colors have insisted, the historical woman Mary of Nazareth is not the Mary of the "holy pictures." Nor is she the Mary of the "happily-ever-after fairy-tale ending" of Christmas lore and doctrinal malestream projection. Robert McAfee Brown transmits a liturgical exchange in an unspecified Latin American country:

PRIEST: Tell us about Mary of the holy pictures.

RESPONSE: (*displaying a picture*): Here she is. She is standing on a crescent moon. She is wearing a crown. She has rings on her fingers. She has a blue robe embroidered with gold.

PRIEST: That *does* sound like a different Mary from the Mary of the song! Do you think the picture has betrayed the Mary of the song?

RESPONSE: The Mary who said that God "has exalted those of low degree" would not have left all of her friends so she could stand on the moon.

CORPORATE RESPONSE: Take her off the moon!

RESPONSE: The Mary who said that God "has put down the mighty from their thrones" would not be wearing a crown.

CORPORATE RESPONSE: Take off her crown! ...

RESPONSE: The Mary who said that God "has filled the hungry with good things" would not have left the people who were still hungry to wear a silk robe embroidered with gold.

CORPORATE RESPONSE: Take off her robe!

ANGUISHED RESPONSE: But, Father, this is not right! (*embarrassedly*) We're, we're doing a striptease of the Virgin.

PRIEST: Very well, if you don't like the way Mary looks in this picture, what do you think the Mary of the song would look like?

RESPONSE: The Mary of the song would not be standing on the moon. She would be standing in the dirt and dust where we stand.

RESPONSE: The Mary of the song would not be wearing a crown. She would have an old hat like the rest of us, to keep the sun from causing her to faint.

RESPONSE: The Mary of the song would not be wearing a silk robe embroidered with gold. She would be wearing old clothes like the rest of us.

EMBARRASSED RESPONSE: Father, it may be awful to say this, but it sounds as though Mary would look just like me! My feet are dirty, my hat is old, my hands are rough and my clothes are torn.[85]

Although the anguished voice of the dialogue referring to the strip-tease of the Virgin alludes to sexual violence, it still speaks from a moralistic male perspective. Nonetheless, this voice articulates an "opening" for addressing issues of sexual violence that the priest alludes to rather than addresses. He does so by turning the discussion back to the Mary of the song who does not speak specifically from the perspective of a pregnant woman. The imagination of liberation theology still sees Mary as the sexually untainted "pure" virgin and mother. She is not imagined as a raped, molested, and sexually violated young woman. She is understood as a poor woman and contrasted with the mighty and rich. Insofar as liberation theology does not address the question of sexual violence against women and Mary's possible subjection to it, the Mary of the "holy pictures" lives on in the image of Mary as an impoverished and hungry woman. The infancy stories of the Gospels and especially the Magnificat, which are generally held to provide a revelatory *topos* for liberation theology, foster such an elision of possible sexual violence suffered by Mary, although they do not completely eradicate traces of it. They speak of poverty, marginality, and hunger but not of the specific danger of sexual violence against women in occupied territories.

The "Visitation" in the Context of Occupation and Sexual Violence

Through the centuries the tellers of the so-called infancy stories have articulated that the mighty, be it Herod, Pilate, or the generals of Haiti, will attempt to kill those who carry the vision of a different "world order" of justice and well-being. The Proto-Gospel of James, dating probably from the first or second century C.E., for instance, expresses this experience:

Then Elizabeth, having heard that they searched for John, took him and climbed the mount and looked around where to hide him: and there was no shelter. Then moaning, Elizabeth said in a loud voice: "Receive, O Mountain, the mother and her child!" Because Elizabeth could climb no farther. And at once, the mount was split and accepted her. And a light was visible for them; because an angel of the Lord was with them to watch over them. (22, 3)[86]

Today, those who carry on this vision of justice and well-being still experience daily the violence evoked by it. I have interrupted the writing of this chapter to meet with the Christian Palestinian liberation theologian Mitri Raheb in Jerusalem.[87] After his doctoral studies in Germany, he returned as a Lutheran pastor to his birthplace, Bethlehem, where his family has lived for generations. In his book he recounts an experience similar to that of Elizabeth in the Proto-Gospel of James:

> I can well remember the six-day war in 1968. Shortly after the beginning of the war, Israel began to shell Bethlehem. My mother brought me in her arms to the Church of the Nativity. There we found shelter together with many other Christian families from Bethlehem. During the war we lived together in the rooms of the church. There we felt safe and protected despite the shelling and bombing.[88]

Our conversation centered not on war, occupation, and intifada, however, but on Raheb's vision for an "intellectual" women's center in Bethlehem where Palestinian Christian and Muslim women who have studied abroad and returned to Palestine could come together with women who have never left to discuss their experiences of alienation and mediation between different cultures. Such a center also would provide Palestinian initiative and space for dialogue between Christian, Muslim, and Jewish women who face similar difficulties in patriarchal biblical religions. In the face of increasing nationalist fundamentalism women could come together to name the emancipatory traditions of their religion and the possibilities of resistance to kyriarchal domination that these traditions offer. The "visitation" would become a living reality. It would take place again and again in Bethlehem, Jerusalem, Ain Karim, and many other places.[89]

The two women students who had arranged the meeting between us felt challenged into action by this daring vision and practical suggestion. They proposed that after their return to Germany they would organize a network that could link not only Palestinian and German Christian women but also Christian and Islamic women. Such a network could introduce into feminist Jewish-Christian dialogue issues raised by women of the third biblical religion, Islam. We were all very conscious, however, that the starting point and shaping model for such a network could not be the joyous event of Mary's "visiting" with Elizabeth, an event that presupposed familiarity and spiritual kinship.

Instead such a dialogue would have to begin by critically exploring the difficult relations between European or American and Palestinian women. Such strained relations between Christian, Jewish, and Muslim women are biblically articulated in the story of Sarah and Hagar. This story of the free woman and the bondwoman has found a broad resonance in feminist liberation discourses. African American feminists see in Hagar the slave woman, Latin American feminists behold her as the destitute woman, and Asian feminists understand her as the culturally alienated woman.[90] Sarah and Hagar symbolically prefigure the pitfalls and possibilities of a critical dialogue between Palestinian and European or American Christian women, between Christian, Jewish, and Muslim women living in "the holy land" of biblical religions. This dialogue must first focus on the problematic relations exemplified in these two biblical foremothers since they are paradigmatic for women's relations under kyriarchal conditions. Only after such a critical exploration may feminists hope to continue the conversations between Elizabeth and Mary in Ain Karim.

With Bethlehem and Ain Karim as symbolic boundary markers, the infancy stories provide the imaginative site for feminist dialogue. In their center stands Mary of Nazareth. But what kind of Mary? we might ask. Is she the "beloved daughter of the fathers" or the young frightened woman who undertakes the arduous journey through the hill country to seek support from another woman? The infancy stories might very well have been women's stories retold again and again before they received their written form in Matthew's and Luke's Gospels.[91] Although written down, they have never been brought to closure. They have been repeated, amplified, and totally changed in countless ways. They have been told through the centuries and still are told today.

As "Christmas" stories that preach capitalist consumerism in the name of religion these stories have become privatized and functionalized. The Bethlehem of the Christmas stories is a legendary place of singing angels and the babe in the manger. Like Santa's shop at the North Pole, the stable of Bethlehem with the sweet baby boy has become part of the cultural repertoire that fosters holiday spending. Together with the shepherds in the fields, his adoring mother Mary sustains the romantic emotions of the holiday spirit. Christmas has become the foremost shopping feast in the global village. For the most part women are the high priestesses of this consumer ritual. Not only in the United States, which consumes 70 percent of the world's resources, but throughout the whole industrialized world, the weeks before Christmas are dedicated to retail sales and shopping frenzies.

Several years ago, I visited Hong Kong during the Advent season for a Jewish-Christian dialogue conference on Wisdom. I had looked forward to an encounter with Asian culture and religions but was overwhelmed by the commercial Christmas decorations in a society where the majority of people are not Christian. Santa Claus and Mrs. Claus, Frosty the Snowman, and Rudolf the Red-nosed Reindeer, candy-glazed ginger bread houses and snow-powdered Christmas trees, jingle bells and elves carrying presents, neon stars and season's greetings in all colors

and scripts blazed from every tall building. This advertising spectacle
had turned the <u>birth of Jesus in Bethlehem into a fairy tale among the</u>
<u>many fairy tales and wonderland scenes of the holiday pastiche.</u> Preach-
<u>ers who insist on spiritual rather than materialist consumerism do not</u>
<u>dislodge but reenforce the cultural fairy tale of Christmas by turning the</u>
<u>stories about Mary and Jesus into one more edifying story for religious</u>
<u>consumption.</u>

The cultural orgy of shopping and gift-giving has its largely unrec-
ognized but deep religious roots in the biblical story of G*d's love
embodied in a newborn child and offered to the world as the promise
of heretofore unrealized possibility. The infancy stories probably were
originally folk tales that were rewritten in the canonical and extracanonical Gospels. These stories tell about wo/men, slaves, shepherds,
the hungry, and the homeless who experience the good tidings of salvation. They are stories of open-ended salvation for all, not fairy tales of
rich and glamorous people. Even their contemporary commercialization
and romanticization has not been able to eradicate their revolutionary
imaginative power of transformation.

Biblical scholarship points out, however, that the infancy narratives
of the canonical Gospels of Matthew and Luke already began to turn
the story about Mary and her child into a fairy tale — or, as scholars
say, into two quite different mythical or miraculous accounts that are
historically suspect. Critical exegesis has sought to trace the literary development of the two versions and to contextualize them in the religious
cultural ambiance of the first century. In contrast to biblical literalists
who insist on the historical facticity of the infancy narratives, critical
scholars stress their religious-symbolic meaning and spiritualized reality. Thus both approaches, the literalist and the scholarly, confirm the
fairy-tale mentality.

In line with biblical studies, feminist scholars have suggested that de-
spite their differences, the Gospels agree that Jesus is the child of Mary.
Against all patriarchal custom Jesus is called in Mark 6:3 "the son of
Mary," which the Gospel of Matthew modified with the designation
"the carpenter's son" (Matt. 13:55) and Luke corrected with "son of
Joseph" (4:22). The infancy narratives of the Gospels of Matthew and
Luke also concur that Mary became pregnant in the period between be-
trothal and completed marriage. And finally, the Matthean and Lukan
Gospels also know that Joseph was not the biological father of Jesus.
This information has lent itself to two different feminist theological
interpretations.[92]

Those feminist theologians who accept the Gospels' statement that
Mary "was found to be with child of a holy spirit" (Matt. 1:18, 20;

Luke 1:34) interpret this text as positive. They stress Mary's independence from a man as well as her free choice and active self-determination in consenting to her unexpected pregnancy. As we saw in chapter 2, Sojourner Truth espoused this line of reasoning in the last century. Answering a clergyman who had objected to equal rights for women on the grounds that Jesus was a man and not a woman, Sojourner Truth asserted: "Where did your Christ come from? From G*d and a woman. Man had nothing to do with him."

Those feminist scholars in religion who hold that divine agency does not miraculously replace male agency in conception either believe that Mary was seduced by Joseph or someone else during the time of their betrothal, or they point to the persistent rumor found in Jewish and Christian ancient literature that Mary was raped by a Roman soldier. In the latter case she joins the countless women ravished by soldiers in war and occupation. Bangladesh, Kuwait, and Sarajevo intrude into the mythology of the perpetual virgin and Queen of Heaven.

In Luke's account, the unwed pregnant Mary does not remain alone with her anxieties but seeks support from another woman, Elizabeth. Filled with the Holy Spirit who exalts the violated and makes the fruit of illegitimacy holy, the two women rejoice in G*d's liberating action. In the Magnificat, the pregnant Mary enunciates G*d's salvation and well-being to the humiliated and downtrodden. The future of G*d's well-being for all without exception is not to be awaited passively. It is being born among us today, from our flesh and blood, from our commitments and struggles for justice. It becomes born as the hope for those who are without hope.

To place the agency of Mary, the "single" mother, at the center of our attention interrupts the kyriocentric celebration of the eternal feminine. Such a feminist move is dangerous in the eyes of both ecclesiastical and political authorities. For instance, German theologian Dr. Sylvia Schroer was denied a distinguished professorship by the bishop of Tübingen simply because she had written a popular article pointing out that the Gospel of Matthew pictures Mary in "bad company," namely, that of Tamar, Rahab, Ruth, and Bathsheba. Closer to home, Professor Jane Schaberg has been attacked and vilified by the Catholic right because of her book *The Illegitimacy of Jesus*.

The assaults of former Vice-president Dan Quayle on the TV character Murphy Brown for having a baby out of wedlock provide a political example. Quayle's intervention was ridiculed by the press, but he nevertheless made it acceptable again to speak about "illegitimacy" as if the legitimacy of a child depends solely on the father. The present discussion on welfare reform documents the growing power of the religious right to define the problem and to undo the feminist achievements of the past twenty years.

The "dangerous memory" of the young woman and teenage mother Miriam of Nazareth, probably not more than twelve or thirteen years old, pregnant, frightened, and single, who sought help from another woman, can subvert the tales of mariological fantasy and cultural femininity. In the center of the Christian story stands not the lovely "white lady" of artistic and popular imagination, kneeling in adoration before her son. Rather it is the young pregnant woman, living in occupied territory and struggling against victimization and for survival and dignity. It is she who holds out the offer of untold possibilities for a different christology and theology.

In Place of a Conclusion:
On the Open Road to Galilee

The chapters of this book have not been concerned with establishing "definite" closed readings of biblical texts nor with providing closure to debated issues in feminist christology. Rather they have sought critically to engage biblical and feminist discourses on Jesus, Miriam's child and Sophia's prophet, and to position them symbolically on the "road to Galilee." Against the allurement of literalist certainty and the enticement of playful excess, I have argued that the road of a critical feminist christological inquiry must be variegated, inclusive, and open-ended but still remain engaged and committed.

Like the women of the resurrection narratives on the way to the tomb, I was particularly concerned with how to remove the "commonsense" stone that closes and contains potentially transformative readings within the preconstructed frame/tomb of the kyriarchal sex/gender system. I have argued that the very early, still open-ended Jesus' traditions might be helpful for articulating feminist interreligious christological discourses today. These traditions understand John and Jesus as standing in a long line of messengers and prophets whom Divine Wisdom sent to announce "good news" not only to men but also to women, not to those who have made it but to those who are poor, hungry, and weeping now. Like John the Baptizer and Jesus the Galilean, or like Elizabeth of Ain Karim and Miriam of Nazareth, feminist theologians today continue the long line of Sophia's prophets and messengers that spans the centuries and points to an open-ended future.

Like the women of the infancy narratives, the women disciples, Mary of Magdala, and the women around her enunciate the open-endedness of the journey. They proclaim that the executed Jesus is believed to be the Resurrected One. The Living One goes ahead of them and enables the disciples of the *basileia* to continue the tradition and vision of Sophia's messengers by announcing the good news of G*d's new "world order" of justice and well-being for every wo/man without exception. The Living One is present wherever the disciples of the *basileia* practice the inclusive discipleship of equals, making it a present reality among poor, hungry, abused, and alienated wo/men. As Katie G. Cannon has underscored, central for struggling communities such as the Black Church are three things: the notion of *imago dei,* justice and love, and last but not least solidarity in community.[93]

Instead of assuming that a "feminine" style of thinking or a mode of theologizing from "the woman's perspective" promotes liberationist christological discourses in the interest of wo/men, I have argued that we need to explore critically how even such discourses can perpetrate kyriarchal mind-sets. In addition, we have to inquire whether and to what degree the textualized wo/men characters of the Christian Testament communicate kyriarchal values and visions. We must also consider that women, sometimes even more than men, have internalized cultural-religious feminine values and hence are in danger of reproducing the preconstructed kyriarchal politics of either womanly submission or feminine glorification in their own speaking and writing. Feminist theological discourses have to position themselves in such a way that they are "crossing" the "double cross" of the preconstructed kyriarchal sex/gender frame of meaning that is especially determinative of christology.

Consequently, I have insisted, the category of "woman" must be critically assessed rather than presupposed or idealized as a special source of christological insight. It must be shown for what it is, the "common-sense" construct of the cultural-religious sex/gender system that serves kyriarchal interests.[94] Fortunately today, more and more diverse and resistant discourses of emerging feminist movements around the world are interrupting those discourses of middle-class academic gender or women's studies that have conceptualized feminist inquiry in terms of reading or speaking *as a woman.* These feminist discourses challenge universalistic kyriarchal claims that all women have a feminine nature in common that defines them as "others" or as "subordinates" to men.

If feminist christology is to displace the politics of meaning that is determined by the preconstructed kyriarchal sex/gender system, feminist theologians must no longer articulate wo/men's identity in essentialist universalistic terms. Instead they must carefully analyze their own assumptions as well as those of malestream christological discourses to determine how much they take into account the diverse cultural-religious contexts, the historically shaped subjectivity, and the diverse voices of wo/men. By so doing, feminist theologies can unravel the unitary exclusive conceptualizations of christological and other cultural-religious discourses that define woman as the "naturalized" or "revealed" Other of men, an Otherness that is in reality that of *elite Woman to elite Man*. The insights into the collusion of theological discourses with the kyriarchal structures of race, class, heterosexuality, and colonialist oppression compel us not to duplicate or multiply those white malestream christological discourses that are drawn upon the preconstructed rock of the cultural sex/gender system.

Instead, feminist scholars in religion must firmly situate their theological discourses within the emancipatory movements of wo/men around the globe. Biblically based women's liberation movements have their historical roots in the liberation from slavery and oppression announced by Miriam, in the repentance preached by John, and in the *basileia* vision proclaimed by Jesus. Those wo/men who have been engaged in such emancipatory *basileia* movements have sought through the centuries again and again to realize the *basileia* of G*d not only as a power for abolishing kyriarchal domination and exploitation but also as a force for establishing the salvation and well-being of all, which Mary announced in the Magnificat. At the same time this Christian vision of the discipleship praxis of equals realizes that the *basileia* is not yet here, not yet an accomplished reality. Wo/men still have to struggle and hope for the liberation and well-being of all, a vision still to be realized by G*d in the future. Nevertheless, like Mary, feminist liberation theologians proclaim that the *basileia,* that is, G*d's different world and renewed creation symbolized in the abundant table set by Divine Wisdom, is promised especially to wo/men suffering from multiple oppressions and dehumanizations.

For that reason I have argued here that G*d-language, discourses about Jesus Christ, and Marian symbolism must remain embedded in feminist liberation movements and practices of transformation. They are to be contextualized in the praxis of the discipleship of equals, which provides the fecund ground and theological matrix in which new symbols, images, songs, hymns, prayers, rituals, and feast days are growing. A critical feminist discourse on Jesus and Mary will be able to bring about the transformation of patriarchal church and kyriarchal society for the liberation of all only if it does not limit itself to intellectual theological speculations and emotional devotional piety. Instead it must engage in an uncompromising liberationist practice that consciously seeks to transcend its kyriarchal predicaments, locations, and limitations.

We have arrived at the end of our arduous journey through the mountainous country of christological discourses. The meeting and conversation between Elizabeth and Mary, which is supposed to have taken place in Ain Karim, have provided the imaginative space for our critical feminist conversations. The "visitation" celebrated here is between two women of Wisdom. I hope they have become a symbolic paradigm of wo/men coming together for theological reflection in their struggles for liberation. Jesus, Miriam's child and Sophia's prophet, goes ahead of us on the open-road to Galilee signifying the beginnings of the still-to-be-realized *basileia* discipleship of equals.

Notes

Chapter 1: The Oratory of Euphemia and the Ekklēsia of Wo/men

1. For the problematic use of the term "woman"/"women" see Denise Riley, *"Am I That Name?": Feminism and the Category of Women in History* (Minneapolis: University of Minnesota Press, 1988); Judith Butler, *Gender Trouble: Feminism and the Subversion of Identity* (New York: Routledge, 1990). My way of spelling "wo/men" seeks to underscore not only the incoherent, destabilized character of the term "woman"/"women" but also to retain the expression "women" as a political category. Since the term "woman"/"women" is often read as referring to white women only, my unorthodox writing of the term seeks to draw to the attention of readers that those kyriarchal structures that determine women's lives and status also have an impact on men of subordinated races, classes, countries, and religions, albeit in a different way. Hence the spelling "wo/men" seeks to communicate that whenever I speak of "wo/men" I mean not only to include *all women* but also to speak of oppressed and marginalized men. "Wo/men" must therefore be understood as an inclusive expression rather than as an exclusive universalized gender term.

2. Edward W. Said, "Nationalism, Human Rights, and Interpretation," in Barbara Johnson, ed., *Freedom and Interpretation: The Oxford Amnesty Lectures 1992* (New York: Basic Books, 1993), 198.

3. In order to mark the inadequacy of our language about G*d, I had adopted the Jewish orthodox spelling "G-d" in my books *Discipleship of Equals: A Critical Feminist Ekklesia-logy of Liberation* (New York: Crossroad, 1993) and *But She Said: Feminist Practices of Biblical Interpretation* (Boston: Beacon Press, 1992). However, Jewish feminists have pointed out that such a spelling is offensive to many of them because it suggests a very conservative, if not reactionary, theological frame of reference. Hence I have changed my way of writing the word again in this book. Although I realize that such a change causes problems for secretaries and copy editors, I do think it is theologically necessary to visibly destabilize our way of thinking and speaking about G*d.

4. For a review of such malestream discourses to construct a Christian Testament christology see, e.g., William M. Thompson, *The Jesus Debate: A Survey and Synthesis* (New York: Paulist Press, 1985); Horst Robert Balz, *Methodische Probleme der neutestamentlichen Christologie,* Wissenschaftliche Monographien zum Alten und Neuen Testament 25 (Neukirchen-Vluyn: Neukirchener Verlag, 1967); A. Roy Eckardt, *Reclaiming the Jesus of History: Christology Today* (Minneapolis: Fortress Press, 1992).

5. See for instance, Marinus de Jonge, *Christology in Context: The Earliest Christian Responses to Jesus* (Philadelphia: Westminster Press, 1988); Paula Fredricksen, *From Jesus to Christ: The Origins of the New Testament Images of Jesus* (New Haven: Yale University Press, 1988); Richard A. Horsley, *Jesus and the Spiral of Violence* (San Francisco: Harper & Row, 1989); John D. Crossan, *The Historical Jesus: The Life of a Mediterranean Jewish Peasant* (San Francisco: Harper, 1991); John P. Meier, *A Marginal Jew: Rethinking the Historical Jesus,* vol. 1 (New York: Doubleday, 1991); Eugene M. Boring, *The Continuing Voice of Jesus: Christian Prophecy and the Gospel Tradition* (Louisville: Westminster/John Knox Press, 1991); E. P. Sanders, *The Historical Figure of Jesus* (London: Allen Lane, 1993).

6. For reviews see, e.g., Marcus J. Borg, "Portraits of Jesus in Contemporary American Scholarship," *Harvard Theological Review* 84, no. 1 (1991): 1–22; Marcus J. Borg, *Jesus in Contemporary Scholarship* (Philadelphia: Trinity Press International, 1994); James H. Charlesworth, "Annotated Bibliography," in James H. Charlesworth, ed., *Jesus' Jewishness: Exploring the Place of Jesus within Early Judaism* (New York: Crossroad/American Interfaith Institute, 1991); John F. O'Grady, "The Present State of Christology," *Chicago Studies* 32, no. 1 (April 1993): 77–91; Werner G. Kümmel, "Jesusforschung seit 1981," *Theologische Rundschau* N.F. 53 (1988): 229–49 and 54 (1989): 1–53; Daniel Kosch, "Neue Jesusliteratur," *Bibel und Kirche* 48 (1993): 40–44; Ferdinand Hahn, "Umstrittenes Jesusbild?" *Münchener Theologische Zeitschrift* 44 (1993): 95–107.

7. For instance Jacquelyn Grant, *White Women's Christ and Black Women's Jesus* (Atlanta: Scholars Press, 1989); Maryanne Stevens, ed., *Reconstructing the Christ Symbol: Essays in Feminist Christology* (New York: Paulist Press, 1993); Kelly Brown Douglas, *The Black Christ* (Maryknoll, N.Y.: Orbis Books, 1994); María Pilar Aquino, *Our Cry for Life: Feminist Theology from Latin America,* trans. Dinah Livingstone (Maryknoll, N.Y.: Orbis Books, 1993); Doris Strahm and Regula Strobel, *Vom Verlangen nach Heilwerden: Christologie in feministisch-theologischer Sicht* (Fribourg: Exodus, 1991); Chung Hyun Kyung, *Struggle to Be the Sun Again: Introducing Asian Women's Theology* (Maryknoll, N.Y.: Orbis Books, 1990); Rita Nakashima Brock, "And a Little Child Will Lead Us: Christology and Child Abuse," in Joanne Carlson Brown and Carole R. Bohn, eds., *Christianity, Patriarchy and Abuse: A Feminist Critique* (New York: Pilgrim Press, 1989), 42–61; Rosemary Radford Ruether, "Feminism and

Jewish-Christian Dialogue: Particularism and Universalism in Search for Religious Truth," in John Hick and Paul Knitter, eds., *The Myth of Christian Uniqueness: Toward a Pluralistic Theology of Religions* (Maryknoll, N.Y.: Orbis Books, 1987), 137–48; Susan Brooks Thistlethwaite, *Sex, Race and God: Christian Feminism in Black and White* (New York: Crossroad, 1989); Elizabeth A. Johnson, *She Who Is: The Mystery of God in Feminist Theological Discourse* (New York: Crossroad, 1992); Elizabeth A. Johnson, "The Incomprehensibility of God and the Image of God Male and Female," *Theological Studies* 45 (1984): 441–65; Elizabeth A. Johnson, "Redeeming the Name of Christ: Christology," in Catherine Mowry LaCugna, ed., *Freeing Theology: The Essentials of Theology in Feminist Perspective* (San Francisco: Harper, 1993), 115–37; Verena Wodtke, ed., *Auf den Spuren der Weisheit* (Freiburg: Herder, 1991).

8. Since the designations "Old Testament" and "New Testament" as parts of the Christian Bible suggest anti-Jewish supersessionism, in my own text I replace the appellations "Old Testament" with "Common Testament" and "New Testament" with "Christian Testament"; the latter designation points to the Christian authorship and ownership of those first-century canonical writings that have been named "New Testament." Other scholars use "First and Second Testament" to underscore the secondary character of the New Testament (see James A. Sanders, "First Testament and Second," *Biblical Theology Bulletin* 17 [1987]: 47–49). A widely accepted new way of designating both Testaments is not likely to emerge as long as popular and academic Christian discourses maintain the kind of supersessionist anti-Jewish theological rhetoric that is associated with the appellation "New Testament."

9. See John Dominic Crossan, *Jesus: A Revolutionary Biography* (San Francisco: Harper & Row, 1994).

10. See David W. Odell-Scott, *A Post-Patriarchal Christology,* American Academy of Religion Series 78 (Atlanta: Scholars Press, 1991).

11. Ain Karim is alternately spelled "Ain Karem," "En Kerem," "Ein Karim," and "Ein Karem."

12. For example, Greer Fay Cashman, *Essential Jerusalem* (Basingstoke, Hampshire: The Automobile Association, 1991), 47.

13. For a theoretical discussion of the politics of gender see, e.g., the essays collected by Seyla Benhabib and Drucilla Cornell, *Feminism as Critique: On the Politics of Gender* (Minneapolis: University of Minnesota Press, 1987).

14. On the social construction of economics and gender see the contributions in Marianne A. Ferber and Julie A. Nelson, eds., *Beyond Economic Man: Feminist Theory and Economics* (Chicago: University of Chicago Press, 1993).

15. For this expression see Donna Haraway, "A Manifesto for Cyborgs: Science, Technology and Socialist Feminism in the 1980s," *Socialist Re-*

view 80 (1985): 65–105; repr. in Elizabeth Weed, ed., *Coming to Terms: Feminism, Theory, Politics* (New York: Routledge, 1989), 173–204.

16. See, e.g., John Fiske, *Television Culture* (New York: Methuen, 1987).

17. For feminist analyses of communication see among others Robin Tolmach Lakoff, *Talking Power: The Politics of Language* (New York: Basic Books, 1990); Linda A. M. Perry, Lynn Turner, and Helen M. Sterk, *Constructing and Reconstructing Gender: The Links among Communication, Language and Gender* (Albany: State University of New York Press, 1992).

18. For an excellent "case study" and critical analysis of the involvement of religion in this global struggle see especially the works of the journalist Penny Lernoux, *Cry of the People* (New York: Penguin, 1982); *In Banks We Trust* (New York: Penguin, 1986); and her last book before her untimely death, *People of God: The Struggle for World Catholicism* (New York: Penguin, 1989).

19. See, for instance, Robert B. Reich, *The Work of Nations* (New York: Vintage Books, 1992).

20. Joan Smith, "The Creation of the World We Know: The World-Economy and the Re-Creation of Gendered Identities," in Valentine M. Moghadam, ed., *Identity Politics and Women: Cultural Reassertions and Feminisms in International Perspective* (Boulder, Colo.: Westview Press, 1994), 27–41.

21. See especially the declaration of the Division for the Advancement of Women on "International Standards of Equality and Religious Freedom: Implications for the Status of Women," in Moghadam, *Identity Politics and Women*, 425–38.

22. See, e.g., Rebecca E. Klatch, "Women of the New Right in the United States: Family, Feminism, and Politics," in Moghadam, *Identity Politics and Women*, 367–88.

23. Most of the contributions in Moghadam, *Identity Politics and Women*, are on women and Islam in different parts of the world.

24. See Madeleine Tress, "Halakha, Zionism and Gender: The Case of Gush Emunim," in Moghadam, *Identity Politics and Women*, 307–28, and Debra Renee Kaufman, "Paradoxical Politics: Gender Politics among Newly Orthodox Jewish Women in the United States," ibid., 349–66.

25. Sucheta Mazumdar, "Moving Away from a Secular Vision? Women, Nation, and the Cultural Construction of Hindu India," in Moghadam, *Identity Politics and Women*, 243–73, and Radha Kumar, "Identity Politics and the Contemporary Indian Feminist Movement," ibid., 274–92.

26. For documentation and analysis see the award-winning three-part PBS series *God and Politics,* in which Bill Moyers explores the connections between state and church and its impact on U.S. foreign policy.

27. See Valentine M. Moghadam, "Introduction: Women and Identity Politics in Theoretical and Comparative Perspective," in Moghadam, *Identity Politics and Women,* 3–26; Hanna Papanek, "The Ideal Woman and the Ideal State: Control and Autonomy in the Construction of Identity," ibid.,

42–75; and Ira Yuval-Davis, "Identity Politics and Women's Ethnicity," ibid., 408–24.

28. Diana L. Eck, *Encountering God: A Spiritual Journey from Bozeman to Banaras* (Boston: Beacon Press, 1993), 176, writes: "A new wave of exclusivism is cresting around the world today. Expressed in social and political life, exclusivism becomes ethnic or religious chauvinism, described in South Asia as communalism.... As we have observed, identity-based politics is on the rise because it is found to be a successful way of arousing political energy."

29. See the book jacket of John Dominic Crossan, *Jesus: A Revolutionary Biography* (San Francisco: Harper & Row, 1994).

30. See the critical review of N. T. Wright, "Taking the Text with Her Pleasure: A Post-Post-Modernist Response to J. Dominic Crossan, *The Historical Jesus: The Life of a Mediterranean Jewish Peasant* (Edinburgh: T. & T. Clark; San Francisco: HarperSanFrancisco, 1991), (with apologies to A. A. Milne, St. Paul and James Joyce)," *Theology* 96, no. 112 (1993): 303–10, from the perspective of a critical realistic reading. It is regrettable, however, that Wright's critical essay resorts to sexist "figuration."

31. See my critique of positivism in biblical studies in "Text and Reality — Reality as Text: The Problem of a Feminist Social and Historical Reconstruction on the Basis of Texts," *Studia Theologica* 43 (1989): 19–34, and *But She Said,* 79–101.

32. See also Rita Felski, *Beyond Feminist Aesthetics: Feminist Literature and Social Change* (Cambridge: Harvard University Press, 1989), 168f.: "Some form of appeal to collective identity and solidarity is a necessary precondition for the emergence and effectiveness of an oppositional movement; feminist theorists who reject any notion of a unifying identity as a repressive fiction in favor of a stress on absolute difference fail to show how such diversity and fragmentation can be reconciled with goal-oriented political struggles based upon common interests."

33. For instance, Jacquelyn Grant, "The Sin of Servanthood and the Deliverance of Discipleship," in Emily M. Townes, ed., *A Troubling in My Soul: Womanist Perspectives on Evil and Suffering* (Maryknoll, N.Y.: Orbis Books, 1993), 199–218, and I address the question of servanthood and emphasize discipleship in very similar ways, although we come from quite different social and religious backgrounds. Since Grant does not refer to my own theoretical analysis — see my article " 'Waiting at Table': A Critical Feminist Theological Reflection on Diakonia," *Concilium* 198 (1988): 84–94, and my book *Discipleship of Equals,* 290–306 — I feel justified in surmising that a comparable multiplicative analysis of kyriarchy results in coinciding theoretical proposals.

34. Katie Geneva Cannon's womanist ethical method, which she has developed in interaction with the Black women's literary tradition, for example, is not only useful for delegitimizing the patriarchal teachings of the Black Church but equally for critiquing the hegemonic preaching of white

churches. See her article " 'The Wounds of Jesus': Justification of Goodness in the Face of Manifold Evil," in Townes, *A Troubling in My Soul*, 219–31.

35. See Hedwig Meyer-Wilmes, *Rebellion auf der Grenze: Ortsbestimmung feministischer Theologie* (Freiburg: Herder, 1990), which soon will be available in English.

36. See especially my books *But She Said* and *Discipleship of Equals*.

37. See the contributions in Elisabeth Schüssler Fiorenza and Mary Collins, eds., *Women — Invisible in Church and Theology*, Concilium 182 (Edinburgh: T. & T. Clark, 1985).

38. For such an analysis see Patricia Hill Collins, *Black Feminist Thought: Knowledge, Consciousness, and the Politics of Empowerment* (Boston: Unwin Hyman, 1990), esp. 3–42 and 201–38.

39. See Gustavo Gutiérrez, *The Power of the Poor in History* (Maryknoll, N.Y.: Orbis Books, 1983).

40. For the articulation of such a feminist social analytic see especially the work of Rosemary Hennessy, *Materialist Feminism and the Politics of Discourse* (New York and London: Routledge, 1993).

41. On this problem see literature and discussion in Elisabeth Schüssler Fiorenza and Shawn M. Copeland, eds., *Violence against Women*, Concilium 1994/1 (Maryknoll, N.Y.: Orbis Books, 1994).

42. See Chris Weedon, *Feminist Practice and Poststructuralist Theory* (Oxford: Blackwell, 1987); Linda Hutcheon, *The Politics of Postmodernism* (New York: Routledge, 1989); Linda Nicholson, ed., *Feminism/Postmodernism* (New York: Routledge, 1990).

43. See Nancy C. M. Hartsock, *Money, Sex and Power: Toward a Feminist Historical Materialism* (Boston: Northeastern University Press, 1985).

44. For a feminist discussion of Michel Foucault's work see Irene Diamond and Lee Quinby, eds., *Feminism and Foucault: Reflections on Resistance* (Boston: Northeastern University Press, 1988); Caroline Ramazanoglu, ed., *Up against Foucault: Explorations of Some Tensions between Foucault and Feminism* (New York: Routledge, 1993).

45. Hennessy, *Materialist Feminism and the Politics of Discourse*, 32.

46. "Patriarchy" is generally either understood in the sense of sexism and gender dualism or used as an undefined label. The term in the "narrow sense" is best understood as "father-right and father-might." However, this translation overlooks that the father as the head of household was in antiquity also lord, master, and husband. Consequently, "patriarchy" connotes a complex system of subordination and domination. Moreover, the patriarchal system of the household was the paradigm for the order of society and state. For a review of the common feminist understanding of patriarchy see V. Beechey, "On Patriarchy," *Feminist Review* 3 (1979): 66–82; G. Lerner, *The Creation of Patriarchy* (New York: Oxford University Press, 1986), 231–41; Christine Schaumberger, "Patriarchat als feminis-

tischer Begriff," in *Wörterbuch der feministischen Theologie* (Gütersloh: Mohn, 1991), 321–23, with literature.

47. See my article "The Politics of Otherness: Biblical Interpretation as a Critical Praxis for Liberation," in Marc H. Ellis and Otto Maduro, *The Future of Liberation Theology: Essays in Honor of Gustavo Gutiérrez* (Maryknoll, N.Y.: Orbis Books, 1989), 311–25.

48. See Klaus Thraede, "Zum historischen Hintergrund der 'Haustafeln' des Neuen Testaments," in *Pietas: Festschrift B. Kötting* (Münster: Aschendorff, 1980), 359–68; D. Lührmann, "Neutestamentliche Haustafeln und antike Ökonomie," *New Testament Studies* 27 (1980/81): 83–97; D. Balch, *Let Wives Be Submissive: The Domestic Code in 1 Peter* (Chico, Calif.: Scholars Press, 1981); D. Balch, "Household Codes," in D. Aune, ed., *Greco-Roman Literature and the New Testament* (Atlanta: Scholars Press, 1988), 25–50.

49. Susan Moller Okin, *Women in Western Political Thought* (Princeton: Princeton University Press, 1979), 15–98; Elizabeth V. Spelman, *Inessential Woman: Problems of Exclusion in Feminist Thought* (Boston: Beacon Press, 1988), 19–56. For Roman patriarchal structures see W. K. Lacey, "Patria Potestas," in Beryl Rawson, ed., *The Family in Ancient Rome: New Perspectives* (Ithaca, N.Y.: Cornell University Press, 1986), 121–44.

50. Page duBois, *Torture and Truth* (New York: Routledge, 1991), 123; for Roman slavery see K. R. Bradley, *Slaves and Masters in the Roman Empire: A Study in Social Control* (New York: Oxford University Press, 1986); Dale B. Martin, *Slavery as Salvation: The Metaphor of Slavery in Pauline Christianity* (New Haven: Yale University Press, 1990), 1–49, paints a positive picture of slavery, probably in order to justify Paul's use of this metaphor.

51. See also M. E. Hawkesworth, *Beyond Oppression: Feminist Theory and Political Strategy* (New York: Continuum, 1990); Hannelore Schröder, "Feministische Gesellschaftstheorie," in Luise F. Pusch, ed., *Feminismus: Inspektion der Herrenkultur* (Frankfurt: Suhrkamp, 1983), 449–78.

52. Cynthia Farrar, *The Origins of Democratic Thinking: The Invention of Politics in Classical Athens* (Cambridge: Cambridge University Press, 1988), 165. However, this work is limited because of its inattention to androcentric language and a lack of awareness that, for instance, the statement "man is the measure" does not refer in general to the individual but only to the autonomy of elite Athenian man.

53. See also chapter 4 in *Bread Not Stone: The Challenge of Feminist Biblical Interpretation* (Boston: Beacon Press, 1985) and Clarice Martin, "The 'Haustafeln' (Household Codes) in African American Biblical Interpretation: 'Free Slaves' and 'Subordinate Women,'" in Cain Hope Felder ed., *Stony the Road We Trod: African American Biblical Interpretation* (Minneapolis: Fortress Press, 1991), 206–31, for a feminist/womanist discussion of the household code texts.

54. These structures have produced kyriocentric theology and spirituality. For instance, Teresa of Avila articulates a notion of obedience according to which even the heavenly Christ submits to church authorities insofar as she has to subject her revelations in obedience to her spiritual "father" and confessor. See Udo Maria Schiffers, "Weisheit des Gehorsams bei Theresa von Avila," in Walter Beier, ed., *Weisheit Gottes — Weisheit der Welt* (St. Ottilien: EOS Verlag, 1987), 2:835–62.

55. For discussion see my article "A Discipleship of Equals: Ekklesial Democracy and Patriarchy in Biblical Perspective," in Eugene C. Bianchi and Rosemary Radford Ruether eds., *A Democratic Catholic Church* (New York: Crossroad, 1992), 17–33.

56. Carol C. Gould, *Rethinking Democracy: Freedom and Social Cooperation in Politics* (Cambridge: Cambridge University Press, 1988); Anne Phillips, *Engendering Democracy* (University Park: Pennsylvania State University Press, 1991).

57. For France see Joan B. Landes, *Women and the Public Sphere in the French Revolution* (Ithaca, N.Y.: Cornell University Press, 1988), who shows that the French Revolution created a rigidly gendered public male sphere that relegated women to the private sphere of the home. Stated baldly, the early modern classical revival — with its political, linguistic, and stylistic overtones — invested public action with a decidedly masculinist ethos. She then goes on to argue that "although women failed to achieve political emancipation, the Revolution bequeathed them an oral identity and a political constitution. Gender became a socially relevant category in post-revolutionary life. Indeed both domesticity — including republican motherhood — and feminism might be viewed as two variant but inter-related outcomes of the transformation of the absolutist public sphere" (13).

58. Joan Cocks, *The Oppositional Imagination: Feminism, Critique, and Political Theory* (New York: Routledge, 1989), 212f.

59. For a fascinating history of the social construction of sex see Thomas Laqueur, *Making Sex: Body and Gender from the Greeks to Freud* (Cambridge: Harvard University Press, 1990).

60. See, e.g., Gayatri Chakravorty Spivak, in Sarah Harasym, ed., *The Post-Colonial Critic: Interviews, Strategies, Dialogues* (New York: Routledge, 1990); Caroline Ramazanoglu, *Feminism and the Contradictions of Oppression* (London: Routledge, 1989).

61. bell hooks, *Talking Back* (Boston: South End Press, 1989), 175.

62. See Aloys Grillmeier, *Christ in Christian Tradition*, vol. 1, *From the Apostolic Age to Chalcedon* (Atlanta: John Knox Press, 1975), 451; Karl-Heinz Ohlig, *Fundamentalchristologie im Spannungsfeld von Christentum und Kultur* (Munich: Kösel, 1986); Michel Clévenot, *Der Triumph des Kreuzes: Geschichte des Christentums im IV. und V. Jahrhundert* (Fribourg: Exodus, 1988).

63. See Jochen Schmidt, *Die Geschichte des Genie-Gedankens in der*

deutschen Literatur, Philosophie und Politik 1750–1945, 2 vols. (Darmstadt: Wissenschaftliche Buchgesellschaft, 1985).

64. Helmut Köster, "The Divine Human Being," *Harvard Theological Review* 78 (1985): 251. However, Köster stresses that the Christian message democratizes the concept of *imitatio Christi* insofar as in the teaching of Jesus the idea of the "imitation of the divine man" is completely absent. "Perfection is giving oneself rather than becoming oneself" (246).

65. Jacob Neusner, *Jews and Christians: The Myth of a Common Tradition* (Philadelphia: SCM/Trinity Press International, 1991). See also Arthur Cohen, *The Myth of the Judeo-Christian Tradition* (New York: Harper & Row, 1969).

66. In her response to this text (communication of July 12, 1994) Julie Miller observed: "I know this is not your primary concern but I would also suggest that resistance to challenges such as yours is not wholly based on a desire for superiority but rather a fundamental fear of losing one's intellectual/ontological/religious identity, i.e., one's 'self' as one always has known it, no matter how debilitating or oppressive that may be. What you are arguing for and against can send people into true spiritual/identity crises; thus resistance to concepts which challenge one's known world can be viewed as a form of psychological self-defense."

67. Regula Strobel, "Feministische Kritik an traditionellen Kreuzestheologien," in Doris Strahm and Regula Strobel, eds., *Vom Verlangen nach Heilwerden: Christologie in feministisch-theologischer Sicht,* 52–65.

68. For a similar argument see Dieter Georgi, "The Interest in Life of Jesus Theology as a Paradigm for the Social History of Biblical Criticism," *Harvard Theological Review* 85, no. 1 (1992): 71–79.

69. See Charles Joseph Hefele, *A History of the Christian Councils from the Original Documents,* ed. and trans. William R. Clark, 2d ed. (Edinburgh: T. & T. Clark, 1894), 1:260.

70. For critical discussion and literature see the paper of Vasiliki Limberis, "The Council of Ephesos," given at the Ephesus Symposium, March 25–29, 1994, at Harvard Divinity School. I am grateful to professor Limberis for sharing her manuscript with me.

71. For the meaning of the term see the excellent study of J. H. Reumann, "The Uses of 'Oikonomia' and Related Terms in Greek Sources to about A.D. 100 as a Background for Patristic Application," dissertation, University of Pennsylvania, 1957.

72. President Bush's "new world order" seems to have here its historical roots. For a somewhat uncritical assessment of the impact of this "new world order" on women see Patricia Aburdene and John Naisbitt, *Megatrends for Women* (New York: Villard Books, 1992), 265–318.

73. T. Herbert Bindley, ed., *The Oecumenical Documents of the Faith* (London: Methuen, 1950), 232. It is interesting to note that the text does not mention the empress Pulcheria, the sister of Theodosius II, but only her

husband, Marcian, although her powerful influence controlled the synodal process. This example not only illustrates the silencing functions of kyrio-centric texts, but also underscores the implication of elite women in the maintenance of kyriarchal power. See Henry Chadwick, *The Early Church* (Grand Rapids: Eerdmans, 1968).

74. Bindley, *The Oecumenical Documents of the Faith*, 232.

75. For the imperial politics that determined the "politics of meaning" that the council promulgated, see especially Grillmeier, *Christ in Christian Tradition*, vol. 1, *From the Apostolic Age to Chalcedon*.

76. Odell-Scott, *A Post-Patriarchal Christology*, 100.

77. Ibid., 113.

78. This comes clearly to the fore in the discussion of Galatians 3:28, where he insists that economic, political, and sexual difference is not abol-ished in baptism. That he is especially interested in sexual difference comes to the fore in his discussion of 1 Corinthians 11:2–16, where he argues that Paul opposes patriarchal relations in favor of equality between the sexes. However, in order to sustain this argument he must ascribe the hierarchical/kyriarchal arguments to the Corinthian community. This is a familiar ploy of exegetes to "rescue" Paul from his feminist critics. For a feminist read-ing of the text see especially Antoinette Clark Wire, *The Corinthian Women Prophets: A Reconstruction through Paul's Rhetoric* (Minneapolis: Fortress Press, 1990).

79. See, however, Basil Studer, "Consubstantialis Patri — Consubstan-tialis Matri: une antithese cristologique chez Leon le Grand" *Studia Patris-tica* 13, no. 2 (1975): 286–94. Studer argues that this formulation expresses the "double solidarity" of Christ.

80. Bindley, *The Oecumenical Documents of the Faith*, 234–35.

81. For this concept see Michel Pecheux, *Language, Semantics, and Ide-ology* (New York: St. Martin's Press, 1975). In any discursive formation the "preconstructed" produces the effect of an "always already given," the "common-sense" meaning, or "what everyone already knows."

82. Grillmeier, *Christ in Christian Tradition*, 543.

83. For the elaboration of this expression see Hazel V. Carby, "On the Threshold of Women's Era: Lynching, Empire and Sexuality," in Henry L. Gates, ed., *Race, Writing, and Difference* (Chicago: University of Chicago Press, 1986), 301–28. See also the article by Kwok Pui-lan, "The Image of the White Lady: Gender and Race in Christian Mission," in Anne Carr and Elisabeth Schüssler Fiorenza, eds., *The Special Nature of Women?* Concilium (London: SCM Press, 1991), 19–27.

84. For a location and discussion of this problem in feminist discourses see, e.g., Tania Modleski, *Feminism without Women: Culture and Criticism in a "Postfeminist" Age* (New York: Routledge, 1991), as well as references in note 1 above.

85. See Hennessy, *Materialist Feminism and the Politics of Discourse*, 33–36.

86. Ibid., 75.

87. Ibid., 76.

88. I use the term here in both senses of the word's meaning: (*a*) brought into being and (*b*) defined in terms of gender.

89. For elaboration see *But She Said*, 125–32. For a psychological analysis of why women collaborate in their own oppression see Jessica Benjamin, *The Bonds of Love: Psychoanalysis, Feminism, and the Problem of Domination* (New York: Pantheon Books, 1988).

90. See my introduction to the tenth anniversary edition of *In Memory of Her: A Feminist Theological Reconstruction of Christian Origins* (New York: Crossroad, 1994).

91. Amy Jill Levine, "Who Caters the Q Affair? Feminist Observations on Q Paraenesis," *Semeia* 50 (1990): 145–61.

92. See, for instance, Bruce J. Malina, *The New Testament World: Insights from Cultural Anthropology* (Atlanta: John Knox, 1981), and Bruce J. Malina and Jerome H. Neyrey, "First-Century Personality: Dyadic, Not Individual," in Jerome H. Neyrey, ed., *The Social World of Luke-Acts: Models for Interpretation* (Peabody, Mass.: Hendrickson Publishers, 1991), 67–96. For a critical assessment see Mary Ann Tolbert, "Social, Sociological, and Anthropological Methods," in Elisabeth Schüssler Fiorenza, ed., *Searching the Scriptures*, vol. 1, *A Feminist Introduction* (New York: Crossroad, 1993), 255–72.

93. For a critical assessment of the anthropological construct of "the Mediterranean" see especially the articles by Michael Herzfeld, "The Horns of the Mediterranean Dilemma," *American Ethnologist* 11 (1984): 439–55, and " 'As in Your Own House': Hospitality, Ethnography, and the Stereotype of the Mediterranean Society," in David Gilmore, ed., *Honor and Shame and the Unity of the Mediterranean* (Washington, D.C.: American Anthropological Association, 1987).

94. Basil Studer, "Das Christusdogma der Alten Kirche und das neutestamentliche Christusbild," *Münchener Theologische Zeitschrift* 44 (1993): 13–22. See also his book *Gott und unsere Erlösung im Glauben der alten Kirche* (Düsseldorf: Patmos, 1985).

95. However, a footnote in "Das Christusdogma der Alten Kirche," 21 n. 31, discloses his kyriarchal interests: "In an explanation of the history of trinitarian doctrine, one cannot stress too much that from the very beginning the relation between God and Jesus was expressed with the metaphor of fatherhood-sonship.... Regrettably the relation between father and son at first was determined too one-sidedly in a cosmological frame of reference (*per quem omnia facta sunt*) whereas the Easter event (the acceptance of the son's obedience by the father) was not sufficiently attended to. However, Augustine had already resolved the tension between these two ways of determining the relation between father and son; he anchors the obedience of the only righteous one in his eternal sonship." This a classic statement of a kyriarchal relationship.

Chapter 2: And Mary Went
into the Hill Country

1. Dorothy E. Smith, *Texts, Facts, and Femininity: Exploring the Relations of Ruling* (New York: Routledge, 1993), 159.

2. Elaine Showalter, "Feminist Criticism in the Wilderness," in Elaine Showalter, ed., *Feminist Criticism: Essays on Women, Literature and Theory* (New York: Pantheon Books, 1985), 243–70.

3. Annette Kolodny, "Dancing through the Minefield: Some Observations on the Theory, Practice and Politics of a Feminist Literary Criticism," in Showalter, *Feminist Criticism,* 144–67.

4. For discussion and literature see Michael E. Lodahl, *Shekinah/Spirit: Divine Presence in Jewish and Christian Religion* (New York: Paulist Press, 1992).

5. For instance, twenty years ago scholars could use the terms "maleness," "masculinity," and "manhood" with reference to Jesus without recognizing that such discourse posed a theological problem. See, e.g., C. F. D. Moule, "The Manhood of Jesus in the New Testament," in S. W. Sykes and J. P. Clayton, eds., *Christ, Faith and History,* Cambridge Studies in Christology (Cambridge: Cambridge University Press, 1972), 95–110.

6. For an overview of different christological proposals see Mary Gerhart, "Imaging Christ in Art, Politics, Spirituality: An Overview," in Francis A. Eigo, ed., *Imaging Christ: Politics, Art, Spirituality* (Villanova, Pa.: Villanova University Press, 1991), 1–46, and Ellen Leonard, "Women and Christ: Toward Inclusive Christologies," *Toronto Journal of Theology* 6, no. 2 (1990): 266–85.

7. In her Marion Thomson Wright lecture on February 20, 1993, at Rutgers University, Nell Irvin Painter pointed out that Frances Dana Gage published this speech twelve years after the event as a response to Harriet Beecher Stowe's profile article "Sojourner Truth, the Libyan Sibyl," which had appeared in the *Atlantic Monthly.* See Nell Irvin Painter, "The Writing and Selling of Sojourner Truth," in her study packet *An Introduction to Black Women's Studies* (Princeton University, Fall 1993). For further discussion and bibliography see Nell Painter, "Truth, Sojourner (c. 1799–1885)," in Darlene Clark Hine, ed., *Black Women in America: A Historical Encyclopedia* (Brooklyn: Carlson, 1993), 1172–76; see also Margaret Washington, ed., *Narrative of Sojourner Truth* (New York: Vintage, 1993), especially the introduction, and Karen Baker-Fletcher, "Anna Julia Cooper and Sojourner Truth: Two Nineteenth-Century Black Interpreters of Scripture," in Elisabeth Schüssler Fiorenza, ed., *Searching the Scriptures,* vol. 1, *A Feminist Introduction* (New York: Crossroad, 1993), 41–51.

8. For the elaboration of this notion and discussion of the literature on this concept see Elisabeth Schüssler Fiorenza, *But She Said: Feminist Practices of Biblical Interpretation* (Boston: Beacon Press, 1992), 105–14.

9. Smith, *Texts, Facts, and Femininity,* 160.

10. See Maria Mies, *Patriarchy and Accumulation on a World Scale: Women in the International Division of Labor* (London: Zed Books, 1986).

11. See the excellent systemic analyses in Elisabeth Schüssler Fiorenza and Anne Carr, eds., *Women, Work and Poverty*, Concilium 194 (Edinburgh: T. & T. Clark, 1987).

12. Susan Moller Okin, *Women in Western Political Thought* (Princeton: Princeton University Press, 1979), 73–96.

13. See Elisabeth List, "Homo Politicus — Femina Privata: Thesen zur Kritik der politischen Anthropologie," in J. Conrad and U. Konnertz, *Weiblichkeit in der Moderne: Ansätze feministischer Vernunftkritik* (Tübingen: edition diskord, 1986), 75–95.

14. See, e.g., the biographical reflection and analysis of apartheid as an ideology and institution to maintain a "servant people" by Mark Mathabene, *Kaffir Boy: The True Story of a Black Youth's Coming of Age in Apartheid South Africa* (New York: Macmillan, 1986).

15. Genevieve Lloyd, *Man of Reason: Male and Female in Western Philosophy* (Minneapolis: University of Minnesota Press, 1984); see also her article, "The Man of Reason," in Ann Garry and Marilyn Pearsall, eds., *Women, Knowledge, and Reality: Explorations in Feminist Philosophy* (New York: Routledge, 1992), 111: "By the Man of Reason I mean the ideal of rationality associated with the rational philosophers of the seventeenth century. And, secondly, something more nebulous — the residue of that ideal in our contemporary consciousness.... The main feature of the Man of Reason that I am concerned to bring into focus is his maleness." See also Sarah Coakley, "Gender and Knowledge in Western Philosophy: The 'Man of Reason' and the 'Feminine Other' in Enlightenment Thought," in Anne Carr and Elisabeth Schüssler Fiorenza, eds., *The Special Nature of Women?* Concilium (London: SCM Press, 1991), 75–84.

16. See, e.g., Joan Jacobs Brumberg, "The Ethnological Mirror: American Women and Their Heathen Sisters, 1870–1910," in Barbara J. Harris and JoAnn K. McNamara, eds., *Women and the Structure of Society: Selected Research from the Fifth Berkshire Conference on the History of Women* (Durham, N.C.: Duke University Press, 1984), 108–28.

17. See my article "The Politics of Otherness: Biblical Interpretation as a Critical Praxis for Liberation," in Marc H. Ellis and Otto Maduro, eds., *The Future of Liberation Theology: Essays in Honor of Gustavo Gutiérrez* (Maryknoll, N.Y.: Orbis Books, 1989), 311–25, and Kwok Pui-lan, "The Image of the 'White Lady': Gender and Race in Christian Mission," in Carr and Schüssler Fiorenza, *The Special Nature of Women?* 19–27; see also Kwok Pui-lan, *Chinese Women and Christianity, 1860–1927* (Atlanta: Scholars Press, 1992).

18. Rosemary Radford Ruether, "Male Clericalism and the Dread of Women," *The Ecumenist* 11 (1973): 65–69.

19. See the analysis of this situation in my keynote address at the Second Ordination Conference in 1978, reprinted in *Discipleship of Equals:*

A Critical Feminist Ekklesia-logy of Liberation (New York: Crossroad, 1993), 129–50, esp. 140–44. For a comparative ecumenical view see also Jacqueline Field-Bibb, *Women towards Priesthood: Ministerial Politics and Feminist Practice* (New York: Cambridge University Press, 1991).

20. For the right-wing, conservative tendencies of such a "biologization" process see, e.g., Renate Bridenthal, Atina Grossmann, and Marion Kaplan, eds., *When Biology Became Destiny: Women in Weimar and Nazi Germany* (New York: Monthly Review Press, 1984).

21. Elizabeth A. Johnson, "Redeeming the Name of Christ: Christology," in Catherine Mowry LaCugna, ed., *Freeing Theology: The Essentials of Theology in Feminist Perspective* (San Francisco: Harper, 1993), 118f.

22. As Ann Oakley, *Sex, Gender and Society* (New York: Harper & Row, 1972), 191, already observed in 1972: "One expert on intersexuality has said that it is impossible to define male and female genital morphologies as distinct: they exist as a continuum of possible developments and are thus a constant reminder, not of biological polarity of male and female but of their biological identity."

23. N. Leys Stepan, "Race and Gender," in Sandra Harding, ed., *The "Racial" Economy of Science: Toward a Democratic Future* (Bloomington: Indiana University Press, 1993), 361.

24. Dennis Baron, *Grammar and Gender* (New Haven: Yale University Press, 1986).

25. Robert H. Robins, *A Short History of Linguistics* (London: Longmans, 1979), 137.

26. *English Grammar,* 1795; see Baron, *Grammar and Gender,* 24.

27. See Casey Miller and Kate Swift, *Words and Women: New Language in New Times* (Garden City, N.Y.: Doubleday Anchor Books, 1977).

28. See Denise Riley, *"Am I That Name?" Feminism and the Category of 'Women' in History* (Minneapolis: University of Minnesota Press, 1988).

29. The same can be said for race classifications; see Gloria A. Marshall, "Racial Classifications: Popular and Scientific," in Harding, *The "Racial" Economy of Science,* 116–27.

30. For a comparison of sexist and racist language see the contributions in Mary Vetterling-Braggin, ed., *Sexist Language: A Modern Philosophical Analysis* (Totowa, N.J.: Rowman and Littlefield, 1981), 249–319.

31. Okin, *Women in Western Political Thought,* 135.

32. For a feminist discussion of the interplay between language and identity see, for instance, the contributions in Joyce Penfield, ed., *Women and Language in Transition* (Albany: State University of New York Press, 1987).

33. Mary Daly, *Beyond God the Father: Toward a Philosophy of Women's Liberation* (Boston: Beacon Press, 1973), 69.

34. Daphne Hampson and Rosemary Radford Ruether, "Is There a Place for Feminists in a Christian Church?" *Blackfriars* (January 1987): 2.

35. Daphne Hampson, *Theology and Feminism* (Oxford: Blackwell, 1990), 51.

36. Hampson and Ruether, "Is There a Place for Feminists?" 7.

37. For an appreciative review see Mary Hembrow Snyder, *The Christology of Rosemary Radford Ruether: A Critical Introduction* (Mystic, Conn.: Twenty-Third Publications, 1988).

38. Her most recent discussion on christology is entitled "Can Christology Be Liberated from Patriarchy?" in Maryanne Stevens, ed., *Reconstructing the Christ Symbol: Essays in Feminist Christology* (New York: Paulist Press, 1993), 7–29; it basically follows the same course of argument.

39. Rosemary Radford Ruether, *Sexism and God-Talk: Toward a Feminist Theology* (Boston: Beacon Press, 1983), 137.

40. Ibid., 138.

41. See Nancy Tuana, *The Less Noble Sex: Scientific, Religious, and Philosophical Conceptions of Woman's Nature* (Bloomington: Indiana University Press, 1993).

42. Jacquelyn Grant, *White Women's Christ, Black Women's Jesus* (Atlanta: Scholars Press, 1989), 144.

43. Ibid., 6.

44. See, e.g., Virginia Fabella, "A Common Methodology for Diverse Christologies," in Virginia Fabella and Mercy Amba Oduyoye, eds., *With Passion and Compassion: Third World Women Doing Theology* (Maryknoll, N.Y.: Orbis Books, 1988), 108–17; Teresa M. Hinga, "Jesus Christ and the Liberation of Women in Africa," in Mercy Amba Oduyoye and Musimbi R. A. Kanyoro, eds., *The Will to Arise: Women, Tradition, and the Church in Africa* (Maryknoll, N.Y.: Orbis Books, 1992), 183–94.

45. For an excellent elaboration of such a theological analysis see María Pilar Aquino, *Our Cry for Life: Feminist Theology from Latin America,* trans. Dinah Livingstone (Maryknoll, N.Y.: Orbis Books, 1993).

46. Grant, *White Women's Christ, Black Women's Jesus,* 220.

47. Isabel Carter Heyward, *Speaking of Christ: A Lesbian Feminist Voice* (New York: Pilgrim Press, 1989), 21.

48. Isabel Carter Heyward, *The Redemption of God: A Theology of Mutual Relation* (New York: University Press of America, 1980), 30.

49. Heyward, *Speaking of Christ,* 84.

50. Isabel Carter Heyward, *Touching Our Strength: The Erotics of Power and the Love of God* (San Francisco: Harper & Row, 1989), 192–93 (glossary).

51. Rita Nakashima Brock, *Journeys by Heart: A Christology of Erotic Power* (New York: Crossroad, 1988), 57.

52. Ibid., 66.

53. Ibid., 52.

54. Ibid., 67.

55. Ibid., 115 n. 8.

56. Susan Brooks Thistlethwaite, *Sex, Race and God: Christian Feminism in Black and White* (New York: Crossroad, 1989), 107.

57. Mary Grey, *Feminism, Redemption, and the Christian Tradition*

(Mystic, Conn.: Twenty-Third Publications, 1990), 300. See also her most recent book *The Wisdom of Fools? Seeking Revelation for Today* (London: SPCK, 1993).

58. Mary Grey, "Jesus — Einsamer Held oder Offenbarung beziehungs-hafter Macht?" in Doris Strahm and Regula Strobel, eds., *Vom Verlangen nach Heilwerden: Christologie in feministisch-theologischer Sicht* (Fribourg: Exodus, 1991), 167.

59. Mary Grey, *Feminism, Redemption and the Christian Tradition*, 211.

60. Manuela Kalsky, "Vom Verlangen nach Heil: Eine feministische Christologie oder messianische Heilsgeschichten?" in *Vom Verlangen nach Heilwerden*, 226.

61. Cathy Kelsey, "Feminist Reconstructions of Christology," research paper written for the Harvard Divinity School colloquium on Religion, Gender, and Culture, which I chaired in the spring semester 1992.

62. In her review of *Vom Verlangen nach Heilwerden* ("Zwischen Patri-archat, Antijudaismus und Totalitarismus: Anmerkungen zu einer Theolo-gie in feministisch-theologischer Sicht," *Orientierung* 56 [1992]: 130–35), Dorothee Soelle chides feminist theologians for writing in the intellectual-ized language of the academy and suggests that they should explore the language of love in prayer and liturgy as a more appropriate source for feminist christology. She quotes explicitly as such a recommended example the medieval language about the "most beautiful Lord Jesus" (*Schönster Herr Jesus*).

63. See, e.g., Janice Radway, *Reading the Romance: Women, Patriarchy and Popular Literature* (Chapel Hill: University of North Carolina Press, 1991); Linda K. Christian-Smith, *Becoming a Woman through Romance* (New York: Routledge, 1990).

64. See her very significant lecture "Jesus the Christ and the Woman Prot-estant Minister in the Pastoral Praxis of the Congregation," which she gave in the Evangelische Akademie Hofgeismar in April 1993. I want to thank Julie Hopkins for making available to me the manuscript of this paper, which to my knowledge has not yet appeared in published form.

65. Erlene Stetson, ed., *Black Sister: Poetry by Black American Women, 1746–1980* (Bloomington: Indiana University Press, 1981), 24f.

66. Participants in workshops and seminars generally object to this state-ment because they think I glorify the Christian evangelical experience of Sojourner Truth and advocate that feminists ought to take it at face value or come up with a similar one. However, I am concerned here with the *structural significance* of this experience and argue that it must be critically elaborated and explored in a feminist hermeneutics of liberation.

67. Most recently see Gutiérrez's article and the replies by John de Gruchy and Stephen May as well as his reply to them: Gustavo Gutiérrez, "Joy in the Midst of Suffering," in Hilary D. Regan and Alan J. Torrance, eds., *Christ and Context: The Confrontation between Gospel and Culture* (Edinburgh: T. & T. Clark, 1993), 78–104.

68. See also Sharon D. Welch, *Communities of Resistance and Solidarity* (Maryknoll, N.Y.: Orbis Books, 1985), and *A Feminist Ethics of Risk* (Minneapolis: Fortress, 1991).

69. Mary McClintock Fulkerson, "Contesting Feminist Canons: Discourse and the Problem of Sexist Texts," *Journal of Feminist Studies in Religion* 7, no. 2 (1991): 53–75, rightly has criticized the ascription of sexism to texts and argues that feminists should respect fundamentalist biblical readings by women as potentially self-affirming. However, rather than further developing a critical hermeneutics of proclamation for liberation, she is too much concerned to prove the "originality" of her own approach. Hence she not only engages in fruitless polemics that misconstrue other feminist positions but also adopts uncritically a postmodern "ludic" reading. For the distinction between "ludic," i.e., "playfully relativistic," and "resistance" postmodernism see Teresa Ebert, "The 'Difference' of Postmodern Feminism," *College English* 53 (1991): 886–904.

Chapter 3: The Power of Naming

1. Judith Plaskow, "Feminist Anti-Judaism and the Christian God," *Journal of Feminist Studies in Religion* 7, no. 2 (1991): 106.

2. For this expression see the book by Haig A. Bosmajian, *The Language of Oppression* (Lanham, Md.: University Press of America, 1983).

3. See Josef Imbach, *Wem gehört Jesus? Seine Bedeutung für Juden, Christen und Moslems* (Munich: Kösel, 1989).

4. For such an articulation see Hans Küng and Karl-Josef Kuschel, *A Global Ethic: The Declaration of the World Parliament of Religions* (New York: Continuum, 1994).

5. For a review of christological discourses see Eugene B. Borowitz, *Contemporary Christologies: A Jewish Response* (New York: Paulist, 1980).

6. See the diverse contributions in Hans Küng and Jürgen Moltmann, eds., *Fundamentalism as an Ecumenical Challenge*, Concilium 1992/3 (London: SCM Press, 1992).

7. See John Hick and Paul F. Knitter, eds., *The Myth of Christian Uniqueness: Toward a Pluralistic Theology of Religions* (Maryknoll, N.Y.: Orbis Books, 1987); see especially the contributions of Marjorie Hewitt Suchocki, "In Search of Justice: Religious Pluralism from a Feminist Perspective," 149–61, and Paul F. Knitter, "Toward a Liberation Theology of Religions," 178–200.

8. On Jewish-Christian dialogue from the perspectives of political and liberation theologies, see Dan Cohn-Sherbok, *On Earth as It Is in Heaven: Jews, Christians, and Liberation Theology* (Maryknoll, N.Y.: Orbis Books, 1987); Marc H. Ellis, *Toward a Jewish Theology of Liberation* (Maryknoll, N.Y.: Orbis Books, 1987); and the contributions in David Tracy and Elis-

abeth Schüssler Fiorenza, eds., *The Holocaust as Interruption,* Concilium 175 (Edinburgh: T. & T. Clark, 1984).

9. For such a positioning see also Rosemary Radford Ruether, "Feminism and Jewish-Christian Dialogue: Particularism and Universalism in the Search for Religious Truth," in Hick and Knitter, *The Myth of Christian Uniqueness,* 137–48; for the pros and cons of feminist interreligious dialogue see Ursula King, "Das verschüttete Erbe der Frauen," in Brigitte Hübner and Hartmut Meesmann, eds., *Streitfall feministische Theologie* (Düsseldorf: Patmos, 1993), 287–95, and Michael von Bück, "Ein Wandel des Bewusstseins kündigt sich an," ibid., 296–304.

10. See, e.g., Leonard Swidler et al., eds., *Bursting the Bonds? A Jewish-Christian Dialogue on Jesus and Paul* (Maryknoll, N.Y.: Orbis Books, 1990).

11. For the German discussion see Marie Therese Wacker, "Feminist Theology and Anti-Judaism: The Status of the Discussion and the Context of the Problem in the Federal Republic of Germany," *Journal of Feminist Studies in Religion* 7, no. 2 (1991): 109–16, and Leonore Siegele Wenschkewitz, ed., *Verdrängte Vergangenheit, die uns bedrängt: Feministische Theologie in der Verantwortung für die Geschichte* (Munich: Kaiser, 1988). See also Christine Schaumberger, ed., *Weil wir nicht vergessen wollen... Zu einer feministischen Theologie im deutschen Kontext,* AnFragen 1 (Münster: Morgana Frauenbuchverlag, 1987).

12. Annette Daum and Deborah McCauley, "Jewish Christian Feminist Dialogue: A Wholistic Vision," *Union Seminary Quarterly Review* 38 (1983): 147–218.

13. On Jewish-Christian dialogue in Germany see also Marianne Wallach-Faller, "Wenn Frauen die männliche Sicht verinnerlichen," in Hübner and Meesmann, *Streitfall feministische Theologie,* 269–76, and Martin Stöhr, "Die verheissene Einheit steht auf dem Spiel," ibid., 277–86.

14. James H. Charlesworth, ed., *Jews and Christians: Exploring the Past, Present and Future* (New York: Crossroad, 1990), 14.

15. James H. Charlesworth, ed., *Jesus' Jewishness: Exploring the Place of Jesus within Early Judaism* (New York: Crossroad/American Interfaith Institute, 1991).

16. A. Roy Eckardt, "Salient Jewish-Christian Issues of Today: A Christian Exploration," ibid., 151–78.

17. My first attempt to participate in the discussion was at the Seventh Jewish-Christian Dialogue held in 1983 in Boston.

18. Judith Plaskow, "Christian Feminism and Anti-Judaism, *Cross Currents* 33 (1978): 306–9.

19. See Plaskow's most recent contribution, "Anti-Judaism in Feminist Christian Interpretation," in Elisabeth Schüssler Fiorenza, ed., *Searching the Scriptures,* vol. 1, *A Feminist Introduction* (New York: Crossroad, 1993), 117–29.

20. See also Susannah Heschel, "Jüdisch-feministische Theologie und

Antijudaismus in christlich-feministischer Theologie," in Wenschkewitz, *Verdrängte Vergangenheit, die uns bedrängt,* 54–103; see also Susannah Heschel, "Anti-Judaism in Christian Feminist Theology," *Tikkun* 5, no. 3 (1990): 26–28.

21. This expression seems to have been coined by Leonard Swidler, but this line of argument is found in many publications. See Leonard Swidler, "Jesus Was a Feminist," *Catholic World* 212 (1971): 177–83. See also his book *Biblical Affirmations of Women* (Philadelphia: Westminster, 1979).

22. Alan Segal, *Rebecca's Children* (Cambridge: Harvard University Press, 1987).

23. I want to thank Judith Plaskow for her careful reading of a previous draft of this chapter. In her letter of October 28, 1992, she points out that in the course of my discussion I have never answered this rhetorical question. However, I do not think that a Christian feminist should or can answer this question. Rather, I suggest, it is up to Jewish feminists to wrestle with it. Hence, I will focus in this chapter on the problems which anti-Judaism poses for a Christian feminist theological discourse.

24. Luke T. Johnson, "The New Testament's Anti-Jewish Slander and the Conventions of Ancient Polemic," *Journal of Biblical Literature* 108, no. 3 (1989): 419–41, cavalierly solves the problem of anti-Judaism in the Christian Testament by pointing out that such slanderous behavior was common in the first century. He seems not to have read anything I have written when he characterizes my approach as liberationist censorship, "which is frequently based on the premise that texts should reflect our liberated self-understanding and practice. If they offend our sensibilities, they are dispensable" (421). In a footnote (n. 4) he credits Rosemary Radford Ruether as having defined the "basic liberationist approach" and me for having extensively developed it in *In Memory of Her.* Such sloppy but politically expedient scholarship still seems to be acceptable in biblical studies today!

25. For a concise introduction to the various methodological approaches in biblical scholarship see, e.g., Steven L. McKenzie and Stephen R. Haynes, eds., *To Each Its Own Meaning: An Introduction to Biblical Criticisms and Their Applications* (Louisville: Westminster/John Knox Press, 1993).

26. On the problem of a "New Testament Theology" see Hendrikus Boers, *What Is New Testament Theology?* (Philadelphia: Fortress Press, 1979); Heikki Räisänen, *Beyond New Testament Theology: A Story and a Programme* (London: SCM Press, 1990); John Reumann, ed., *The Promise and Practice of Biblical Theology* (Minneapolis: Augsburg Fortress, 1991).

27. For discussions of biblical arguments see, for instance, Krister Stendahl, *The Bible and the Role of Women* (Philadelphia: Fortress Press, 1966), and more recently Karen Jo Torjesen, *When Women Were Priests: Women's Leadership in the Early Church and the Scandal of Their Subordination in the Rise of Christianity* (San Francisco: Harper & Row, 1993). For discussions of the Vatican's argument against the ordination of women see Arlene

and Leonard Swidler, eds., *Women Priests: A Catholic Commentary on the Vatican Declaration* (New York: Paulist Press, 1977); Carroll Stuhlmueller, ed., *Women and Priesthood: Future Directions* (Collegeville, Minn.: Liturgical Press, 1978). For the ecumenical discussion see Brita Stendahl, *The Force of Tradition: A Case Study of Women Priests in Sweden* (Philadelphia: Fortress Press, 1985), and Jacqueline Field-Bibb, *Women towards Priesthood: Ministerial Politics and Feminist Praxis* (Cambridge: Cambridge University Press, 1991) with extensive documentation.

28. For literature and discussion see Robert Jewett, "New Testament Christology: The Current Dialogue between Systematic Theologians and Biblical Scholars," Larry Hurtado, "New Testament Christology: Retrospect and Prospect," and Patrick R. Keifert, "Interpretive Paradigms: A Proposal Concerning New Testament Christology," in Robert Jewett, ed., *Christology and Exegesis: New Approaches,* Semeia 30 (Decatur, Ga.: Scholars Press, 1984).

29. For instance, in her review of *Vom Verlangen nach Heilwerden* Dorothee Soelle criticizes the editors Doris Strahm and Regula Strobel for not incorporating more biblical essays, because in her opinion such an inclusion would have "modified the modernist slant of the book." Dorothee Soelle, "Zwischen Patriarchat, Antijudaismus und Totalitarismus: Anmerkungen zu einer Christologie in feministisch theologischer Sicht," *Orientierung* 56 (1992): 130–35.

30. Pamela Dickey Young, *Feminist Theology/Christian Theology* (Minneapolis: Fortress Press, 1990), 80–90.

31. See also Harvey Cox, "Rabbi Yeshua Ben Yoseph: Reflections on Jesus' Jewishness and the Interfaith Dialogue," in Charlesworth, *Jesus' Jewishness,* 27–62.

32. For the elaboration of the kyriarchal sex/gender system see chap. 2.

33. For malestream accounts see, e.g., Gerd Theissen, *The Shadow of the Galilean: The Quest for the Historical Jesus in Narrative Form* (Philadelphia: Fortress, 1987); Björn Krondorfer, ed., *Body and Bible: Interpreting and Experiencing Biblical Narratives* (Philadelphia: Trinity Press International, 1992).

34. For instance, Renita J. Weems, *Just a Sister Away: A Womanist Vision of Women's Relationships in the Bible* (San Diego: LuraMedia, 1988); Alicia Suskin Ostriker, *Feminist Revision and the Bible* (Oxford: Blackwell, 1993); Martha A. Kirk, C.C.V.I., *Tears, Milk and Honey: Celebrations of Biblical Women's Stories* (Kansas City, Mo.: Sheed & Ward, 1987); and especially the work of Miriam Therese Winter.

35. For the theoretical elaboration of such a hermeneutics see my book *Bread Not Stone: The Challenge of Feminist Biblical Interpretation* (Boston: Beacon Press, 1984).

36. Rachel Conrad Wahlberg, *Jesus according to a Woman* (New York: Paulist Press, 1975), and *Jesus and the Freed Woman* (New York: Paulist Press, 1978).

37. Elisabeth Moltmann-Wendel, *The Women around Jesus* (New York: Crossroad, 1982).

38. Hanna Wolff, *Jesus, der Mann* (Stuttgart and Berlin: Kreuz Verlag, 1979).

39. Christa Mulack, *Jesus, der Gesalbte der Frauen* (Stuttgart and Berlin: Kreuz Verlag, 1987). See also her books *Die Weiblichkeit Gottes: Matriarchale Voraussetzungen des Gottesbildes* (Stuttgart and Berlin: Kreuz Verlag, 1983) and *Maria — Die geheime Göttin im Christentum* (Stuttgart and Berlin: Kreuz Verlag, 1985). However, see the critical discussion of Mulack's work by Doris Brockmann, "Die Weiblichkeit Gottes: Zu Christa Mulack's Programmatik der Neubestimmung des Göttlichen," in Marie-Theres Wacker, ed., *Der Gott der Männer und die Frauen* (Düsseldorf: Patmos, 1987), 70–92, as well as Jutta Flatters, "Von der Aufwertung des 'Weiblichen' und seinem Preis: Kritische Anmerkungen zu Christa Mulack's 'Jesus — der Gesalbte der Frauen,' " in Wenschkewitz, ed., *Verdrängte Vergangenheit,* 164–80. Both review articles underscore the anti-Jewish implications of such a conceptualization and interpretation of Jesus in terms of cultural "femininity/womanhood" (*Weiblichkeit*).

40. Elisabeth Moltmann-Wendel, "Beziehung — die vergessene Dimension der Christologie: Neutestamentliche Ansatzpunkte feministischer Christologie," in Strahm and Strobel, *Vom Verlangen nach Heilwerden,* 100–111. See also her "Christ in Feminist Context," in Hilary Regan and Alan J. Torrance, eds., *Christ and Context: The Confrontation between Gospel and Culture* (Edinburgh: T. & T. Clark, 1993), 105–16.

41. Moltmann-Wendel, "Christ in Feminist Context," 116.

42. In Regan and Torrance, *Christ and Context,* 128.

43. Gail Paterson Corrington, *Her Image of Salvation: Female Saviors and Formative Christianity* (Louisville: Westminster/John Knox Press, 1992), 33. For a different discussion and critical evaluation of the same biblical text see my book *But She Said,* 51–78.

44. Virginia Burrus, "Word and Flesh: The Bodies and Sexuality of Ascetic Women in Christian Antiquity," *Journal of Feminist Studies in Religion* 10, no. 1 (1994): 26–51; see also Patricia Cox Miller, "The Devil's Gateway: An Eros of Difference in the Dream of Perpetua," *Dreaming* 2 (1992): 62.

45. See the contributions in Elizabeth Struthers Malbon and Adele Berlin, eds., *Characterization in Biblical Literature,* Semeia 63 (Atlanta: Scholars Press, 1993), especially the article by Alice Bach, "Signs of the Flesh: Observations on Characterization in the Bible," ibid., 61–79.

46. Vernon K. Robbins, "Using a Socio-Rhetorical Poetics to Develop a Unified Method: The Woman Who Anointed Jesus as a Test Case," in Eugene H. Lovering, Jr., ed., *Society of Biblical Literature, 1992 Seminar Papers* (Atlanta: Scholars Press, 1992), 311.

47. See, for instance, the fresco at Dura Europos. See Warren G. Moon, "Nudity and Narrative: Observations on the Frescoes from the Dura

Synagogue," *Journal of the American Academy of Religion* 40 (1992): 587–658.

48. Robbins, "Using a Socio-Rhetorical Poetics," 313.

49. Ben Witherington III, *Women and the Genesis of Christianity* (Cambridge: Cambridge University Press, 1990), xii and 245f.

50. For a discussion of the book's reception see my introduction to the tenth anniversary edition: Elisabeth Schüssler Fiorenza, *In Memory of Her: A Feminist Theological Reconstruction of Christian Origins* (New York: Crossroad, 1994).

51. Witherington, *Women and the Genesis of Christianity,* 248.

52. For a historical review and bibliography see Richard H. Hiers, *Jesus and Ethics: Four Interpretations: Adolf von Harnack, Albert Schweitzer, Rudolf Bultmann and C. H. Dodd* (Philadelphia: Westminster Press, 1968); Dieter Georgi, "Historischer Jesus," *Theologische Realenzyklopädie* 20 (1990): 566–75; Dieter Georgi, "The Interest in Life of Jesus Theology as a Paradigm for the Social History of Biblical Criticism," *Harvard Theological Review* 85, no. 1 (1992): 51–83; Marcus J. Borg, "A Renaissance in Jesus Studies," *Theology Today* 45 (1988): 280–92; Marcus J. Borg, "Portraits of Jesus in Contemporary North American Scholarship," *Harvard Theological Review* 84, no. 1 (1991): 1–22; Marcus J. Borg, *Jesus in Contemporary Scholarship* (Philadelphia: Trinity Press International, 1994); Ferdinand Hahn, "Umstrittenes Jesusbild?" *Münchener Theologische Zeitschrift* 44 (1993): 95–107; Daniel J. Harrington, "The Jewishness of Jesus as an Approach to Christology: Biblical Theology and Christian-Jewish Relations," in John Reumann, ed., *The Promise and Practice of Biblical Theology* (Minneapolis: Fortress Press, 1991), 71–86.

53. Rita Nakashima Brock, *Journeys by Heart: A Christology of Erotic Power* (New York: Crossroad, 1988).

54. For discussion see the chapter on the historical Jesus in Niels A. Dahl, *The Crucified Messiah and Other Essays* (Minneapolis: Augsburg, 1974), 48–89.

55. For introductions to critical methods of biblical interpretation see, e.g., Christopher Tuckett, *Reading the New Testament: Methods of Interpretation* (Philadelphia: Fortress, 1987); Steven L. McKenzie and Stephen R. Haynes, eds., *To Each Its Own Meaning: An Introduction to Biblical Criticisms and Their Applications* (Louisville: Westminster/John Knox Press, 1993); and especially the section on method in Schüssler Fiorenza, *Searching the Scriptures,* 1:189–312.

56. For a helpful discussion of the criteria of authenticity and their problems see M. Eugene Boring, "The Historical-Critical Method's 'Criteria of Authenticity': The Beatitudes in Q and Thomas as a Test Case," *Semeia* 44 (1988): 9–44.

57. See James H. Charlesworth, "From Barren Mazes to Gentle Rappings: The Emergence of Jesus Research," *Princeton Seminary Bulletin* 7, no. 3 (1986): 221–30 with annotated bibliography.

58. See Barbara H. Geller Nathanson, "Toward a Multicultural Ecumenical History of Women in the First Century/ies C.E.," in Schüssler Fiorenza, *Searching the Scriptures,* 1:272–89.

59. See *Zu ihrem Gedächtnis,* trans. Christine Schaumberger (Munich: Kaiser Verlag, 1988). Whereas English does not require that one decide whether a term such as "Pharisees" refers to men and to women, German does not allow for such an "easy out."

60. For such a criticism see Susanne Heine, "Brille der Parteilichkeit: Zu einer feministischen Hermeneutik," *Evangelische Kommentare* 23 (1990): 354–57, and the replies by Luise Schottroff and Dorothee Soelle, "Subtile Unterstellungen," and Anette Noller, "Liebgewonnene Vorurteile über eine unliebsame Forschungsrichtung," *Evangelische Kommentare* 23 (1990): 563–65.

61. Sally Overby Langford, "On Being a Religious Woman: Women Proselytes in the Greco-Roman World," in Peter J. Haas, ed., *Recovering the Role of Women: Power and Authority in Rabbinic Jewish Society,* South Florida Studies in the History of Judaism 59 (Atlanta: Scholars Press, 1992), 113–30; see also my contribution to the Georgi Festschrift entitled "The Rhetoricity of Historical Knowledge" (in press).

62. Since *In Memory of Her* was published, several important works on Jewish women in the Greco-Roman world have appeared. See for instance, Judith Romney Wegner, *Chattel or Person? The Status of Women in the Mishnah* (New York: Oxford University Press, 1988); Amy Jill Levine, ed., *"Women Like This": New Perspectives on Jewish Women in the Greco-Roman World* (Atlanta: Scholars Press, 1991); Cheryl Ann Brown, *No Longer Be Silent: First-Century Jewish Portraits of Biblical Women* (Louisville: Westminster/John Knox Press, 1992); Ross Shepard Kraemer, *Her Share of the Blessing: Women's Religions among Pagans, Jews and Christians in the Greco-Roman World* (New York: Oxford University Press, 1992).

63. See the discussion of John Dominic Crossan, "Materials and Methods in Historical Jesus Research," *Foundations and Facets Forum* 4 (1988): 3–24; John Dominic Crossan, "Divine Immediacy and Human Immediacy: Towards a New First Principle in Historical Jesus Research," *Semeia* 44 (1988): 121–40. See also John P. Meier, "Reflections on Jesus of History Research Today," in Charlesworth, ed., *Jesus' Jewishness,* 84–107.

64. For an account of the work of the "Jesus Seminar" see also Marcus J. Borg, *Meeting Jesus Again for the First Time: The Historical Jesus and the Heart of Contemporary Faith* (San Francisco: Harper, 1994), 20–45.

65. James R. Butts, "Probing the Polling: Jesus Seminar Results on the Kingdom Sayings," *Foundations and Facets Forum* 3, no. 1 (1987): 99 n. 3.

66. Jacob Neusner, "What Do We Study When We Study the Bible?" *Proceedings of the Irish Biblical Association* 10 (1986): 1–12.

67. Dorothy E. Smith, *The Conceptual Practices of Power: A Feminist Sociology of Knowledge* (Boston: Northeastern University Press, 1990), 63.

68. The argument for the understanding of Jesus as a Cynic philosopher has been especially developed in Q (Sayings Source) Studies. For a critical discussion see Richard A. Horsley, "Q and Jesus: Assumptions, Approaches and Analyses," *Semeia* 55 (1991): 175–212; see also Pheme Perkins, "Jesus before Christianity: Cynic and Sage?" *Christian Century* 110 (1993): 749–51 (review of Burton L. Mack, *The Lost Gospel: The Book of Q and Christian Origins* [San Francisco: HarperCollins, 1993]).

69. One of my readers interjected here: "Do we reject the maleness of Jesus or the theological significance of his maleness?" My point is that the common-sense distinction between biological sex as a "fact" and cultural gender meanings is sustained by the modern sex/gender system.

70. Mary Rose D'Angelo, "Re-membering Jesus: Women, Prophecy and Resistance in the Memory of the Early Churches," *Horizons* 19 (1992): 199–218, basically follows the reconstructive historical model that I have articulated. However, she seems to position her alternative notion of "shared prophecy in which women and men participated in a common spirit" (202) in the early Christian revelatory "appearance" tradition, which tends to eclipse the historical particularity of Jesus. She thereby reinscribes the feminist trend that adopts as a feminist frame of reference the culturally preconstructed notion of "feminine" relationality that eclipses the contributions of individuals in favor of an ostensibly "leaderless" collective.

71. For such a (deliberate?) misreading see Ross Kraemer's reviews of *In Memory of Her* in *Religious Studies Review* 11, no. 1 (1985): 107, and in *Journal of Biblical Literature* 104, no. 4 (1985): 722. See also my response in the introduction to the tenth anniversary edition of the book.

72. For a comprehensive review of the meaning of this expression in contemporary Judaism see Anna Maria Schwemer, "Gott als König und seine Königsherrschaft," in Martin Hengel and Anna Maria Schwemer, eds., *Königsherrschaft Gottes und himmlischer Kult in Judentum, Urchristentum und in der hellenistischen Welt* (Tübingen: J. C. B. Mohr, 1991), 45–118. For the discussion of the *basileia* discourse in early Christianity see Helmut Merkel, "Die Gottesherrschaft in der Verkündigung Jesu," ibid., 119–61.

73. See Marinus De Jonge, "The Christological Significance of Jesus' Preaching of the Kingdom of God," in Abraham J. Malherbe and Wayne A. Meeks, eds., *The Future of Christology: Essays in Honor of Leander E. Keck* (Minneapolis: Fortress Press, 1993), 7: "Notwithstanding the intrinsic difficulties in reconstructing Jesus' message concerning the kingdom, there is a surprising consensus" in understanding it as meaning "the time and place where God's power and kingly rule will hold sway." See G. N. Stanton, *The Gospels and Jesus* (Oxford: Oxford University Press, 1989), 196.

74. Ellis Rivkin, "What Crucified Jesus?" in Charlesworth, *Jesus' Jewishness*, 242.

75. For this expression see Norman Perrin, *Jesus and the Language of the Kingdom* (Philadelphia: Fortress Press, 1976).

76. See especially the work of Kathleen E. Corley, *Private Women, Public*

Meals: Social Conflict in the Synoptic Tradition (Peabody, Mass.: Hendrickson Publishers, 1993); "Were the Women around Jesus Really Prostitutes? Women in the Context of Greco-Roman Meals," in Eugene H. Lovering, ed., *Society of Biblical Literature, 1989 Seminar Papers* (Atlanta: Scholars Press, 1989), 487–521; "Jesus' Table Practice: Dining with 'Tax Collectors and Sinners,' including Women," in Eugene H. Lovering, ed., *Society of Biblical Literature, 1993 Seminar Papers* (Atlanta: Scholars Press, 1993), 444–59.

77. Joanna Dewey, "Jesus' Healings of Women: Conformity and Non-Conformity to Dominant Cultural Values as Clues for Historical Reconstruction," in Eugene H. Lovering, ed., *Society of Biblical Literature, 1993 Seminar Papers* (Atlanta: Scholars Press, 1993), 178–93.

78. Alan F. Segal, "Jesus, the Jewish Revolutionary," in Charlesworth, *Jesus' Jewishness*, 212.

79. Ibid., 213: "... but also to people more generally with ordinary feelings of low self-esteem (Mk 10:31; Mt 19:30; Lk 13:30)" or "... few confident and successful people would have entered the movement at first. Those whose wealth had not brought with it feelings of achievement or worth would have been better targets for evangelism" (214).

80. I want to thank Judith Plaskow for alerting me to this possible misreading. In her letter of October 28, 1992, she queries: "My biggest question is in some ways apart from the issue of anti-Judaism. I agree that understanding Christianity as one of a number of emancipatory movements in first-century Israel is a reading that does not reinforce traditional anti-Judaism — on the contrary, it encourages Jews to look at other emancipatory elements in our tradition. But in terms of Christian theological issues, aren't you simply shifting the theological weight from Jesus to the Jesus movement? In other words, while you talk about New Testament texts reinscribing patriarchy as they present the Jesus movement in the Greco-Roman context, you don't talk about non-emancipatory elements in the Jesus movement itself. Did none exist? Are you open to the possibility of their existing?"

81. Schüssler Fiorenza, *In Memory of Her*, 148.

82. See Robert Holst, "The Anointing of Jesus: Another Application of the Form-Critical Method," *Journal of Biblical Literature* 95 (1976): 435–46; Claus-Peter März, "Zur Traditionsgeschichte von Mk 14, 3–9 und Parallelen," *New Testament Studies* 67 (1981–82): 89–112.

83. For a discussion of Mark's account see Monika Fander, *Die Stellung der Frau im Markusevangelium unter besonderer Berücksichtigung kultur — und religionsgeschichtlicher Hintergründe* (Altenberge: Telos Verlag, 1989), 118–35; for Matthew see the excellent analysis of Elaine M. Wainwright, *Towards a Feminist Critical Reading of the Gospel according to Matthew*, Beihefte zur Zeitschrift für die neutestamentliche Wissenschaft 60 (Berlin: Walter de Gruyter, 1991), 252–83.

84. Raymond E. Brown, *The Death of the Messiah: From Gethsemane*

to the Grave, vol. 1 (New York: Doubleday, 1994), 1395; see also James Brownson, "Neutralizing the Intimate Enemy: The Portrayal of Judas in the Fourth Gospel," in Eugene H. Lovering, Jr., ed., *Society of Biblical Literature, 1992 Seminar Papers* (Atlanta: Scholars Press, 1992), 49–60.

85. For a general bibliography on the Passion Narratives see Brown, *The Death of the Messiah,* 94–106.

Chapter 4: Proclaimed by Women

1. Wesley W. Isenberg, "The Gospel of Philip," in James M. Robinson, ed., *The Nag Hammadi Library,* 2d rev. ed. (San Francisco: Harper, 1990), 145.

2. Kelly Brown Douglas, *The Black Christ* (Maryknoll, N.Y.: Orbis Books, 1994), 177.

3. For a contemporary interpretation see Elga Sorge, *Religion und Frau: Weibliche Spiritualität im Christentum,* Kohlhammer Taschenbücher 1038 (Stuttgart and Berlin: Verlag W. Kohlhammer, 1985), 94–138; see also the review article by W. W. Berry, "Images of Sin and Salvation in Feminist Theology," *Anglican Theological Review* 60 (1978): 25–54.

4. Mary Daly, *Beyond God the Father* (Boston: Beacon Press, 1973), 77.

5. For a critique of the theology of the cross similar to that of Daly see Sheila Collins, *A Different Heaven and Earth* (Valley Forge, Pa.: Judson, 1974), 203, and the critique of Jürgen Moltmann, *The Crucified God* (London: SCM Press, 1974) by Elga Sorge, "Wer leiden will, muss lieben: feministische Gedanken über die Liebe der christlichen Vorstellung vom gekreuzigten Gott," *Feministische Studien* 11, no. 1 (1983): 54–69. For a critique of Jürgen Moltmann from a liberation theological perspective see Dorothee Soelle, *Suffering* (Philadelphia Fortress Press, 1975).

6. Joanne Carlson Brown, Rebecca Parker, and Carol R. Bohn, eds., *Christianity, Patriarchy and Abuse: A Feminist Critique* (New York: Pilgrim Press, 1989), 2.

7. Ibid., 26.

8. Sheila Redmond, "Christian 'Virtues' and Recovery from Child Sexual Abuse," in *Christianity, Patriarchy and Abuse,* 73–74.

9. Elisabeth Moltmann-Wendel, "Gibt es eine feministische Kreuzestheologie," in Eveline Valtink, ed., *Das Kreuz mit dem Kreuz Hofgeismarer Protokolle* (Hofgeismar: Evangelische Akademie, 1990), 92.

10. Mary Grey, *Feminism, Redemption, and the Christian Tradition* (London: SCM Press, 1989), 157.

11. Hans Küng, *Christ-Sein* (Munich: Pieper Verlag, 1974), 400.

12. Grey, *Feminism, Redemption and the Christian Tradition,* 156.

13. Especially with reference to Romans 8.

14. Carol Ochs, *An Ascent to Joy: Transforming Deadness of Spirit* (Notre Dame, Ind.: University of Notre Dame Press, 1986).

15. Grey, *Feminism, Redemption and the Christian Tradition,* 186.

16. Regula Strobel, "Feministische Kritik an traditionellen Kreuzestheologien," in Doris Strahm and Regula Strobel, eds., *Vom Verlangen nach Heilwerden Christologie in feministisch-theologischer Sicht* (Fribourg: Exodus, 1991), 52–64.

17. Strobel, "Das Kreuz im Kontext feministischer Theologie: Versuch einer Standortbestimmung," ibid., 182–93.

18. See the doctoral dissertation (1975) of Judith Plaskow, *Sex, Sin, and Grace: Women's Experience and the Theologies of Reinhold Niebuhr and Paul Tillich* (Lanham, Md.: University Press of America, 1980). For an exploration of sin and guilt from the perspective of feminist liberation theology see Christine Schaumberger, "Subversive Bekehrung: Schulderkenntnis, Schwesterlichkeit, Frauenmacht: Irritierende und inspirierende Grundmotive kritisch-feministischer Befreiungstheologie," in Christine Schaumberger and Luise Schottroff, *Schuld und Macht: Studien zu einer feministischen Befreiungstheologie* (Munich: Chr. Kaiser, 1988), 153–288.

19. Regula Strobel, "Feministische Kritik," *Vom Verlangen nach Heilwerden,* 57–58. See also her paper "Dahingegeben für unsere Schuld: Feministisch-theologische Bemerkungen zum Kreuz-Schuld-Sühne-Modell in der christlichen Tradition," in Valtink, *Das Kreuz mit dem Kreuz,* 7–28.

20. Chung Hyun Kyung, *Struggle to Be the Sun Again: Introducing Asian Women's Theology* (Maryknoll, N.Y.: Orbis Books, 1990), 54.

21. Ibid., 56.

22. Kwok Pui-lan, "God Weeps with Our Pain," *East Asia Journal of Theology* 2, no. 2 (1984): 220–32.

23. Chung, *Struggle to Be the Sun Again,* 71.

24. Delores S. Williams, "Black Women's Surrogate Experience and the Christian Notion of Redemption," in Paula M. Cooey, William R. Eakin, and Jay B. McDaniel, eds., *After Patriarchy: Feminist Transformations of the World Religions* (Maryknoll, N.Y.: Orbis Books, 1990), 8. See also Delores S. Williams, *Sisters in the Wilderness: The Challenge of Womanist God-Talk* (Maryknoll, N.Y.: Orbis Books, 1993), 15–83.

25. Williams, "Black Women's Surrogate Experience," 9.

26. Ibid., 9.

27. Elisabeth Schüssler Fiorenza, *In Memory of Her: A Feminist Theological Reconstruction of Christian Origins* (New York Crossroad, 1983), 135.

28. See John P. Galvin, "Jesus Christ," in Francis Schüssler Fiorenza and John P. Galvin, *Systematic Theology: Roman Catholic Perspectives* (Minneapolis: Fortress Press, 1991), 1:278, for a discussion on Anselm's theology and the bibliographical documentation of his discussion.

29. For a critical review of the role of the death of Jesus in modern theologies of redemption see the still very significant contribution of Francis Schüssler Fiorenza, "Critical Social Theory and Christology: Toward an Understanding of Atonement and Redemption as Emancipatory Solidarity,"

Proceedings of the Thirtieth Annual Convention of the Catholic Theological Society of America 30 (1975): 63–110.

30. See J. Swetnam, *Jesus and Isaac: A Study of the Epistle to the Hebrews in the Light of the Aqedah,* Analecta Biblica 94 (Rome: PBI, 1981); W. R. G. Loader, *Sohn und Hoherpriester: Eine traditionsgeschichtliche Untersuchung zur Christologie des Hebräerbriefes,* Wissenschaftliche Monographien zum Alten und Neuen Testament 53 (Neukirchen-Vluyn: Neukirchener Verlag, 1981).

31. Rita Nakashima Brock, "And a Little Child Will Lead Us: Christology and Child Abuse," in Brown, Parker, and Bohn, *Christianity, Patriarchy, and Abuse,* 43. See also her book *Journeys by Heart: A Christology of Erotic Power* (New York: Crossroad, 1988).

32. Christine E. Gudorf, *Victimization: Examining Christian Complicity* (Philadelphia: Trinity Press International, 1992), 14–15. Cf. René Girard, *Job: Victim of His People* (Stanford: Stanford University Press, 1977), and *Violence and the Sacred* (Stanford: Stanford University Press, 1977); see also James G. Williams, *The Bible, Violence, and the Sacred* (San Francisco: Harper, 1989), 184–257, on the "Gospels and the Innocent Victim."

33. For a feminist discussion of sacrifice and ritual by a sociologist of religion see Nancy Jay, *Throughout Your Generations Forever: Sacrifice, Religion and Paternity* (Chicago: University of Chicago Press, 1992).

34. Brian Wren, *What Language Shall I Borrow? God-Talk in Worship: A Male Response to Feminist Theology* (New York: Crossroad, 1990), 119, passim.

35. For an exhaustive (in every sense of the word) discussion of the divergent interpretations of the canonical and extracanonical Gospels as well as a comprehensive accounting of the secondary literature, see Raymond E. Brown, *The Death of the Messiah: From Gethsemane to the Grave,* 2 vols. (New York: Doubleday, 1994).

36. See among others Williams, "Black Women's Surrogate Experience," 13.

37. For the understanding of rhetoric in Christian Testament studies see my book *Revelation: Vision of a Just World* (Minneapolis: Augsburg Fortress, 1991) and my Society of Biblical Literature presidential address "The Ethics of Biblical Interpretation: Decentering Biblical Scholarship," *Journal of Biblical Literature* 107, no. 1 (1988): 3–17; see also Wilhelm Wuellner, "Hermeneutics and Rhetorics: From 'Truth and Method' to 'Truth and Power,'" *Scriptura S* 3 (1989): 1–54, and Burton L. Mack, *Rhetoric and the New Testament* (Minneapolis: Augsburg Fortress, 1990).

38. For instance, Joseph Blinzler insists on Jewish responsibility in *The Trial of Jesus* (Westminster, Md.: Newman, 1959), whereas Paul Winter, *On the Trial of Jesus,* 2d rev. ed. (Berlin: Walter de Gruyter, 1961), and H. Cohn, *Reflections on the Trial and Death of Jesus* (Jerusalem: Israel Law Review Association, 1967), have argued that the Romans alone were

responsible. Today most scholars assume that Jesus was crucified by the Romans but with the collaboration of some Jewish leaders.

39. David Seeley, "Was Jesus like a Philosopher? The Evidence of Martyrological and Wisdom Motifs in Q, Prepauline Traditions and Mark," in David J. Lull, ed., *Society of Biblical Literature, 1989 Seminar Papers* (Atlanta: Scholars Press, 1989), 540–49.

40. Burton L. Mack, *A Myth of Innocence: Mark and Christian Origins* (Philadelphia: Fortress, 1988), 282.

41. Such an assumption is found, for instance, in the Gnostic Acts of John. The apostle John reveals in a sermon given in Ephesus that he fled to the Mount of Olives and hid in a cave. Jesus appeared to him during the time of his dying on the cross in Jerusalem explaining that he was dying in Jerusalem for the people. See Heinz Wolfgang Kuhn, " 'Jesus als Gekreuzigter' in der frühchristlichen Verkündigung bis zur Mitte des 2. Jahrhunderts," *Zeitschrift für Theologie und Kirche* 72 (1975), 12.

42. See Luise Schottroff, "Die Kreuzigung Jesu: Feministisch-theologische Rekonstruktion der Kreuzigung Jesu und ihrer Bedeutung im frühen Christentum," in Valtink, *Das Kreuz mit dem Kreuz,* 7–28.

43. For an excellent discussion of Jewish resistance to Roman occupation and imperialism see Richard A. Horsley, *Jesus and the Spiral of Violence: Popular Jewish Resistance in Roman Palestine* (San Francisco: Harper & Row, 1987), 1–146.

44. Flavius Josephus, *Jewish Wars* 2.13.4 no. 259.

45. Martin Hengel, *Crucifixion in the Ancient World and the Folly of the Message of the Cross* (Philadelphia: Fortress, 1977); Heinz Wolfgang Kuhn, "Die Kreuzestrafe während der frühen Kaiserzeit," *Aufstieg und Niedergang der römischen Welt* 2:25.1 (1985): 648–793.

46. The expression "the King of the Jews" as well as the name of Jesus is found in all four Gospels, although the overall wording of the *titulus* differs somewhat. The extracanonical Gospel of Peter reads "This is the King of Israel" (4:11). See E. Bammel, "The Titulus," in E. Bammel and C. F. D. Moule, eds., *Jesus and the Politics of His Day* (Cambridge: Cambridge University Press, 1986), 353–64.

47. Brian C. McGing, "Pontius Pilate and the Sources," *Catholic Biblical Quarterly* 53 (1991): 416–38.

48. Ellis Rivkin, "What Crucified Jesus?" in James H. Charlesworth, ed., *Jesus' Jewishness: Exploring the Place of Jesus within Early Judaism* (New York: Crossroad/American Interfaith Institute, 1991), 257.

49. Most recently, Craig C. Evans, "From Public Ministry to the Passion: Can a Link Be Found between the (Galilean) Life and the (Judean) Death of Jesus?" in Eugene H. Lovering, Jr., ed., *Society of Biblical Literature, 1993 Seminar Papers* (Atlanta: Scholars Press, 1993), 460–72.

50. S. G. F. Brandon, *Jesus and the Zealots: A Study of the Political Factor in Primitive Christianity* (Manchester: Manchester University Press, 1967).

51. E. P. Sanders, *Jesus and Judaism* (Philadelphia: Fortress Press, 1985).

52. Geza Vermes, *Jesus, the Jew* (London: Collins, 1973), and *The Religion of Jesus, the Jew* (London: SCM Press, 1993).

53. "David Hill, "Jesus before the Sanhedrin — On What Charge?" *Irish Biblical Studies* 7 (1985): 174–85.

54. Howard Snyder, "Models of the Kingdom: Sorting out the Practical Meaning of God's Reign," *Transformation* 10 (1993): 1–6; Brian Rice McCarthy, "Jesus, the Kingdom, and Theopolitics," in David J. Lull, ed., *Society of Biblical Literature, 1990 Seminar Papers* (Atlanta: Scholars Press, 1990), 311–21.

55. See also Walter Wink, "Jesus and the Domination System," in Eugene H. Lovering, Jr., ed., *Society of Biblical Literature, 1991 Seminar Papers* (Atlanta: Scholars Press, 1991), 265–86.

56. See Norman Perrin, *Jesus and the Language of the Kingdom of God: Symbol and Metaphor in New Testament Interpretation* (Philadelphia: Fortress, 1976) for the distinction between steno- and tensive symbol. Perrin derived this distinction from the work of Philipp E. Wheelwright. See Philip Wheelwright, *Metaphor Reality* (Bloomington: Indiana University Press, 1962), and *The Burning Fountain: A Study in the Language of Symbolism*, 2d ed. (Gloucester: P. Smith, 1983).

57. For a similar understanding of *basileia* see also John Dominic Crossan, *The Historical Jesus: The Life of a Mediterranean Jewish Peasant* (San Francisco: Harper, 1991), 265–99: "What was described by his parables and aphorisms as a here and now Kingdom of the nobodies and the destitute is precisely a Kingdom performed rather than just proclaimed." Although Crossan then goes on to describe the "enactment of the Kingdom of the nobodies" in an antipatriarchal fashion similar to what I have done in *In Memory of Her,* he tends to existentialize and "liturgize" rather than "politicize" such a "performance of the Kingdom."

58. For a feminist discussion of the historical-critical method of interpretation see the contribution of Monika Fander, "Historical Critical Methods," in Elisabeth Schüssler Fiorenza, ed., *Searching the Scriptures,* vol. 1, *A Feminist Introduction* (New York: Crossroad, 1993), 205–24.

59. For a comparison of form criticism and rhetorical criticism see Klaus Berger, "Rhetorical Criticism, New Form Criticism, and New Testament Hermeneutics," in Stanley E. Porter and Thomas H. Olbricht, eds., *Rhetoric and the New Testament,* Journal for the Study of the New Testament Supplement Series 90 (Sheffield: JSOT Press, 1993), 390–96.

60. For Paul see, e.g., Alexandra R. Brown, "Seized by the Cross: The Death of Jesus in Paul's Transformative Discourse," in Eugene H. Lovering, Jr., ed., *Society of Biblical Literature, 1993 Seminar Papers* (Atlanta: Scholars Press, 1993), 740–57.

61. For the following see especially Klaus Wengst, *Christologische Formeln und Lieder des Urchristentums,* Studien zum Neuen Testament 7 (Gütersloh: Gerd Mohn, 1973); and by the same author, "Glaubensbekenntnisse, IV," in *Theologische Realenzyklopädie* 13:392–99.

62. See, e.g., Romans 8:11; Galatians 1:1; Romans 10:9; 1 Corinthians 6:14.

63. See Jürgen Becker, "Die neutestamentliche Rede vom Sühnetod Jesu," in *Die Heilsbedeutung des Kreuzes für Glaube und Hoffnung des Christen,* Zeitschrift für Theologie und Kirche 8 (Tübingen: Mohr, 1990), 29–49.

64. See Willem S. Foster, "The Religio-historical Context of the Resurrection of Jesus and Resurrection Faith in the New Testament," *Neotestamentica* 23 (1989): 159–75.

65. On the resurrection see, e.g., Pheme Perkins, *Resurrection: New Testament Witness and Contemporary Reflection* (Garden City, N.Y.: Doubleday, 1984); Paul Hoffmann, "Auferstehung, ii/1" *Theologische Realenzyklopädie* 4:478–93; Reginald H. Fuller, *The Formation of the Resurrection Narratives* (Philadelphia: Fortress, 1980); Gerald O'Collins, *Interpreting the Resurrection* (New York: Paulist Press, 1988).

66. In her response to a previous draft of this chapter Shelly Matthews pointed out that in the next chapter the Wisdom of Solomon likens the suffering of the righteous to a "sacrificial burnt offering accepted by God" (3:5–6). This observation is important because it shows that in the language world of early Christians suffering and sacrifice are already associated in a metaphorical way.

67. See Odil Hannes Steck, *Israel und das gewaltsame Geschick der Propheten,* Wissenschaftliche Monographien zum Alten und Neuen Testament 23 (Neukirchen-Vluyn: Neukirchener Verlag, 1967).

68. See also L. Ruppert, *Jesus als der leidende Gerechte? Der Weg Jesu im Lichte eines alt- und zwischentestamentlichen Motivs,* Stuttgarter Bibelstudien 59 (Stuttgart: Katholisches Bibelwerk, 1972).

69. See Robert Doran, "The Martyr: A Synoptic View of the Mother and Her Seven Sons," in George W. Nickelsburg and John J. Collins, eds., *Ideal Figures in Ancient Judaism: Profiles and Paradigms,* Society of Biblical Literature Septuagint and Cognate Studies 12 (Chico, Calif.: Scholars Press, 1980), 189–221, and especially Robin Darling Young, "The 'Woman with the Soul of Abraham,' Traditions about the Mother of the Maccabean Martyrs," in Amy Jill Levine, ed., *"Women Like This": New Perspectives on Jewish Women in the Greco-Roman World* (Atlanta: Scholars Press, 1991), 67–82.

70. Burton L. Mack, *The Lost Gospel: The Book of Q and Christian Origins* (San Francisco: Harper, 1993), 216f. argues: "The clue to the logic of the kerygma lies in the phrase that Christ died 'for us,' namely the congregation of Christians. Such a notion cannot be traced to old Jewish and/or Israelite traditions, for the very idea of a vicarious human sacrifice was anathema in these cultures.... The notion of a resurrection from the dead, on the other hand, offended hellenic sensibility.... As an idea it was born in the fusion of an apocalyptic imagination with an age-old narrative plot sometimes called a wisdom tale."

71. For example, in Romans 5:6, 8; 14:15; 1 Corinthians 8:11; 1 Thessalonians 5:10; Galatians 2:21b; 2 Corinthians 5:14f.; 1 Corinthians 1:13.

72. For an interpretation of the Fourth Gospel in terms of a "community of friends," see Wes Howard-Brook, *Becoming Children of God: The Fourth Gospel and Radical Discipleship* (Maryknoll, N.Y.: Orbis Books, 1994); for a critical reading of the Fourth Gospel from a Jewish feminist perspective see the commentary of Adele Reinhartz in Elisabeth Schüssler Fiorenza, ed., *Searching the Scriptures,* vol. 2, *A Feminist Commentary* (New York: Crossroad, 1994); on a feminist theology of friendship see Mary E. Hunt, *Fierce Tenderness: A Feminist Theology of Friendship* (New York: Crossroad, 1991).

73. For example, Exodus 24:6–8; Psalm 50:5; Zechariah 9:11.

74. Becker, "Die neutestamentliche Rede," 38–43.

75. See Elsa Tamez, *The Amnesty of Grace: Justification by Faith from a Latin American Perspective* (Maryknoll, N.Y.: Orbis Books, 1993), 86.

76. The Greek does not read *hyper hēmōn* (for us) but *anti pollōn* (in return for all who are many). The image here is not of atonement for sins but manumission, i.e., the setting free of slaves.

77. See my discussion in "The Phenomenon of Early Christian Apocalyptic," in David Hellholm, ed., *Apocalypticism in the Mediterranean World and the Near East* (Tübingen: J. C. B. Mohr, 1983), 295–316; for a somewhat different emphasis see J. C. H. Lebram, "The Piety of the Jewish Apocalyptists," ibid., 171–210.

78. See my article "Redemption as Liberation," *Catholic Biblical Quarterly* 36 (1974): 220–32, which appeared in a revised form in my book *Judgment and Justice* (Philadelphia: Fortress Press, 1985), 68–81. See Also Hans Kessler, *Erlösung als Befreiung* (Düsseldorf: Patmos Verlag, 1972).

79. Alan Segal, " 'He Who Did Not Spare His Own Son': Jesus, Paul, and the Akedah," in Peter Richardson and John C. Hurd, eds., *From Jesus to Paul: Studies in Honor of Francis Wright Beare* (Waterloo, Ont.: Wilfred Laurier University Press, 1984), 169–84.

80. Niels Alstrup Dahl, *The Crucified Messiah and Other Essays* (Minneapolis: Augsburg, 1974), 149.

81. Ibid., 156.

82. See Mark 9:37, par. Luke 9:48; Matthew 10:40 and Luke 10:16 (Q); John 13:20.

83. Eduard Schweizer, "What Do We Really Mean When We Say 'God Sent His Son...?' " in John T. Carroll et al., eds., *Faith and History: Essays in Honor of Paul W. Meyer* (Atlanta: Scholars Press, 1990), 304–5.

84. See the next chapter for a fuller discussion and literature.

85. This parable is patterned after Isaiah's poem of the vineyard (Isa. 5:1–7). As Ched Myers, *Binding the Strong Man: A Political Reading of Mark's Story of Jesus* (Maryknoll, N.Y.: Orbis Books, 1988), 309, sums up: "The son is killed and cast off.... For all this, the parable threatens the tenants will be slaughtered, and the vineyard turned over to someone else

(12:8f.). The violence and counterviolence of this climax are true to Isaiah's condemnation."

86. Franz Mussner, "Ursprünge und Entfaltung der neutestamentlichen Sohneschristologie," in Heinrich Fries et al., eds., *Grundfragen der Christologie heute* (Freiburg: Herder, 1975), 77–113.

87. R. P. Martin, *Carmen Christi: Phil ii.5–11 in Recent Interpretation and in the Setting of Early Christian Worship*, 2d ed., Society for New Testament Study Monograph Series 4 (Cambridge: Cambridge University Press, 1983), and a more recent discussion of Philippians 2:6–11 and Colossians 1:15–20 by N. T. Wright, *The Climax of the Covenant: Christ and the Law in Pauline Theology* (Minneapolis: Fortress, 1992), 56–119.

88. See Mark 14:32–42 par.; John 18:11.

89. The classic work on christological titles is Ferdinand Hahn, *The Titles of Jesus in Christology* (London: Lutterworth, 1969).

90. For a discussion of the literary roles of women in the passion and resurrection narratives see Dorothy A. Lee, "Presence or Absence? The Question of Women Disciples at the Last Supper," *Pacifica* 6 (1993): 1–20; see also Patrick J. Hartin, "The Role of the Women Disciples in Mark's Narrative" *Theologia Evangelica* 26, no. 2 (1993): 91–102; for bibliography and a comprehensive chart of the Gospel texts about the Galilean women disciples before and after Jesus' death and resurrection see Brown, *The Death of the Messiah*, 2:1014–26.

91. Susanne Heine, "Eine Person von Rang und Namen: Historische Konturen der Magdalenerin," in *Jesu Rede von Gott und ihre Nachgeschichte im frühen Christentum: Festschrift für Willi Marxsen zum 70. Geburtstag* (Gütersloh: Gerd Mohn, 1989), 179–94; see also Helen Schüngel-Straumann, "Maria von Magdala — Apostolin und erste Verkünderin der Osterbotschaft," in Dietmar Bader, ed., *Maria Magdalena zu einem Bild der Frau in der christlichen Verkündigung* (Munich: Verlag Schnell & Steiner, 1990), 8–32.

92. For a comprehensive discussion of the literature on the traditions of Mary of Magdala see Susan Haskins, *Mary Magdalen: Myth and Metaphor* (New York: Harcourt Brace & Co., 1994) and the contributions in Bader, *Maria Magdalena zu einem Bild der Frau in der christlichen Verkündigung*.

93. See Mark 16:6: "Do not be alarmed; you are looking for Jesus of Nazareth, who was crucified. He has been raised; he is not here. Look, there is the place they laid him"; and Matthew 28:5–7: "Do not be afraid; I know that you are looking for Jesus who was crucified. He is not here; for he has been raised, as he said. Come, see the place where he lay. Then go quickly and tell his disciples, 'He has been raised from the dead."

94. For a careful exegetical analysis and bibliographical discussion of the "state of the question" see Elaine Wainwright, *Towards a Feminist Critical Reading of the Gospel according to Matthew*, Beihefte zur Zeitschrift für die neutestamentliche Wissenschaft 60 (Berlin: de Gruyter, 1991), 284–318.

95. Gerald O'Collins, S.J., and Daniel Kendall, S.J., "Mary Magdalen

as Major Witness to Jesus' Resurrection," *Theological Studies* 48, no. 4 (1987): 640–43.

96. Their "politics of meaning" comes nicely to the fore in the attempt to play out Pheme Perkins's scholarship against my own, although they acknowledge that Perkins favorably reviewed *In Memory of Her.* Observe their emotive, suggestive, and prejudicial language: "Perkins, however, approaches her subject more from an exegetical point of view than from one which attempts to recruit the early Christian story for the purposes of feminist theological reconstruction" (643).

97. See, for instance, the conclusion of Daniel Kendall, S.J., and Gerald O'Collins, S.J., "The Uniqueness of the Easter Appearances," *Catholic Biblical Quarterly* 54, no. 2 (1992): 287–307, who argue against "those like Schillebeeckx who underplay the special nature of the Easter appearances and so reduce the role of the apostolic witnesses as authoritative founders of the church."

98. Anthony J. Tambasco, *A Theology of Atonement and Paul's Vision of Christianity* (Collegeville, Minn.: Liturgical Press, 1991), 70.

99. Chung, *Struggle to Be the Sun Again,* 73.

Chapter 5: Prophets of Sophia

1. I became fascinated with the Wisdom tradition in the Christian Testament in the context of the 1973 Rosenstil Seminar on Wisdom in Early Judaism and Christianity sponsored by the Department of Theology at the University of Notre Dame. See my contribution, "Wisdom Mythology and the Christological Hymns of the New Testament," in Robert L. Wilken, ed., *Aspects of Wisdom in Judaism and Early Christianity* (Notre Dame, Ind.: University of Notre Dame Press, 1975), 17–42. This article does not indicate any awareness of androcentric language. My then still timid attempts to change such language were edited out by my student assistants as the "problem" of a writer whose native language was not English. The same applies to my contribution in *Aspects of Religious Propaganda in Judaism and Christianity* (Notre Dame, Ind.: University of Notre Dame Press, 1976), which I edited. Some of this research on Wisdom was incorporated into *In Memory of Her: A Feminist Theological Reconstruction of Christian Origins* (New York: Crossroad, 1994) but was spread over different sections of the book. My own discourses on Sophia were articulated partially in response to Elaine Pagels's work *The Gnostic Gospels* (New York: Random House, 1979) and Joan Chamberlain Engelsman's book *The Feminine Dimension of the Divine* (Philadelphia: Westminster Press, 1979). Susan Cady, Marion Ronan, and Hal Taussig, *Sophia: The Future of Feminist Spirituality* (San Francisco: Harper & Row, 1986), in turn were inspired by my work to explore the spiritual-liturgical aspect of Divine Wisdom. The New Testament exposition of Hal Taussig, however, simultaneously seeks to uti-

lize and to "curb" the feminist implications of this tradition. In various publications Elizabeth Johnson has taken over my work but recast it in dogmatic-systematic terms. For a Jewish feminist discussion of Divine Wisdom see Asphodel P. Long, *In a Chariot Drawn by Lions: The Search for the Female in Deity* (London: Women's Press, 1992).

2. See also my article "Auf den Spuren der Weisheit, Weisheits-theologisches Urgestein," in Verena Wodtke, ed., *Auf den Spuren der Weisheit: Sophia — Wegweiserin für ein neues Gottesbild* (Freiburg: Herder, 1991), 24–40.

3. Adrienne Rich, *The Dream of a Common Language* (New York: Norton, 1978), 60–67.

4. Ibid., 60.

5. *Chokmah* is the Hebrew and *sophia* the Greek word for the English term "wisdom."

6. For the Gospels see Leo G. Perdue, "The Wisdom Sayings of Jesus," *Foundations and Facets Forum* 2, no. 3 (1986): 3–35, who has catalogued such sapiential sayings.

7. See Carol A. Newsome, "Woman and the Discourse of Patriarchal Wisdom: A Study of Proverbs 1–9," in Peggy L. Day, ed., *Gender and Difference in Ancient Israel* (Minneapolis: Fortress Press, 1989), 142–60, who concludes her study with a helpful methodological insight: "Having learned from the father how to resist interpolation by hearing the internal contradictions in discourse, one is prepared to resist the patriarchal interpolation of the father as well. For the reader who does not take up the subject position offered by the text, Proverbs 1–9 ceases to be a simple text of imitation and becomes a text about the problematic nature of discourse itself" (159).

8. See, e.g., W. C. Trenchard, *Ben Sira's View of Women* (Chico, Calif.: Scholars Press, 1982). Claudia V. Camp, "Understanding a Patriarchy: Women in Second-Century Jerusalem through the Eyes of Ben Sira," in Amy Jill Levine, ed., *"Women Like This": New Perspectives on Jewish Women in the Greco-Roman World* (Atlanta: Scholars Press, 1991), 1–40, suggests that Ben Sira's "shrill, sometimes virulent instructions on women" are due to stress generated by two social forces: "One is the loss of control that the sage experienced in the larger social realm, which may have translated into an obsession for control in the closer sphere, specifically his sexuality and his household. The second is the conflict of social values which this stress exacerbates" (38).

9. For a general introduction, which, however, does not deal with the androcentric character of the Wisdom literature, see Dianne Bergant, C.S.A., *What Are They Saying about Wisdom Literature?* (New York: Paulist Press, 1984). In a private dedication, the author answers the question of the book's title: "They are saying — Search for it in experience!! Feminist experience."

10. See, for instance, Luise Schottroff, "Wanderprophetinnen: Eine femi-

nistische Analyse der Logienquelle," *Evangelische Theologie* 51 (1991): 332–34.

11. Claudia V. Camp, *Wisdom and the Feminine in the Book of Proverbs*, Bible and Literature Series 14 (Sheffield: Almond, 1985).

12. See also Camp's contribution, "The Female Sage in Ancient Israel and in the Biblical Wisdom Literature," in J. Gammie and L. Perdue, eds., *The Sage in Ancient Israel* (Winona Lake, Ind.: Eisenbrauns, 1990).

13. See Silvia Schroer, "Weise Frauen und Ratgeberinnen in Israel: Vorbilder der personifizierten Chokmah," in Wodtke, *Auf den Spuren der Weisheit*, 9–23.

14. Silvia Schroer, "Die göttliche Weisheit und der nachexilische Monotheismus," in Marie-Theres Wacker and Erich Zenger, eds., *Der eine Gott und die Göttin: Gottesvorstellungen des biblischen Israel im Horizont feministischer Theologie*, Quaestiones Disputatae 135 (Freiburg: Herder, 1991), 151–83.

15. Dieter Georgi, "Frau Weisheit oder das Recht auf Freiheit als schöpferisische Kraft," in Leonore Siegele Wenschkewitz, ed., *Verdrängte Vergangenheit, die uns bedrängt: Feministische Theologie in der Verantwortung für die Geschichte* (Munich: Kaiser, 1988), 258ff.; see also his commentary *Weisheit Salomos*, Jüdische Schriften aus hellenistisch-römischer Zeit ii/4 (Gütersloh: Mohn, 1980).

16. See Ross Shepard Kraemer, "Monastic Jewish Women in Greco-Roman Egypt: Philo Judaeus on the Therapeutrides, *Signs* 14 (1989): 342–70.

17. See the work of Sarah Pomeroy, *Women in Hellenistic Egypt: From Alexander to Cleopatra* (New York: Schocken Books, 1984).

18. See Ross Shepard Kraemer, *Her Share of the Blessing: Women's Religions among Pagans, Jews, and Christians in the Greco-Roman World* (Oxford: Oxford University Press, 1992), 106–27, on Jewish women's religious lives and offices in the Greco-Roman Diaspora.

19. See, however, Judith Romney Wegner, "Philo's Portrayal of Women — Hebraic or Hellenic?" in Levine, *"Women Like This,"* 44–66, who argues that Philo's views on women owe "far more to Greek ideas, mediated through Hellenistic culture, than to the Jewish Scripture he inherited from his ancestors" (65). However, the assumption of such a clear-cut opposition between Greek and Jewish literatures and ideas does not take into account that Philo's "Jewish Scriptures" were already "translated" into Greek in more than the literal sense.

20. See the forthcoming commentary by Silvia Schroer in Elisabeth Schüssler Fiorenza, ed., *Searching the Scriptures*, vol. 2, *A Feminist Commentary* (New York: Crossroad, 1994); see also David Winston, *The Wisdom of Solomon*, Anchor Bible (Garden City, N.Y.: Doubleday, 1979).

21. Helmut Engel, "Was Weisheit ist und wie sie entstand, will ich verkünden," in Georg Hetschel and Erich Zenger, eds., *Lehrerin der Gerechtigkeit*, Erfurter theologische Schriften 19 (Leipzig, 1991), 67–102.

22. James M. Reese, *Hellenistic Influences on the Book of Wisdom and Its Consequences,* Analecta Biblica 41 (Rome: Biblicum, 1970); John S. Kloppenborg, "Isis and Sophia in the Book of Wisdom," *Harvard Theological Review* 75 (1982): 57–84, for a review of the literature.

23. Hermann von Lips, "Christus als Sophia? Weisheitliche Traditionen in der urchristlichen Christologie," in Cilliers Breytenbach and Henning Paulsen, eds., *Anfänge der Christologie: Festschrift Ferdinand Hahn* (Göttingen: Vandenhoeck & Ruprecht, 1991), 75–96.

24. Apuleius, *Metamorphoses,* 11. 25.

25. John S. Kloppenborg, "Isis and Sophia," 72.

26. See Marie-Theres Wacker, "Feministisch-theologische Blicke auf die neuere Monotheismus-Diskussion," in *Der eine Gott und die Göttin,* 45.

27. "The Mother of Wisdom," in James M. Robinson, ed., *The Future of Our Religious Past* (1964; New York: Harper & Row, 1971). In the English-speaking context W. L. Knox, "The Divine Wisdom," *JST* 38 (1937): 230–37, even before Conzelmann had pointed to this connection between Isis and Sophia.

28. Richard A. Baer, *Philo's Use of the Categories of Male and Female* (Leiden: Brill, 1970).

29. See ibid., 42.

30. Philo, *De fuga et inventione,* 51ff., with reference to Genesis 25:20.

31. Georgi, "Frau Weisheit oder das Recht auf Freiheit als schöpferische Kraft," 251.

32. Burton Mack, *Logos and Sophia: Analysis of the Wisdom Theology in Hellenistic Judaism,* Studien zur Umwelt des Neuen Testaments 10 (Göttingen: Vandenhoeck & Ruprecht, 1973), 188; see also his "Wisdom Myth and Mythology," *Interpretation* 24 (1970): 46–60.

33. Martin Hengel, "Jesus als messianischer Lehrer der Weisheit und die Anfänge der Christologie," in Edmond Jacob, ed., *Sagesse et Religion* (Paris: Presses Universitaires de France, 1979), 147–90.

34. James M. Robinson, "Logoi Sophōn: On the Gattung of Q," in Helmut Koester and James M. Robinson, eds., *Trajectories through Early Christianity* (Philadelphia: Fortress, 1971), 71–113.

35. For a very interesting, albeit overstated, sociopolitical history of the Two-Source Theory and its ideological roots in Bismarck's *Kulturkampf,* see William R. Farmer, *The Gospel of Jesus: The Pastoral Relevance of the Synoptic Problem* (Louisville: Westminster/John Knox Press, 1994).

36. Richard A. Horsley, "Q and Jesus: Assumptions, Approaches and Analyses," *Semeia* 55 (1991): 206.

37. Ibid., 206.

38. Richard Horsley, "Questions about Redactional Strata and the Social Relations Reflected in Q," in David J. Lull, ed., *Society of Biblical Literature, 1989 Seminar Papers* (Atlanta: Scholars Press, 1989), 186–203. According to him it expresses the sentiment of Galilean men against the central might of Jerusalem.

39. Felix Christ, *Jesus Sophia: Die Sophia-Christologie bei den Synoptikern,* Abhandlungen zur Theologie des Alten und Neuen Testaments 57 (Zurich: Zwingli, 1970), 81–93.

40. John S. Kloppenborg, "Wisdom Christology in Q," *Laval Théologique et Philosophique* 34 (1978): 141.

41. Newsome, "Women and the Discourse of Patriarchal Wisdom," 151.

42. Mary Rose D'Angelo, "Theology in Mark and Q: Abba and 'Father' in Context," *Harvard Theological Review* 85, no. 2 (1992): 171f., suggests that this logion is part of a larger redactional unit in which seven of the nine Q references to G*d as "father" occur. However, in her eagerness to assert that it cannot be shown from Q and Mark that Jesus used either "abba" or the "father" title and to prove that "abba"/"father" is used in a patriarchal sense, she neither distinguishes between the "father" and the "father-son" language nor considers that such language can have antipatriarchal functions. See also her article "Abba and 'Father': Imperial Theology and the Jesus Traditions," *Journal of Biblical Literature* 111, no. 4 (1992): 611–30. However, Klaus W. Müller, "König und Vater: Streiflichter zur metaphorischen Rede über Gott in der Umwelt des Neuen Testaments," in Martin Hengel and Anna Maria Schwemer, eds., *Königsherrschaft Gottes und himmlischer Kult in Judentum, Urchristentum und in der hellenistischen Welt* (Tübingen: J. C. B. Mohr, 1991), 21–44, points out that in difference to the Greco-Roman imperial use of "Father-King" language, G*d is called "king" only 5 times but "father" 245 times in the Christian Testament. The use of "king" is found twice in a metaphorical/parabolic context in Matthew and three times in 1 Timothy (1:17; 6:15, 16).

43. Philo, *Quis rerum divinarum heres,* 127f.

44. Silvia Schroer, "The Spirit, Wisdom and the Dove," *Freiburger Zeitschrift für Philosophie und Theologie* 33 (1986): 213f.

45. Hengel, "Die Anfänge der Christologie," 175.

46. See Philippians 2:6–11; 1 Timothy 3:16; Colossians 1:15–20; Ephesians 2:14–16; Hebrews 1:3; 1 Peter 3:18; John 1:1–14.

47. Elisabeth Schüssler Fiorenza, "Wisdom Mythology and the Christological Hymns of the New Testament," in Wilken, *Aspects of Wisdom,* 17–42.

48. Mack, *Logos and Sophia,* 61: "The scheme of the return to heaven after the resurrection from earth is a form of Isis-Osiris myth of the hellenistic time" (see Plutarch, *De Iside,* 25ff.).

49. Sheila Briggs, "Can an Enslaved God Liberate? Hermeneutical Reflections on Philippians 2:6–11," in Katie Geneva Cannon and Elisabeth Schüssler Fiorenza, eds., *Interpretation for Liberation,* Semeia 47 (Atlanta: Scholars Press, 1989), 141–56.

50. Klaus Wengst, *Christologische Formeln und Lieder des Urchristentums,* Studien zum Neuen Testament 7 (Gütersloh: Mohn, 1972), 170.

51. To trace the footprints of Sophia in Gnostic writings would require

a separate article. See the discussions in Karen King, ed., *Images of the Feminine in Gnosticism* (Philadelphia: Fortress, 1988); Deirdre J. Good, *Reconstructing the Tradition of Sophia in Gnostic Literature*, SBL Monograph Series 32 (Atlanta: Scholars Press, 1987); and Deirdre J. Good, "Ein Bild voller Spannungen — Sophia in der Gnosis," in Wodtke, *Auf den Spuren der Weisheit*, 41–54; see also the work of Elaine Pagels.

52. See, e.g., David Adamo, "Wisdom and Its Importance to Paul's Christology in 1 Corinthians," *Bulletin of Biblical Studies* 7 (1988): 31–43.

53. Birger A. Pearson, "Hellenistic-Jewish Wisdom Speculation and Paul," in Wilken, *Aspects of Wisdom*, 43–66.

54. See Elisabeth Schüssler Fiorenza, "Rhetorical Situation and Historical Reconstruction in 1 Corinthians," *New Testament Studies* 33 (1987): 386–403; and especially Antoinette Clark Wire, *The Corinthian Women Prophets: A Reconstruction through Paul's Rhetoric* (Minneapolis: Augsburg Fortress Press, 1990).

55. See Martin Scott, *Sophia and the Johannine Jesus*, Journal for the Study of the New Testament Supplement Series 71 (Sheffield: JSOT Press, 1992).

56. This interpretation has been pioneered by M. J. Suggs, *Wisdom Christology and Law in Matthew's Gospel* (Cambridge: Harvard University Press, 1970); see also Celia Deutsch, *Hidden Wisdom and the Easy Yoke: Wisdom Torah and Discipleship in Mt 11:25–30*, Journal for the Study of the New Testament Supplement Series 18 (Sheffield: Sheffield Academic Press, 1987). For a dissenting view see Marshall D. Johnson, "Reflections on a Wisdom Approach to Matthew's Christology," *Catholic Biblical Quarterly* 46 (1974): 44–64; see also D. Orten, *The Understanding Scribe: Matthew and the Apocalyptic Ideal*, Journal for the Study of the New Testament Supplement Series 25 (Sheffield: Sheffield Academic Press, 1989).

57. Fred W. Burnett, *The Testament of Jesus-Sophia: A Redaction-Critical Study of the Eschatological Discourse in Matthew* (Washington, D.C.: University Press of America, 1979); see also his articles: "Characterization and Christology in Matthew: Jesus in the Gospel of Matthew," in David J. Lull, ed., *Society of Biblical Literature, 1989 Seminar Papers* (Atlanta: Scholars Press, 1989), 588–603, and "Exposing the Anti-Jewish Ideology of Matthew's Implied Author: The Characterization of God as Father," *Semeia* 59 (1992): 155–91.

58. For a review of scholarship on this question, see Graham Stanton, "The Origins and Purpose of Matthew's Gospel: Matthean Scholarship from 1945–1980," *Aufstieg und Niedergang der römischen Welt* 25, no. 3 (1985): 1906–21.

59. Daniel Patte, " 'Love Your Enemies' — 'Woe to You, Scribes and Pharisees': The Need for a Semiotic Approach in New Testament Studies," in Theodore W. Jennings, Jr., ed., *Text and Logos: The Humanistic Interpretation of the New Testament* (Atlanta: Scholars Press, 1990): 81–96, provides

a very helpful hermeneutical reflection on Matthew as well as exegetical anti-Jewish discourses. He suggests that "Matthew's intentional message is not anti-Jewish. On the contrary, it advocates a return to a more Jewish understanding of the gospel in general, and more particularly of Christ and of discipleship.... The audience that he envisions... is a church that is totally separated from Judaism... and radically rejects any continuity with the Jews and their Judaism" (95).

60. See Antoinette Clark Wire, "Gender Roles in a Scribal Community," in David L. Balch, ed., *Social History of the Matthean Community: Cross-Disciplinary Approaches* (Minneapolis: Fortress, 1991), 87–121.

61. See Celia Deutsch, "Wisdom in Matthew: Transformation of a Symbol," *Novum Testamentum* 32 (1990): 13–47.

62. See Helmut Gese, "Wisdom, Son of Man, and the Origins of Christology: The Consistent Development of Biblical Theology," *Horizons in Biblical Theology* 3 (1981): 45.

63. For a more differentiated and carefully argued view see Elaine Wainwright, *Towards a Feminist Critical Reading of the Gospel according to Matthew,* Beihefte zur Zeitschrift für die neutestamentlich Wissenschaft 60 (Berlin: Walter de Gruyter, 1991).

64. See, e.g., John Ashton, "The Transformation of Wisdom: A Study of the Prologue of John's Gospel," *New Testament Studies* 32 (1986): 161–86.

65. Rudolph Schnackenburg, "Der Vater, der mich gesandt hat: Zur johanneischen Christologie," in Breytenbach and Paulsen, *Anfänge der Christologie,* 275–92, argues that the "father-son" christology of the Fourth Gospel is late in comparison to the prophetic emissary christology. However, Schnackenburg does not discuss the Wisdom traditions in this context.

66. Raymond E. Brown, *The Gospel according to John,* vol. 1, Anchor Bible (New York: Doubleday, 1966), cxxii.

67. Norman R. Petersen, *The Gospel of John and the Sociology of Light: Language and Characterization in the Fourth Gospel* (Philadelphia: Trinity Press International, 1993), 128, 131.

68. Deborah Cameron, *Feminism and Linguistic Theory* (London: Macmillan, 1985), 140.

69. Luise Schottroff, "Wanderprophetinnen: Eine feministische Analyse der Logienquelle," *Evangelische Theologie* 51 (1991): 322–34.

70. Amy-Jill Levine, "Who's Catering the Q Affair? Feminist Observations on Q Paraenesis," *Semeia* 50 (1990): 145–61.

71. D'Angelo, "Theology in Mark and Q," 173.

72. Silvia Schroer, "Jesus Sophia: Erträge der feministischen Forschung zu einer frühchristlichen Deutung der Praxis und des Schicksals Jesu von Nazaret," in Doris Strahm and Regula Strobel, eds., *Vom Verlangen nach Heilwerden: Theologie in feministisch-theologischer Sicht* (Fribourg: Exodus, 1991), 112–28.

73. R. S. Sugirtharajah, "Wisdom, Q, and a Proposal for a Christology,"

Expository Times 102 (1990): 42–46. This proposal comes close to my own, although the article does not refer to *In Memory of Her*.

74. For a malestream attempt to underscore the significance of Wisdom christology see Walter Kasper, "Gottes Gegenwart in Jesus Christus: Vorüberlegungen zu einer weisheitlichen Christologie," in Walter Baier, ed., *Weisheit Gottes — Wesheit der Welt* (St. Ottilien: EOS Verlag, 1987), 1:311–27.

75. Joan Chamberlain Engelsman, *The Feminine Dimension of the Divine* (Philadelphia: Westminster, 1979), 95–148. Somewhat different arguments are found in Rosemary Radford Ruether, *Sexism and God-Talk: Toward a Feminist Theology* (Boston: Beacon Press, 1983), 57–61. Chamberlain Engelsman utilizes the Jungian archetypal theory; Radford Ruether is rightfully critical of the Jungian masculine-feminine symbol system, in which the feminine is always ranked in second place.

76. Stevan L. Davies, *The Gospel of Thomas and Christian Wisdom* (New York: Seabury Press, 1983).

77. Ibid., 129f.

78. Ibid., 171.

79. Marvin W. Meyer, "Making Mary Male: The Categories 'Male' and 'Female' in the Gospel of Thomas," *New Testament Studies* 31 (1985): 554.

80. Davies, *The Gospel of Thomas*, 153.

81. Radford Ruether, *Sexism and God-Talk*, 61.

82. Ibid., 138.

83. Patricia Hill Collins, *Black Feminist Thought: Knowledge, Consciousness and the Politics of Empowerment* (Boston: Unwin Hyman, 1990), distinguishes an Afrocentric notion of humanism from that criticized by Western feminists. Such a different "humanism" grows from the experience of the "oppressed Others." It is a "humanist vision of self-actualization, self-definition, and self-determination" (224).

84. For this position see James M. Robinson, "Very Goddess and Very Man: Jesus' Better Self," in King, *Images of the Feminine in Gnosticism*, 113–27, and Elizabeth A. Johnson, "Jesus the Wisdom of God: A Biblical Basis for Non-Androcentric Christology," *Ephemerides Theologicae Lovanienses* 61 (1985): 261–94.

85. See, e.g., Christa Mulack, *Jesus der Gesalbte der Frauen* (Stuttgart and Berlin: Kreuz Verlag, 1987).

86. Elizabeth V. Spelman, *Inessential Woman: Problems of Exclusion in Feminist Thought* (Boston: Beacon, 1988), has graphically depicted these relationships in antiquity and the modern world.

87. Susan Brooks Thistlethwaite, *Sex, Race, and God: Christian Feminism in Black and White* (New York: Crossroad, 1989).

88. See, e.g., Ean Beck, *The Cult of the Black Virgin* (Boston: Arkana, 1985); Ivan Van Sertima, ed., *Black Women in Antiquity* (New Brunswick, N.J.: Transaction Books, 1988); Martin Bernal, *Black Athena: The Afroasiatic Roots of Classical Civilization* (New Brunswick, N.J.: Rutgers

University Press, 1988); China Galland, *Longing for Darkness: Tara and the Black Madonna* (New York: Penguin Books, 1990).

89. See, e.g., the practical exercises and liturgical rituals in Susan Cady, Marian Ronan, and Hal Taussig, *Wisdom's Feast: Sophia in Study and Celebration* (New York: Harper & Row, 1989).

Chapter 6: In Her Image and Likeness

1. Gerhard G. Meersseman, ed., *Der Hymnos Akathistos im Abendland: Die älteste Andacht zur Gottesmutter* (Freiburg: Universitätsverlag, 1958); English translation of quoted text by Barbara Newman, "The Pilgrimage of Christ-Sophia," *Vox Benedictina* 9, no. 1 (1992): 20.

2. Pope John Paul II, *Apostolic Letter on Reserving Priestly Ordination to Men Alone,* Vatican, Pentecost, May 22, 1994. See also the discussion of this statement in *America* 171, no. 3 (1994): 16–26.

3. Vatican II, *Lumen gentium,* 53.

4. Dorothee Soelle, "Maria ist eine Sympathisantin," in Dorothee Soelle, *Sympathie: Theologisch-politische Traktate* (Stuttgart: Kreuz Verlag, 1978), 56.

5. Mary Gordon, "Coming to Terms with Mary," *Commonweal* (January 15, 1982): 11.

6. Demosthenes Savramis, "Die Stellung der Frau im Christentum: Theorie und Praxis unter besonderer Berücksichtigung Marias," in Walter Schöpsdau, ed., *Mariologie und Feminismus* (Göttingen: Vandenhoeck, 1985), 29.

7. Kari Elisabeth Børresen, "Männlich-Weiblich: Eine Theologiekritik," *Una Sancta* 35 (1980): 325–34.

8. Helga Sciurie, "Maria-Ecclesia als Mitherrscherin Christi: Zur Funktion des Sponsus-Sponsa Modells in der Bildkunst des 13. Jahrhunderts," in H. Röckelein, C. Opitz, and R. Bauer, eds., *Maria, Abbild oder Vorbild: Zur Sozialgeschichte mittelalterlicher Marienverehrung* (Tübingen: edition diskord, 1990), 120.

9. Ursula Nilgen, "Maria Regina — ein politischer Kultbildtyp?" *Römisches Jahrbuch für Kunstgeschichte* 19 (1981): 1–33.

10. Barbara Corrado Pope, "Immaculate and Powerful: The Marian Revival in the Nineteenth Century," in Clarissa W. Atkinson, Constance H. Buchanan, and Margaret R. Miles, eds., *Immaculate and Powerful: The Female in Sacred Image and Social Reality* (Boston: Beacon Press, 1985), 173–201.

11. See, for instance, the report of Richard N. Ostling, "The Search for Mary: Handmaid or Feminist?" *Time* (December 30, 1991): 62–66.

12. See the analysis of the Latin American context by Ivone Gebara and Clara Maria Bingemer, *Mary — Mother of God, Mother of the Poor* (Maryknoll, N.Y.: Orbis Books, 1987), 128–58.

13. Elisabeth Gössmann, "Reflexionen zur mariologischen Dogmengeschichte," in Röckelein, Opitz, and Bauer, *Maria, Abbild oder Vorbild,* 19–36; Elisabeth Gössmann, "Mariologische Entwicklungen im Mittelalter: Frauenfreundliche und frauenfeindliche Aspekte," in E. Gössmann and D. R. Bauer, eds., *Maria für alle Frauen oder über allen Frauen?* (Freiburg: Herder, 1989), 63–85.

14. See the critical analysis of Eva Schirmer, *Eva-Maria: Rollenbilder von Männern für Frauen* (Offenbach: Laetare Verlag, 1988).

15. With reference to the Beguines see, for instance, Martina Wehrli-Johns, "Haushälterin Gottes: Zur Mariennachfolge der Beginen," in Röckelein, Opitz, and Bauer, *Maria, Abbild oder Vorbild,* 147–67. However, one must not forget that the "women's tradition" was always suspected of heresy and was under surveillance by the Inquisition. See P. Segl, "Die religiöse Frauenbewegung in Südfrankreich im 12. und 13. Jahrhundert zwischen Häresie und Orthodoxie," in P. Dinzelbacher and D. R. Bauer, eds., *Religiöse Frauenbewegung und mystische Frömmigkeit im Mittelalter* (Cologne: Bohlau, 1988); Johannes Thiele, "Die religiöse Frauenbewegung des Mittelalters: Eine historische Orientierung," in Johannes Thiele, ed., *Mein Herz schmilzt wie Eis am Feuer: Die religiöse Frauenbewegung des Mittelalters in Porträts* (Stuttgart: Kreuz Verlag, 1988), 9–34, with discussion of the literature.

16. For further information see the contributions in Wolfgang Beinert and Heinrich Petri, eds., *Handbuch der Marienkunde* (Regensburg: Pustet, 1984).

17. See, e.g., Rosemary Radford Ruether, *Mary — The Feminine Face of the Church* (Philadelphia: Westminster Press, 1977); Christa Mulack, *Maria: Die geheime Göttin im Christentum* (Stuttgart: Kreuz Verlag, 1985).

18. For such a criticism see also Gabriela Signori, "Marienbilder im Vergleich: Marianische Wunderbücher zwischen Weltklerus, städtischer Ständevielfalt und ländlichen Subsistenzproblemen (10.–13. Jahrhundert)," in Röckelein, Opitz, and Bauer, *Maria, Abbild oder Vorbild,* 58–90.

19. Marina Warner, *Alone of All Her Sex: The Myth and the Cult of the Virgin Mary* (New York: Knopf, 1976).

20. Leonardo Boff, *The Maternal Face of God: The Feminine and Its Religious Expressions* (San Francisco: Harper & Row, 1987).

21. See G. Heintze, "Maria im Urteil Luthers und in evangelischen Äusserungen der Gegenwart," in Wolfgang Beinert, ed., *Maria — Eine ökumenische Herausforderung* (Regensburg: Pustet, 1984), 57–74; G. Maron, "Die Protestanten und Maria," in Elisabeth Moltmann-Wendel, Hans Küng, and Jürgen Moltmann, eds., *Was geht uns Maria an? Beiträge zur Auseinandersetzung in Theologie, Kirche, und Frömmigkeit* (Gütersloh: Mohn, 1988), 60–71.

22. Eberhard Wölfel, "Erwägungen zu Struktur und Anliegen der Mariologie," in Schöpsdau, *Mariologie und Feminismus,* 77.

23. See the critique of the work of Carl G. Jung, for instance, in ibid., 96, n.52.

24. As representative of this discussion see, e.g., Nelle Morton, *The Journey Is Home* (Boston: Beacon, 1985), and Ursula Krattinger, *Die perlmutterne Mönchin: Reise in eine weibliche Spiritualität* (Zurich: Kreuz Verlag, 1983).

25. See Chung Hyun Kyung, *Struggle to Be the Sun Again: Introducing Asian Women's Theology* (Maryknoll, N.Y.: Orbis Books, 1990), 76.

26. See Els Maeckelberghe, "'Mary': Maternal Friend or Virgin Mother?" in Anne Carr and Elisabeth Schüssler Fiorenza, eds., *Motherhood: Experience, Institution, Theology,* Concilium 206 (Edinburgh: T. & T. Clark, 1989), 120, 127.

27. However, Mechthild can also say about Mary: "Her son is God and she is Goddess."

28. For a historical discussion see R. E. Brown, K. P. Donfried, and J. A. Fitzmyer, eds., *Mary in the New Testament* (Philadelphia: Fortress, 1978); F. Mussner, "Die Mutter Jesu im Neuen Testament," in Wolfgang Beinert, ed., *Maria — Eine ökumenische Herausforderung* (Regensburg: Pustet, 1984), 9–30; Otto Knoch, "Maria in der Heilgen Schrift," in Wolfgang Beinert and Heinrich Petri, eds., *Handbuch der Marienkunde* (Regensburg: Friedrich Pustet, 1984), 15–92.

29. For an excellent discussion see María Pilar Aquino, *Our Cry for Life: Feminist Theology from Latin America,* trans. Dinah Livingstone (Maryknoll, N.Y.: Orbis Books, 1993).

30. See, e.g., the work of Gebara and Bingemer and of Christa Mulack.

31. See, for instance, the discussion and bibliography in my book *But She Said: Feminist Practices of Biblical Interpretation* (Boston: Beacon Press, 1992), esp. 51–78, 195–219. See also Brigitte Kahl, *Armenevangelium und Heidenevangelium* (Berlin: Evangelische Verlagsanstalt, 1987), 86–149, and Itumeleng J. Mosala, *Biblical Hermeneutics and Black Theology in South Africa* (Grand Rapids: Eerdmans, 1989), 137–89.

32. Jane Schaberg, *The Illegitimacy of Jesus* (San Francisco: Harper & Row, 1987); "Die Stammütter und die Mutter Jesu," Concilium 25 (1989): 528–33.

33. For such an articulation of a critical feminist hermeneutics of liberation see my books *Bread Not Stone: The Challenge of Feminist Biblical Interpretation* (Boston: Beacon Press, 1985) and *Discipleship of Equals: A Critical Feminist Ekklesia-logy of Liberation* (New York: Crossroad, 1993).

34. See Herlinde Pissarek-Hudelist, "Maria — Schwester oder Mutter im Glauben? Chancen und Schwierigkeiten in Verkündigung und Katechese," in Gössmann and Bauer, *Maria für alle Frauen oder über allen Frauen?* 146–67.

35. See Elizabeth A. Johnson, "Saints and Mary," in Francis Schüssler Fiorenza and John P. Galvin, eds., *Systematic Theology: Roman Catholic Perspectives* (Minneapolis: Fortress Press, 1991), 2:146–77, 155–163.

36. For this evaluation see also Anne Carr, "Mary in the Mystery of the Church: Vatican Council II," in Carol Frances Jegen, ed., *Mary according to Women* (Kansas City, Mo.: Leaven Press, 1985), 5–32.

37. See Joseph Ratzinger, *Die christliche Brüderlichkeit* (Munich: Kösel, 1960), whose theological outlook influenced the council's theology.

38. See, e.g., Anne Carr, "Mary: Model of Faith," in Doris Donnelly, ed., *Mary, Woman of Nazareth: Biblical and Theological Perspectives* (New York: Paulist Press, 1989), 7–24.

39. Radford Ruether, *Mary — The Feminine Face of the Church,* 86.

40. Rosemary Radford Ruether, *Sexism and God-Talk: Toward a Feminist Theology* (Boston: Beacon Press, 1983), 152.

41. Ibid., 157.

42. Ibid., 155.

43. Ivone Gebara and Clara Maria Bingemer, *Mary — Mother of God, Mother of the Poor,* 43. However, it must not be overlooked that their chapter on "Mary in Scripture" is riddled with anti-Jewish supersessionist statements.

44. Ibid., 163.

45. Ibid.

46. This has been argued repeatedly especially by Catharina J. M. Halkes, *Gott hat nicht nur starke Söhne: Grundzüge einer feministischen Theologie* (Gütersloh: GTB Siebenstern, 1980), 92–109; see also her articles "Maria, die Frau: Mariologie und Feminismus," in Schöpsdau, *Mariologie und Feminismus,* 42–70, and "Maria," *Wörterbuch der feministischen Theologie* (Gütersloh: G. Mohn, 1991), 268–74.

47. Mary Daly, *Beyond God the Father: Toward a Philosophy of Women's Liberation* (Boston: Beacon Press, 1973), 89.

48. The same reference to the ambivalent and ambiguous character of hegemonic mariology is found frequently in feminist literature.

49. See, for instance, Elizabeth Johnson, "Reconstructing a Theology of Mary," in Donnelly, *Mary, Woman of Nazareth,* 69–91.

50. Kari Elisabeth Børresen, "Maria in der katholischen Theologie," in Moltmann-Wendel, Küng, and Moltmann, *Was geht uns Maria an?* 84, arrives at a similar judgment: "Finally, the interrelation between femininity and subordination remains fundamental to ecclesiology and mariology. In a similar fashion the incompatibility between the Divine and femaleness remains basic to the discourse about God and to christology."

51. See my article "Feminist Theology as a Critical Theology of Liberation," *Theological Studies* 36 (1975): 606–26 (reprinted in revised form in *Discipleship of Equals*).

52. See especially John R. Shinners, "Mary and the People: The Cult of Mary and Popular Belief," in Donnelly, *Mary, Woman of Nazareth,* 161–86.

53. The text in translation reads: "I see thee, Mary, in a thousand ways / So beautifully expressed, / But no Image can express the way / In which my soul can see thee."

54. Schalom Ben Chorin, "A Jewish View of the Mother of Jesus," in Küng and Moltmann, *Mary in the Churches,* 12–16.

55. This is not to be understood as a genealogical, causative derivation of the cult of Mary from the local cult of the G*ddesses but rather must be seen as its cooptation and usurpation. See, e.g., Edith Specht, "Kulttradition einer weiblichen Gottheit: Beispiel Ephesos," in Röckelein, Opitz, and Bauer, *Maria, Abbild oder Vorbild,* 37–47, and Françoise Jeanlin, "Konstantinopel, die Stadt der Theotokos," ibid., 48–57; see also the work of Marina Warner and Josefine Schreier, *Göttinnen: Ihr Einfluss von der Urzeit bis zur Gegenwart* (Munich: Verlag Frauenoffensive, 1977).

56. See, e.g., Hugo Rahner, *Greek Myths and Christian Mysteries* (New York: Harper & Row, 1963); Jean Daniélou, "Le culte marial et la paganisme," in D'Hubert du Manoir, ed., *Maria: Études sur la Sainte Vierge* (Paris: Beauchesne, 1949), 159–81; H. Leclercq, "Marie, Mère de Dieu," *Dictionnaire d'archéologie chrétienne et de liturgie* 10/2 (Paris, 1932): 1982–2043.

57. Elizabeth Johnson, "Mary and the Image of God," in Donnelly, *Mary, Woman of Nazareth,* 34–37.

58. See, for instance, Christa Mulack, *Natürlich weiblich: Die Heimatlosigkeit der Frau im Patriarchat* (Stuttgart: Kreuz Verlag, 1990).

59. See, e.g., Marie-Theres Wacker, "Die Göttin kehrt zurück: Kritische Sichtung neuer Entwürfe," in Marie-Theres Wacker, ed., *Der Gott der Männer und die Frauen* (Düsseldorf: Patmos Verlag, 1987), 11–38; Doris Brockmann, "Die Weiblichkeit Gottes: Zu Christa Mulack's Programmatik der Neubestimmung des Göttlichen," ibid., 93–100; Jutta Flatters, "Von der Aufwertung des 'Weiblichen' und ihrem Preis: Kritische Anmerkungen zu Christa Mulack's 'Jesus — der Gesalbte der Frauen,'" in L. Siegele-Wenschkewitz, *Verdrängte Vergangenheit, die uns bedrängt: Feministische Theologie in der Verantwortung für die Geschichte* (Munich: Kaiser Verlag, 1988), 164–80; Marie-Theres Wacker, "Matriarchale Bibelkritik — ein antijüdisches Konzept?" ibid., 181–242.

60. See, for instance, Elisabeth Gössmann, "Mariologische Thesen in Feministischer Theologie: Darstellung und Kritik," in Gössmann and Bauer, *Maria für alle Frauen oder über allen Frauen?* 168–79.

61. See among others Hermann Häring, "Die Mutter als die Schmerzensreiche: Zur Geschichte des Weiblichen in der Trinität," in *Der Gott der Männer und der Frauen,* 38–69, and the book of Frederic Raurell, *Der Mythos vom männlichen Gott* (Freiburg: Herder, 1989).

62. Among others G. K. Kaltenbrunner, "Ist der Heilige Geist weiblich?" *Una Sancta* 32 (1977): 273–80; M. Meyer, "Das 'Mutter-Amt' des Heiligen Geistes in der Theologie Zinzendorfs," *Evangelische Theologie* 43 (1983): 415–22.

63. See Verena Wodtke, *Auf den Spuren der Weisheit: Sophia — Wegweiserin für ein weibliches Gottesbild* (Freiburg: Herder, 1991).

64. See Elizabeth Johnson, "Mary and the Image of God," 62, esp. nn. 26, 28, 29.

65. Edward Schillebeeckx, *Mary, Mother of the Redemption* (New York: Sheed and Ward, 1964), 113–14.

66. Virgil Elizondo, "Mary and the Poor: A Model of Evangelizing Ecumenism," in Küng and Moltmann, *Mary in the Churches,* 61.

67. See, e.g., Mary DeCock, "Our Lady of Guadalupe: Symbol of Liberation?" in Jegen, *Mary according to Women,* 113–41; Ena Campbell, "The Virgin of Guadalupe and the Female Self-Image: A Mexican Case History," in James Preston, ed., *Mother Worship: Theme and Variations* (Chapel Hill: University of North Carolina Press, 1982), 5–24; Evelyn Stevens, "Marianismo: The Other Face of Machismo in Latin America," in Ann Pescatello, ed., *Male and Female in Latin America* (Pittsburgh: University of Pittsburgh Press, 1973), 90–100; Lillian Comas-Diaz, "Feminist Therapy with Hispanic/Latina Women: Myth or Reality?" in Lenora Fulani, ed., *The Psychopathology of Everyday Racism and Sexism* (New York: Harrington Park Press, 1988), 39–62.

68. Boff, *The Maternal Face of God,* 96.

69. Andrew Greeley, *The Mary Myth: On the Femininity of God* (New York: Seabury, 1977), 13.

70. Gerda Weiler, *Ich brauche die Göttin: Zur Kulturgeschichte eines Symbols* (Basel: Mond-Buch Verlag, 1990).

71. Christa Mulack, *Maria — die geheime Göttin im Christentum* (Stuttgart: Kreuz Verlag, 1983).

72. For such an intra-feminist thealogical debate see Emily Erwin Culpepper, "Contemporary Goddess Thealogy: A Sympathetic Critique," in Clarissa Atkinson, Margaret Miles, and Constance Buchanan, eds., *Shaping New Vision: Gender and Values in American Culture* (Ann Arbor: University of Michigan Press, 1987), 51–71; see also the contributions of Mary Jo Weaver, "Who Is the Goddess and Where Does She Get Us?"; Jo Ann Hackett, "Can a Sexist Model Liberate Us? Ancient Near Eastern 'Fertility' Goddesses"; Howard Eilberg-Schwartz, "Witches of the West: Neopaganism and the Goddess Worship as Enlightenment Religions," in *Journal of Feminist Studies in Religion* 5, no. 1 (1989): 47–100, as well as the roundtable discussion on "If God Is God She Is Not Nice," ibid., 103–18.

73. The conservative political tendency of this direction of thought is underscored by feminist philosophical criticisms of the theoretical frameworks of Mary Daly and Luce Irigaray. See Ruth Grossmass, "Von der Verführungskraft der Bilder: Mary Daly's Elemental — Feministische Philosophie," in Ruth Grossmass, ed., *Feministischer Kompass, patriarchales Gepäck: Kritik,* 56–116; and Alexandra Busch, "Der metaphorische Schleier des ewig Weiblichen — Zu Luce Irigaray's Ethik der sexuellen Differenz," ibid., 117–71; see also the evaluation of Mary Daly's thought by Rosi

Braidotti, *Patterns of Dissonance: A Study of Women in Contemporary Philosophy* (New York: Routledge, 1991), 204–8.

74. Judith Plaskow, *Standing Again at Sinai: Judaism from a Feminist Perspective* (San Francisco: Harper & Row, 1990), 121–69.

75. For an extensive annotated bibliography see Anne Carson, *Goddesses and Wise Women: The Literature of Feminist Spirituality 1980–1992* (Freedom, Calif.: Crossing Press, 1992); for an interreligious discussion see Carl Olsen, ed., *The Book of the Goddess: Past and Present* (New York: Crossroad, 1983); For a personal thealogical account see especially Carol P. Christ, *Laughter of Aphrodite: Reflections on a Journey to the Goddess* (San Francisco: Harper & Row, 1987).

76. For the interconnection of G*d-language and self-esteem see Carol Saussy, *God Images and Self-Esteem: Empowering Women in a Patriarchal Society* (Louisville: Westminster/John Knox Press, 1991).

77. On this question see the important work of Sallie McFague, *Models of God: Theology for an Ecological, Nuclear Age* (Philadelphia: Fortress, 1987), and by the same author, *The Body of God: An Ecological Theology* (Minneapolis: Fortress, 1993).

78. See Susan Heckman, *Gender and Knowledge: Elements of Postmodern Feminism* (Boston: Northeastern University Press, 1990), 152–90. For theology see the very important book of Rebecca S. Chopp, *The Power to Speak: Feminism, Language, God* (New York: Crossroad, 1989).

79. See, for instance, Eberhard Wölfel, "Erwägungen zu Struktur und Anliegen der Mariologie," in Schöpsdau, *Mariologie und Feminismus,* 88–96. Johannes Thiele, *Madonna mia: Maria und die Männer* (Stuttgart: Kreuz Verlag, 1990), argues that the Madonna as "the girl, the bride, the mother, and the sorrowful" confronts every man "in his feelings, religious emotionality, even in his completely missing or only barely developed erotic culture" (93).

80. In his encyclical *Mother of the Redeemer* (section 46) Pope John Paul II makes a direct connection between the essence of woman and the motherhood of Mary. With reference to Mary he valorizes feminine virtues such as generous self-sacrifice, the power of love to suffer great pain, limitless fidelity, tireless commitment, relationality, and the ability to combine empathetic insight with words of consolation and encouragement. See the collection of papal addresses in English by Seamus O'Byrne, ed., *Pope John Paul II: Mother of the Church* (Dublin: Mercier Press, 1987).

81. See especially the proposals of Gebara and Bingemer and Elizabeth Johnson, who advocate the integration of the cult of Mary into the general cult of the saints. As a historical figure, Mary, like all the saints, belonged to the *basileia* movement, and from heaven, "the world of God," still supports emancipatory struggles.

82. Such a mode of multifaceted theological associations and imaginative amplifications is apparent in *Akathistos,* a Marian hymn of the Eastern

church. This hymn applies to Mary the biblical images of the Exodus, which Paul uses to characterize Christ's saving activity:

> Hail, you sea that has devoured the holy Pharaoh;
> Hail, you rock that has given drink to those who thirst for life;
> Hail, you column of fire that led those in the dark...
> Hail, O land of promises,
> Hail, you, from whom flows honey and milk.
> Hail, you inviolate mother.

See Meersseman, *Hymnos Akathistos,* 52.

83. The importance of this turn toward practical mariology has been stressed by Paul Schmidt, *Maria, Modell der neuen Frau: Perspektiven einer zeitgemässen Mariologie* (Kevelaer: Butzon & Bercker, 1974); see also the contribution of Herlinde Pissarek-Hudelist, "Thesen zur Befreiungs-mariologie," in Gössmann and Bauer, *Maria für alle Frauen oder über allen Frauen?* 180–90.

84. See Ruth C. Duck, *Gender and the Name of God: The Trinitarian Baptismal Formula* (New York: Pilgrim Press, 1991).

85. Robert McAfee Brown, *Theology in a New Key: Responding to Liberation Themes* (Philadelphia: Westminster Press, 1978), 99–100.

86. As quoted by Maria Teresa Petrozzi, *Ain Karim* (Jerusalem: Franciscan Publishing Press, n.d.), 38. After this account, Elizabeth and Ain Karim are mentioned again only in the Jerusalem lectionary, which dates to the fifth–eighth century ("28, August. In the village of Encharim, in the church of the just Elizabeth, her commemoration" [ELS 44]). Petrozzi points to a possible reason for this lacuna: "Judeo-Christian communities have been traced in Jerusalem, Bethlehem, Bethany, Capharnaum, Nazareth, and Ain Karim. The lack of information about our site might be attributed to that conspiracy of silence maintained by the Fathers of the official Greek Church with regard to all places of worship kept by Judeo-Christians. The most outstanding example is supplied by the sanctuary of the Annunciation, Nazareth: The official Church neglected it as long as it was the property of Judeo-Christians" (42).

87. Mitri Raheb, *Ich bin Christ und Palestinenser: Israel, Seine Nachbarn und die Bibel,* Gütersloher Taschenbücher 1307 (Gütersloh: Gütersloher Verlagshaus, 1994); to be published in English by Fortress Press.

88. Ibid., 16.

89. For the elaboration of such a feminist interreligious dialogue see, for instance, Paula M. Cooey, William R. Eakin, and Jay B. McDaniel, eds., *After Patriarchy: Feminist Transformations of the World Religions* (Maryknoll, N.Y.: Orbis Books, 1991).

90. See Kwok Pui-lan, "Racism and Ethnocentrism in Feminist Biblical Interpretation," in Elisabeth Schüssler Fiorenza, ed., *Searching the Scriptures,* vol. 1, *A Feminist Introduction* (New York: Crossroad, 1993).

91. For literature and exegetical discussion of these texts see Raymond E. Brown, *The Birth of the Messiah: A Commentary of the Infancy Narra-*

tives in Matthew and Luke (Garden City, N.Y.: Doubleday, 1977), and Richard A. Horsley, *The Liberation of Christmas: The Infancy Narratives in Social Context* (New York: Crossroad, 1989).

92. For two quite different feminist biblical interpretations see Luise Schottroff, *Let the Oppressed Go Free: Feminist Perspectives on the New Testament* (Louisville: Westminster/John Knox Press, 1993), 158–67, and Janice Capel Anderson, "Mary's Difference: Gender and Patriarchy in the Birth Narratives," *Journal of Religion* 67, no. 2 (1987): 183–202.

93. Katie Geneva Cannon, *Black Womanist Ethics* (Atlanta: Scholars Press, 1988).

94. Christiane Schmerl and Ruth Grossmass, " 'Nur im Streit wird die Wahrheit geboren'...Gedanken zu einer prozessbezogenen feministischen Methodologie," in Christiane Schmerl and Ruth Grossmass, eds., *Feministicher Kompass, patriarchales Gepäck: Kritik konservativer Anteile in neueren feministichen Theorien* (New York, Frankfurt: Campus Verlag, 1989).

Select Bibliography

Aquino, María Pilar. *Our Cry for Life: Feminist Theology from Latin America.* Trans. Dinah Livingstone. Maryknoll, N.Y.: Orbis Books, 1993.

Ashton, John. "The Transformation of Wisdom: A Study of the Prologue of John's Gospel." *New Testament Studies* 32 (1986): 161–86.

Bader, Dietmar, ed. *Maria Magdalena: Zu einem Bild der Frau in der christlichen Verkündigung.* Schriftenreihe der Katholischen Akademie der Erzdiözese Freiburg. Munich: Verlag Schnell & Steiner, 1990.

Balch, David L., ed. *Let Wives Be Submissive: The Domestic Code in 1 Peter.* Chicago: Scholars Press, 1981.

———. "Household Codes." In *Greco-Roman Literature and the New Testament,* ed. D. Aune, 25–50. Atlanta: Scholars Press, 1988.

———. *Social History of the Matthean Community: Cross-Disciplinary Approach.* Minneapolis: Fortress Press, 1991.

Balz, Horst Robert. *Methodische Probleme der neutestamentlichen Christologie.* Wissenschaftliche Monographien zum Alten und Neuen Testament 25. Neukirchen-Vluyn: Neukirchener Verlag, 1967.

Barrett, C. K. "What Is New Testament Theology? Some Reflections." *Horizons in Biblical Theology* 3 (1981): 1–22.

Baudler, Georg. *Jesus im Spiegel seiner Gleichnisse.* Stuttgart: Calwer Verlag, 1986.

Beavis, Mary Ann. "Ancient Slavery as an Interpretive Context for the New Testament Servant Parables with Special Reference to the Unjust Steward (Lk 16:1–8)," *Journal of Biblical Literature* 11 (1992): 37–54.

Becker, Jürgen. "Die neutestamentliche Rede vom Sühnetod Jesu." In *Die Heilsbedeutung des Kreuzes für Glaube und Hoffnung des Christen,* ed. Eberhard Jüngel, 29–49. Tübingen: J. C. B. Mohr/Paul Siebeck, 1990.

Beechey, V. "On Patriarchy." *Feminist Review* 3 (1979): 66–82.

Beinert, Wolfgang. *Maria in der feministischen Theologie.* Kevelaer: Verlag Butzon & Bercker, 1988.

Beinert, Wolfgang, and Heinrich Petri, eds. *Handbuch der Marienkunde.* Regensburg: Verlag Friedrich Pustet, 1984.

Belenky, Mary F., et al. *Women's Ways of Knowing: The Development of Self, Voice, and Mind.* New York: Basic Books, 1986.

Belsey, C. "Constructing the Subject: Deconstructing the Text." In *Feminist Criticism and Social Change: Sex, Class, and Race in Literature and Culture,* ed. J. Newton and D. Rosenfelt, 45–64. New York: Methuen, 1985.

Benhabib, S., and D. Cornell, eds. *Feminism as Critique: On the Politics of Gender.* Minneapolis: University of Minnesota Press, 1987.

Benjamin, Jessica. *The Bonds of Love: Psychoanalysis, Feminism, and the Problem of Domination.* New York: Pantheon Books, 1988.

Berger, Klaus. "Rhetorical Criticism, New Form Criticism, and New Testament Hermeneutics." In *Rhetoric and the New Testament,* ed. Stanley E. Porter and Thomas H. Olbricht, 390–96. Journal for the Study of the New Testament Supplement Series 90. Sheffield: JSOT Press, 1993.

Bindley, Herbert T., ed. *The Oecumenical Documents of the Faith.* London: Methuen, 1950.

Bloomquist, Karen L. "Sexual Violence: Patriarchy's Offense and Defense." In *Christianity, Patriarchy, and Abuse: A Feminist Critique,* ed. Joanne Carlson Brown and Carole R. Bohn, 62–69. New York: Pilgrim Press, 1989.

Boers, Hendrikus. *What Is New Testament Theology?* Philadelphia: Fortress Press, 1979.

———. "Polysemy in Paul's Use of Christological Expressions." In *The Future of Christology: Essays in Honor of Leander E. Keck,* ed. Abraham J. Malherbe and Wayne A. Meeks, 91–108. Minneapolis: Fortress Press, 1993.

Boff, Leonardo. *The Maternal Face of God: The Feminine and Its Religious Expressions.* San Francisco: Harper & Row, 1987.

Børresen, Kari Elisabeth. "Männlich-Weiblich: Eine Theologiekritik." *Una Sancta* 35 (1980): 325–34.

Boring, M. Eugene. "The Historical-Critical Method's 'Criteria of Authenticity': The Beatitudes in Q and Thomas as a Test Case." *Semeia* 44 (1988).

———. *The Continuing Voice of Jesus: Christian Prophecy and the Gospel Tradition.* Louisville: Westminster/John Knox Press, 1991.

Borg, Marcus J. "Portraits of Jesus in Contemporary North American Scholarship," *Harvard Theological Review* 84, no. 1 (1991): 1–22.

———. *Jesus in Contemporary Scholarship.* Philadelphia: Trinity Press International, 1994.

———. *Meeting Jesus Again for the First Time: The Historical Jesus and the Heart of Contemporary Faith.* San Francisco: Harper, 1994.

Borowitz, Eugene B. *Contemporary Christologies: A Jewish Response.* New York: Paulist, 1980.

Bosmajian, Haig A. *The Language of Oppression.* Lanham, Md.: University Press of America, 1983.

Botha, C. J. "What Is the Kingdom of God?" *Theologia Evangelica* 22, no. 3 (1989): 30–35.

Botha, Jan. "On the 'Reinvention' of Rhetoric." *Scriptura* 31 (1989): 14–31.

Brandon, D. *Grammar and Gender.* New Haven: Yale University Press, 1986.

Brandon, S. G. F. *Jesus and the Zealots: A Study of the Political Factor in Primitive Christianity.* Manchester: Manchester University Press, 1967.

Breytenbach, Cilliers, and Henning Paulsen, eds. *Anfänge der Christologie: Festschrift für Ferdinand Hahn zum 65. Geburtstag.* Göttingen: Vandenhoeck & Ruprecht, 1991.

Bridenthal, Renate, Atina Grossmann, and Marion Kaplan, eds. *When Biology Became Destiny: Women in Weimar and Nazi Germany.* New York: Monthly Review Press, 1984.

Briggs, Sheila. "Can an Enslaved God Liberate?" *Semeia* 47 (1989): 141–56.

Brooks Thistlethwaite, Susan. "Every Two Minutes: Battered Women and Feminist Interpretation." In *Feminist Interpretation of the Bible,* ed. Letty M. Russell, 96–110. Philadelphia: Westminster Press, 1985.

———. *Sex, Race, and God: Christian Feminism in Black and White.* New York: Crossroad, 1989.

Brooks Thistlethwaite, Susan, and Mary Potter Engel, eds. *Lift Every Voice: Constructing Christian Theologies from the Underside.* San Francisco: Harper & Row, 1990.

Brooten, Bernadette. *Women Leaders in the Ancient Synagogue.* Chico, Calif.: Scholars Press, 1982.

———. "Jewish Women's History in the Roman Period: A Task for Christian Theology." *Harvard Theological Review* 79 (1986): 22–30.

Brown, Alexandra R. "Seized by the Cross: The Death of Jesus in Paul's Transformative Discourse." In *Society of Biblical Literature, 1993 Seminar Papers,* ed. Eugene H. Lovering, Jr., 740–57. Atlanta: Scholars Press, 1993.

Brown, Cheryl Ann. *No Longer Be Silent: First-Century Jewish Portraits of Biblical Women.* Louisville: Westminster/John Knox Press, 1992.

Brown, Raymond E. *The Birth of the Messiah: A Commentary on the Infancy Narratives in Matthew and Luke.* Garden City, N.Y.: Doubleday, 1977.

———. *The Death of the Messiah: From Gethsemane to the Grave.* 2 vols. Garden City, N.Y.: Doubleday, 1994.

Brown, Raymond E., K. P. Donfried, and J. A. Fitzmyer, eds. *Mary in the New Testament.* Philadelphia: Fortress Press, 1978.

Brown Douglas, Kelly. *The Black Christ.* Maryknoll, N.Y.: Orbis Books, 1994.

Brownson, James. "Neutralizing the Intimate Enemy: The Portrayal of Judas in the Fourth Gospel." In *Society of Biblical Literature, 1992 Seminar Papers,* ed. Eugene H. Lovering, Jr., 49–60. Atlanta: Scholars Press, 1992.

Bultmann, Rudolf Karl. *Theology of the New Testament.* Trans. K. Grobel. New York: Scribners, 1955.

———. *History of the Synoptic Tradition.* New York: Harper & Row, 1963.

Burnett, Fred W. *The Testament of Jesus-Sophia: A Redaction-Critical Study of the Eschatological Discourse in Matthew.* Washington, D.C.: University Press of America, 1979.

———. "Exposing the Anti-Jewish Ideology of Matthew's Implied Author: The Characterization of God as Father." In David Jobling and Tina Pippin, eds., *Ideological Criticism of Biblical Texts,* Semeia 59 (1992): 155–91.

Burrus, Virginia. "The Heretical Woman as Symbol in Alexander, Athanasius, Epiphanius and Jerome." *Harvard Theological Review* 84 (1991): 229–48.

———. "Word and Flesh: The Bodies and Sexuality of Ascetic Women in Christian Antiquity." In *Journal of Feminist Studies in Religion* 10, no. 1 (1994): 26–51.

Butts, James R. "Probing the Polling: Jesus Seminar Results on the Kingdom Sayings." *Foundations and Facets Forum* 3, no. 1 (1987): 98–128.

Cady Stanton, Elizabeth, ed. *The Original Feminist Attack on the Bible: The Woman's Bible.* Facsimile edition. New York: Arno Press, 1974.

Cameron, Deborah. *Feminism and Linguistic Theory.* London: Macmillan & Co., 1985.

Camp, Claudia. "Female Voice, Written Word: Women and Authority in Hebrew Scripture." In *Embodied Love,* ed. P. M. Cooey, S. A. Farmer, M. E. Ross, 97–113. San Francisco: Harper & Row, 1987.

———. "Woman Wisdom as Root Metaphor: A Theological Consideration." In *The Listening Heart: Essays in Wisdom and the Psalms in Honor of Roland E. Murphy, O. Carm.,* ed. Kenneth G. Hogland et al., 46–76. Journal for the Study of the Old Testament Supplement Series 58. Sheffield: JSOT Press, 1987.

Cannon, Katie G. *Black Womanist Ethics.* Atlanta: Scholars Press, 1988.

———. "Slave Ideology and Biblical Interpretation." In *Interpretation for Liberation,* ed. Katie G. Cannon and Elisabeth Schüssler Fiorenza, 9–23. Atlanta: Scholars Press, 1989.

———. "Womanist Perspectival Discourse and Canon Formation." *Journal of Feminist Studies in Religion* 9 (1993).

Cannon, Katie G., and Elisabeth Schüssler Fiorenza, eds. *Interpretation for Liberation.* Semeia 47. Atlanta: Scholars Press, 1989.

Capel Anderson, Janice. "Matthew: Gender and Reading." In *The Bible and Feminist Hermeneutics,* ed. Mary Ann Tolbert, 3–28. Semeia 28. Chico, Calif.: Scholars Press, 1983.

———. "Mary's Difference: Gender and Patriarchy in the Birth Narratives." *Journal of Religion* 67 (1987): 183–202.

Carby, Hazel V. "On the Threshold of Women's Era: Lynching, Empire and Sexuality." In *Race, Writing, and Difference,* ed. H. L. Gates, 301–28. Chicago: University of Chicago Press, 1986.

Carlson Brown, Joanne, and Carol R. Bohn, eds. *Christianity, Patriarchy, and Abuse: A Feminist Critique.* New York: Pilgrim Press, 1989.

Castelli, Elizabeth A. "Les belles infideles/Fidelity or Feminism? The Meaning of Feminist Biblical Translation." *Journal of Feminist Studies in Religion* 6, no. 2 (1990): 25–40.

———. *Imitating Paul: A Discourse of Power.* Louisville: Westminster/John Knox Press, 1991.

Chadwick, Henry. *The Early Church.* Grand Rapids: Eerdmans, 1968.

Chakravorty Spivak, Gayatri. *In Other Words: Essays in Cultural Politics.* New York: Metheun, 1987.

———. *The Post-Colonial Critic: Interviews, Strategies, Dialogues.* Ed. Sarah Harasym. New York: Routledge, 1990.

Chamberlain Engelsman, Joan. *The Feminine Dimension of the Divine.* Philadelphia: Westminster, 1979.

Charlesworth, James H. "From Barren Mazes to Gentle Rappings: The Emergence of Jesus Research. *Princeton Seminary Bulletin* n.s. 7 (1986): 221–30.

Charlesworth, James H., ed. *Jews and Christians: Exploring the Past, Present and Future.* New York: Crossroad/American Interfaith Institute, 1990.

———. *Jesus' Jewishness: Exploring the Place of Jesus within Early Judaism.* New York: Crossroad/American Interfaith Institute, 1991.

Chopp, Rebecca S. "Feminism's Theological Pragmatics: A Social Naturalism of Women's Experience." *Journal of Religion* 67, no. 2 (1987): 239–56.

———. *The Power to Speak: Feminism, Language, and God.* New York: Crossroad, 1989.

Christ, Carol P. *Laughter of Aphrodite: Reflections on a Journey to the Goddess.* San Francisco: Harper & Row, 1987.

———. "Embodied Thinking: Reflections on Feminist Theological Method." *Journal of Feminist Studies in Religion* 5, no. 1 (1989): 7–15.

Christ, Carol P., and Judith Plaskow, eds. *Weaving the Visions.* New York: Harper & Row, 1988.

Christian-Smith, Linda K. *Becoming a Woman through Romance.* New York: Routledge, 1990.

Chung Hyun Kyung. *Struggle to Be the Sun Again: Introducing Asian Women's Theology.* Maryknoll, N.Y.: Orbis Books, 1990.

Clark Wire, Antoinette. *The Corinthian Women Prophets: A Reconstruction through Paul's Rhetoric.* Minneapolis: Augsburg Fortress Press, 1990.

Clévenot, Michel. *Der Triumph des Kreuzes: Geschichte des Christentums im IV. und V. Jahrhundert.* Fribourg: Exodus, 1988.

Cocks, Joan. *The Oppositional Imagination: Feminism, Critique, and Political Theory.* New York: Routledge, 1989.

Code, Lorraine. *What Can She Know?* Ithaca, N.Y.: Cornell University Press, 1991.

Cohen, Arthur. *The Myth of the Judeo-Christian Tradition.* New York: Harper & Row, 1969.

Conzelmann, Hans. *An Outline of the Theology of the New Testament.* New York: Harper & Row, 1969.

Cooey, Paula M., William R. Eakin, Jay B. McDaniel, eds. *After Patriarchy: Feminist Transformations of the World Religions.* Maryknoll, N.Y.: Orbis Books, 1991.

Corley, Kathleen E. "Jesus' Table Practice: Dining with 'Tax Collectors and Sinners,' including Women." In *Society of Biblical Literature, 1993 Seminar Papers,* ed. Eugene H. Lovering, Jr., 444–59. Atlanta: Scholars Press, 1993.

———. *Private Women, Public Meals: Social Conflict in the Synoptic Tradition.* Peabody, Mass.: Hendrickson Publishers, 1993.

Corrado Pope, Barbara. "Immaculate and Powerful: The Marian Revival in the Nineteenth Century." In *Immaculate and Powerful: The Female in Sacred Image and Social Reality,* ed. Clarissa W. Atkinson, Constance H. Buchanan, and Margaret R. Miles, 173–201. Boston: Beacon Press, 1985.

Cousar, Charles B. *A Theology of the Cross: The Death of Jesus in the Pauline Letters.* Minneapolis: Fortress, 1992.

Coyle, J. Kevin. "Mary Magdalene in Manichaeism?" *Muséon* 104 (1991): 39–55.

Craig, K. M., and M. A. Kristjansson. "Women Reading as Men/Women Reading as Women: A Structural Analysis for the Historical Project." In *Poststructural Criticism and the Bible: Text/History/Discourse,* ed. Gary A. Phillips, 119–36. Semeia 51. Atlanta: Scholars Press, 1990.

Craighead, M. *The Mother's Song: Images of God the Mother.* New York: Paulist Press, 1986.

Crossan, John Dominic. "Materials and Methods in Historical Jesus Research." *Foundations and Facets Forum* 4, no. 4 (1988): 3–24.

———. *The Historical Jesus: The Life of a Mediterranean Jewish Peasant.* San Francisco: Harper & Row, 1991.

D'Angelo, Mary Rose. "Abba and 'Father': Imperial Theology and the Jesus Traditions," *Journal of Biblical Literature* 111 (1992): 611–30.

———. "Re-membering Jesus: Women, Prophecy, and Resistance in the Memory of the Early Churches." *Horizons* 19 (1992): 199–218.

———. "Theology in Mark and Q: *Abba* and 'Father' in Context." *Harvard Theological Review* 85 (1992): 149–74.

Dahl, Nils Alstrup. *The Crucified Messiah and Other Essays.* Minneapolis: Augsburg, 1974.

———. *Jesus the Christ: The Historical Origins of Christological Doctrine.* Ed. Donald H. Juel. Minneapolis: Fortress Press, 1991.

Daly, Mary. *Beyond God the Father: Toward a Philosophy of Women's Liberation.* Boston: Beacon Press, 1973.

Danker, F. "Who Put Jesus to Death?" In *Political Issues in Luke-Acts,* ed. Richard Cassidy and Philip J. Scharper. Maryknoll, N.Y.: Orbis Books, 1983.

Daum, Annette, and Deborah McCauley. "Jewish Christian Feminist Dialogue: A Wholistic Vision." *Union Seminary Quarterly Review* 38 (1983): 147–218.

Davies, Stevan L. *The Gospel of Thomas and Christian Wisdom.* New York: Seabury Press, 1983.

Day, Peggy L., ed. *Gender and Difference in Ancient Israel.* Minneapolis: Augsburg/Fortress, 1989.

De Jonge, Marinus. *Christology in Context: The Earliest Christian Response to Jesus.* Philadelphia: Westminster Press, 1988.

Deutsch, Celia. *Hidden Wisdom and the Easy Yoke: Wisdom, Torah and Discipleship in Matthew 11.25–30.* Journal for the Study of the New Testament Supplement Series 18. Sheffield: JSOT Press, 1987.

———. "Wisdom in Matthew: Transformation of a Symbol." *Novum Testamentum* 32 (1990): 13–47.

Dewey, Joanna. "Jesus' Healings of Women: Conformity and Non-Conformity to Dominant Cultural Values as Clues for Historical Reconstruction." In *Society of Biblical Literature, 1993 Seminar Papers,* ed. Eugene H. Lovering, Jr., 178–93. Atlanta: Scholars Press, 1993.

Dickey Young, Pamela. *Feminist Theology / Christian Theology: In Search of Method.* Minneapolis: Fortress, 1990.

Dillenberger, Jane. "The Magdalene: Reflections on the Image of the Saint and Sinner in Christian Art." In *Women, Religion and Social Change,* ed. Yvonne Yazbeck Haddad and Ellison Banks Findly, 115–45. Albany: State University of New York Press, 1985.

Dillistone, F. W. "Wisdom, Word, and Spirit: Revelation in the Wisdom Literature." *Interpretation* 2 (1948): 275–87.

Dinzelbacher P., and D. R. Bauer, eds. *Religiöse Frauenbewegung und mystische Frömmigkeit im Mittelalter.* Cologne: Bohlau, 1988.

Domeris, Bill. "Christology and Community: A Study of the Social Matrix of the Fourth Gospel." *Journal of Theology for Southern Africa* 64 (September 1988): 49–56.

Doran, Robert. "The Martyr: A Synoptic View of the Mother and Her Seven Sons." In *Ideal Figures in Ancient Judaism: Profiles and Paradigms,* ed.

George W. Nickelsburg and John J. Collins, 189–221. Society of Biblical Literature Septuagint and Cognate Studies 12. Chico, Calif.: Scholars Press, 1980.

duBois, Page. *Centaurs and Amazons: Women and the Pre-History of the Great Chain of Being.* Ann Arbor: University of Michigan Press, 1982.

———. *Torture and Truth: The New Ancient World.* New York: Routledge, 1991.

Duffy, Stephen J. "The Galilean Christ: Particularity and Universality." *Journal of Ecumenical Studies* 26 (1989): 154–74.

Dunn, James D. G. *Christology in the Making.* Philadelphia: Westminster, 1980.

Dyke, Doris Jean. *Crucified Woman.* Toronto: United Church Publishing House, 1991.

Ebert, Teresa L. "The Romance of Patriarchy: Ideology, Subjectivity, and Postmodern Feminist Cultural Theory." *Cultural Critique* 10 (1988): 25–36.

Eckardt, A. Roy. *Reclaiming the Jesus of History: Christology Today.* Minneapolis: Fortress Press, 1992.

Ehrman, Bart D. "The Cup, the Bread, and the Salvific Effect of Jesus' Death in Luke-Acts." In *Society of Biblical Literature, 1991 Seminar Papers,* ed. Eugene H. Lovering, Jr., 576–91. Atlanta: Scholars Press, 1991.

Evans, Craig A. "From Public Ministry to the Passion: Can a Link Be Found between the (Galilean) Life and the (Judean) Death of Jesus?" In *Society of Biblical Literature, 1993 Seminar Papers,* ed. Eugene H. Lovering, Jr., 460–72. Atlanta: Scholars Press, 1993.

Fabella, Virginia. "A Common Methodology for Diverse Christologies." In *With Passion and Compassion: Third World Women Doing Theology,* ed. V. Fabella and M. Amba Oduyoye, 108–17. Maryknoll, N.Y.: Orbis Books, 1988.

Fander, Monika. *Die Stellung der Frau im Markusevangelium unter besonderer Berücksichtigung kultur- und religionsgeschichtlicher Hintergründe.* Altenberge: Telos Verlag, 1989.

———. "Historical Critical Methods." In Elisabeth Schüssler Fiorenza, ed., *Searching the Scriptures,* vol. 1, *A Feminist Introduction,* 205–24. New York: Crossroad, 1993.

Farrar, Cynthia. *The Origins of Democratic Thinking: The Invention of Politics in Classical Athens.* Cambridge: Cambridge University Press, 1988.

Feber, Marianne A., and Julie A. Nelson, eds. *Beyond Economic Man: Feminist Theory and Economics.* Chicago: University of Chicago Press, 1993.

Felski, Rita. *Beyond Feminist Aesthetics: Feminist Literature and Social Change.* Cambridge: Harvard University Press, 1989.

Field-Bibb, Jacqueline. *Women towards Priesthood: Ministerial Politics and Feminist Practice.* New York: Cambridge University Press, 1991.

Fitzmyer, Joseph. "Abba and Jesus' Relation to God." *A cause de l'Évangile: Études sur les synoptiques et les Actes offertes au P. Jacques DuPont, O.S.B. à l'occasion de son 70e anniversaire,* 15–30. Lectio Divina 123. Paris: Cerf, 1985.

Fossum, Jarl. "The New *Religionsgeschichtliche Schule*: The Quest for Jewish Christology." In *Society of Biblical Literature, 1991 Seminar Papers,* ed. Eugene H. Lovering, Jr., 638–46. Atlanta: Scholars Press, 1991.

Foster, Willem S. "The Religio-historical Context of the Resurrection of Jesus and Resurrection Faith in the New Testament. *Neotestamentica* 23 (1989): 159–75.

Fowler, Robert M. "Postmodern Biblical Criticism." *Foundations and Facets Forum* 5, no. 3 (1989): 3–30.

Frankenberg, Ruth. *White Women, Race Matters: The Social Construction of Whiteness*. Minneapolis: University of Minnesota Press, 1993.

Fredricksen, Paula. *From Jesus to Christ: The Origins of the New Testament Images of Jesus*. New Haven: Yale University Press, 1988.

Freyne, Sean. "The Charismatic." In *Ideal Figures in Ancient Judaism: Profiles and Paradigms*, ed. George W. Nickelsburg and John J. Collins, 223–58. Society of Biblical Literature Septuagint and Cognate Studies 12. Chico, Calif.: Scholars Press, 1980.

———. *Galilee, Jesus and the Gospels: Literary Approaches and Historical Investigations*. Dublin: Gill & Macmillan, 1988.

Frymer-Kensky, Tikva. *In the Wake of the Goddesses: Women, Culture, and the Biblical Transformation of Pagan Myth*. New York: Free Press, 1992.

Gebara, Ivone, and Clara Maria Bingemer. *Mary — Mother of God, Mother of the Poor*. Maryknoll, N.Y.: Orbis Books, 1987.

Geller Nathanson, Barbara H. "Toward a Multicultural Ecumenical History of Women in the First Century/ies C.E. In Elisabeth Schüssler Fiorenza, ed., *Searching the Scriptures*, vol. 1, *A Feminist Introduction*, 272–89. New York: Crossroad, 1993.

Georgi, Dieter. "Das Wesen der Weisheit nach der Weisheit Salomos." In *Religionstheorie und Politische Theologie*. Vol. 2, *Gnosis und Politik*, ed. Jacob Taubes, 66–81. Munich: Wilhelm Fink Verlag/Verlag Ferdinand Schöning, 1984.

———. "Leben-Jesu-Theologie/Leben-Jesu-Forschung." *Theologische Realenzyklopädie* 20 (1991): 566–75.

———. "The Interest in Life of Jesus Theology as a Paradigm for the Social History of Biblical Criticism." *Harvard Theological Review* 85, no. 1 (1992): 51–83.

Gerhart, Mary. "Imaging Christ in Art, Politics, Spirituality: An Overview." In *Imaging Christ: Politics, Art, Spirituality*, ed. Francis A. Eigo, O.S.A., 1–45. Villanova, Pa.: Villanova University Press, 1991.

———. *Genre Choices, Gender Questions*. Oklahoma Project for Discourse and Theory 9. Norman: University of Oklahoma Press, 1992.

Gerhart, Mary, and Allan Melvin Russell. *Metaphoric Process: The Creation of Scientific and Religious Understanding*. Fort Worth: Texas Christian University Press, 1984.

Gese, Hartmut. "Wisdom, Son of Man, and the Origins of Christology: The Consistent Development of Biblical Theology." *Horizons in Biblical Theology* 3 (1981): 23–57.

Girard, René. *Job: Victim of His People*. Stanford: Stanford University Press, 1977.

———. *Violence and the Sacred*. Stanford: Stanford University Press, 1977.

Good, Deirdre J. "Sophia in Valentinianism." *The Second Century* 4, no. 4 (1984): 193–201.

————. *Reconstructing the Tradition of Sophia in Gnostic Literature.* Atlanta: Scholars Press, 1987.

Gordon, Mary. "Coming to Terms with Mary." *Commonweal* (January 15, 1982): 11–14.

Gössmann, Elisabeth, and D. R. Bauer, eds. *Maria für alle Frauen oder über allen Frauen?.* Freiburg: Herder, 1989.

Grant, Jacquelyn. *White Women's Christ, Black Women's Jesus.* Atlanta: Scholars Press, 1990.

Greene, G., and C. Kaplan, eds. *Making a Difference: Feminist Literary Criticism.* New York: Methuen, 1985.

Grey, Mary. *Feminism, Redemption, and the Christian Tradition.* London: SCM Press, 1989.

————. *The Wisdom of Fools? Seeking Revelation for Today.* London: SPCK, 1993.

Grillmeier, Aloys. *Christ in Christian Tradition.* Vol. 1: *From the Apostolic Age to Chalcedon (451).* Trans. John Bowden. 2d ed. Atlanta: John Knox Press, 1975.

Gudorf, Christine E. *Victimization: Examining Christian Complicity.* Philadelphia: Trinity Press International, 1992.

Gutiérrez, Gustavo. *The Power of the Poor in History.* Maryknoll, N.Y.: Orbis Books, 1983.

Haas, Peter J., ed. *Recovering the Role of Women: Power and Authority in Rabbinic Jewish Society.* South Florida Studies in the History of Judaism 59. Atlanta: Scholars Press, 1992.

Habermas, J. *The Theory of Communicative Action.* Boston: Beacon Press, 1987.

Hahn, Ferdinand. *The Titles of Jesus in Christology.* London: Lutterworth, 1969.

————. "Umstrittenes Jesusbild?" *Münchener Theologische Zeitschrift* 44 (1993): 95–107.

Hammerton-Kelly, Robert. *God the Father.* Philadelphia: Fortress Press, 1979.

————. *Sacred Violence: Paul's Hermeneutic of the Cross.* Minneapolis: Fortress Press, 1992.

Hanig, Roman. "Christus als 'wahrer Salomo' in der frühen Kirche." *Zeitschrift für die neutestamentliche Wissenschaft* 84 (1993): 111–34.

Haraway, Donna. "A Manifesto for Cyborgs: Science, Technology and Social Feminism in the 1980s." *Socialist Review* 80 (1985): 65–105.

Harding, Sandra, ed. *The "Racial" Economy of Science: Toward a Democratic Future.* Bloomington: Indiana University Press, 1993.

Harrington, Daniel J. "The Jewishness of Jesus as an Approach to Christology: Biblical Theology and Christian-Jewish Relations." In *The Promise and Practice of Biblical Theology,* ed. John Reumann, 71–86. Minneapolis: Fortress Press, 1991.

Harrisville, Roy A. "In Search of the Meaning of 'The Reign of God.'" *Interpretation* 47 (1983): 140–51.

Hartman, Lars. "Is the Crucified Christ the Center of a New Testament Theology?" In *Text and Logos: The Humanistic Interpretation of the New Testament,* ed. Theodore W. Jennings, Jr., 175–88. Homage Series. Scholars Press: Atlanta, 1990.

Haskins, Susan. *Mary Magdalene: Myth and Metaphor.* London: Harcourt Brace & Company, 1993.

Hawkesworth, M. E. *Beyond Oppression: Feminist Theory and Political Strategy.* New York: Continuum, 1990.

Heine, Susanne. "Eine Person von Rang und Namen: Historische Konturen der Magdalenerin." In *Jesu Rede von Gott und ihre Nachgeschichte im frühen Christentum: Festschrift für Willi Marxsen zum 70. Geburtstag,* 179–94. Gütersloh: Gerd Mohn, 1989.

———. "Brille der Parteilichkeit: Zu einer feministischen Hermeneutik." *Evangelische Kommentare* 23 (1990): 354–57.

Hefele, Charles Joseph. *A History of the Christian Councils from the Original Documents.* Ed. and trans. William R. Clark. 2d ed. Edinburgh: T. & T. Clark, 1984.

Hengel, Martin. "Jesus als messianischer Lehrer der Weisheit und die Anfänge der Christologie." In *Sagesse et Religion, [actes du] Colloque de Strasbourg, Octobre 1976,* 147–88. Travaux du Centre d'Etudes Supérieures spécialisé d'Histoire des Religions de Strasbourg. Paris: Presses universitaires de France, 1979.

———. *Crucifixion in the Ancient World and the Folly of the Message of the Cross.* Philadelphia: Fortress, 1977.

Hengel, Martin, and Anna Maria Schwemer, eds. *Königsherrschaft Gottes und himmlischer Kult in Judentum: Urchristentum und in der hellenistischen Welt.* Tübingen: J. C. B. Mohr (Paul Siebeck), 1991.

Hennessy, Rosemary. *Materialist Feminism and the Politics of Discourse.* New York and London: Routledge, 1993.

Herzfeld, Michael. "Honor and Shame: Problems in the Comparative Analysis of Moral Systems." *MAN* 15 (1980): 339–51.

———. "The Horns of the Mediterraneanist Dilemma." *American Ethnologist* 11 (1984): 439–54.

Heschel, Susannah. "Jüdisch-feministische Theologie und Antijudaismus in christlich-femistischer Theologie." In *Verdrängte Vergangenheit, die uns bedrängt: Feministische Theologie in der Verantwortung für die Geschichte,* ed. Leonore Siegele Wenschkewitz, 54–103. Munich: Chr. Kaiser, 1988.

———. "Anti-Judaism in Christian Feminist Theology." *Tikkun* 5, no. 3 (1990): 26–28.

Hiers, Richard H. *Jesus and Ethics — Four Interpretations: Adolf von Harnack, Albert Schweitzer, Rudolf Bultmann, and C. H. Dodd.* Philadelphia: Westminster Press, 1968.

Hill, David. "Jesus before the Sanhedrin — On What Charge?" *Irish Biblical Studies* 7 (1985): 174–85.

Hill Collins, Patricia. *Black Feminist Thought: Knowledge, Consciousness and the Politics of Empowerment.* Boston: Unwin Hyman, 1990.

Hinga, Teresa M. "Jesus Christ and the Liberation of Women in Africa." In *The Will to Arise: Women, Tradition and the Church in Africa,* ed. Mercy Amba Oduyoye and Musimbi R. A. Kanyoro, 183–94. Maryknoll, N.Y.: Orbis Books, 1992.

Hoffmann, Paul. "Auferstehung, ii/1." *Theologische Realenzyklopädie* 4:478–93.

Holladay, Carl R. "New Testament Christology: Some Considerations of Method." *Novum Testamentum* 25 (1983): 257–78.

Hollenbach, Paul. "The Historical Jesus Question in North America Today." *Biblical Theology Bulletin* 19 (1989): 11–22.

Holst, Robert. "The Anointing of Jesus: Another Application of the Form-Critical Method." *Journal of Biblical Literature* 95 (1976): 435–46.

hooks, bell. *Feminist Theory: From Margin to Center.* Boston: South End Press, 1984.

———. *Sisters of the Yam: Black Women and Self Recovery.* Boston: South End Press, 1993.

Horsley, Richard A. "Wisdom of Word and Words of Wisdom in Corinth." *Catholic Biblical Quarterly* 39 (1977): 224–39.

———. *Jesus and the Spiral of Violence.* San Francisco: Harper & Row, 1989.

———. *The Liberation of Christmas.* New York: Crossroad, 1989.

———. *Sociology and the Jesus Movement.* New York: Crossroad, 1989.

———. "Q and Jesus: Assumptions, Approaches and Analyses." *Semeia* 55 (1991): 175–212.

Howard-Brook, Wes. *Becoming Children of God: The Fourth Gospel and Radical Discipleship.* Maryknoll, N.Y.: Orbis Books, 1994.

Hübner, Hans. "Zur Ethik der Sapientia Salomonis." In *Studien zum Text und zur Ethik des neuen Testaments: Festschrift zum 80. Geburtstag von Heinrich Greeven,* ed. Wolfgang Schrage, 166–87. Berlin: Walter de Gruyter, 1986.

Hultgren, Arland J. *Christ and His Benefits: Christology and Redemption in the New Testament.* Philadelphia: Fortress Press, 1987.

Humphrey, Hugh M. "Jesus as Wisdom in Mark." *Biblical Theology Bulletin* 19, no. 2 (1989): 48–53.

Hunt, Mary E. *Fierce Tenderness: A Feminist Theology of Friendship.* New York: Crossroad, 1991.

Hurtado, L. W. "Jesus as Lordly Example in Philippians 2:5–11." In *From Jesus to Paul: Studies in Honor of Francis Wright Beare,* ed. Peter Richardson and John C. Hurd, 113–26. Waterloo, Ont.: Wilfred Laurier University Press, 1984.

Imbach, Josef. *Wem gehört Jesus? Seine Bedeutung für Juden, Christen und Moslems.* Munich: Kösel, 1989.

Jacobsen Buckley, Jorunn. "The Mandaean Appropriation of Jesus' Mother, Mirai." *Novum Testamentum* 35 (1993): 181–96.

Jay, Nancy. *Throughout Your Generations Forever: Sacrifice, Religion and Paternity.* Chicago: University of Chicago Press, 1992.

Jewett, Robert, ed. *Christology and Exegesis: New Approaches.* Semeia 30. Decatur, Ga.: Scholars Press, 1984.

Johnson, Barbara, ed. *Freedom and Interpretation: The Oxford Amnesty Lectures 1992.* New York: Basic Books, 1993.

Johnson, Elizabeth. "Redeeming the Name of Christ: Christology." *Theological Studies* 45 (1984): 441–65.

———. *She Who Is: The Mystery of God in Feminist Theological Discourse.* New York: Crossroad, 1992.

————. "The Incomprehensibility of God and the Image of God: Male and Female." In *Freeing Theology: The Essentials of Theology in Feminist Perspective,* ed. Catherine Mowry LaCugna, 115–37. San Francisco: Harper, 1993.

Johnson, Luke Timothy. "The New Testament's Anti-Jewish Slander and the Conventions of Ancient Polemic." *Journal of Biblical Literature* 108 (1989): 419–41.

Johnson, Marshall D. "Reflections on a Wisdom Approach to Matthew's Christology." *Catholic Biblical Quarterly* 36 (1974): 44–64.

Johnson, William Stacy. "The Reign of God in Theological Perspective." *Interpretation* 47 (1993): 127–39.

Kahl, Brigitte. *Armenevangelium und Heidenevangelium.* Berlin: Evangelische Verlagsanstalt, 1987.

Katz, Steven. "Issues in the Separation of Judaism and Christianity after 70 C.E." *Journal of Biblical Literature* 103 (1984): 43–76.

Kelber, Werner H. "The Birth of a Beginning: John 1:1–18." *Semeia* 52 (1991): 121–43.

King, Karen L., ed. *Images of the Feminine in Gnosticism.* Studies in Antiquity and Christianity. Philadelphia: Fortress Press, 1988.

Kirk, Martha A. *Tears, Milk and Honey: Celebrations of Biblical Women's Stories.* Kansas City, Mo.: Sheed & Ward, 1987.

Kloppenborg, John S. "Isis and Sophia in the Book of Wisdom." *Harvard Theological Review* 75 (1982): 57–84.

————. *The Formation of Q: Trajectories in Ancient Wisdom Collections.* Philadelphia: Fortress, 1987.

————. *"The Formation of Q* Revisited: A Response to Richard Horsley." In *Society of Biblical Literature, 1989 Seminar Papers,* ed. David J. Lull, 204–15. Atlanta: Scholars Press, 1989.

Kloppenborg, John S., et al. "Wisdom Christology in Q." *Laval Théologique et Philosophique* 34 (1978): 129–47.

Knox, Wildred L. "The Divine Wisdom." *Journal of Theological Studies* 38 (1937): 230–37.

Koch, Dietrich-Alex. "Jesu Tischgemeinschaft mit Zöllnern und Sündern: Erwägungen zur Entstehung von Mk 2, 13–17." In *Jesu Rede von Gott und ihre Nachgeschichte im frühen Christentum: Festschrift für Willi Marxsen zum 70. Geburtstag,* 57–73. Gütersloh: Gerd Mohn, 1989.

Koester, Helmut. "The Divine Human Being." *Harvard Theological Review* 78 (1985): 243–52.

————. *Ancient Christian Gospels: Their History and Development.* London, Philadelphia: SCM Press/Trinity Press International, 1990.

————. "Jesus the Victim." *Journal of Biblical Literature* 111 (1992): 3–15.

Kosch, Daniel. "Neue Jesusliteratur." *Bibel und Kirche* 48 (1993): 40–44.

Kraemer, Ross Shepard. *Her Share of the Blessing: Women's Religions among Pagans, Jews and Christians in the Greco-Roman World.* New York: Oxford University Press, 1992.

Kretschmar, Georg. " 'Natus ex Maria Virgine': Zur Konzeption und Theologie des Protevangelium Jacobi." In *Anfänge der Christologie: Festschrift für*

Ferdinand Hahn zum 65. Geburtstag, ed. Cilliers Breytenbach and Henning Paulsen, 417–28. Göttingen: Vandenhoeck & Ruprecht, 1991.

Kuhn, Heinz-Wolfgang. "Jesus als Gekreuzigter in der frühchristlichen Verkündigung bis zur Mitte des 2. Jahrhunderts." *Zeitschrift für Theologie und Kirche* 72 (1975): 3–46.

Kümmel, Werner George. *The Theology of the New Testament.* Trans. J. E. Steedy. Nashville: Abingdon Press, 1973.

————. "Jesusforschung seit 1981 I. Forschungsgeschichte, Methodenfragen." *Theologische Rundschau* 53 (1988): 229–49.

————. "Jesusforschung seit 1981 II. Gesamtdarstellungen. *Theologische Rundschau* 54 (1989): 1–53.

Küng, Hans, and Jürgen Moltmann, eds. *Mary in the Churches.* Concilium 268. Edinburgh: T. & T. Clark, 1983.

Kwok Pui-lan. "God Weeps with Our Pain." *East Asian Journal of Theology* 22 (1984): 228–32.

————. "Discovering the Bible in the Non-Biblical World." *Semeia* 47 (1989): 25–42.

————. "The Image of the White Lady: Gender and Race in Christian Mission." In *The Special Nature of Women?* ed. Anne Carr and Elisabeth Schüssler Fiorenza, 19–27. Concilium. London: SCM Press, 1991.

————. *Chinese Women and Christianity, 1860–1927.* Atlanta: Scholars Press, 1992.

LaCugna, Catherine Mowry, ed. *Freeing Theology: The Essentials of Theology in Feminist Perspective.* San Francisco: Harper, 1993.

Leonard, Ellen, C.S.J. "Women and Christ: Toward Inclusive Christologies." *Toronto Journal of Theology* 6 (1990): 266–85.

————. "Women: Confronting Images of Christ." In *Imaging Christ: Politics, Art, Spirituality,* ed. Francis A. Eigo, O.S.A., 171–96. Villanova, Pa.: Villanova University Press, 1991.

Levine, Amy-Jill, ed. *"Women Like This": New Perspectives on Jewish Women in the Greco-Roman World.* Atlanta: Scholars Press, 1991.

————. "Who's Catering the Q Affair? Feminist Observations on Q Paraenesis." In Leo G. Perdue and John G. Gammie, eds., *Paraenesis: Act and Form. Semeia* 50 (1990): 145–61.

Lips, Hermann von. "Christus als Sophia? Weisheitliche Traditionen in der urchristlichen Christologie." In *Anfänge der Christologie: Festschrift für Ferdinand Hahn zum 65. Geburtstag,* ed. Cilliers Breytenbach and Henning Paulsen, 75–95. Göttingen: Vandenhoeck & Ruprecht, 1991.

Lloyd, Genevieve. *The Man of Reason: "Male" and "Female" in Western Philosophy.* Minneapolis: University of Minnesota Press, 1993.

Lodahl, Michael E. *Shekinah/Spirit: Divine Presence in Jewish and Christian Religion.* New York: Paulist Press, 1992.

Mack, Burton L. "Wisdom Myth and Mythology: An Essay in Understanding a Theological Tradition." *Interpretation* 24 (1970): 46–60.

————. *A Myth of Innocence: Mark and Christian Origins.* Philadelphia: Fortress Press, 1988.

————. *Rhetoric and the New Testament.* Minneapolis: Fortress Press, 1990.

————. *The Lost Gospel: The Book of Q and Christian Origins*. San Francisco: HarperCollins, 1993.

Maeckelberghe, Els. " 'Mary': Maternal Friend or Virgin Mother?" In *Motherhood: Experience, Institution, Theology*, ed. Anne Carr and Elisabeth Schüssler Fiorenza, 120–27. Concilium 206. Edinburgh: T. & T. Clark, 1989.

Malchow, Bruce V. "Social Justice in the Wisdom Literature." *Biblical Theology Bulletin* 12 (1982): 120–24.

Malherbe, Abraham J., and Wayne A. Meeks, eds. *The Future of Christology: Essays in Honor of Leander E. Keck*. Minneapolis: Fortress Press, 1993.

Malina, Bruce J., and Jerome H. Neyrey. "First-Century Personality: Dyadic, Not Individual." In *The Social World of Luke-Acts: Models for Interpretation*, ed. Jerome H. Neyrey, 67–96. Peabody, Mass.: Hendrickson Publishers, 1991.

Martin, Clarice. "Womanist Interpretation of the New Testament: The Quest for Holistic and Inclusive Translation and Interpretation." *Journal of Feminist Studies in Religion* 6, no. 2 (1990): 41–62.

————. "The 'Haustafeln' (Household Codes) in African American Biblical Interpretation: 'Free Slaves' and Subordinate Women." In *Stony the Road We Trod: African American Biblical Interpretation*, ed. Cain Hope Felder, 206–31. Minneapolis: Fortress Press, 1991.

Martin, Dale B. *Slavery as Salvation: The Metaphor of Slavery in Pauline Christianity*. New Haven: Yale University Press, 1990.

Mays, James Luther, ed. "The Language of the Reign of God." *Interpretation* 47 (1993): 117–26.

Meersseman, Gerhard G. *Der Hymnos Akathistos im Abendland: Die älteste Andacht zur Gottesmutter*. Freiburg: Universitätsverlag, 1958.

Meier, John P. "Why Search for the Historical Jesus?" *Bible Review* 9 (1993): 30–32, 57.

Metz, Johannes-Baptist, and Edward Schillebeeckx, eds. *God as Father*. Concilium 143. Edinburgh: T. & T. Clark, 1981.

Meyer, Marvin W. "Making Mary Male: The Categories 'Male' and 'Female' in the Gospel of Thomas." *New Testament Studies* 31 (1983): 554–70.

————. "The Beginning of the Gospel of Thomas." *Semeia* 52 (1991): 161–73.

Meyer-Wilmes, Hedwig. *Rebellion auf der Grenze: Ortsbestimmung feministischer Theologie*. Freiburg: Herder, 1990.

Mies, Maria. *Patriarchy and Accumulation on a World Scale: Women in the International Division of Labor*. London: Zed Books, 1986.

Míguez Bonino, José, ed. *Faces of Jesus: Latin American Christologies*. Maryknoll, N.Y.: Orbis Books, 1984.

Myers, Ched. *Binding the Strong Man: A Political Reading of Mark's Story of Jesus*. Maryknoll, N.Y.: Orbis Books, 1988.

Modleski, Tania. *Feminism without Women: Culture and Criticism in a "Postfeminist" Age*. New York: Routledge, 1991.

Moghadam, Valentine, ed. *Identity Politics and Women: Cultural Reassertions and Feminisms in International Perspective*. Boulder, Colo.: Westview Press, 1993.

Mohanty, G. T., A. Russo, and L. Torres, eds. *Third World Women and the Politics of Feminism*. Bloomington: Indiana University Press, 1991.

Moller Okin, S. *Women in Western Political Thought*. Princeton: Princeton University Press, 1979.

Moltmann-Wendel, Elisabeth. *The Women around Jesus*. New York: Crossroad, 1982.

———. "Christ in Feminist Context." In *Christ and Context: The Confrontation between Gospel and Culture*, ed. Hilary Regan and Alan J. Torrance, 105–16. Edinburgh: T. & T. Clark, 1993.

Moon, Warren G. "Nudity and Narrative: Observations on the Frescoes from the Dura Synagogue." *Journal of the American Academy of Religion* 40 (1992): 587–658.

Morton, Nelle. *The Journey is Home*. Boston: Beacon Press, 1985.

Mosala, Itumeleng J. *Biblical Hermeneutics and Black Theology in South Africa*. Grand Rapids: Eerdmans, 1989.

Mulack, Christa. *Maria — Die geheime Göttin im Christentum*. Stuttgart and Berlin: Kreuz Verlag, 1985.

———. *Jesus, der Gesalbte der Frauen*. Stuttgart and Berlin: Kreuz Verlag, 1987.

Mussner, Franz. "Rückfrage nach Jesus: Bericht über Neue Wege und Methoden." *Theologische Berichte: Methoden der Evangelien-Exegese* 13 (1985): 165–82.

———. "Ursprünge und Entfaltung der neutestamentlichen Sohneschristologie." In *Grundfragen der Christologie heute*, ed. Leo Scheffczyk, 77–113. Quaestiones Disputatae 72. Freiburg: Herder, 1975.

Nakashima Brock, Rita. *Journeys by Heart: A Christology of Erotic Power*. New York: Crossroad, 1988.

———. "And a Little Child Will Lead Us: Christology and Child Abuse." *Christianity, Patriarchy, and Abuse: A Feminist Critique*, ed. Joanne Carlson Brown and Carol R. Bohn, 42–61. New York: Pilgrim Press, 1989.

Neirynck, Frans. "John and the Synoptics: The Empty Tomb Stories." *New Testament Studies* 30 (1984): 161–87.

Neusner, Jacob. "What Do We Study When We Study the Bible?" *Proceedings of the Irish Biblical Association* 10 (1986): 1–12.

———. *Jews and Christians: The Myth of a Common Tradition*. Philadelphia: SCM/Trinity Press International, 1991.

———. *A Rabbi Talks with Jesus: An Intermillennial, Interfaith Exchange*. New York: Doubleday, 1993.

Newman, Barbara. "The Pilgrimage of Christ-Sophia." *Vox Benedictina* 9 (1992): 9–37.

———. "Woman and the Discourse of Patriarchal Wisdom: A Study of Proverbs 1–9." In *Gender and Difference in Ancient Israel*, ed. Peggy L. Day, 142–60. Minneapolis: Fortress Press, 1989.

Neyrey, Jerome H., S.J. *An Ideology of Revolt: John's Christology in Social-Science Perspective*. Philadelphia: Fortress Press, 1988.

Nickelsburg, George W. E., and George MacRae, S.J., eds. *Christians among Jews and Gentiles*. Philadelphia: Fortress Press, 1986.

Nilgen, Ursula. "Maria Regina — ein politischer Kultbildtyp?" *Römisches Jahrbuch für Kunstgeschichte* 19 (1981): 1–33.

Noller, Anette. "Liebgewonnene Vorurteile über eine unliebsame Forschungs-richtung," *Evangelische Kommentare* 23 (1990): 563–65.

Oakley, Ann. *Sex, Gender and Society.* New York: Harper & Row, 1972.

Oakman, Douglas E. *Jesus and the Economic Questions of His Day.* Studies in the Bible and Early Christianity 8. Lewiston, N.Y., and Queenston, Ont.: Edwin Mellen Press, 1986.

O'Collins, Gerald, S.J., and Daniel Kendall, S.J. "Mary Magdalene as Major Witness to Jesus' Resurrection." *Theological Studies* 48 (1987): 631–46.

Odell-Scott, David W. *A Post-Patriarchal Christology.* American Academy of Religion Series 78. Atlanta: Scholars Press, 1991.

O'Grady, John F. "The Present State of Christology." *Chicago Studies* 32, no. 1 (April 1993): 77–91.

O'Neill, J. C. "The Kingdom of God." *Novum Testamentum* 35 (1993): 130–41.

Ostling, Richard N. "The Search for Mary: Handmaid or Feminist?" *Time* (December 30, 1991): 62–66.

Ostriker, Alicia Suskin. *Feminist Revision and the Bible.* Oxford: Blackwell, 1993.

Painter, Nell. "Truth, Sojourner (c. 1799–1885)." In *Black Women in America: A Historical Encyclopedia,* ed. Darlene Clark Hine, 1172–76. Brooklyn: Carlson, 1993.

Pagels, Elaine H. *The Gnostic Gospels.* New York: Random House, 1979.

Paterson Corrington, Gail. "The Milk of Salvation: Redemption by the Mother in Late Antiquity and Early Christianity." *Harvard Theological Review* 82 (1989): 393–420.

——. *Her Image of Salvation: Female Saviors and Formative Christianity.* Gender and the Biblical Tradition. Louisville: Westminster/John Knox Press, 1992.

Patte, Daniel. " 'Love Your Enemies' — 'Woe to You, Scribes and Pharisees': The Need for a Semiotic Approach in New Testament Studies." In *Text and Logos: The Humanistic Interpretation of the New Testament,* ed. Theodore W. Jennings, Jr., 81–96. Homage Series. Scholars Press: Atlanta, 1990.

Pecheux, Michel. *Language, Semantics, and Ideology.* New York: St. Martin's Press, 1975.

Pelikan, Jaroslav. *Jesus through the Centuries.* New Haven: Yale University Press, 1985.

Perdue, Leo G. "The Wisdom Sayings of Jesus." *Foundations and Facets Forum* 2, no.3 (1986): 3–35.

——. "The Death of the Sage and Moral Exhortation: From Ancient Near Eastern Instructions to Graeco-Roman Paraenesis." *Semeia* 50 (1990): 81–109.

Perkins, Pheme. "Jesus: God's Wisdom." *Word and World* 7 (1987): 273–80.

——. "Jesus before Christianity: Cynic and Sage?" *Christian Century* 110 (1993): 749–51.

Perrin, Norman. *Jesus and the Language of the Kingdom: Symbol and Metaphor in New Testament Interpretation.* Philadelphia: Fortress Press, 1976.

Phillips, Anne. *Engendering Democracy.* University Park, Pa.: Pennsylvania State University Press, 1991.

Plaskow, Judith. "Christian Feminism and Anti-Judaism." *Cross Currents* 33 (1978): 306–9.

———. *Sex, Sin, and Grace: Women's Experience and the Theologies of Reinhold Niebuhr and Paul Tillich.* Lanham, Md.: University Press of America, 1980.

———. *Standing Again at Sinai: Judaism from a Feminist Perspective.* San Francisco: Harper & Row, 1990.

———. "Feminist Anti-Judaism and the Christian God." *Journal of Feminist Studies in Religion* 7 (1991): 95–134.

Pokorny, Petr. *The Genesis of Christology: Foundations for a Theology of the New Testament.* Trans. Narus Lefébure. Edinburgh: T. & T. Clark, 1987.

Pope-Levison, Priscilla, and John R. Levison. *Jesus in Global Contexts.* Louisville: Westminster/John Knox Press, 1992.

Radford Ruether, Rosemary. "Male Clericalism and the Dread of Women." *The Ecumenist* 11 (1973): 65–69.

———. *Mary — The Feminine Face of the Church.* Philadelphia: Westminster Press, 1977.

———. *Sexism and God-Talk: Toward a Feminist Theology.* Boston: Beacon Press, 1983.

———. "Feminism and Jewish-Christian Dialogue: Particularism and Universalism in Search for Religious Truth." In *The Myth of Christian Uniqueness: Toward a Pluralistic Theology of Religions,* ed. John Hick and Paul Knitter, 137–48. Maryknoll, N.Y.: Orbis Books, 1987.

Radway, Janice A. *Reading the Romance: Women, Patriarchy, and Popular Literature.* Chapel Hill: University of North Carolina Press, 1991.

Räisänen, Heikki. *Beyond New Testament Theology: A Story and a Programme.* Philadelphia: Trinity Press International, 1990.

Ramazanoglu, Caroline. *Feminism and the Contradictions of Oppression.* London: Routledge, 1989.

Regan, Hilary, and Alan J. Torrance, eds. *Christ and Context: The Confrontation between Gospel and Culture.* Edinburgh: T. & T. Clark, 1993.

Reich, Robert B. *The Work of Nations.* New York: Vintage Books, 1992.

Reumann, John H., ed. *The Promise and Practice of Biblical Theology.* Minneapolis: Fortress Press, 1991.

———. "The Uses of 'Oikonomia' and Related Terms in Greek Sources to about A.D. 100 as a Background for Patristic Application." Dissertation, University of Pennsylvania, 1957.

Richard, Earl. *Jesus — One and Many: The Christological Concept of New Testament Authors.* Wilmington, Del.: Michael Glazier, 1988.

Riesner, Rainer. "Der Ursprung der Jesus-Überlieferung." *Theologische Zeitschrift* 38 (1982): 493–513.

Robbins, Vernon K. *Jesus the Teacher: A Socio-Rhetorical Interpretation of Mark.* Philadelphia: Fortress Press, 1984; Minneapolis: Fortress, 1992.

———. "Using a Socio-Rhetorical Poetics to Develop a Unified Method: The Woman Who Anointed Jesus as a Test Case." In *Society of Biblical Literature, 1992 Seminar Papers,* ed. Eugene H. Lovering, Jr., 302–19. Atlanta: Scholars Press, 1992.

Roberts Gaventa, Beverly. "The Rhetoric of Death in the Wisdom of Solomon and the Letters of Paul." In *The Listening Heart: Essays in Wisdom and the Psalms in Honor of Roland E. Murphy, O. Carm.*, ed. Kenneth G. Hogland, et al., 127–45. Journal for the Study of the Old Testament Supplement Series 58. Sheffield: JSOT Press, 1987.

Robinson, James M. "Very Goddess and Very Man: Jesus' Better Self." In *Images of the Feminine in Gnosticism*, ed. Karen L. King, 113–35. Philadelphia: Fortress Press, 1988.

Röckelein, H., C. Opitz, and R. Bauer, eds. *Maria, Abbild oder Vorbild: Zur Sozialgeschichte mittelalterlicher Marienverehrung.* Tübingen: edition diskord, 1990.

Romney Wegner, J. *Chattel or Person: The Status of Women in the Mishnah.* New York: Oxford University Press, 1988.

Russell, Letty M., ed. *Feminist Interpretation of the Bible.* Philadelphia: Westminster, 1985.

Sanders, E. *Jesus and Judaism.* Philadelphia: Fortress Press, 1985.

Sanders, Jack T. "Nag Hammadi, Odes of Solomon, and New Testament Christological Hymns." In *Gnosticism and the Early Christian World: In Honor of James M. Robinson,* ed. James E. Goehring, et al., 51–66, 162–84. Sonoma, Calif.: Polebridge Press, 1990.

Sanders, James A. "First Testament and Second." *Biblical Theology Bulletin* 17 (1987): 47–49.

Saussy, Carroll. *God and Self-Esteem: European Women in a Patriarchal Society.* Louisville: Westminster/John Knox Press, 1991.

Schaberg, Jane. *The Illegitimacy of Jesus: A Feminist Theological Interpretation of the Infancy Narratives.* San Francisco: Harper & Row, 1987.

———. "How Mary Magdalene Became a Whore." *Bible Review* 8, no. 5 (1992): 30–37, 51–52.

Schaumberger, Christine. *Weil wir nicht vergessen wollen... Zu einer feministischen Theologie im deutschen Kontext.* AnFragen 1. Münster: Morgana Frauenbuchverlag, 1987.

———. "Patriarchat als feministischer Begriff." In *Wörterbuch der feministischen Theologie.* Gütersloh: Mohn, 1991.

Schaumberger, Christine, and Luise Schottroff. *Schuld und Macht: Studien zu einer feministischen Befreiungstheologie.* Munich: Chr. Kaiser, 1988.

Schmidt, Jochen. *Die Geschichte des Genie-Gedankens in der deutschen Literatur: Philosophie und Politik 1750–1945.* 2 vols. Darmstadt: Wissenschaftliche Buchgesellschaft, 1985.

Schirmer, Eva. *Eva-Maria: Rollenbilder von Männern für Frauen.* Offenbach: Laetare Verlag, 1988.

Schnell, C. W. "Tendencies in the Synoptic Resurrection Tradition: Rudolf Bultmann's Legacy and an Important Christian Tradition." *Neotestamentica* 23 (1989): 177–96.

Schnelle, Udo. *Antidoketische Christologie im Johannesevangelium: Eine Untersuchung zur Stellung des vierten Evangeliums in der johannischen Schule.* Göttingen: Vandenhoeck & Ruprecht, 1987.

Schottroff, Luise. *Let the Oppressed Go Free: Feminist Perspectives on the New Testament.* Louisville: Westminster/John Knox Press, 1993.

Schottroff, Luise, and Wolfgang Stegemann, eds. *Jesus and the Hope of the Poor.* Maryknoll, N.Y.: Orbis Books, 1986.

Schürmann, Heinz. "Das Zeugnis der Redenquelle für die Basileia-Verkündigung Jesu." In *Logia: Les Paroles de Jesus. The Sayings of Jesus. Mémorial Joseph Coppens,* ed. Joël Delobel, 121–200. Bibliotheca Ephemeridum Theologicarum Lovaniensium 59. Louvain: University Press, 1982.

Schüssler Fiorenza, Elisabeth. *In Memory of Her: A Feminist Theological Reconstruction of Christian Origins.* New York: Crossroad, 1983.

———. *Bread Not Stone: The Challenge of Feminist Biblical Interpretation.* Boston: Beacon Press, 1985.

———. "The Ethics of Biblical Interpretation: Decentering Biblical Scholarship." *Journal of Biblical Literature* 107, no. 1 (1988): 3–17.

———. "Rhetorical Situation and Historical Reconstruction in 1 Corinthians." *New Testament Studies* 33 (1987): 386–403.

———. *Revelation: Vision of a Just World.* Philadelphia: Fortress Press, 1991.

———. *But She Said: Feminist Practices of Biblical Interpretation.* Boston: Beacon Press, 1992.

———. *Discipleship of Equals: A Critical Feminist Ekklesia-logy of Liberation.* New York: Crossroad, 1993.

Schüssler Fiorenza, Elisabeth, ed., *Searching the Scriptures,* vol. 1, *A Feminist Introduction.* New York: Crossroad, 1993.

Schüssler Fiorenza, Francis. "Critical Social Theory and Christology: Toward an Understanding of Atonement and Redemption as Emancipatory Solidarity." *Proceedings of the Thirtieth Annual Convention of the Catholic Theological Society of America* 30 (1975): 63–110.

Schüssler Fiorenza, Francis, and John P. Galvin, ed. *Systematic Theology: Roman Catholic Perspectives.* Vol. 1. Minneapolis: Fortress Press, 1991.

Schweizer, Eduard. "What Do We Really Mean When We Say, 'God Sent His Son'?" In *Faith and History: Essays in Honor of Paul W. Meyer,* ed. John T. Carroll, Charles H. Cosgrove, and Elizabeth Johnson, 298–312. Atlanta: Scholars Press, 1990.

Seeley, David. "Was Jesus like a Philosopher? The Evidence of Martyrological and Wisdom Motifs in Q, Prepauline Traditions and Mark." In *Society of Biblical Literature, 1989 Seminar Papers,* ed. David J. Lull, 540–49. Atlanta: Scholars Press, 1989.

———. "Rulership and Service in Mark 10:41–45." *Novum Testamentum* 35 (1993): 234–50.

Segal, Alan F. *Rebecca's Children.* Cambridge: Harvard University Press, 1987.

Smith, Dennis E. "The Historical Jesus at Table." In *Society of Biblical Literature, 1989 Seminar Papers,* ed. David J. Lull, 466–86. Atlanta: Scholars Press, 1989.

Smith, Dorothy E. *The Everyday World as Problematic: A Feminist Sociology.* Boston: Northeastern University Press, 1987.

———. *The Conceptual Practices of Power: A Feminist Sociology of Knowledge.* Boston: Northeastern University Press, 1990.

———. *Texts, Facts, and Femininity: Exploring the Relations of Ruling.* New York: Routledge, 1993.

Smith, Joan. "The Creation of the World We Know: The World Economy and the Re-Creation of Gendered Identities." In *Identity Politics and Women: Cultural Reassertions and Feminism in International Perspective.* Ed. Valentine M. Moghadam, 27–41. Boulder, Colo.: Westview Press, 1994.

Snyder, Howard. *Political Theology.* Trans. John Shelley. Philadelphia: Fortress Press, 1974.

———. "Models of the Kingdom: Sorting Out the Practical Meaning of God's Reign." *Transformation* 10 (1993): 1–6.

Soelle, Dorothee. "Maria ist eine Sympathisantin." In Dorothee Soelle, *Sympathie: Theologisch-politische Traktate.* Stuttgart: Kreuz Verlag, 1978, 56.

———. "Zwischen Patriarchat, Antijudaismus, und Totalitarismus: Anmerkungen zu einer Theologie in feministisch-theologischer Sicht." *Orientierung* 56 (1992): 130–35.

Spelman, Elizabeth V. *Inessential Women: Problems of Exclusion in Feminist Thought.* Boston: Beacon Press, 1988.

Stegemann, Hartmut. "Die Bedeutung der Qumranfunde für das Verständnis Jesu und des frühen Christentums." *Bibel und Kirche* 48 (1993): 10–19.

Stendahl, Krister. *Meanings: The Bible as Document and as Guide.* Philadelphia: Fortress Press, 1984.

Sternberger, Günter. *Pharisäer, Sadduzäaer, Essener.* Stuttgart: Verlag Katholisches Bibelwerk GmbH, 1991.

Steven, Maryanne, ed. *Reconstructing the Christ Symbol: Essays in Feminist Christology.* New York: Paulist Press, 1993.

Strahm, Doris, and Regula Strobel, eds. *Vom Verlangen nach Heilwerden: Theologie in feministisch-theologischer Sicht.* Freiburg/Fribourg: Exodus, 1991.

Stratton Hawley, John, ed. *Fundamentalism and Gender.* Oxford University Press, 1993.

Studer, Basil, O.S.B. *Gott und unsere Erlösung im Glauben der alten Kirche.* Düsseldorf: Patmos, 1985.

———. "Das Christusdogma der alten Kirche und das neutestamentliche Christusbild." *Münchener Theologische Zeitschrift* 44 (1993): 13–22.

Stuhlmueller, Carroll, ed. *Women and Priesthood: Future Directions.* Collegeville, Minn.: Liturgical Press, 1978.

Sugirtharajah, R. S. "Wisdom, Q, and a Proposal for a Christology." *Expository Times* 102 (1990): 42–46.

———. "'What Do Men Say Remains of Me?' Current Jesus Research and Third World Christologies." *Asia Journal of Theology* 5 (1991): 331–37.

Swidler, Arlene, and Leonard Swidler, eds. *Women Priests: A Catholic Commentary on the Vatican Declaration.* New York: Paulist Press, 1977.

Swidler, Leonard, et al., eds. *Bursting the Bonds? A Jewish-Christian Dialogue on Jesus and Paul.* Maryknoll, N.Y.: Orbis Books, 1990.

———. "Jesus Was a Feminist." *Catholic World* 212 (1971): 177–83.

Tambasco, Anthony J. *A Theology of Atonement and Paul's Vision of Christianity.* Collegeville, Minn.: Liturgical Press, 1991.

Tamez, Elsa. *The Amnesty of Grace: Justification by Faith from a Latin American Perspective.* Maryknoll, N.Y.: Orbis Books, 1993.

Theissen, Gerd. *The Shadow of the Galilean: The Quest for the Historical Jesus in Narrative Form.* Philadelphia: Fortress Press, 1987.

Thiele, Johannes, ed. *Mein Herz schmilzt wie Eis am Feuer: Die religiöse Frauenbewegung des Mittelalters in Porträts.* Stuttgart: Kreuz Verlag, 1988.

Thompson, William M. *The Jesus Debate: A Survey and Synthesis.* New York: Paulist Press, 1985.

Tolbert, Mary Ann. "Social, Sociological, and Anthropological Methods." In Elisabeth Schüssler Fiorenza, ed., *Searching the Scriptures,* vol. 1, *A Feminist Introduction,* 255–72. New York: Crossroad, 1993.

Torjesen, Karen Jo. *When Women Were Priests: Women's Leadership in the Early Church and the Scandal of Their Subordination in the Rise of Christianity.* San Francisco: Harper & Row, 1993.

Townes, Emilie M., ed. *A Troubling in My Soul: Womanist Perspectives on Evil and Suffering.* Maryknoll, N.Y.: Orbis Books, 1993.

Tracy, David, and Elisabeth Schüssler Fiorenza, eds. *The Holocaust as Interruption.* Concilium 175. Edinburgh: T. & T. Clark, 1984.

Trible, Phyllis. "Subversive Justice: Tracing the Miriamic Traditions." In *Justice and the Holy: Essays in Honor of Walter Harrelson,* ed. Douglas A. Knight and Peter J. Paris, 99–109. Atlanta: Scholars Press, 1989.

Tyson, Joseph B. "The Birth Narratives and the Beginning of Luke's Gospel." *Semeia* 52 (1991): 103–20.

Valtink, Eveline, ed. *Das Kreuz mit dem Kreuz Hofgeismarer Protokolle.* Hofgeismar: Evangelische Akademie, 1990.

Van der Horst, Pieter W. "Einige Beobachtungen zum Thema Frauen im antiken Judentum." *Berliner Theologische Zeitschrift* 10 (1993): 77–93.

Vermes, Geza. *Jesus, the Jew.* London: Collins, 1973.

———. *The Religion of Jesus, the Jew.* London: SCM Press, 1994.

Vorster, Willem S. "The Religio-historical Context of the Resurrection of Jesus and Resurrection Faith in the New Testament." *Neotestamentica* 23 (1989): 159–75.

Wacker, Marie-Theres. *Der Gott der Männer und die Frauen.* Düsseldorf: Patmos, 1987.

———. "Feminist Theology and Anti-Judaism: The Status of the Discussion and the Context of the Problem in the Federal Republic of Germany." *Journal of Feminist Studies in Religion* 7, no. 2 (1991): 109–16.

Wahlberg, Rachel Conrad. *Jesus according to a Woman.* New York: Paulist Press, 1975.

———. *Jesus and the Freed Woman.* New York: Paulist Press, 1978.

Wainwright, Elaine Mary. *Towards a Feminist Critical Reading of the Gospel according to Matthew.* Beihefte zur Zeitschrift für die neutestamentliche Wissenschaft 60. Berlin: Walter de Gruyter, 1991.

Warner, Marina. *Alone of All Her Sex: The Myth and the Cult of the Virgin Mary.* New York: Knopf, 1976.

Washington, Margaret, ed. *Narrative of Sojourner Truth.* New York: Vintage, 1993.

Weems, Renita J. *Just a Sister Away: A Womanist Vision of Women's Relationships in the Bible.* San Diego: LuraMedia, 1988.

————. "Reading Her Way through the Struggle." *Stony the Road We Trod: African American Biblical Interpretation,* ed. Cain Hope Felder, 57–80. Minneapolis: Fortress, 1991.

Wengst, Klaus. *Christologische Formeln und Leider des Urchristentums.* Studien zum Neuen Testament 7. Gütersloh: Gerd Mohn, 1973.

————. *Pax Romana: Anspruch und Wirklichkeit.* Munich: Chr. Kaiser Verlag, 1986.

Wiebe, Ben. "Messianic Ethics: Response to the Kingdom of God." *Interpretation* 45 (1991): 29–42.

Willett, Michael E. *Wisdom Christology in the Fourth Gospel.* San Francisco: Mellen Research University Press, 1992.

Williams, Delores S. "Black Women's Surrogate Experience and the Christian Notion of Redemption." In *After Patriarchy: Feminist Transformations of the World Religions,* ed. Paula M. Cooey, William R. Eakin, and Jay B. McDaniel. Maryknoll, N.Y.: Orbis Books, 1990.

————. *Sisters in the Wilderness: The Challenge of Womanist God-Talk.* Maryknoll, N.Y.: Orbis Books, 1993.

Williams, James G. *The Bible, Violence, and the Sacred: Liberation from the Myth of Sanctioned Violence.* San Francisco: Harper, 1991.

Wink, Walter. "Jesus' Reply to John: Matt 11:2–6 / Luke 7:18–23." *Foundations and Facets Forum* 5, no. 1 (1989): 121–28.

————. "Jesus and the Domination System." In *Society of Biblical Literature, 1991 Seminar Papers,* ed. Eugene H. Lovering, Jr., 265–86. Atlanta: Scholars Press, 1991.

Witherington, Ben, III. *Women in the Ministry of Jesus.* Society for New Testament Studies Monograph Series 51. Cambridge: Cambridge University Press, 1984.

————. *Women in the Earliest Churches.* Cambridge: Cambridge University Press, 1988.

Wodtke, Verena., ed. *Auf den Spuren der Weisheit.* Freiburg: Herder, 1991.

Wolff, Hanna. *Jesus, der Mann.* Stuttgart and Berlin: Kreuz Verlag, 1979.

Wren, Brian. *What Language Shall I Borrow? God-Talk in Worship: A Male Response to Feminist Theology.* New York: Crossroad, 1989.

Wright, N. T. "Taking the Text with Her Pleasure: A Post-Post Modernist Response to J. Dominic Crossan, *The Historical Jesus: The Life of a Mediterranean Jewish Peasant* (Edinburgh: T. & T. Clark; San Francisco: HarperSanFrancisco, 1991), (with Apologies to A. A. Milne, St. Paul and James Joyce)," *Theology* 96, no. 112 (1993): 303–10.

Wuellner, Wilhelm. "Hermeneutics and Rhetorics: From 'Truth and Method' to 'Truth and Power,'" *Scriptura S* 3 (1989): 1–54

Wyatt, Jean. *Reconstructing Desire: The Role of the Unconscious in Women's Reading and Writing.* Chapel Hill: University of North Carolina Press, 1990.